BURGESS
CAMPING
SERIES

Burgess

CAMPING SERIES

Consulting Editors
BARBARA ELLEN JOY and MARJORIE CAMP

PROGRAMS IN
OUTDOOR EDUCATION

by

WILLIAM H. FREEBERG, CHAIRMAN

Recreation and Outdoor Education Department
Southern Illinois University

and

LOREN E. TAYLOR

Outdoor Education Specialist
Recreation and Outdoor Education Department
Southern Illinois University
Carbondale, Illinois

Burgess Publishing Company

426 South Sixth Street • Minneapolis 15, Minnesota

INTRODUCTION

If the reception accorded the authors' previous book, *Philosophy of Outdoor Education,* is any criterion, this companion volume should have equally wide success wherever schools are community centered and teachers and administrators are concerned with more than desk-work and book-work.

To be sure, the authors do not regard outdoor education as some new panacea or as a replacement for classroom teaching. Their point of view is simply stated: Whenever desirable learnings can be more effectively accomplished out-of-doors than in the classroom, they should take place out-of-doors. Just as libraries, audio-visual materials, language laboratories, and so on are important adjuncts to the modern school, so outdoor education has a unique contribution to make.

Too many of us equate outdoor education with school camping. Outdoor education can take place just outside the schoolroom entrance--wherever nature can be studied first-hand.

Starting with the irrefutable premise that all knowl dge is interrelated, a "seamless web," the authors explore in this volume useful principles and techniques, types of outdoor programs, the strengthening of the conventional subject areas by outdoor study and activity, and finally, applications to special interest groups.

The authors are in the forefront of what is now definitely identifiable as the "outdoor education movement." This volume, like its predecessor, charts new paths and merits wide use.

> Arthur E. Lean
> Dean, College of Education
> Southern Illinois University

PREFACE

In recent years there has been a growing concern among citizens of America regarding the quality and kind of education provided by the public schools. It is claimed that education has become too artificial, verbal and superficial. Children are taught early to read and then they read their way, one textbook after another, through the elementary school, high school and then college. The more students advance in formal education the greater becomes his insulation from the real problems of life. Educators are wary of leaving the classroom or straying too far from the textbook. They, as well as many parents, cannot conceive of any learning worthwhile unless it takes place in the classroom.

The objectives of this book are to present one of many techniques which might be used to make education more real and meaningful not only for public schools but for all agencies and institutions involved in the education of children and adults. Outdoor education programs are an integral part of many school curricula in America and abroad. These have contributed a great deal toward understanding and interpretation of formal classroom instruction. The emphasis and extensive use of outdoor education programs can contribute immeasurably to current social and educational needs of youth.

Part one of this book lays the groundwork, defines outdoor education and suggests principles for guidance in outdoor education programs. Part two deals with the various types of outdoor education and emphasizes that outdoor education is much more than camping. The third section of the book suggests ways and means of enriching subject-matter areas through outdoor education. The final section deals with evaluation and research.

It is hoped that this book might serve as a curriculum guide and as a curriculum supplement for teachers of all grade levels and of all areas of subject-matter specialization.

William H. Freeberg
Loren E. Taylor

TABLE OF CONTENTS

ACKNOWLEDGMENTS

The authors wish to acknowledge the writings and research in outdoor education over the past many years which have given outdoor education the respect and status it enjoys today. Without this past labor by so many unnamed authors and the experimentations of so many creative teachers this book would not be possible.

There is a vast amount of literature in the educational and sociological fields that directly relates to outdoor education. The authors are greatly indebted to those who have made this literature available to help interpret in our own way the many ramifications involved in outdoor education programs. The authors assume responsibility for any shortcomings involved in the use of this literature for interpretive purposes.

The authors owe a great deal to D. W. Morris, President of Southern Illinois University for his vision and his courage in providing the university with an extensive outdoor education laboratory; to John E. Grinnell, Vice-President for Operations, and John S. Rendleman, Executive Director of Business Affairs, for their encouragement and guidance in the development of the outdoor education program at Southern Illinois University representing various departments who have assisted in developing the outdoor education program in terms of instruction and research.

The authors acknowledge with special thanks the many other leaders in the field of outdoor education including L. B. Sharp, executive director of the Outdoor Education Association; Reynold E. Carlson, Indiana University; Howard Weaver, University of Illinois, George Donaldson, Tyler, Texas; Don Hammerman, Northern Illinois University; Paul Harrison, Northern Illinois University; Jean Samford, Antioch College; and countless other creative teachers who are working and experimenting with children in outdoor education programs.

The authors owe special thanks and appreciation to Joann Lilly, Margie Schoenberger, Linda Lemmon, and Henrietta Eicher for typing and proofreading the manuscript. The authors also wish to acknowledge graduate assistants Denver Bennett and Wesley Upton for their help on the manuscript.

Part 1

Outdoor Education
A Method of Teaching
and a Way of Learning

With millions of acres of woods and valleys and hills
and streams and fishes . . . or with streets and shop windows
and crowds and vehicles and all sorts of city delights at
the door, you are forced to sit, not in a room with some
human grace and comfort . . . but in a stalled pound with a
lot of other children, beaten if you talk, beaten if you
move, beaten if you cannot prove by answering idiotic questions
that even when you escaped from the pound and from the eye of
your gaoler, you were still agonizing over his detestable sham
books instead of daring to live.

—*G. B. Shaw*

Outdoor education is a method of education. It involves intelligent planning by all teachers using nature and real life experiences in interpreting subject matter areas found in the school curriculum. Through direct experiences with nature, people, objects, things, places, and by actually "learning by doing, "there is scientific evidence that "the learning process is faster, what is learned is retained longer, and there is greater appreciation and understanding for those things that are learned firsthand. "[1]

Every subject-matter field in the present day curriculum may be enriched through outdoor education. Moreover, subject-matter areas tend to lose their bounds and become related and integrated as ideas and facts take on meaning and perspective. Planned programs for all levels of instruction from kindergarten through college have demonstrated the values of the outdoor education method.

Outdoor education is not a separate discipline or a separate area of study such as history, English, arithmetic, or other subject-matter areas. There are no clearly defined

[1] L. B. Sharp, "Basic Considerations in Outdoor and Camping Education" The Bulletin of the National Association of Secondary School Principals, May, 1947. p. 43.

principles and objectives specifically designed for outdoor education as a subject. General principles and objectives must be formulated within the framework of education and the school curriculum. Each specific subject-matter area must be carefully studied and analyzed to discover how and when direct learning experiences outside the classroom will make textbook learning more meaningful.

Outdoor education is not intended to replace textbook learning. It is not a substitute for abstract teaching. Rather it is a method that can be successfully and intelligently introduced by all teachers, in all subject-matter areas, to supplement and complement written and oral expression.

It is not in conflict with the child-centered, subject matter-centered, or the society-centered approaches to learning. In fact, many rewarding teaching experiences are possible which complement all three approaches.

Every teacher should be skilled in the outdoor education method. The attitudes and appreciations, the skills and knowledges, the adventure and enjoyment associated with outdoor education experiences should be an important part of every educational program.

Many educators erroneously regard the outdoors as a laboratory for the science department. As a result of this concept, more science classes use the outdoors for instructional materials than any other subject-matter area. However, teaching of English, history, arithmetic, civics and every subject in the curriculum can find materials outside the classroom which will make their subject matter more meaningful, more interesting, and more enjoyable. Teachers in all subject-matter areas should plan outdoor experiences as a part of their regular classroom work.

It is impossible for any teacher to know all there is to know about the out-of-doors, or about the many experiences they encounter through field trips and other outdoor learning situations. Learning becomes a mutual process by both pupil and teacher as a result of firsthand experiences and as a result of the skillful techniques used by teachers to get the most out of the learning situation. This is a vital contribution that makes outdoor education a real method of acquiring knowledge.

The method by which teachers provide the learning experience is most important; it should be closely associated with and accompanied by adequate library materials, textbooks, classroom lessons, and other aids to learning. Teachers are not required to have all the knowledge necessary to explain and interpret things they study in an outdoor education program. It is more important to provide diversified learning experiences for the students and to skillfully guide and direct these experiences into purposeful and meaningful study.

Outdoor education methods involve a coordination of many ideas and involve the borrowing of many desirable educational techniques that have been proposed throughout the history of education. Some of these ideas, techniques, and proposals most frequently recommended in education and which are more nearly descriptive of the outdoor education method are:

1. Education is a social process.
2. Experience is the best teacher.
3. Man learns to do by doing.
4. Learning is best when information is obtained through all the senses.
5. The mind proceeds from the known to the unknown, from the particular to the general, and from the concrete to the abstract.
6. Education is growth.
7. Knowledge should be acquired through experience and the written word, not merely through the written word.
8. It is difficult to teach a person but possible to help him learn.
9. A skilled teacher must know what to teach as well as how to teach.
10. The "what" and the "how" are inseparable counterparts for good teaching. One is no more important than the other for the learning process is affected by all aspects of the teacher-learner situation. To be a successful teacher requires sound educational methods and techniques as a means of challenging, motivating, and imparting knowledge to students.

Some of the more apparent contributions to learning inherent in well-established outdoor education programs consist of observation, investigation, cooperation, integration, correlation, meditation, informality, creativity, and active participation.[2]

At the very outset outdoor education promised to make a new and original contribution to education. Many schools in the United States have experimented with outdoor education programs. Experimental programs in school camping have also been conducted successfully throughout the United States. The public schools in many states now accept outdoor education programs as an important and integral part of the school curriculum. Laws permitting and encouraging outdoor education programs may be found in several states, e.g., Michigan, New York, California, Illinois, Ohio. This trend will gain momentum as research and practice prove its value as an educational technique. With proper planning and administration outdoor education offers to the schools opportunities for creativity and resources not available through present formal education. As more and more schools experiment in this phase of the school program and as research and practice prove its value, outdoor education will gain momentum and become well established in the schools of the United States as a valuable teaching technique.

The outdoor education program cannot afford to function with procedures and methods that are now employed through traditional teaching methods. An outdoor education program loses much of its value when present teaching methods and teaching techniques are merely transferred outside the classroom. Some of the frequent abuses of the outdoor education program include the use of traditional teaching procedures; dictatorial and authoritative relationships between teachers, counselors, and students; fixed activity programs; the use of competition, prizes and awards to motivate and stimulate effort and interest; the over-emphasis on athletic and recreational activities; the regimentation of classes; and the formal approach to learning.

---

[2]For further discussion see: William H. Freeberg and Loren E. Taylor, Philosophy of Outdoor Education, Minneapolis: Burgess Publishing Co., 1961, pp. 96-131.

Chapter I

A REALISTIC APPRAISAL
OF EDUCATION

The school system of the United States has frequently been challenged and has undergone periodic attacks for poor educational standards, for a narrow curriculum, for a broad curriculum, for poor curriculum content, for not keeping up with the times and many other similar charges. In recent years many desirable changes have occurred and our educational standards have improved.

Today the United States is confronted with scientific and social change that has caused citizens to renew their attack on the educational system. A great deal of the criticism is justifiable. However, much of the fault finding is based on opinion rather than fact. Educational, psychological and sociological research is lacking and what is available is slow to be interpreted in terms of today's educational needs.

The problems cannot be answered by crash programs, intuitive criticisms, hysterical demands, proposals and recriminations. We cannot solve the problem by adopting the Russian system, the German system, or the English system of education. It is not advisable to turn back to the educational system of one-hundred years ago. Today, individuals and groups in the United States are advocating nationalism and internationalism, more academic courses and more vocational courses, a more traditional school system and a more progressive system of education. Strong and vehement arguments are made in behalf of change but equally strong opposition pleads for the status quo and a return to old methods.

One outstanding educator in viewing the urgent and complex problems of society wrote:

> As things are. . .mankind are by no means agreed about
> the things to be taught, whether we look to virtue or
> the best life. Neither is it clear whether education
> is more concerned with intellectual or moral virtue.
> The existing practice is perplexing; no one knowing
> on what principle we should proceed--should the useful
> in life, or should virtue, or should the higher knowl-
> edge be the aim of our training; all three opinions
> have been entertained. Again about the means there
> is no agreement; for different persons, starting with
> different ideas about the nature of virtue, naturally
> disagree about the practice of it.

Many readers may be surprised to know that the
above statement was written over twenty-five hundred years
ago by Aristotle when Greece was in the midst of a political
and social upheaval.

Thus, there have always been difficulties and differences for no society has ever had a completely perfect educational system. Yet this fact provides little comfort to
modern day educators for never in history has the world
undergone a social, political, scientific, and economic revolution of such magnitude as modern society. The rapidity
of this change and the magnitude of its scope has brought
education the most insistent, elusive, and perplexing problems in the history of education. What are the objectives
of education? Who sets these objectives? How can the objectives best be achieved? What should we teach? How
should it be taught? Is the modern day curriculum meeting
the demands of society? Who shall be taught? Who shall
teach?

An examination of the objectives of education and a
parallel study of society reveals that through the ages the
educational objectives of a given era gave expression to the
goals of society. For example, Comenius (1592-1670) emphasized usefulness and practicality in his teachings. He
was living in a utilitarian society. Informal education designed to acquire food, clothing, and shelter was the order
of the day.

After many centuries the utilitarian societies became
more and more involved in their organizations and education

undertook to teach youth the means of preserving the existing social order. As these cultures became more permanent, they acquired a system of values and morals and it became the purpose of education to inculcate these values in the youth of the society. It soon became apparent that purposes could not be automatically achieved through mastery of school subjects. This realization ushered in the mental discipline theory of education. Subject matter was classified and formalized and every student was given the same course of study in order to train his mind. Although each of these theories have been discarded for the most part, their influence is still felt in varying degrees in the modern school curricula.

It is generally agreed among educators today that the primary purposes of education are: (1) Keeping alive and passing on the cultural heritage from one generation to the next and (2) equipping children for useful lives.

The greatest disagreement among lay citizens, as well as educators, is the degree to which one of the above stated purposes is stressed to the neglect of the other. In the past educators have been too much concerned with passing on the cultural heritage and not enough concerned with equipping children and adults with the special skills needed to live in his particular society.

EDUCATION AND SOCIETY

The purposes of the public school system of the United States are determined by the American democratic philosophy and the needs of her citizens--both children and adult --for living in a democracy. In a government of the people, by the people, and for the people, it is obvious that the people must be educated. Thomas Jefferson pretty well sums up the feeling of the early proponents of universal education when he said: "I know of no safety depository of the ultimate powers of society but the people themselves; and if we think them not enlightened enough to exercise their control with a wholesome discretion the remedy is not to take it from them, but to inform them their discretion by education."

The American Constitution and the Bill of Rights grant to all citizens certain unalienable rights among which are life, liberty, and the pursuit of happiness. The American way of life is based on a recognition of the worth and dignity of each individual. The responsibility for enjoying the American way of life and for preserving these fundamental beliefs rest on the shoulders of each individual citizen. Each and every individual is entitled to the development of his abilities and talents to the fullest extent. The schools, the home, churches, and many other community agencies and institutions must accept the responsibility for perpetuating and reinforcing the beliefs and ideals of democracy. The school curriculum should be planned to allow the fullest practice in American ideals in order that students may learn to live and act democratically and to learn and practice mutual respect.

Changing conditions in American society have brought new challenges to the schools in preparing students for modern living. There are strong and persistent pressures on the schools to maintain and preserve all content in the present curriculum. Likewise, there is pressure to maintain the traditional methods of teaching. It is understandable that the general objectives of education which have been formulated over the past hundred years and expressed in the Seven Cardinal Principles of Education in 1918 and later by the Educational Policies Commission in 1938 are resistant to change.

An examination of the above-mentioned objectives show that they are well stated and comprehensive enough to provide for the needs of individuals in modern society. The fault seems to lie in the fact that educators are not providing a curriculum to achieve these objectives. In fitting children for life, the schools must examine the demands of contemporary society; the society the children are living in now and will live in the future. Much of the content of the fixed curriculum and many of the methods now being used need a reevaluation and revision to meet the present day needs. The educational objectives may change very little but they must be interpreted in light of the present day changes in society.

At the turn of the century a student prepared himself for a very limited number of vocations or professions. The total number of positions to be filled were limited in number and scope. Today, with specialization in industry and work and changes brought about by science and technology, the choice of professions, vocations, and avenues of employment number in the twenty thousands. For example, in the medical profession the general practitioner of one hundred years ago is rapidly being replaced by the pediatrician, the obstetrician, the optician, the urologist, the pathologist, the radiologist, the psychologist, and many other specialists in such fields as heart or eye, ear, nose and throat. In industry the craftsman no longer finishes a complete product as did the cabinet maker, the harness maker, or the blacksmith of one hundred years ago. Today, many people must prepare for special tasks in mass production and many others must be ready to handle personnel and supervise their work.

Furthermore, the public schools are not keeping abreast of the tremendous progress of the society which it is supposed to serve. Today, the United States is plagued with widespread unemployment and at the same time a large number of technical and semi-technical jobs are unfilled because of a lack of skilled manpower. The country is short of teachers, short of nurses and hospital technicians, short of scientists, short of doctors, and short of specially trained people in practically every field. Yet the public schools seem oblivious to the situation.

There is a new and changing concept of quantity and space that confronts the students of today. The old methods of teaching mathematics and related subjects must be revised so students can move where their interests and abilities lie. There is a need for shift in emphasis that will permit all students who are endowed with different talents an opportunity to learn and appreciate the new concepts of quantity and space.

There is also a new concept in education which challenges the schools in educating for world understanding. In the modern age it is imperative that schools help students develop respect for opinions, beliefs, attitudes, and needs of people around the world. The modern improvements of transportation and communication has shrunk the world into

a neighborhood. America does not have the economic su-
premacy she once enjoyed; she can no longer be complacent
and smug to other nations. As President John Kennedy says,
"America is no longer in a position to solve all the world
problems." This is a task of many nations. Pupils must
understand and appreciate world conditions and influences.
They must realize several factors which have been well outlined by Slay and Monahan:[1]

1. That conditions in any part of the world affect all
   people of the world;
2. That nations with an abundance of materials, technological, and human resources have a moral responsibility for sharing these with less favored nations
3. That the common needs of mankind are the foundations
   for world cooperation: an adequate level of food,
   clothing, and shelter, basic medical care, and full
   access to man's accumulated knowledge;
4. That the values, goals, and aspirations of a people
   are to be respected and recognized as desirable;
5. That world cooperation must be carried forward
   within a philosophy that insures the dignity and
   sense of worth of all concerned;
6. That world cooperation shall transcend regimes and
   political differences;
7. That the interdependence of nations is inescapable.

New inventions have caused a need for a new education
for life. Automation and the push button era demand change
in the school curriculum. Both the physical and mental
health of each individual is at stake and this in turn directly
affects the health and vitality of the nation. Knowing how to
adjust to a sedentary life of leisure and relative luxury
brings with it responsibilities for educating for creativity
and progress.

Man's new found leisure presents a new kind of problem for education. Leisure once considered a sin is today
a rich and rewarding part of every citizen's life. The promises of tomorrow should make it an even larger share of
man's life. Dubin states, "work is no longer a central life

[1]Ronald J. Slay and Tom Monahan, "World Cooperation: A Challenge To Teacher
Education." Phi Delta Kappan, November, 1960, p. 104.

interest for workers. These life interests have moved out into the community. "[2]

The rapidly increasing leisure hours are, of course, accompanied by a reduction of the work week. In agricultural work, the work week in 1850 was 72 hours; in 1956, the work week dropped to 47 hours. In non-agricultural industries the work week in 1850 was 66 hours and this dropped to 40.9 hours in 1956. By 1975, it is predicted by sociologists and others that the work week will drop as low as 30 hours per week.

In addition to a shrinking work week, the leisure hours are ever expanding due to the fact that over 90 per cent of all industrial workers are enjoying paid vacations averaging a two week period. As far back as 1937 when the paid vacation began to build momentum over 75 per cent of all office and retail employees were already enjoying paid vacations.

Earlier retirement and the increased life span must also be considered by modern educators who must equip citizens for living in the new age of leisure.

The amazing and ever-increasing scientific achievements of twentieth-century America are the product and result of the ability as a nation to perpetuate the democratic principles. Without freedom, cooperation, competition, and eagerness for knowledge, and without dedicated interest in the moral and religious principles of democracy, America would not enjoy the high standard of living she now has. The progress and mutual respect and understanding of all neighbors is the present challenge to the public schools.

Passing on the cultural heritage is not enough. When education stresses culture and heritage with little thought of equipping citizens to live in society here and now, that society fails to develop. It becomes stagnant and eventually disintegrates. The school curriculum of such a society stresses bookish facts and information concerning the past, most of which is useless in helping the student to live in his society.

China with her respect for the past and emphasis on memorization of old books and past laws surely proved without doubt in her 4,000 year experiment that education is

[2]Eric Larrabee and Rolf Meyersohn (Editors), Mass Leisure, Glencoe, Illinois: The Free Press, 1958, p. 226.

more than passing on the cultural heritage.

Today educators and lay citizens are beginning to realize that passing on the cultural heritage, though important, is not enough. The schools must provide education for mass leisure, for a longer life, and for sedentary living; education for a vocation, and for professional services; education for family living, individual living, for community living, and for world living; and education to cope with a technical and sociological advancement.

EDUCATION AND THE INDIVIDUAL

It is a recognizable fact that the public schools cannot improve society without first improving the citizens of that society. By helping individuals grow through teaching democratic skills and by enriching their lives through education, society will be improved. Our democratic form of government rests its faith and confidence in the individual. It provides a government for the purpose of helping each individual to a fuller and richer life. It demands of the individual education, government participation, respect for world citizens, and beliefs in the democratic principles.

In recent years, educators have been aware that subject matter is not enough to fulfill the various functions commonly ascribed to the public schools. Education is now thought to include any desirable change in behavior through the physical, mental, emotional, social, and spiritual growth acquired through interaction with the total environment. In this context the public school is only one of many agencies of education in the community. The family, the neighborhood, the church, the Young Men's Christian Association, the Young Women's Christian Association, the public library, television, radio, movies and theaters, government agencies, and many other agencies, clubs, and organizations in the community influence and modify behavior of the human being either for good or bad.

In the past, schools have assumed that they were solely responsible for education. History and social studies consisted largely of learning dates and historical facts.

Literature was entirely classical, reading what others had written with little effort to encourage creativity in writing or speaking. Mathematics textbooks were filled with abstract facts and processes and with problems unrelated to life needs or life situations. Science consisted chiefly in the acquisition of scientific classifications and terminology. Language dealt largely with diagramming sentences and sentence structure rather than clear expression.

Such a curriculum was ideal for most teachers because this is the method that was used to teach them. Teaching was formal, stereotyped, and it was not a good practice to deviate from the textbook or to alter methods to any great extent. Daily lesson plans were made directly from the main textbook and from other references. This was the easy way to teach, because all the information came from the textbook or manual. The answers were in the book and there was little need for interpreting the facts with related experiences. Teachers had strict control over the class since the students remained in their seats and recited only when called upon. Recitation of memorized facts was awarded more than creative inquiries and questions concerning related and associated interests.

In a small school in Southern Illinois a group of sixth graders spent a week at camp. The parents of these youngsters were asked to evaluate the program and were also asked to make comments regarding the regular school program. Many interesting responses were received and most parents were enthusiastic about the school camp program. One parent's comment stated:

> The classroom program seems to lack consistency and direction. The children themselves seem to have less interest than their teachers and the program's proponents. We are living in a fast moving rocket age and the youngsters would be grateful and more enthusiastic if education could be tied more closely to the things they know; the things that are happening; the things that are really important to them. The program at camp was apparently very good because it did these things and the children were inspired by being with dedicated people and in the outdoors.

It is a sad commentary on education leadership that community pressures are necessary to force the public schools to acknowledge a need for improved programs. Parents are becoming alarmed at the lack of knowledge children have about the commonplace things; about their ability to work complicated arithmetic problems from the workbook but inability to make simple computations necessary in their everyday lives.

Outstanding educators are beginning to ask questions:

> "Why is it," asked a principal who had watched students come and go in one school for over twenty years, "Why is it that so many of our students who participate in student activities while in school have so little interest in civic affairs after they graduate? We try to make our schools democratic. We try to give every student a chance to take a responsible part in class work and student activities, but the amount of carry over to life after graduation is disappointingly small. There seems to be a gap between the school and the out-of-school world which we haven't been able to bridge."[3]

It is appalling, even alarming, in a democratic nation for a fifty per cent turnout in a national election to be considered good. The widespread indifference of public concern is a grave danger to a democratic society. The inability on the part of the rank and file to deal intelligently with the problems of society or worse still their lack of interest in these problems points up a real challenge to the public and private schools of America. The schools are the only agency equipped to prepare young people to meet the difficulties of the complicated society of twentieth-century America.

The Institute of School Experimentation comments on this glaring weakness of modern education:

> The school which never gives children and youth experience in dealing with real situations sends out into the life of the community young people who are indifferent

---

[3]J. E. Grinnell and Raymond J. Young, The School and The Community, New York: The Ronald Press Company, 1955, pp. 21-22.

to or even unaware of some of the fundamental problems of society.[4]

From the very beginning of American history with the signing of the Declaration of Independence and the adoption of the Constitution, the public schools have lagged behind American life. As the United States grew and developed economically, politically, and socially the gap between the curricula of her schools and society has grown wider and wider. Industrialization has quickly transformed the nation and the world into a totally new civilization--a mode of life unlike any that has been known to man. The task of the school is to help people adjust their modes of living to a fast changing society.

Many critics of the schools say that their curricula has been influenced too much by professors working in laboratories and libraries and not enough by the needs of children and the vital affairs of current life.

MacConnell comments on the rigid and unchanging social curriculum and the tendency of schools to become slaves to academic tradition:

> In the school of tomorrow the aristocratic, cultural traditions of education must be completely and finally abandoned. Scholarship must become functional. This does not mean that it will be concerned only with the material wants of man or that it will lack creativeness or intelligent stimulation, but it will cease to rattle the bones of the dead past solely for pleasure, or worse, out of a sense of academic duty.[5]

Dr. Delyte W. Morris, President of Southern Illinois University, further expands the function of the public schools in an address before a public forum on educational reform in Havana, Cuba, in 1958. Morris said:

---

[4] F. B. Stratemeyer and Others, _Developing A Curriculum For Modern Living_, New York: Teachers College, Columbia University, 1947, p. 408.

[5] C. M. MacConnell, E. O. Melby, and C. O. Arndt, _New Schools For A New Culture_, New York: Harper and Brothers, 1943, pp. 171-174.

Public schools in a democracy must stay close to the
needs of the people . . .

Rather than remain apart from daily living, the
public schools should so entwine themselves into the
daily life of the communities about them that they
furnish intellectual leadership and stimulate dynamic
social growth . . .

The vast world changes in our generation are causing
a reappraisal of many things in our country. They have
caused us, as they are causing you, to reappraise, re-
evaluate and re-orient public education.

It is my belief that our nation could not exist as
it is today had there not been from the beginning a
desire for universal free education and the will to
achieve it. That our nation is not a perfect nation
is due to the fact that our educational system has not
been perfect. However, we have endured and grown strong
er as a democratic nation because we have staked our
democracy on the belief that an enlightened electorate
will be able to govern itself. Or, to put it another
way, we have held that the greatest good of the greatest number, in the long run, will result from full
franchises of an educated populace.

Events both at home and abroad which have made Amer·
icans question public schools and have led outstanding educators to denounce the traditional approach to education have
resulted in the modern community approach. Educators
have seen the importance of selecting learning experience
based on mandates from psychology and social theory. The
following six criteria have been generally agreed upon by
educators in the selection of learning experiences:

1. The experience must meet the need of the learner.
2. The curriculum must be tied closely to the learner's
   experience.
3. The curriculum must extend the horizon and stimulate creative imagination.
4. The curriculum must develop a social conscience
   and democratic ideals.
5. The curriculum must use the community as a laboratory for learning--a resource area, and
6. The cultural heritage must be regarded as a means
   to achieving these objectives and not as an end of
   learning.

Planning educational programs in light of the above criteria calls for a closer look at both the curriculum content and the method of teaching used. It calls for a break from the traditional textbook approach to education and the sacred formalized method of teaching to the emergence of a more realistic approach to education.

Schooling for a society of industrialization and urbanization certainly must be different than that used in the day of hand production and rural living; it must be different in a society of interactive group life and world interdependence than it was in the day of individualistic order and isolationism.

Grinnell and Young[6] list ten valuable guides which should be helpful to teachers in planning learning experiences for children in modern society:

1. Teach more of the applications of subject matter to life problems and situations.
2. Organize instruction around life problems and needs.
3. Take learners into the community-field trips, excursions, assignments, interviews, camping, work experience, and similar activities.
4. Bring the community into the schools through a wide variety of audio-visual materials.
5. Make learning situations in the school more like life in the community.
6. Greater participation of individuals and groups of the community in planning and improving instructional materials and learning activities, especially through the use of advisory groups.
7. Acquaint the community with the purposes, programs, activities, achievements, and changes in the work of the schools.
8. Develop more comprehensive and effective understanding and good will on the part of the lay persons.
9. Employ laymen with particular information to lead discussions in classes, to be interviewed, or to lecture.
10. Use objects and printed materials available in the community as learning materials.

[6]J. E. Grinnell and Raymond J. Young, The School and The Community, New York: The Ronald Press Company, 1955, pp. 20-21.

IMPLICATIONS FOR THE TEACHER

Teachers are often thought of as people who tell children what to do. This idea of the teacher's role has come about from past experience in group life. In the family group, the parents told what could or could not be done; at school, the teacher ruled the class; at church, the pastor told what life to lead; and on the job, the "bosses" directed the daily work. Most people have experienced and have been subjected to this type of leadership. A high value has been placed on domineering leadership and it is too often accepted without challenge or question.

Today, however, children are beginning to experience a new kind of leadership--that of democracy. Democracy is based on the assumption that the class or group has the right and the capacity to make its own decisions, and the teacher's function is to help it to do so in the best possible way. Democracy provides positive leadership.

T. V. Smith[7] makes a significant distinction between the domineering teacher and the democratic teacher when he states that the autocratic leader is "strong in proportion to the ignorance of his followers" whereas the democratic leader is "strong in proportion to the intelligence of his followers." This same idea has a great deal of significance for the classroom teacher.

Today, freedom is at stake. No longer can the schools afford to drift along with the same curriculum and the same methods of teaching with little regard to the demands of society. The schools either assume leadership or society disintegrates. In the battle for the minds of men and the hoped for emergence of democratic principles of living for all people of all nations the burden rests upon the shoulders of the classroom teacher.

It behooves every community to provide the most creative and the best teacher possible. The loss to a community and to its children is too great not to do otherwise. The time has come when the public must look upon money spent for teachers' salaries as being fully as important as money

---

[7] T. V. Smith, The Democratic Way of Life, Chicago: University of Chicago Press, 1926, p. 186.

spent on getting a man to the moon.

In the new appraisal of education which is in process, ways and means must be found which will give every citizen a real and meaningful education for living here and now on this planet. The cost of transportation to the moon will be too expensive. The citizens of every community must face facts and give more time to their schools. If left to educators alone, the past has shown that they are apt to get involved in academic matters and debate such issues as "the role of liberal arts" versus "the role of vocational education." Too many educators line up on an "either - or" basis. It has been said that war is "too important to be left to generals." Education which can bring about forces for peace is too important to be left to a few scholars. In a democracy it must be the concern of every citizen. Discussions of educational problems by parent groups, P.T.A.'s, civic and community clubs bring a more democratic and more practical climate to the solution of educational problems. An examination of schools where community groups and parents are actively involved in the educational program reveals both stability and flexibility in the curriculum. Good education demands stress on cultural values, but not to the extent that problems of everyday living, community enrichment and individual fulfillment are excluded or neglected.

Every classroom teacher must know and heed the psychological and sociological findings which have been established in recent years. It is not enough to know how to teach; every teacher must keep up with research in the field and operate at maximum efficiency.

The schools of today sorely need unusual teaching abilities in every classroom. Dedicated and creative teaching is rare, too little appreciated, and often not encouraged. Social and economic factors have sometimes left school administrators with little choice in the quality of teachers they must select. These factors are causing prospective teachers who are talented and creative to seek employment in other fields. Many college students ask, "Why should I teach when I can double or triple my salary in other fields?" Much headway has been made in recent years toward enticing many well qualified and creative individuals to accept teaching as their life's work. Much is left to be done in teacher recruitment. American society can only be perpetuated with assurance from society that good teachers will be provided in large enough numbers so that every boy and girl will benefit from a good education.

Literature in psychology and education reveals ten basic concepts which every teacher should consider in guiding the learning activities of children.

1. EDUCATION IS LIFE

Traditional educators have regarded the purpose of education as a preparation for life. The child is prepared in the elementary school for junior high school, in junior high school for high school and so on until he graduates from college and is ready to take his place in the stream of life. His diploma is a permit to start living; proof that he has enough knowledge stored in reserve and ready to use for meeting life's problems.

In such a school the child is always preparing for something. Knowledge and information is imparted so that it may be used in the future--sometime when they become adults. As Kelley points out, he does not know quite what it is that he is preparing for, and the teacher is often ill-equipped to help him to know. Kelley further comments:

> Since education is supplementary and preparatory, we build school buildings designed to shut out life so that the child can give complete attention to our abstractions or tools for conveying these abstractions, to books, blackboards, and chalk. The windows of the classroom are often purposely built high so that the child cannot look out of them and be distracted. The whole atmosphere of the place where education goes on is exclusive and forbidding in its nature. We build our colleges out in isolated places where the world will not intrude. We segregate the most similar ones together, where they cannot learn from different kinds of people. Often we do not let them associate with their own kind, unless they are also of the same sex. Perhaps the place where a visitor from another country could learn the least about life in America would be on a typical college campus or for that matter in a typical American schoolroom.

> All of this isolation is consistent with the assumption that children are not living but are preparing for life, that knowledge set out to be learned can be acquired and kept in cold storage, that it is of no use now but will come in handy sometime.[8]

Such schooling held no immediate satisfaction for the student. Rather than helping children to live richly and fully at all ages and on all grade levels the schools were getting them prepared for the future. Much emphasis was given to marks, credits, awards, honors, promotions, and finally graduation. Children worked their way through the elementary school, high school, and finally college with the idea that armed with the diplomas they were ready to start living.

Modern educators regard education as something more than a preparation for life. They help children live richly and fully at all grade levels and education becomes a functioning process for the present as well as the future. Today's experience is used to build on past experiences, and knowledge, skills, attitudes and appreciations are developed for a here and now situation that may be used tomorrow, next week, or anytime in the future. Education, thus, does not prepare for life ahead, nor does it stop at graduation. It is a continuous process from birth to death and may take place both in and outside the classroom.

This philosophy of education is more acceptable to the student who sometimes feels that he has to spend most of his life in school learning to live.

2. LEARNING IS AN ACTIVE PROCESS

A child learns by his own activity. He cannot receive an education in a passive way; the school cannot give the child his education. Knowledge cannot be passed directly from one person to another. There must be some measure of desire and interest; some attention given to the learning situation. The function of the school is to set up learning situations and provide an environment whereby the child

---

[8] Earl C. Kelley, Education For What Is Real. New York: Harper and Brothers, 1947, pp. 18-19.

may learn through his own activity. Learning is strengthened and is made more meaningful when children are actively engaged and actively involved in the educational process.

"Experience is the best teacher." This age-old proverb was not originated in school or by educators but was well established long before the first formal school. No one has yet been able to disprove the wisdom of its words.

"I would have a child say not, 'I know,' but 'I have experienced,'" says John Dewey, the force behind the revolution in democracy's new school.

The truisms that "we learn by doing" and "experience is the best teacher" imply that children should share in planning, conducting, and evaluating the learning process. In the traditional assign-study-test method of schooling the student is involved only in the passive activity of study and recitation. The teacher does most of the talking and the thinking under the false impression that they are imparting knowledge. The teacher makes the assignments, evaluations and grades the pupils. Much of the educational values obviously are lost in this process since testing and giving grades seems to be the chief objective.

Good teachers involve their pupils in planning activities, in carrying out activities, and in evaluating their own activities. They recognize that self-activity is the only way of learning; that teaching is not a process of imparting knowledge but a process of stimulating and guiding the student in the learning process.

John Dewey, probably more than any educator, popularized the activity-school and the basic concept of "learning by doing." It is hard to understand how any objective thinkers can argue with this fundamental tenet of modern education. Traditionalists are afraid that through the activity approach children will not learn basic educational fundamentals (reading, writing, and arithmetic); these subjects have been taught in a passive way since the beginning of formalized education. It is a strange paradox in education that great scholars are equally as adverse to making this change as are those who do not have scientific evidence to make judgment. The passive "listening school" is hard to replace. "We have always done it this way" seems to end all arguments.

Modern educators realize that teachers cannot give children their education but they can provide learning situations and guidance so that children may learn through their own activities. In this climate, learning takes on significance as it becomes meaningful, interesting, and alive. Furthermore, children not only learn reading, writing, and arithmetic, but they learn to work together democratically; they learn oral expression; they learn and experience healthful living; they are provided with wholesome recreation and many other important learnings important to living in a democratic society. In the activity-school children learn democracy by living it.

3. THE MIND CANNOT BE TRAINED

It has taken many years for the schools to outgrow the "mental discipline" concept of education. In too many schools, however, this idea of education still persists. The mind was regarded as being like a muscle and abstract materials, difficult foreign languages and mathematical formulas were supposed to exercise the mind. The more difficult and "stiffer" the materials the more efficiently the mind was trained. It made little difference to these early educators what they taught or what knowledge was useful so long as the children didn't like it.

Experiments by Thorndike and other psychologists which were conducted around the turn of the century have exploded beyond all doubt the mental discipline theory of learning. The mind could no longer be regarded as a muscle. Thorndike exploded the formal discipline theory of education and with other psychologists exposed the limitations of formal mind training.

It was chiefly due to the findings of these psychologists that Latin has been dropped as a requirement for graduation by most schools. It was not dropped because it was too difficult but because educators needed more realistic and lifelike materials for teaching. The notion that Latin will improve English gave way to better methods of mastering English by studying English, writing and speaking English. Such subjects as Latin and geometry are offered in

today's curriculum for a real-life purpose and not to train
the mind.

Teachers realize that the best way to teach is to teach
through experience and firsthand direct relationships. Children must see relationships if effective learning is to occur.
Good teachers, of course, will always depend upon textbooks
and subject matter materials but they will be used as a
means to an end and not as ends in themselves. Subject
matter will be used along with audio visual aids, community
resources, outdoor education and other instructional aids to
meet both student needs and instructional goals. Disciplina-
ry values will not be attributed to any textbooks or to subject
matter areas; knowledge for knowledge sake and materials
for training the mind left the school systems when administrators and teachers realized that the mind is not a muscle.

4. KNOWLEDGE IS NOT THE ONLY GOAL OF EDUCA-
TION

For many centuries imparting knowledge was considered the chief goal of education. Culture in the Middle
Ages remained static for century after century. This was
not due to the fact that there was a lack of knowledge but
because of the acceptance of knowledge, and knowledge
alone, as the chief purpose of education.

Since knowledge was exalted as the mark of an educated man, facts and information were gathered and put into
textbooks. For years such textbooks have guided both the
content and the methods of formal instruction in the schools.

All knowledge was classified and organized into a doz-
en or so school subjects. Reading and memorization of
textbooks in these subject areas was the basic purpose of
education. Textbooks were written for every grade level
all with the idea of preparing the student for college entrance
examinations regardless of whether or not the student would
ever enter college. Critical thinking or the wisdom to use
knowledge did not receive as high a mark in the traditional
school as the ability to repeat facts, either written or oral.

Today, teachers are beginning to realize that textbooks set a limit on knowledge. Rather than teach from

one textbook, the modern teacher uses many textbooks, the library, the community, audio-visual aids, field trips and other outdoor education activities in order to gain knowledge and make this knowledge more meaningful.

In the modern classroom knowledge and factual materials are used in helping the student to meet his problems, to refine his own conceptual system, and to help him organize and use his own experience effectively. Education begins with the child and is expanded through his own experience and through his own environment. The refined system of knowledge of the adult world will not be forced upon the student unless it is of value to him here and now. If he needs such knowledge in the future, he will have been taught to find it as a lawyer or a medical doctor may at times consult their journals for information. The student will not be expected to store all pertinent information in his mind until such time that there is a need for it. It is beyond the power of any teacher to know what each individual student should know.

In the modern school, not knowledge but the art of the utilization of knowlege, is important. Knowledge alone is useless if the pupil does not know how to use it. Knowledge although important, is only one aspect of education. Wisdom is more important.

Educators of the past who stressed facts, textbooks, and encyclopedia knowledge are now concerned more with wisdom to use this knowledge--for knowledge alone is not enough in our rapid changing civilization. Educators of the past assumed that all thoughts had long been put down in books and all imaginations already expressed in poems and compositions. To have memorized the books and poems seemed enough. But the prophetic Emerson said over a century ago, "The world is new and untried. Do not believe the past. I give you the universe, a virgin today."

Schools today must continue to help children acquire the information and tools required by the complexity of modern life. Abilities in reading, writing, listening, speaking, and computation are more essential in modern society than ever before. Imparting knowledge, not for knowledge sake, but as a basis for critical thinking in the solution of individual and social problems and the development of independent study habits for specialized learnings in later years, is the task of the modern day teacher.

5. HABITS, VALUES, ATTITUDES AND APPRECIATIONS ARE IMPORTANT OUTCOMES OF EDUCATION

A child's learning is influenced by his established patterns of behavior. When he enters school, he has many fixed habits of health, nutrition, speech, interests, and perceptions relating to himself, to individuals and to groups. These habits influence considerably his social interactions. Education must help pupils clarify their understanding, shape their values and direct them into satisfying channels.

Modern teachers are concerned with strengthening positive habits in children and with eliminating those habits that are not desirable for successful living. In addition, the teacher aids the child in developing new habits as they grow and learn together.

In the past schools have too often emphasized drill without understanding or purpose, and as a consequence the acquisition of skills has been a dull, tiresome and meaningless routine. Children must understand thoroughly the need for and purposes of the learning task to be accomplished. They must see the need for repetitious drill and the need for perfection in performance of the task. Correct habits in observation, investigations, skill, study, reading and listening form the basis to other learnings. Since habit is so difficult to establish or to change it is important that the teacher follow through in establishing essential habits.

One of the fundamental purposes of public education is to inculcate and perpetuate the values which society believes to be essential for continued existence. It is vital in a democracy and to the American way of life that the schools uphold and teach successfully the values inherent in the democratic tradition.

Attitudes are feelings. Wholesome attitudes are fundamental to learning. A child who hates school will be difficult to teach. A child who believes that art is for girls will not enjoy his classes. As long as singing is considered effeminate, music lessons for boys will surely be rejected.

Children often learn their attitudes from others. This makes the teacher's role most important in establishing wholesome attitudes. Fortunately, attitudes are easier to establish and to change than habits. Living in a climate where the approach to learning is objective and positive, where the emphasis is on democratic principles and the worth of the individual, a child will tend to adapt wholesome attitudes which will help him live in a world of neighbors.

Children need to develop an endless variety of appreciation in addition to developing skills, values, attitudes and knowledges.

In the past the appreciation subjects have usually been thought of as music, art, crafts, literature, dance and drama. Today, educators realize that appreciation cannot be wholly confined to these specific subjects. Appreciation overflows into all areas of life, into all subject matter and into the learning of skills. Appreciation can give meaning and beauty to the routine daily tasks. Understanding brings appreciation of people, of the world and of other cultures.

Interest, attitude, understanding and interpretation are pre-requisites to appreciation. Teachers need to provide an environment which is rich in opportunities for listening, seeing, hearing, doing, and experimenting if they are to develop appreciations of selected studies. Teachers must provide sympathetic understanding; a climate for freedom of expression and originality; and encouragement and acceptance of a child's work in order to develop appreciations in a subject matter area.

6. TEST SCORES RATE THE TEACHER AS WELL AS THE PUPILS

The administering of teacher-made examinations and tests have become a common procedure in schools throughout the nation. If used right, this can be an important aspect of the education process, but if tests are given to classify students into certain slots, A, B, C, D, E, they are of questionable value. If a large proportion of pupils fail a test, a wise teacher will wonder if he did a good job in presenting the assignment, if his techniques are effective, if the test was too difficult, if the wording was obscure, or if he has demanded the questions to be answered in his own words.

Intelligence quotients, reading scores, and other test results should not be substituted for close personal relationships and individual guidance. Tests and evaluations discussed and administered with the students may help the teacher in determining efficiency in reaching teacher expectations as well as determining the progress of the students. They test both the teacher and the pupil. The college teacher who boasts that over one half of his class will fail his course cannot necessarily claim to be a good teacher.

Kelley says that teachers assume that it is more important to measure what has been learned than it is to learn. He produces evidence that this is a correct assumption by pointing out that:

> Since much of the time in school is spent in recitation we are really using our time evaluating what has been learned somewhere else. In our programs of testing and examining we are deceived by a student's ability to return abstractions to us, and we call it evidence of learning. We seem to assume that evaluation is an outside process--that is, that a person can truly evaluate somebody else, and supposedly, if he himself is to be evaluated, that it should be done by somebody else. Evaluation of what has been done hence becomes more important than doing, because more time is devoted to it.[9]

Finally, it must be stated that our most popular tests cannot measure the most important outcome of education. It can measure facts acquired and knowledges gained, but these may soon be forgotten after the examination. Imagination and creative thinking are not usually measured.

Grouping students by ability, so that the above-average are in one class, the average or below-average in another, doesn't seem to increase the achievement of either

[9]Earl C. Kelley, _Education For What Is Real_, Harper and Brothers, 1947, p. 22.

group according to a recent study at the State University of Iowa.

The study covered 500 students in 23 classes, some grouped by ability and some in regular classes. Fourth, fifth, and sixth grades were studied, with grouping occurring by IQ, age, sex, reading ability and teacher's appraisal. The investigator recording the study, Bradley Loomer, reported that the reading, language, vocabulary, word study and arithmetic "do not support the claimed advantage of grouping as opposed to no grouping." The disadvantage of grouping, in Loomer's view, is that slow students need the presence of the able students to stimulate and encourage them.

Loomer concluded: "The key to good education for children evidently rests with good teaching. The claim that the mechanical process of grouping will automatically produce better teaching and more skilled pupils is not supported by the evidence--at least in this study."

Cooperative Research projects[10] at the Universities of Chicago and Minnesota have documented the significant fact that creative ability and measured intelligence (I.Q.) are not identical. This discovery may well change educational procedures from kindergarten through graduate schools. In the past, and still in most situations, schools have operated on the assumption that the child with the high intelligence rating would also be the most creative. Some individuals do possess both kinds of abilities; some do not. The latter group may be ignored by teachers or excluded from educational opportunities that would ripen their creative powers into peak performances.

A second outcome of these investigations, equally important as the first, has been the development of substantial evidence that creative ability, unlike intelligence which remains relatively constant, can be developed, extended and improved. The implications of this possibility for school programs are obvious.

The next steps for research on creative ability are to discover the kinds of factors that make for creativity in a

---

[10]Taken from mimeographed report on the Cooperative Research Program by Lindley J. Stiles, Dean, School of Education, University of Wisconsin.

person, in any field, and to design educational programs and procedures that produce maximum development. When such knowledge is available, schools and teachers can be geared to the discovery and development of creativity. Achievement of this objective is of paramount importance to the nation as well as to the individuals whose potential creative talents are currently being ignored.

Einstein failed mathematics in grade school because his mind was above the trivial and insignificant mathematical formulas and problems for which he was being tested. An even more contemporary example of an outstanding scholar who failed mathematics is Werner Von Braun, the expert in America's space project.

7. EDUCATION IS MOST EFFECTIVE WHEN SUBJECT MATTER RELATES TO LIFE

Education cannot be divorced from life; it cannot be fragmented. Education is a whole process. It starts at birth and continues through elementary, junior high, high school, college and university, and still continues throughout life.

Critics may rant and rave about the "life adjustment" curriculum of the progressive schools, yet it had to have some merit to capture the fancy of a growing and dynamic democratic society--parents as well as educators. Like any other universally accepted philosophy it was not completely understood. John Dewey did not advocate doing away with subject-matter instruction and substituting "fun courses. He did not believe children should be left on their own. He did believe that they should be a partner in the learning process and that their learning should relate to their life here and now. Dewey pointed out that the schools had a responsibility to society and were practically useless unless they accepted this reponsibility.

Dewey describes how the schools have blindly followed scientific classification of knowledge to the point that they are almost completely divorced from experience. Subject matter has become so abstract that a large percentage of it is a waste of the student's time:

Facts are torn away from their original place in experience and rearranged with reference to some general principle. Classification is not a matter of child experience; things do not come to the individual pigeonholed. The vital ties of affection, the connecting bond of activity, hold together the variety of his personal experiences. The adult mind is so familiar with the notion of logically ordered facts that it does not recognize--it cannot realize--the amount of separating and reformulating which the facts of direct experience have to undergo before they can appear as a "study" or branch of learning. A principle, for the intellect, had to be distinguished and defined; facts have to be interpreted in relation to this principle not as they are in themselves. They have to be regathered about a new center which is wholly abstract and ideal...The studies as classified are the product, in a word, of the science of the ages, not of the experience of the child.[11]

Whitehead advocates the eradication of the "fatal disconnection of subjects" which he says kills the vitality of the modern curriculum. The solution which Whitehead urges is a single unity. He says:

There is only one subject-matter for education, and that is Life in all its manifestations. Instead of this single unity, we offer children--Algebra, from which nothing follows; Geometry, from which nothing follows; Science, from which nothing follows; History, from which nothing follows; a Couple of Languages, never mastered; and lastly, most dreary of all, Literature, represented by plays of Shakespeare, with philological notes and short analyses of plot and character to be in substance committed to memory. Can such a list be said to represent Life, as it is known in the midst of the living of it? The best that can be said of it is, that it is a rapid table of contents which a deity might run over in his mind while he was thinking of creating a world, and had not yet determined how to put it together.[12]

[11]John Dewey, The Child and the Curriculum, Chicago: The University of Chicago Press, 1902, pp. 10-11.
[12]Alfred North Whitehead, The Aims of Education, New York: The MacMillan Company, 1929, pp. 18-10

Outdoor education makes its finest contribution in the integration of subject matter. The integration of subject matter helps students see the whole before studying its parts. The best places to see the whole of anything are in its natural setting and this sometimes requires that the teacher leave the classroom.

Integration as found in nature and the out-of-doors before it is isolated and segmented into subject matter areas for classroom use helps children see things as they are and as they relate to their environment.

Furthermore, more efficient and longer-lasting learning and development of attitudes, habits, skills, values, and appreciations for life are best learned when the activities of school are similar to those of life and are learned firsthand.

8. EDUCATION SHOUD INCLUDE TEACHINGS AND EXPERIENCES FOR DEVELOPING EMOTIONAL HEALTH AND EMOTIONAL STABILITY

The twentieth century has often been referred to as the Age of Anxiety. Abnormal behavior is the major health problem in American society. Today, there are 700,000 people in mental institutions, and for every person hospitalized there are at least twenty more that need psychiatric aid. There are 4,000,000 mental defectives in the United States; 8,000,000 neurotic people; 750,000 chronic alcoholics; and over 250,000 Americans in federal, state and local penal institutions. Over 3,000,000 children have emotional and behavior problems. Coleman describes most vividly the conditions in modern society which have brought about this unhappy state:

> Modern man's path to happiness is not an easy one. It is beset by seemingly endless personal and social problems. Wars have disrupted personal life and left their wake of mutilations, loneliness, grief, and social unrest. Periodic breakdowns and runaways of the economic machinery--which has grown gigantically since the Industrial Revolution--have drained human energy and happiness in a way that can be seen only too clearly in the millions of victims of depression and inflation.

Racial discrimination, with its unreasoned feelings of superiority, hatred, and resentment, hurts both the individual and the community. Homes broken by divorce leave emotional scars upon parents and children alike. Excessive competition, conflicting pressure groups, rapid social change, and the threat of global atomic war further aggravate modern man's insecurities. And with all his uncertainties and anxieties, he has few moral beliefs to guide him or to make him feel that his life is meaningful and worth while. His faith in rugged individualism, material possessions, and technology as the ultimate values in life has proved sadly disillusioning. Yet he seems unable to return to his earlier religious values, but stumbles around blindly choosing as best he can among a myriad of religions, philosophies, and social programs.

Small wonder that on every side we see anxious, unhappy, bewildered people who are missing the fulfillment of their best potential because they cannot achieve a satisfactory adjustment to problems that seem just too great. Instead of smooth, effective functioning, we see widespread symptoms of personality maladjustment. In this Age of Anxiety, Americans spend some 10 billion dollars a year on liquor, books on personality adjustment have become best sellers, and stomach ulcers are a national health problem. [13]

A society comprised of men and women who are emotionally unstable is weakened socially, economically and physically. Since the schools in a democracy must be concerned with the problems of the society which support them they must give immediate and full attention to the emotional and physical development of every child. In a democratic society schools are not institutions for intellectual development exclusively. Physical health as well as emotional stability are the concern of the democratic society and, therefore, are important school problems.

A child's behavior is controlled both by his intellect and by his emotions. He develops his personality and character as a result of all the experiences and teachings that he encounters. The student's physical and mental health

[13]James C. Coleman, Abnormal Psychology and Modern Life. Chicago: Scott, Foresman and Company, 1956, pp. 2-3.

should be carefully analyzed and understood by teachers particularly in terms of need for various stages of growth. It is the day to day living at school, home, and in the community that influences the students behavior. The schools must assume a large share of leadership in the emotional development of students.

Unnatural physical conditions of classroom organization often cause tension and emotional disturbances among many students. Likewise classification of students, first by testing and then by room assignment frequently causes emotional problems. The classroom leadership wherein the teacher is strict, domineering and autocratic usually creates emotional problems for many students. Bells, whistles, rigid scheduling, quick lunches, and monitored halls and rooms are frequently additional causes of tensions and emotional problems. Improper lighting, poor ventilation, and other factors of physical plant control are not conducive to good mental health, emotional well being, and stability.

Most of the physical cause of school-centered emotional problems can be temporarily relieved by well-planned outdoor education experiences where the child has a chance to express himself freely and uninhibited in an informal and permissive atmosphere.

Unfortunately many teachers in the modern school are not qualified to carry out or administer these and the many other educational principles which are so necessary for the survival of the democratic society. No parent would want an incompetent physician to perform a major operation on his child. Why, then, should they be satisfied to turn the mind and body of their children over to incompetent teachers? Education, so important for molding children to live successfully and happily in a democracy, cannot be left to unqualified teachers. Education must be recognized as a profession. High professional standards must be set and monies must be available to employ the best teachers possible to guide the lives of the future generation and shape the society of tomorrow.

9. EDUCATION SHOULD FOCUS MORE ATTENTION ON THE AESTHETIC AND ETHICAL NEEDS OF CHILDREN

Every curriculum must be concerned with bringing out the potentialities of the whole child. The present day curriculum has relegated the subject of aesthetics to music and art specialists, thereby limiting aesthetic contentment and necessities to one small part of the child's life.

Gordon comments on the fact that aesthetics should not be regarded as the special domain of the "Fine Arts":

> As I watch people struggling to endow their daily lives with significance and beauty, it seems increasingly clear to me that the key to successful living is awareness. It is the insensitive ones who make the mistakes in taste, who serve the tasteless food, who blunder socially. It is the insensitive who are bored, and fatigued by their boredom. It is almost as though they were dead, because they are living only a fraction of the life that is potentially within them.
>
> The ones who are alive, who find everything interesting, are the ones who have developed a high degree of awareness. Their homes are always filled with beauty, no matter how low their income. They never have empty time on their hands because they are pursuing so many fascinating projects. They find life exciting, no matter their age or social status or educational record. They have learned how to see and to seek. They have achieved the most lasting of riches: They have made the thrill of discovery, which can occur again and again because there is more to discover than can be encompassed in ten lifetimes.
>
> Why are some so blessed and some not? Were they born that way, or is it something they achieved for themselves--or lost for themselves?
>
> I believe that everyone is born with a high endowment of awareness, for all children seem to have it in abundance. Most adults have lost their birthright, in varying degrees depending on how much they have exercised it. The problem is how to regain the use of what has atrophied.[14]

---

[14] Elizabeth Gordon, "Awareness." An Editorial, House Beautiful, January, 1959.

A fundamental need in the United States today is, according
to Walt Whitman in Leaves of Grass: "a class of native
authors, literatures . . . permeating the whole mass of
American mentality, taste, belief . . . begetting appropriate teachers, schools, manners, and as its grandest result
accomplishing . . . a religious and moral character be-
neath the political and productive and intellectual bases
of the State."

Traditional schools have neglected the cultural and
aesthetic aspects of subject matter. They have stressed
knowledges and facts, but have not opened up new vistas
and new appreciations whereby their learnings may reach
the level of creative living. Observation, insight and understanding, imagination manipulation and participation are
all pre-requisites to a rich and meaningful life. It is therefore the responsibility of the school to develop skills and
provide opportunities in singing, dramatics, arts and crafts,
speaking, dancing, and all the creative and aesthetic media
which lead to the wholesome development and adjustment of
all children. Too many children are denied aesthetic experiences in our modern schools because educators feel
that in the crowded curriculum there are too many other
things more important. The little aesthetic education received by too many of our young people today is second-
handed beauty as in pictures. Graduates of public schools,
thus, are unable to recognize and see beauty in real life.

Nature and the so-called useful arts should receive
their just share of aesthetic education. Outdoor education
is unique as a technique for developing aesthetic satisfaction. It is impossible for any teacher, however good or
bad, to exclude aesthetics from the woods, streams, and
meadows. Art pervades the activities of the entire out-of-
doors, is correlated with all activities and is experienced
directly by the students as they seek knowledge and understanding from nature.

Another aspect of educating the whole personality,
closely allied to aesthetic education and equally neglected
by our public schools, is ethical instruction, referred to
by many as character education.

Modern society has brought about a disintegration

of the home and has uprooted man from much of his security and loyalties enjoyed in the past. Behavior problems of children can no longer be left to the home and to the church. The schools must join other community agencies in meeting the ethical necessities of her children.

Grinnell[15] points out that "character building is more than an objective of education--it is the heart of education, the essential meaning of education. Nothing else in education is worth having without rich, significant character."

In the same article Grinnell broadly defines character as: (1) moral values and ethical principles such as honesty, responsibility and justice; (2) spiritual values such as respect for the individual, loyalty and altruism; (3) good citizenship as reflected in the school, the community and the larger world; (4) wisdom, compassion and courage which produces goodness along with greatness in a man or in a society; and (5) judgment and taste, which involves putting into practice all that one has learned concerning the relative worth of actions, things, and people.

A critical examination of the above salient points of character education brings about a realization that they are too important to be left to chance. The moral and ethical problem today is at a crisis. Experience in ethical instruction must be integrated with all subjects and in every aspect of the daily living of children.

10. LEISURE TIME EDUCATION MUST BECOME THE IMMEDIATE CONCERN OF THE SCHOOLS

We are living in a society which has become so highly mechanized and so well organized that leisure time is becoming almost as significant as working time.

Education for leisure is especially important in modern society because people have more leisure hours than ever before in the history of the world; because people need enjoyment and relaxation to ease tensions caused by the complications and strains of modern life; because modern machinery has robbed man of creative, free, and satisfying opportunities that formerly came from work; and, because

[15]John E. Grinnell, "Character Building In Youth." Phi Delta Kappan, February, 1959, p. 213

it is impossible for people to work all the time without recreation and relaxation.

It was not uncommon years ago for educational programs to focus most of their attention on course content that would prepare students for various professional fields of work. The educational programs were designed primarily with preparation for work as their goal. Many work programs were also planned to prepare students primarily for various vocations. Little consideration was given to preparation for leisure time since not as many individuals were privileged to have free time from employment.

We are now living in a society when leisure time is and will increasingly become one of our most significant educational needs.

Legislation, automation and other forces have given our youth an unwanted kind of leisure. Employment is difficult to obtain. Personal enjoyment and creative growth through recreational activities are sorely lacking or too expensive. Idleness and boredom prevail where recognition of leisure time education does not exist. Medical advances and social improvement in laws have provided many oldsters with a longer life and small monthly sustenance checks. Many individuals are retiring either voluntarily or forcefully at the age of 60 to 65 and many can expect to live an additional 10 - 15 or 20 years.

Other inducements to leisure time include paid vacations, shorter working weeks, leaves of absence, and push-button operations.

The schools of America can prepare each citizen for leisure time living through changes in the emphasis on methods of teaching in every school subject matter. There needs to be a balance between learning a subject matter area to prepare for life's work and education for aesthetic appreciation and leisure time enjoyment. Courses such as art and music appreciation might logically include learning activity skills for leisure time enjoyment.

The outdoor education program provides the most desirable laboratory to provide a good balance between education for life's work and education for leisure.

11. CHILDREN MUST BE TAUGHT TO LIVE IN A DEMOCRATIC SOCIETY

Children do not enter school equipped with the skills of living together in a democratic community. If the democratic process is to improve, in fact, if it is to continue in a world of encroaching despotism, the skills of living together must be taught by the schools.

In the past, democracy has been taught from books and in too many cases in a very autocratic manner. Memorization of the Declaration of Independence, the Bill of Rights and other important historical documents and speeches was considered ample in fitting children to live in a democracy.

Today, educators are beginning to realize that true democratic education is more than book knowledge; it is a way of life, a social faith; a belief in the dignity of man. The American Policies Commission of the National Education Association lists six articles of democratic faith:

> First, the individual human being is of surpassing worth.
> Second, the earth and human culture belong to all men.
> Third, men can and should rule themselves.
> Fourth, the human mind can be trusted and should be set free.
> Fifth, the method of peace is superior to that of war.
> Sixth, racial, cultural, and political minorities should be tolerated, respected, and valued.[16]

There are too many discouraging signs in America, today, that indicate much is to be desired in teaching democracy. Too many Americans are apathetic toward their voting privileges either through abuse or neglect. There is still a great deal of animosity toward minority groups on the one hand, and too much abuse of the democratic principles by minority groups on the other. Failure in teaching democracy is further demonstrated in the increased amount of legislation that is being passed to eliminate dis-

---

[16]American Policies Commission. Education of Free Men In American Democracy. Washington, D.C.: National Education Association, 1941, p. 31

crimination of various kinds throughout the country. If the schools were doing a satisfactory job in teaching human relations and democratic group living such legislation would not be necessary.

The schools must stress the political as well as the non-political aspect of education. The schools must, through political education, give children experience in conducting their own affairs in order to prepare them to meet the demands of public life. Children must have an opportunity to exercise their precious right of self-government, to accept responsibility, and to learn to abide by the rules that bring the most good to the most people.

Democracy, in order to flourish, requires an intelligent and enlightened citizenry. The qualities required of a democratic citizen are not inborn; they must be nurtured by the home, the school and the community. In comparison to citizens of almost any European country, the American citizen is almost totally ignorant of the principles and ideals of his government. The majority of the people in the United States cannot name their state and national representatives. Communist countries, on the other hand, realize the importance of education and train every student from kindergarten through college arguments for the communistic system of government. Democratic societies cannot afford to do less.

12. THE SCHOOLS MUST EDUCATE FOR WORLD UNDERSTANDING

It took many decades to develop a spirit of nationalism in the United States.

The thirteen separate and independent colonies did not eliminate local prejudices and ingrained traditions merely by banding together in a Union. For many years schools taught nationalism through memorization of important documents, teaching about their national heroes, and repeating the Pledge of Allegiance to the flag, yet the spirit of patriotism and nationalism did not reach its peak until the early part of the twentieth century.

Just as historical forces replaced local and sectional provincialism with nationalism, new political, economic,

and cultural forces are bringing about drastic modifications
in nationalism. Patriotism, today, has a different meaning
than it did one hundred years ago. Children are taught that
a citizen does not have to die for his country in order to be
patriotic; it is even more important to live for it. Furthermore, in the move from isolationism to a more universal
aspect of government, nationalism is a retarding and re-
actionary force in modern society. It fosters exclusiveness
in an age of cooperation.

Problems, today, are more international in scope
than national. The earth is a much smaller planet than it
was twenty-five years ago. This seeming shrinkage has
been due to the tremendous revolution brought about in
transportation and communication. Today, no city or
country is more than hours away. Many millions of people from all parts of the world visit other countries annu-
ally. Happenings in the remotest part of the world are
common knowledge to every nation within minutes.

Accompanying the revolutions and forces bringing
about closer interdependence in world living is an irre-
sistible trend toward world unity. Two world conflicts
have failed to solve the world's problems and the third
world conflict is too terrible to contemplate. Force, as
a means of settling disputes must be replaced by treaties
and international laws, but even this method of insuring
peace cannot be effective without education for world understanding.

Human societies must be reorganized and re-edu-
cated to live in a world of mutual interdependence and cooperation. The schools must examine their curricula and
become an agency for promoting world understanding and
good will. Womer sums the problem up very clearly:

> The havoc of two world wars makes it evident that some
> agency competent to conserve the peace must be pro-
> vided if modern civilization is to endure, but it is
> open to question whether a league of independent and
> sovereign states in any conceivable form would suffice
> as such an agency. The solution of the problem calls
> for a federal union of peoples as citizens rather than
> a league of states. Such a union, beginning with the

free peoples of the bonafide democracies, and organized
with a view of peaceful growth by the absorption of
other peoples as through advancing culture they become
matured for freedom and self-government, would soon
constitute a political entity more powerful than all
the other peoples of the world, and therefore in a position to command the people of the world. The movement for such a union has already begun, and another
quarter of a century should and probably will see it
well on the way. Possibly the proposed international
organization is a necessary first step that will contribute to a union of peoples. That those who framed
the Charter entertained some such hope is shown by the
opening words of the preamble: "We, the peoples of
the United Nations, determined to save succeeding
generations from the scourge of war. . . ."[17]

The danger of world destruction makes it imperative
for nations to work together through some type of world organization. People from all nations need to come together
to build common world policies. It is either a matter of
cooperation and survival or a matter of isolation and destruction. The United States cannot run the world; no nation can. The atomic bomb has obliviated man-made barriers and national boundary lines. Man has been transformed from a national to a world citizen. Tribal loyalties
and instinct are not appropriate for life in the new world
community. Security can no longer be found in armies
and navies. Wealth and disproportionate abundance of
resources by any nation is no longer needed for coercion
or bargaining purposes. Any nation, however small, is
potentially as strong as the largest nation. Two hundred
well placed atomic bombs can be just as effective as two
thousand bombs.
The whole world is entering a new age of learning as
the mobility of people and ideas is breaking down traditional
beliefs and customary designs for living in each community
of the world. The schools have a tremendous task in helping the United States keep abreast of the new knowledge,
new understandings and new modes of living as nations

[17]Parley Paul Womer, Citizenship And The New Day. New York: Abingdon-Cokesbury
Press, 1945, p. 222

throughout the world join together economically, politically, and socially in mutual trust and world brotherhood.

Former president Dwight D. Eisenhower sums up the need for a realistic approach to education in a commencement speech at Pennsylvania State College a few years ago. He said:

> In this country we emphasize both liberal and practical education. But too often it is a liberal, practical education for the same person . . . Hand and head and heart were made to work together. They must work together. They should be educated together.

When colleges and universities reach the point that they rest their claim for fame not on the number of graduates that make honorary academic societies, but count their greatness in terms of the useful citizens and leaders they have produced, education will have taken a great step forward.

Selected References

American Policies Commission, *Education of Free Men In American Democracy.* Washington, D. C. : National Education Association, 1941.

Bayles, Ernest E. , *The Theory and Practice of Teaching,* New York: Harper, 1950.

Bode, Boyd H. , *Democracy As a Way of Life,* New York: The Macmillan Company, 1939.

Brameld, Theodore, *Education For The Emerging Age Newer Ends and Stronger Means,* New York: Harper and Brothers, 1961.

Brameld, Theodore, *Ends and Means In Education,* New York: Harper and Brothers, 1950.

Brameld, Theodore, *Philosophies of Education In Cultural Perspective,* New York: The Dryden Press, 1955.

Bruner, Jerome S. , *The Process of Education,* Cambridge: Harvard University Press, 1960.

Childs, John L. , *Education and Morals,* New York: Appleton-Century-Crafts, Inc., 1950.

44

Coleman, James C., *Abnormal Psychology and Modern Life*, Chicago: Scott, Foresman and Company, 1956.

Cole, Luella, *Teaching In The Elementary School*, New York: Rinehart, 1939.

Dewey, John, *The Child and the Curriculum*, Chicago: The University of Chicago Press, 1902.

Dewey, John, *Democracy and Education*, New York: The Macmillan Company, 1916.

Dewey, John, *Experience and Education*, New York: The Macmillan Company, 1938.

Drake, William E., *The American School In Transition*, Englewood Cliffs, N. J.: Prentice-Hall, 1955.

Gould, G. and Yoakam, G. A., *The Teacher and His Work*, New York: Harpers, 1951.

Gross, Richard E., Zeleny, Leslie D. and others, *Educating Citizens for Democracy*, New York: Oxford University Press, 1958.

Grinnell, John E., "Character Building In Youth," *Phi Delta Kappan*, February, 1959.

Grinnell, J. E. and Young, Raymond J., *The School and the Community*, New York: The Ronald Press, 1955.

Hildreth, Gertrude, *Child Growth Through Education*, New York: The Ronald Press, 1948.

Kelley, Earl C., *Education For What Is Real*, New York: Harper and Brothers, 1947.

Larrabee, Eric and Meyersohn, Ralf (Editors), *Mass Leisure*, Glencoe, Illinois: The Free Press, 1958.

MacConnell, C. W., Melby, F. O., and Arndt, C. O., *New Schools For a New Culture*, New York: Harper and Brothers, 1943.

Mayer, Frederick, *A History of Educational Thought*, Columbus, Ohio: Charles E. Merrill Books, 1960.

Mayer, Frederick, *Philosophy of Education For Our Times*, New York: The Odyssey Press, 1958.

Mursell, James L., *Education For American Democracy*, New York: Norton, 1943.

Rugg, Harold and Shumaker, Ann, *The Child-Centered School*, New York: World Book Company, 1928.

Slay, Ronald J. and Monahan, Tom, "World Cooperation: A Challenge To Teacher Education," *Phi Delta Kappan*, November, 1960.

Soule, George, *Time For Living*, New York: The Viking Press, 1956.

Smith, T. V., *The Democratic Way of Life*, Chicago: University of Chicago Press, 1926.

Stratemeyer, F. B. and others, *Developing a Curriculum For Modern Living*, New York: Teachers College, Columbia University, 1947.

Washburne, Carleton, *A Living Philosophy of Education*, New York: The John Day Company, 1940.

Whitehead, Alfred North, *The Aims of Education*, New York: The Macmillan Company, 1929.

Womer, Parley Paul, *Citizenship and the New Day*, New York: Abingdon-Cokesbury Press, 1945.

Yoakam, Gerald A. and Simpson, Robert G., *Modern Methods and Techniques of Teaching*, New York: The Macmillan Company, 1948.

Chapter 2

PRINCIPLES OF
PROGRAM PLANNING

The outdoor education program involves all experiences associated with living and learning out of doors. These experiences may vary from a ten minute study of plant life on the school ground to an extended camping experience. The educational values of outdoor experiences are becoming more necessary and more important to all students each day. The needs and interests of youth in today's society are quite different than they were only a generation ago. Future generations will discuss problems of foreign countries as freely as they now discuss our own local problems. They will discuss the scientific exploration of the universe as freely as people today discuss scientific advances in the airplane. They will discuss the effects of cybernation[1] on our way of life as thoroughly as we discuss the effects of the industrial revolution on our way of life. Their leisure-time activities will be real experiences that former generations longed for and dreamed about; and their concepts regarding transportation, communication, medicine, and food will be more phenomenal than present-day concepts regarding jet planes, television, antibiotics and vending machines.

In spite of all the scientific advantages inherited by youth of today at birth, every individual still possesses the same basic human needs and desires that man has possessed for centuries.

The greatest challenge to the educational system today is finding the best curriculum for the schools which

---

[1] For further study see the report to the Center For The Study of Democratic Institutions, Box 4068, Santa Barbara, California. Donald N. Michael, Cybernation: The Silent Conquest.

will provide the scientific and factual information that will
be needed and the curriculum that will also give equal regard to the basic psychological and sociological needs of
all students.

A good outdoor education program which is based on
sound educational principles can be one of the most valuable
complementary or supplementary offerings to the present
day school curriculum.

The outdoor education program provides new ways for
students to learn factual information about man and his universe. It provides a laboratory for directed experiences
where students may learn more about themselves and their
fellow men. It provides teachers with opportunities for accomplishing the objectives of education through an entirely
different and more challenging media. It associates activities and experiences to educational objectives. It makes
education more interesting and enjoyable; and it provides
opportunities to learn many skills to prepare for our new
leisure.

Certain basic principles for planning programs in outdoor education should be observed. By following certain
principles it will insure the successful accomplishment of
the objectives of outdoor education and will also prevent unnecessary duplication of activities which may better be offered in the classroom or by other educational agencies.
The following twelve principles should serve as a guide in
the development of outdoor education programs.

1. The outdoor education program should be planned
   so as to meet the general aims and objectives of
   education.
2. The outdoor education program should be planned
   so it will serve as a catalyst to all subject matter
   areas of the curriculum.
3. The outdoor education program should be closely
   related to the natural environment.
4. The outdoor education program should be planned
   purposefully.
5. The outdoor education program should be planned
   to meet the needs and interests of the participants.
6. The outdoor education program should be planned

in a democratic manner in cooperation with all participants.

7. The outdoor education program should be planned in relation to available facilities and areas.
8. The outdoor education program should be planned with respect to available leadership.
9. The outdoor education program should provide opportunity for repose and meditation.
10. The outdoor education program should be flexible.
11. The outdoor education program should provide for continuing and progressive levels of attainment.
12. The outdoor education program should provide opportunity for creative self expression.

THE OUTDOOR EDUCATION PROGRAM SHOULD MEET THE GENERAL AIMS AND OBJECTIVES OF EDUCATION

All programs associated with the school curriculum must prove their value and contribution to the overall aims and objectives of education. The only justification for introducing new programs into the school curriculum is that it provides a better and more efficient way to accomplish well-established educational objectives.

Research has shown that outdoor education programs contribute as much or more to general education as any other program in the school curriculum. Studies indicate that learning takes place faster and that knowledge is retained longer through outdoor education than through regular formal teachings.

A number of essential plans are needed before an outdoor education program is introduced into the school curriculum. Some of the more important considerations that need to be decided upon in regard to educational aims and objectives include: (1) a review of educational aims and objectives in terms of present-day needs of students, (2) a review of these objectives in terms of how well the present curriculum meets them, (3) a study of the contribution an outdoor education program could make in fulfilling these aims and objectives, (4) an evaluation of existing outdoor education programs, (5) a faculty survey which would indicate how each subject matter area might improve the objectives of their course of study through outdoor education, and (6) a coordinated plan for integrating subject matter areas into planned experiences that would better fulfill the aims and objectives of education.

THE OUTDOOR EDUCATION PROGRAM SHOULD SERVE TO INTEGRATE AND CORRELATE SUBJECT MATTER AREAS

We are living in a day and age when all facets of society have turned to specializations. Our labor force is composed of specialists; our medical profession is composed of specialists; our white-collar workers are composed of specialists and in many vocations and professions there are even specialists in special fields of endeavor. It must be recognized that America's economy, health, and to a large extent general welfare depends upon specializations. When specialization is categorically applied to the educational system it may tend to weaken the aims and objectives of education rather than strengthen them. It is an important function of education to concentrate studies and research in special subject matter areas. It is just as important a function of education to show the inseparable relationships of all subject matter areas found in the school curricula.

The philosophy of outdoor education is based on a study of the whole and the interrelation and inter-dependence of all of its parts. It involves a study of nature and man which encompasses all special subject matter areas of the curriculum.

The outdoor education program includes opportunities for leadership and teaching by all school personnel involved in teaching, guidance, administration, and leadership of youth.

THE OUTDOOR EDUCATION PROGRAM SHOULD BE PLANNED PURPOSEFULLY

Sound educational programs do not just happen. They are purposefully planned. The school curriculum is composed of teachings and activities in many areas of learning that have been accepted only after research and experience has proven them essential to education. Each of these programs have a definite place and a definite responsibility in the total education of the child. The traditional programs now found in the public schools must meet certain educational objectives. These objectives are planned and reviewed by the teacher, curriculum committee, school administrator and finally the school board.

The outdoor education program should be considered an integral part of the total school curriculum.

It is essential that the same study and planning used for traditional programs should also apply to the outdoor education program.

Many years of research and experience have already influenced outdoor educational programs in the United States. The planning process in establishing an outdoor education program for the first time involves a careful analysis of existing programs. The program director must be acquainted with research in outdoor education and in the light of this research guide the planning group to focus their ideas and suggestions on five closely interrelated phases or questions which need to be considered.

What is to be accomplished?

What materials are needed and what activities should be used?

What methods and procedures are to be followed?

What administrative organization is needed for conducting the program? and,

How shall the program be appraised?

In other words, a group faced with planning a program for outdoor education must consider the objectives; materials; activities; methods and techniques; organization; and evaluation.

The above phases of program planning cannot be considered as separate entities or in isolation one from the other. The objectives of outdoor education dictate the program which in turn dictates the organizational structure and the methods employed for learning. Evaluation of the program must consider the degree to which all the above phases contribute to the objectives of education.

The program for outdoor education must be purposefully planned throughout. The basic objectives should be arrived at cooperatively by the staff; each activity and each area of learning should contribute in some way to these objectives. Merely offering a large number of activities will not result in a good program. The ages, abilities, skills, knowledges, needs, and interests of the participants must be considered in order to select program activities which will contribute to the objectives of education. The welfare of the participant is always paramount to education; it is always the focal point in program planning.

Purposeful program planning cannot be accomplished on the spur of the moment, nor can it be accomplished in one meeting. It is a continuous and unending process. Some months before the class goes camping, the program director and his staff may prepare a skeleton outline which will serve as a framework within which the outdoor education program may operate. In pre-planning the outdoor education program or in setting up this skeleton or rough draft, the program director with the help of his staff must determine the capacity and potentialities for learning in the out-of-doors by carefully appraising his leadership and their special abilities, the background of the students, the program possibilities offered by the particular outdoor setting or area, the transportation available for trips and tours, and many other circumstances peculiar to the local situation.

Since the objectives of education and the possibilities of meeting them through outdoor education are the guide posts that indicate the content and direction of the program, the staff should not only keep them in mind but should also understand and analyze the meaning and scope of each objective listed. By cooperatively listing, analyzing, and defining the objectives, the program planners can assure themselves of a unity of purpose and a singleness of direction in the fulfillment of these objectives.

THE OUTDOOR EDUCATION PROGRAM SHOULD BE PLANNED TO MEET THE NEEDS AND INTERESTS OF THE PARTICIPANTS

The program exists to serve the children. In all types and phases of planning for learning in the out-of-doors, the needs and interests of the participants should be uppermost in the minds of the program planners. Areas are set aside, facilities planned, and leadership provided for the primary purpose of helping children find maximum satisfaction in the out-of-doors. Thus, the human element--the needs, interests, capacities, and desires of the participants--is the primary consideration in the development of an outdoor education program. This does not imply that outdoor education should endeavor to meet all the needs of the student. It should, however, meet those which by its unique nature it is better qualified to fulfill.

All people, young and old alike, have certain basic needs. These needs have been listed, classified, and re-listed by psychologists and accepted by educators since the turn of the century. The very process of growing up and living gregariously in a society brings with it acceptance of certain basic needs, drives, or tensions in each individual that determine, or at least influence, action. Although psychologists list many needs of children, those which are more directly related to program planning may be listed as: the need for belonging to a group, the need for security, the need for achievement, the need for recognition, the need to be free from fear, the need to experience success, the need to experience failure, the need to be free from guilt, the need for love and affection, the need for creative self-expression, and the need for understanding.

In 1952 the Educational Policies Commission issued the Imperative Needs of Youth which stressed the social concept of needs rather than the psychological.

1. All youth need to develop salable skills and those understandings and attitudes that make the worker an intelligent and productive participant in economic life. To this end, most youth need supervised work experience as well as education in the

skills and knowledge of their occupations.

2. All youth need to develop and maintain good health and physical fitness.

3. All youth need to understand the rights and duties of the citizen of a democratic society, and to be diligent and competent in the performance of their obligations as members of the community and citizens of the state and nation.

4. All youth need to understand the significance of the family for the individual and society and the conditions conducive to successful family life.

5. All youth need to know how to purchase and use goods and services intelligently, understanding both the values received by the consumer and the economic consequences of their acts.

6. All youth need to understand the methods of science, the influence of science on human life, and the main scientific facts concerning the nature of the world and of man.

7. All youth need opportunities to develop their capacities to appreciate beauty in literature, art, music, and nature.

8. All youth need to be able to use their leisure time well and to budget it wisely, balancing activities that yield satisfactions to the individual with those that are socially useful.

9. All youth need to develop respect for other persons, to grow in their insight into ethical values and principles, and to be able to live and work cooperatively with others.

10. All youth need to grow in their ability to think rationally, to express their thoughts clearly, and to read and listen with understanding.[2]

While it is imperative that the program director keep the interests of the participants in mind while planning their program, it is equally important that he consider their needs. Very little can be taught unless the child is interested in learning, but on the other hand little learning occurs if the teacher does not challenge children to new interests.

[2]Educational Policies Commission. Education For All American Youth. Washington, D.C.: National Education Association, 1952.

The outdoor education program must be built around both the needs and interests of the participant. Many of the activities are so universal that there is little doubt as to their appeal. However, outdoor education should expand and cultivate interests and provide for older children whose interests have become more diverse. Common interests give the program a starting point; from here the program may be expanded and enriched according to each individual's interests through other activities which yield a pleasant experience.

The implication for outdoor education, once the needs and interests theory is accepted, will be more significant. Volumes have been written on such basic educational concepts as accept the child as he is and where he is, be sensitive to the child's feelings and desires, be friendly to the child, reassure the child, help the child develop his own values, treat the child as an individual, love the child, make the child feel wanted and accepted, praise the child, recognize the child, encourage the child in self-expression and limitless other suggestions for fulfilling the desires and wishes of the individual.

Another implication for education in general, and outdoor education in particular, is the fact that teachers and counselors must have a background in child psychology and the psychology of learning. It is a mark of good leadership to be able to identify the needs and interests of the children on the one hand, and to provide a stimulating and educational sound program to fulfill these needs and interests on the other. A teacher or counselor with an educational background in psychology and child growth and development will not make the mistake of imposing his own interests and experience as a guide for the student. Furthermore, he will know the technique in bringing the participants into the process of identifying their own needs and will be able to help them recognize less obvious needs. This requires an understanding of the background of the student, to the extent that this can be determined, and a sharing by the student in program planning and selection of the activities. Giving the students a part in planning and conducting the program helps assure the type of program that meets their needs and interests.

THE OUTDOOR EDUCATION PROGRAM SHOULD BE PLANNED IN A DEMOCRATIC MANNER IN COOPERATION WITH ALL THE PARTICIPANTS

Self government is the very essence of democracy. To perpetuate a society, including its form of government, has always been one of the chief purposes of education. A basic assumption in a democracy is that intelligent participation in government by everyone results in the best possible decisions for all. Only through cooperative effort in solving group problems and by having a hand in shaping and governing his own affairs can an individual achieve the highest level of attainment in a democratic society. This is true freedom. This, in itself, is the acceptance of the dignity of man.

Every school administrator in the country would agree that teaching democracy and self government as a function of the school is one of the objectives of education in the United States. Practically every professional education committee or group who have listed the function and purposes of education agree that the general function of education has two aspects: (1) to recognize the dignity of each individual and to develop his personality for maximum use in a society, and (2) to perpetuate the democratic form of government.

John Dewey's statement that "we learn by doing" has withstood the test of many critics of education. Skills in democratic living are learned. The best way to teach democracy is to practice it. Students who do not have skills in self government should be given a chance to experience them and as their understanding increases and their ability grows they should be given the opportunity for practice in, and responsibility for, the governing of their own affairs. Children learn democracy by living democratically. They learn to assume responsibilities by having opportunites to assume them. Handing out pre-planned and prescribed programs is not educationally sound nor does it contribute greatly to personality development or democratic living.

The more experience children get in managing their own affairs under proper supervision, the more likely they are to accept responsibility to cooperate in all phases of the program. Furthermore, the democratic process strengthens the outdoor education program by developing leadership traits in all children.

The extent to which a program director has children share in program planning will be the extent to which one of the basic purposes of outdoor education is being achieved. Children who are guided through the educational process of identifying their needs and planning programs for these needs are getting the best experience possible. Wholesome attitudes, understandings, and appreciations which may last beyond the outdoor education experience are possible through democratic practice in camp.

The school camp program offers the best and most complete laboratory for directed experiences in democratic group living.

Since the teaching of skills in democratic living is one of the objectives of outdoor education it follows that the program should be built around the decentralized unit plan of camping. This allows for more local representation and self identification which is in keeping with our democratic form of government. Furthermore, the division of the campers into small groups enables the counselor to better know the needs and interests of each individual camper.

The National Program Committee of the American Camping Association in 1951 listed sixteen items gauged to measure the degree of democracy in camp. They stated that democracy in camping is actually operating:

1. When counselors are selected on the basis of their understanding of democratic, creative methods of leadership, and when they are democratic in their relationships with each other.
2. When adequate planning is provided for group program planning, the program planning and policy determination become a cooperative experience between campers and adults.
3. When campers have an opportunity to carry out the decisions they have made.
4. When campers are encouraged to engage in spontaneous activity.

5. When living groups are composed of a reasonable age range, so that campers can function on problems with which they are able to cope.
6. When opportunities are provided for the self-expression of individuals and age groups.
7. When the focus of program is the recognized needs of the campers.
8. When campers are given and accept responsibility for their own welfare.
9. When tent or cabin groups are composed of a cross-section of the social, religious, and economic groups that make up the total camp family.
10. When activities are so handled by adult leaders that campers gain a sense of security in their group, a respect for themselves and for others.
11. When the pressure of scheduled activities is so relaxed that campers have sufficient time for contemplation.
12. When major program emphasis is given to developing opportunity for campers to take part in work activities related directly to living experience in the out-of-doors.
13. When the camping experience is characterized by freedom of choice, recognition of campers as persons, opportunity for fullest participation in group living experiences in the out-of-doors, and development of a sense of individual and group responsibility.
14. When individuals or groups have the chance to participate in planning for inter-group or camp-wide activities, through councils, committees and other types of organization.
15. When decisions of such councils are carried back for discussion and action by the groups represented by individual campers.
16. When campers have a chance to evaluate their program and practices.

THE OUTDOOR EDUCATION PROGRAM SHOULD BE PLANNED IN RELATION TO AVAILABLE FACILITIES AND AREAS

The outdoor education program should, ideally, dictate facilities. The outdoor education program does not necessarily have to be conducted in an extensive wilderness area devoted to park, forest or conservation uses. It would be desirable if all school districts could have extensive land holdings of this kind either within or without the school district. These areas are primarily desirable for extended programs in outdoor education usually involving school camping.

A survey of all facilities available for outdoor education purposes should be made. This survey would start with opportunities that exist on the school grounds, vacant lots, local parks, farms, forest preserves, and other similar facilities. Many federal, state, and county agencies have land which may be used either with or without special permits.

Each area of the United States will find different assets in educational ventures for the students. Facilities will range in difference from ocean to desert; from farm pond to lake; from mountain to plain; from forests to sagebrush; and from rich, loam soil to rocky, barren wasteland. Other important factors concerning facilities include varying studies in geography, history, folklore, economics, language arts, and leisure-time pursuits. However, good planning looks beyond the immediate use of existing facilities to the selection and development of new areas and facilities to meet the demands of the future. Long term planning is an important phase of programming for outdoor education.

The outdoor education program is enhanced or limited by available areas and facilities. The location of the outdoor education site or laboratory, whether it is on a lake shore or in the middle of a dense forest; whether it is surrounded by urban or rural life; whether it is one mile from the school or agency or twenty miles away, will affect the program. The availability of, or lack of, facilities determine what activities can profitably be included in the program. Quite frequently the man-made facilities in a school camp will directly influence the outdoor education program.

The number, size, and location of the cabins, dining halls, and other buildings determine the number of children in each group and the organizational set-up which in turn will affect the program.

An outdoor education laboratory or camp site with little in the way of equipment and supplies in many ways is a better facility than those with elaborate resort-type buildings and facilities. Fine tennis courts, volleyball courts, baseball field, and modern dormitories with all the conveniences of a modern city tend to dictate programs which are duplicated by the schools, recreation departments, and other public agencies. On the other hand, a wilderness area with very little to offer in terms of the comforts of home, with little or no commercial equipment and supplies necessitates programming which makes use of the natural environment and indigenous materials. It also allows the teacher to structure the program to give students a better experience in democratic group living.

THE OUTDOOR EDUCATION PROGRAM SHOULD BE PLANNED WITH RESPECT TO AVAILABLE LEADERSHIP

Most classroom teachers should be qualified to teach outside the classroom as well as inside the classroom. In most instances it should be the responsibility of the classroom teacher to plan and conduct outdoor experiences when these experiences are helpful or essential in helping students to better understand what is being taught.

Professional educational literature reveals that there is a definite trend in the public schools towards more and more participation by teachers in class field trips and school journeys. The leadership for beginning programs in outdoor education may be encouraged through the classroom teacher. Some of the fear that many classroom teachers have regarding outdoor education programs includes: lack of class control because of the informal nature of the experiences; public sentiment about being out of class; a lack of comprehensive knowledge concerning nature; administrative difficulties in terms of arrangements and scheduling; and a sense of responsibility for the safety and welfare of their students while off school grounds.

Many schools have overcome these fears through ad-

ministrative changes, in-service training programs, pilot
and experimental programs and by preparing brochures and
booklets with suggested field trips, excursions and school
journeys.

Many schools throughout this country have established
permanent facilities for extended programs in outdoor education. The school camping programs involve a different
problem in educational leadership. The school camping
programs often range from a one week experience to a two
week experience. The selection and planning for leadership
in this kind of program is more involved and requires a
selection of talent among the teachers so the maximum
benefit will be derived from the outdoor experience.

The capacities and limitations of the available leadership in the school may be an enriching or deterring factor
in planning programs for outdoor education. A staff which
is predominately sports minded is apt to direct the program
toward too much stress on this type of activity. Teachers
tend to teach those activities in which they have the most
skill and knowledge.

Ideally, the program content should determine the
leadership requirements for outdoor education. It is the
responsibility of the outdoor education director to appraise
teacher qualifications, determine their special interests,
and stress program activities for which his teachers are
best qualifed. The director will want to improve this leadership and will provide in-service training and workshops
in outdoor education to stimulate interest and develop skills
in teaching in the out-of-doors.

The budget allowed for leadership too often is a limiting factor especially in view of the fact that leadership,
more than any other factor, is necessary for an outdoor
education program and is the key to its success. A camp
director often obtains general counselors as well as special
counselors and activity specialists which will directly affect
the intensity and breadth of the program. Counselors should
be selected because they have certain general qualifications
for the job, but at the same time maximum use should be
made of their special talents. For example, a counselor
with an excellent background in music should be shared as

much as possible by all the campers. A specialist in Indian lore may serve as a counselor and at the same time be able to introduce Indian lore into the entire program through nature, pioneering, and the campfire ceremonies. The program director should select a fully qualified staff with as much variety as possible in interests, abilities, training, and experience to assure a well-rounded, balanced, and rich experience. The quality of the program is directly related to the quality of leadership.

In pre-planning or in the development of the skeleton program consideration must be given to the staff required to provide the guidance and direction needed for fulfillment of the objectives. The director is fortunate if monies are available for hiring this leadership. If the present school staff is to be used then, the director will have to select specialists in the areas where they will be most needed. He then usually provides in-service training to prepare the staff for the highest possible level of knowledge and ability in outdoor education.

In the final analysis the success or failure of the outdoor education program depends upon the quality of leadership. Poor leadership will cause the program to fall short of the philosophy expressed and objectives set for outdoor education. Therefore, it is of utmost importance that great care be given to the selection and training of leaders.

THE OUTDOOR EDUCATION PROGRAM SHOULD BE CLOSELY RELATED TO THE NATURAL ENVIRONMENT

The terms "outdoor education" and "camping" imply living in the open spaces, in the woods, on the lakes and streams, and in wilderness areas as opposed to urban and man-made settings. The term, outdoor education, also implies that it has something unique to offer; otherwise, it would have no excuse for being. This implication leads to an obvious assumption that programs in outdoor education should not duplicate activities which can better be offered at home or in the community by schools, churches, or other educational agencies. If the basic philosophy and the true objectives of outdoor education are understood a duplication of activities will not be reflected by buildings or by commercial supplies such as craft kits, radios and other conveniences of civilization. Unless the program director and staff understand the philosophy of outdoor education and its uniqueness in education, it may not do the things for which it is best suited. Camps which feature radios and television sets, comic books, competitive sports programs, and "nature study" taught in a museum or classroom atmosphere can hardly be said to have an accepted philosophy of outdoor education. It is hard to justify establishing an outdoor education laboratory which includes baseball fields, tennis courts, elaborate buildings and other facilities which already exist on the school ground or are provided by other agencies within the city. It seems illogical to build an elaborate building in which to study nature. Outdoor education has one important and unique contribution to make to education and that is the out-of-doors.

Man's heritage belongs to the soil. The history of civilization is the history of man's struggle with the soil and with the elements. In earlier days every member of the family had a firsthand responsibility in earning his livelihood. One of the greatest deterrents to childhood education is its removal from reality. A good program in outdoor education will explore the outdoors to the fullest. It will stress those things which by its nature it is uniquely fitted to do.

THE OUTDOOR EDUCATION PROGRAM SHOULD PROVIDE OPPORTUNITY FOR REPOSE AND MEDITATION

Since the turn of the century rural life has become, and is becoming, more urban in nature. Not only are more people moving to the city but those who stay on the farm have all the conveniences of city living. The day is past when the entire family had a responsibility in working the soil with hand tools and grappling with nature and the elements for a living. Farm children have about as much leisure time today as their city cousins. The modern farm is equipped with time-saving and labor-saving machinery for every farm chore. Thus, the movement to the cities and the invention of modern farm equipment have divorced children from living intimately with the earth and from their heritage. Schools have become a world of make-believe, a miniature and artificial staging of real life. For both farm and city dwellers this is the age of machines and technology; the age of big business and mass production; the age of specialization; and the age of speed. The typical day in this scientific, machine-dominated age begins with a hurried breakfast prepared over a push-button electric range with coffee from an automatic coffee pot. A quick dash for the bus or subway, or an hour's fight by automobile through city traffic to an office or shop where the stress of competition requires coffee breaks to sooth nerves and maintain sanity throughout the day, until at night the workers force themselves back through crowds and traffic to grab a dinner and fall into bed.

This is the age of neurosis; the age of anxiety; the age of ulcers and nervous breakdowns; the age of aspirins and tranquilizers. Mental hygienists and sociologists are alarmed at the number of patients in mental institutions. For every bed in the mental hospitals of our country at least five patients are waiting to be admitted. Something has to be done.

Educators, religious leaders, and psychologists realize the importance of "time off" for living. Recreation, meditation, rest, and free time are a must if society is to stand the fast pace of living in the twentieth century. Churches are left open in the cities for quiet meditation and prayer. Agencies and schools are providing active as well as passive forms of recreation for those who realize its importance. Quiet and restful havens are more and more being provided in the cities whereby mankind may retreat from the hustle and bustle of civilization. Outdoor education can make a unique contribution to the inner spiritual needs of children and adults alike.

Since the beginning of public education, educators have recognized that the teaching of moral and spiritual values is an important responsibility of the public schools.

The decision of how this is to be done, however, has been rather vague and controversial. Even more vague has been the meaning of spiritual values. The interpretations of spiritual values have ranged from the humanistic, moral, and aesthetic idea to a complete dedication to God and His will among men.

In 1951 the Educational Policies Commission defined moral and spiritual values as "those values which, when applied in human behavior, exalt and refine life and bring it into accord with the standards of conduct that are approved in our democratic culture."[3] The Educational Policies Commission states that the American people are agreed on ten interrelated moral and spiritual values:

1. Human personality ¬ the basic value
2. Moral responsibility
3. Institutions as the servants of man
4. Common consent
5. Devotion to Truth
6. Respect for excellence
7. Moral equality
8. Brotherhood
9. The pursuit of happiness
10. Spiritual enrichment

Stressing spiritual values in outdoor education does not mean religious teaching. It is not the doctrine of any religious group--Protestant, Catholic, or Jewish. Spiritual value, as defined by Dr. Lowell Hazzard, is "a deeper thing which is basic for all of us, the orientation of our souls toward God and toward our fellow men."[4] Dr. Hazzard points out that a natural outdoor education setting has five great advantages in developing spiritual values: (1) closeness to nature, (2) experience of harmony and order, (3) challenge to creativity in response to God's great creativeness, (4) adaptability, and (5) cooperative fellowship.

It is generally agreed among educators that moral

[3]Educational Policies Commission, Moral and Spiritual Values in the Public Schools. Washington, D. C.: National Education Association, 1951, p. 3

[4]Dr. Lowell Hazzard in a speech before the 1952 American Camping Association Convention, "Spiritual Values in Camp."

and spiritual values cannot be labeled and taught as an academic subject in the curriculum. The teaching of values should permeate the entire educational process. Spiritual values transcend preaching and sermonizing.

William Cullen Bryant understood the real sermons that become a part of the student's personality when he wrote the wonderful lines in Thanatopsis. "To him who in the love of nature holds communion with her visible forms, she speaks a various language"...and, "Go forth, under the open sky, and list to nature's teaching, while from all around--earth and her waters, and the depths of air-- comes a still voice."

While much in the way of spiritual and moral values can be achieved in regular scheduled activities such as nature walks, campfires, and nocturnal hikes, a far better job can be done by leaving free time each and every day for every camper to relax and have time to spend as he chooses either in group fellowship or alone in meditation. Every child when given the opportunity will question the "why" and "how" of all things. The child will identify himself with the things that are around him, the stars above him, the fields and woods around him, and the water before him. Here he strikes up a kinship with, and becomes a part of, the world. Every child needs time to think, to dream, to wonder, and to contemplate; it is the birthright of all who are young at heart. Through such meditation, he will develop a greater sense of values, a greater sense of his meaning to life, to himself, and to his fellowmen.

Every camp director and outdoor education leader should pray the prayer of the Indian of long ago who truly had the meaning and understanding of spiritual values.

Great Father, Great Spirit fill us with light.
Give us the strength to understand
    and the eyes to see.
Teach us to walk the soft earth
    as relatives to all that live.

THE OUTDOOR EDUCATION PROGRAM SHOULD BE FLEXIBLE

The outdoor education program, if it is designed to meet the needs and interests of children and if it is adapted to the local situation, will be flexible. Needs and interests of children may vary not only among children but also from one day to the next for each individual child. If a child becomes engrossed in an activity one day or one week and suddenly finds he is no longer interested in it, or another activity becomes more appealing, he should be able to change activities, for all activities should be planned to further the general objective of education.

Flexibility should be practiced in selection, organization, and assignment of children to activities. There are few programs in outdoor education that are so well-planned that last minute changes will not be necessary. When it is considered to be for the best interest of the participants, such changes should be made without hesitation. A program planned in advance provides for specific activities at a specific time and requires specific materials. During the process of immediate preparation or even during the process of the activity itself, if certain materials are not available, students are not interested, or weather is inclement, the counselor should feel free to change the plans.

Informal programs are by nature flexible and outdoor education is informal. The classroom with its separate courses of study and formal methods of teaching makes it difficult to get flexibility in the learning process. Outdoor education does not have the artificiality and formality of the classroom to overcome.

In addition to flexibility as to assignment of children to activities, the entire program should be broad enough to fulfill the wide variety of needs and interests of the children. New activities should be added to meet new interests and other activities should be discontinued when they are no longer popular. There is nothing sacred about a particular activity. Children's needs and interests rather than adult standards should be the primary reason for addition or deletion of activities from the outdoor educating program.

THE OUTDOOR EDUCATION PROGRAM SHOULD PROVIDE FOR CONTINUING AND PROGRESSIVE LEVELS OF ATTAINMENT

The outdoor education program should provide activities, conditions, and situations favorable to the continuous growth and progress of each individual student. Since learning in the out-of-doors is informal, every area of learning is open for adaptation, innovation, and change, all of which are essential to the interest and enthusiasm of the students. The program director has a responsibility of seeing that the program allows for progressive levels of attainment and offers continuity for those students with sustained interest.

There should be progressiveness and continuity within each activity. The program must not be allowed to become static or fixed. When children participate in an activity over and over again without a chance to continue to another level of attainment their interest wanes and enthusiasm dies. A cook-out may be met with enthusiasm a few times, then many children are ready for an overnight campout, and from there they may go on to an extended tour or camping experience. To be more specific, students may enjoy roasting weiners over a fire a few times but in order to keep the enjoyment at a high level, they will have to have an opportunity to build more difficult fires and prepare food in greater varieties and at higher levels of skill. Outdoor education programs should provide for progression of students to higher skills and activities in keeping with their age and past experience. Varied program opportunities, careful groupings and attention to individual needs and ability are needed to accomplish a progression and continuity of interest with each outdoor education activity.

In addition to progressiveness and continuity within an activity, there should be continuity among activities. It is an accepted fact by leading educators that a multi-discipline approach is the only practical way of solving human problems. Students should see the many relationships among various areas of human life. Outdoor education is unique in that it has the opportunity to teach this relationship firsthand. For integration of learning is the very essence, the very heart of an outdoor education program.

Another aspect of continuity is that between school and outdoor education experiences. Outdoor education is not a separate subject - rather an interpretation and integration of all subject matter. Outdoor education should be used when concerned with basic concepts and generalizations which can be made more meaningful in the out-of-doors.

To provide for this progress from one level of attainment to another and to insure continuity of learning experiences, the teacher as counselor must know each child thoroughly. She must know his capacity for learning, his motivating interests, his record of achievement, his physical and mental health pattern, his emotional status and his present achievement level. Physical development, chronological age, social and emotional maturity of the students must be considered in determining the starting point in the continuous growth concept.

THE OUTDOOR EDUCATION PROGRAM SHOULD PROVIDE OPPORTUNITY FOR CREATIVE SELF-EXPRESSION

For centuries philosophers and educators have seen the value of each person being able to express his own unique self--to create something that is his own interpretation of the world around him. In recent years, educators have recognized the social and personal values in creative self-expression. Thus, music, art, drama, crafts, dance, and other forms of creative self-expression have gradually been added to the program.

Opportunity for creativity should be provided in every phase of the outdoor education program. However, not all activities for children are creative, nor should they be. Certain skills and tools of learning which require drill and sometimes intellectual study must be taught. Little progress can be made in any art without a thorough-going master of techniques. But even the teaching of these techniques can be made more enjoyable under the direction of a skilled teacher who knows not only when to teach the techniques, but also how to combine freedom with control and self-expression with direction.

The major emphasis in education today is the teaching of attitudes, appreciations, understanding, and expression --the meaning of life to the child rather than the mastery of techniques and bodies of factual information. The latter are included, to be sure, but only as a means to an end and not ends in themselves.

Because the process of creativity is not completely understood, many teachers do not know how to develop a creative program. Therefore, many of the activities in outdoor education labeled creative become unpopular, or are dropped from the program, because the teacher proceeds in ways that defeat rather than foster the creative process. On the other hand outstanding programs are developed in outdoor education because the teachers recognize that all children have innate creative abilities and provide avenues of self-expression for these abilities in every aspect of living.

Creativity is an approach not an academic subject or an area of study for children. Creativity is a method of teaching for teachers and a way of learning for children. Creativity lies in the child doing the activity himself, prompted by his own imagination and his own inventiveness. The planning, sharing, and thinking that comes from twenty-four hour contact in active participation in group experience is an ideal climate for creative self-expression.

Everyone has creative potentialities. In the past a widely accepted view both within and without the school has been that only the select few, the elite group of artists, musicians, intellects, and writers, are blessed with the gift of creativity. The point of view as to "who is creative still persists in the popular mind. Creativity should be considered as a quality of the everyday living of all people, and not as a privilege for the gifted few. Creativity is not private property; it belongs to humanity.

Programming for creative self-expression in the out-of-doors involves two basic factors: (1) the setting, and (2) leadership.

An attractive and stimulating environment with materials and tools, plenty of time, plenty of space, and a permissive atmosphere lends itself to rich and varied creative experiences. The setting, although a direct responsibility of the teacher, should be shared by the children. They should be encouraged to plan and arrange the setting for carrying out the activity at hand. They should also be encouraged to gather objects and materials which can be used and shared by all in the group project or activity.

The role of the leader in education is twofold--instruction and guidance. Teaching children techniques of learning, teaching them various skills of work and play, helping them master the necessary outdoor education skills and guiding them in the selection of activities is good leadership. The leader discovers talents, sets the mood, enters into work and play with children, and gives recognition and praise for their contributions. All good leaders accept children at their own developmental level, and seek to guide them into activities in terms of their needs, interests, and abilities.

The wise leader or teacher encourages the group to be self-critical and assists them in setting standards of achievement. He encourages group control and interplay among members of the group. While children look to the leader for advice and seek his opinion, they are free to express their own ideas and accept responsibility for the success or failure of the activity. The teacher or leader must be a member of the group. His suggestions open up new possibilities and aid the children to see new relationships; his guidance prevents the development of anti-social habits and attitudes. The leader supplies information and experience needed to enrich the child's daily activities and give them education and recreative significance.

In conclusion, good planning for outdoor education involves attention to certain basic principles. The teacher or camp director no longer dictates the program in outdoor education. The director, counselors, and students plan in accordance with the interests of the participants. The director and counselors serve as guides. They may make suggestions and offer help; but the final choice, within bounds, must be left with the students or campers. Since the process of planning has great educational value, the wider the student participation, the greater will be the benefit to them. Furthermore, representation enhances and encourages cooperation, acceptance of responsibility and practice in democratic group living. Group participation also assures the director that the program be based on the needs and interests of the students.

The program must be planned purposefully with consideration of the objectives, activities and materials, methods and techniques, organization and evaluation. Successful program planning involves a knowledge of the space, facilities, and equipment requirements, as well as the leadership requirements, of each and every activity comprising the program. Although the nature of the area and available facilities does not necessarily limit the activities, it often has a considerable bearing upon the scope and nature of the program.

Since one of the characteristics of a democratic society is change, the program should be flexible, continuing, and progressive in order to meet the needs and interests of each and every individual student.

Lastly, the program must be planned for creative activities which challenge the camper in all aspects of outdoor life. Two ways to plan for creative self-expression is to employ teachers and counselors that understand the techniques of teaching in a creative manner, and secondly, to provide ample free time needed for meditation and repose on the part of the camper. A permissive unhurried atmosphere in an outdoor setting is a big step in encouraging creative activity among students.

Selected References

American Camping Association, *Marks of Good Camping,* New York: Association Press, 1941.

Burns, Gerald P., *Program of the Modern Camp,* Englewood Cliffs, N. J.: Prentice-Hall, 1954.

Clarke, James, *Public School Camping California's Pilot Project In Outdoor Education,* Palo Alto: Stanford University Press, 1951.

Donaldson, George W., *School Camping,* New York: The Association Press, 1952.

Educational Policies Commission, *Education For All American Youth,* Washington, D. C. : National Education Association, 1952.

Education Policies Commission, *Moral and Spiritual Values In The Public Schools,* Washington, D. C. : National Education Association, 1951.

Hutchinson, John L. , *Principles of Recreation,* New York: The Roland Press Company, 1951

Kelly, Earl C. , *Education For What Is Real,* New York: Harper and Brothers, 1947.

Rugg, Harold and Sumaker, Ann, *The Child Centered School,* New York: World Book Company, 1928.

Sharp, L. B. and Partridge, E. DeAlton, "Camping and Outdoor Education, " *The Bulletin of the National Association of Secondary-School Principals,* May, 1947, Vol. 31, No. 147.

Sharp, L. B. , "Schools Go Out of Doors, " Reprinted from *The School Executive,* January, 1944.

Sharp, L. B. and Osborne, Ernest G. , "Schools and Camp-Reprinted from *"Progressive Education, "* April, 1940.

Smith, Julian W. , *Outdoor Education For American Youth,* Washington, D. C. : American Association For Health, Physical Education and Recreation, 1957.

Whitehead, Alfred North, *The Aims of Education,* New York: Macmillan Company, 1929.

Chapter 3

THE OUTDOOR
EDUCATION PROGRAM

"That which can best be learned inside the classroom should be learned there; and that which can best be learned through direct experience outside the classroom, in contact with native materials and life situations, should there be learned."[1]

The above statement is the thesis of outdoor education stated in its simplest terms. Outdoor education is the heritage of all children in all subject matter classes, in all areas of study, and on every grade level. Historically, most outstanding scholars of education have emphasized the importance of real-life experience and the use of nature as a necessary method of teaching. For example, Frank Lloyd Wright, the great architect and designer, said, "I believe now there is no school worth its existence except as it is a form of nature study--true nature study--dedicated to that first, foremost and all the time. Man is a phase of nature, and only as he is related to nature does he really matter, is he of any account whatever, above the dust."

The outdoor education program begins just outside the school building. The facilities and tools of learning are ever present since nature has provided them. Life and living are in constant movement and can be observed and studied from many different and interesting standpoints. A new and exciting method of education can be introduced which has immediate and natural appeal to the students.

[1] L. B. Sharp, "Basic Considerations in Outdoor and Camping Education" The Bulletin of The National Association of Secondary School Principals, May, 1947, p. 43

74

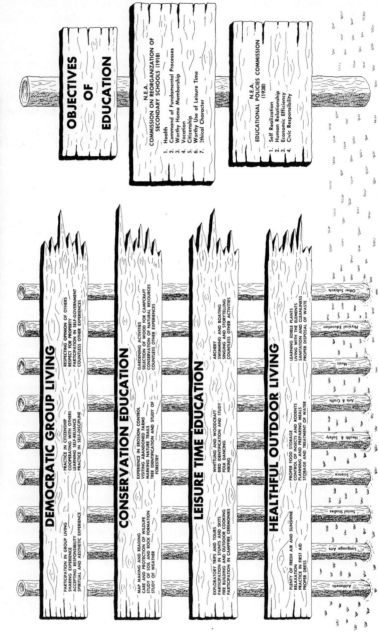

THE OUTDOOR EDUCATION PROGRAM

OBJECTIVES OF EDUCATION

N.E.A. COMMISSION ON REORGANIZATION OF SECONDARY SCHOOLS (1918)

1. Health
2. Command of Fundamental Processes
3. Worthy Home Membership
4. Vocation
5. Citizenship
6. Worthy Use of Leisure Time
7. Ethical Character

N.E.A. EDUCATIONAL POLICIES COMMISSION (1938)

1. Self Realization
2. Human Relationship
3. Economic Efficiency
4. Civic Responsibility

DEMOCRATIC GROUP LIVING

PARTICIPATION IN GROUP LIVING
SHARING EXPERIENCE
ACCEPTANCE RESPONSIBILITY
SPIRITUAL AND AESTHETIC EXPERIENCE

PRACTICE IN CITIZENSHIP
COOPERATING WITH OTHERS
LEARNING SELF-RELIANCE
PRACTICE IN SELF-DISCIPLINE

RESPECTING OPINION OF OTHERS
RESPECT FOR PROPERTY
PARTICIPATION IN SELF-GOVERNMENT
COUNTLESS OTHER EXPERIENCES

CONSERVATION EDUCATION

MAP MAKING AND READING
SELECTION AND PROTECTION OF WILDLIFE
STUDY OF SOIL AND ROCK FORMATION
STUDY OF WEATHER

EXPERIENCE IN EROSION CONTROL
VISITING FISH AND GAME FARMS
MAKING NATURE TRAILS
TREE IDENTIFICATION AND STUDY OF FORESTRY

GARDENING ACTIVITIES
TRIPS TO WEATHER OR CAMPCRAFT
CONSERVATION OF NATURAL RESOURCES
COUNTLESS OTHER EXPERIENCES

LEISURE TIME EDUCATION

EXPLORATORY TRIPS AND TOURS
PARTICIPATION IN STUNTS AND SKITS
FIRE BUILDING AND OUTDOOR COOKING
PARTICIPATION IN CAMPFIRE CEREMONIES

WHITTLING AND WOODCRAFT
BIRD IDENTIFICATION AND STUDY
FOLK DANCING
HIKING

ARCHERY
SWIMMING AND BOATING
SINGING AND STORYTELLING
COUNTLESS OTHER ACTIVITIES

HEALTHFUL OUTDOOR LIVING

PLENTY OF FRESH AIR AND SUNSHINE
RELAXATION
PRACTICE IN FIRST AID
PROPER SIZES

PROPER FOOD STORAGE
CONTROL OF INSECTS AND RODENTS
PLANNING AND PREPARING MEALS
STORAGE AND TREATMENT OF WATER

LEARNING EDIBLE PLANTS
LIVING WITH THE ELEMENTS
SANITATION AND CLEANLINESS
PROPER DISPOSAL OF WASTE

Arithmetic Language Arts Social Studies Science Health & Safety Arts & Crafts Music Physical Education Other Subjects

Opportunities exist for the teacher to associate and interpret the experience and relate them to various classroom subject matter fields.

Programs in outdoor education have in most cases been readily accepted by parents and teachers. There has been an enthusiastic response to these programs by both parents and teachers. Parents may have the opportunity to judge the program from at least two standpoints: they can be brought into the planning of program contents and experience; and they can evaluate their children's reactions to the experience. Children come home from school bubbling over with enthusiasm and telling of the real and meaningful things they learned; asking questions of their parents; engaging them in research to help find answers; and then, go back to school to read further about their experience in library books. Outdoor education is so feasible and its lessons so meaningful that parents wonder why it was not used more when they were in school.

Teachers, too, readily accept the outdoor education method once they have used it as a resource. Teachers who are subject-matter oriented and in the habit of asking questions sometime feel a little disturbed when they are suddenly placed in the midst of nature with eager and enthusiastic children firing questions and seeking answers. Once teachers capture the spirit and have mastered the informal outdoor education technique they are convinced that learning is more meaningful and more real.

It is most important for school administrators and teachers to know that outdoor education is much broader in scope than school camping. Although an extended experience in a good school camp may offer greater opportunity for democratic group living and cooperative learning in the out-of-doors, it is not necessary for a school to own a camp in order to have an outstanding outdoor education program. Some educators and parents who are not acquainted with outdoor education programs too often regard it as camping. They have the "private camp" concept of camping which means elaborate athletic fields, expensive buildings, beautiful lake fronts and other expensive facilities. With a good public relations program and a well-informed public, parents will better understand the importance of learning through the use of resources available to the teacher just outside the classroom. When outdoor education methods are explained, and when the faculty and staff of the school know the philosophy of outdoor education, their program will prove the most realistic and most interesting kind of education available. It is easier to justify a relatively free outdoor laboratory than it is to build an expensive laboratory and carry native materials inside and out of context to teach it.

In the outdoor education program the wonders of nature continually challenge the minds of every individual. There are also many experiences and opportunities for the child to see his relationship to nature, to individuals, to small groups, and to large masses as he works in various ways with his teacher and his classmates. Children find new and creative learning experiences as they explore the secrets of nature with each other and with teachers. Teachers, likewise, learn many new and challenging things about their subject and about methods of education. Many scientists regard the exploration and observation of nature to be one of the most challenging and functional ways in developing critical thinking and creative expression.

The outdoor education program should begin with the kindergarten and should extend through college. The use of real-life experiences and nature can be profitably used at all grade levels. Consideration should be given to planning and interpreting these experiences in terms of the age of the student; the difficulty of subject matters to comprehend; the desire for using the experience to integrate various subject matter fields; the emphasis on short-term or long-term use of a given experience; the use to stimulate further study or research; and the use of the experience to develop new habits of learning and living in the out-of-doors.

The out-of-doors is so large and is so comprehensive for the inexperienced teacher who is used to teaching with everything neatly classified in scientific categories that it is sometimes difficult to know just where to start. The starting point should be determined in the classroom as it grows out of the class activities.

The following guide which is by no means complete and which could not be contained in a single library may offer help to teachers who are using the outdoor education technique for the first time. This list is compiled from many suggestions now being used in various schools in the United States. Education, of course, does not stop with the sixth grade. This outline can be extended through the junior high school, the high school, and on through college. Ideally the outline will be developed by the teacher and the class as they learn together. No two classes will be alike, no two school yards will be alike, and no two sections of the country will be able to use the same outline because of difference in climate, soil, vegetation, animal life, and other natural phenomena.

SUGGESTED OUTDOOR EDUCATION ACTIVITIES

KINDERGARTEN

On The School Ground
1. Gather beautiful leaves in the fall.
2. Dress warmly and play in the first snowfall.
3. Watch for early signs of spring.
4. Observe and smell beautiful flowers.
5. Feel the texture of tree bark.
6. Observe the birds near the school house.
7. Watch the squirrels gather food.
8. Gather wild flowers in the spring.

In The Immediate Neighborhood
1. Visit a neighbor's rock garden.
2. Take a short "look and see" trip.
3. Walk to a busy intersection to practice rules of safety.
4. Visit children's homes to see how pets are housed and fed.
5. Take a walk to learn to appreciate people's property, lawns, flowers, and trees.
6. Take walks to observe numbers on houses, names on streets, mail boxes on houses.

In The Community
1. Take a trip to observe the construction of a new building.
2. Visit the police station.
3. Visit a neighborhood church to hear and see a pipe organ, to see stained glass windows, to observe religious art, and to learn new words.
4. Visit a toy shop to see which toys go on wheels, spin, fly, have engines and propellers.

Beyond The Community
1. Visit a farm.
2. Visit a forest.

FIRST GRADE

On The School Ground
1. Listen to the various sounds.
2. Watch insects at work.
3. Observe the various birds and identify the most common ones.
4. Plant a flower bulb.
5. Watch the buds swell and open in the spring.
6. Gather dandelions or other native wild flowers.
7. Build a snow man.
8. Observe the many colors in nature.
9. Build a feeding station for birds.
10. Plant and care for a lettuce bed.

In The Immediate Neighborhood
1. Take a hike to observe beautiful or unusual plants.
2. Walk to a busy intersection to review and practice safety rules.
3. Walk to and observe a giant spreading tree.
4. Walk to and observe construction of a new house.
5. Take a trip to see and smell flowers.
6. Walk to and observe an interesting thing a classmate found on the way to school.
7. Take walks to observe cloud formations.
8. Take walks to observe kinds of vehicles and their use.

In The Community
1. Take a trip to the park to observe birds and squirrels.
2. Visit the police station and talk to the police.
3. Visit the fire station.
4. Visit a pet shop.
5. Take a walk to see a freight train go by; count the cars and notice their use.
6. Visit a bank to see the people at work, see the vault, and make change for refreshments.

Beyond The Community
1. Visit a farm to learn work of farm family members, care and feeding of farm animals, use of farm buildings and farm machinery.
2. Visit a zoo to see animals read about in class.
3. Take a short ride on a bus and a train to get acquainted with some of the workers.
4. Visit truck gardens and orchards to see how plants and trees grow and to learn names of fruits and vegetables.

SECOND GRADE

On The School Ground
1. View snow flakes with a magnifying glass.
2. Listen to the songs of birds.
3. Plant a few flower bulbs.
4. Learn to recognize several kinds of trees.
5. Build feeding stations for birds.
6. Watch the grounds keeper care for plants.
7. Observe small animals that live on the school ground.
8. Learn to recognize the most common birds.
9. Plant and care for a small school garden.
10. Observe the school ground after a rain.
11. Watch interesting cloud formations.
12. Build bird baths.

In The Immediate Neighborhood
1. Walk to study trees or shrubs.
2. Collect leaves for making crayon prints.

3. Make several trips to watch cycle of life in a bird nest from egg to grown bird.
4. Collect beautiful feathers.
5. Observe the first signs of spring.
6. Gather beautiful nature materials for art work.
7. Visit a neighborhood grocery, meat market, fruit store, delicatessen, bakery, drug store, hardware store, and variety store to get a specific vocabulary that is connected with each, and to extend experiences outside the home, school, and church into the community.

In The Community
1. Take a trip to the store to buy a Halloween pumpkin.
2. Take a trip to the park to observe wild life and plants.
3. Visit a greenhouse.
4. Visit the community flower garden.
5. Visit a poultry farm or hatchery to see how baby fowl grow in the egg and hatch.
6. Visit a neighborhood store to select and purchase seeds for window gardens or garden on school ground.

Beyond The Community
1. Visit a museum or zoo.
2. Visit a turkey farm and bring back feathers.
3. Visit a dairy to see how the dairy is kept clean, how the milk is pasteurized and kept pure.
4. Visit an airport to observe the work and importance of modern transportation.

THIRD GRADE

On The School Ground
1. Examine the texture of soil.
2. Collect insect cocoons and eggs to hatch in a cage in the classroom.
3. Make a snow man, a snow fort, and other snow sculptures.

4. Watch water run down a slope after a heavy rain.
5. Plant and cultivate a small vegetable garden.
6. List all the colors found in nature.
7. Observe the effect of excessive play on grass.
8. Study the homes of birds, animals, and insects.
9. Observe the effect of changing seasons on nature.
10. Plant a tree.
11. Observe the formation and movement of clouds.
12. Add to the list of birds already known.

In The Immediate Neighborhood

1. Take a trip to collect leaves and branches for Thanksgiving decorations.
2. Observe the work of community helpers.
3. Observe decaying tree leaves.
4. Observe unusual rock formations.
5. Observe a creek or branch after a heavy rain.
6. Gather leaves for spatter painting.
7. Visit a flower garden or vegetable garden at the home of a classmate.
8. Observe the construction of a road or building.
9. Visit a bakery to purchase products for a party and to watch the workers and see what is made and sold.
10. Visit a railroad station to purchase tickets for a ride on a train. Observe the cars and the workers --conductor, engineer, brakemen.

In The Community

1. Visit the post office.
2. Visit a florist shop or greenhouse to see the beauty of flowers, to recognize colors, and to learn the names of flowers and other plants.
3. Gather unusual and beautiful rocks from a creek bed.
4. Take a tour through a large factory.

Beyond The Community

1. Visit the school farm.
2. Plan a day's outing at the school forest or state park.
3. Assist in the school garden.
4. Visit a historical landmark.

FOURTH GRADE

On The School Ground
1. Observe and learn to recognize insects.
2. Make a temperature graph of readings during various times of the year.
3. Get a rain gauge and record rainfall for a given month.
4. Make and try out a wind vane.
5. Count the varieties of weeds and plant life on the school ground.
6. Observe the changes in a particular tree throughout the school year.
7. Watch cloud formation and movement during foul and fair weather.
8. Make and try out a weather vane.
9. Lay out and plant a small garden plot.
10. Study the effect of different kinds of soil on plants.
11. Dig a hole to observe layers of soil, then refill.
12. Practice measuring distance by pacing.

In The Immediate Neighborhood
1. Count rings on a tree stump to determine age.
2. Study insects under a magnifying glass.
3. Take a trip to study wild flowers.
4. Watch activity in an ant colony.
5. Observe unusual phenomena in the neighborhood.
6. Collect interesting tree seed and pods.
7. Explore the sandy and rocky bed of a creek.
8. Review known birds and add new ones to recognition list.
9. Visit the pet shop to see how pets are housed and fed and cared for until purchased, to learn the different kinds of animals that make good pets and the diseases that pets have.
10. Take walks to see signs of seasons, to study homes of animals and insects, and to collect seeds, leaves insects, and cocoons.

In The Community
1. Visit a vacant lot and make plans to beautify it.
2. Take a trip to a badly eroded field.

3. Take a trip to the store to buy food for a picnic.
4. Plan a nature hike in the park.
5. Search for beautiful rocks.
6. Collect native materials for an arts and crafts project.
7. Take a trip to a vacant lot or a park in the evening to observe constellations
8. Visit a fruit and vegetable market to see the wide variety of foods that come from farms.

Beyond The Community
1. Take a trip to a forest to observe leaf covering of the soil.
2. Plan an all-day trip to an old whaling port or other point of interest.
3. Visit a limestone quarry.
4. Visit a museum, zoo, or wildlife sanctuary.
5. Collect materials from a forest for a classroom terranium.
6. Plan a day camp experience at a suitable site.
7. Visit a farm to learn about the use of land, types of fertilizer, and rotation of crops.
8. Visit a mill to observe how grain becomes flour.

FIFTH GRADE

On The School Ground
1. Collect several kinds of soil for classroom experiments.
2. Observe and measure shadows; make a sun dial.
3. Construct a weather station.
4. With magnifying glass list all things found in a square foot of ground.
5. Experiment with water evaporation.
6. Test and develop observation skill in variety of nature study.
7. Collect leaves, twigs, pebbles and native materials for nature art.
8. Plan and carry out a school ground beautification project.
9. Observe movement and activities of various insects.

10. Assist grounds keeper in mulching plants.
11. Observe movement and activities of various birds.
12. Record temperature differences in the shade and in the sun.

In The Immediate Neighborhood.
1. Make a weed collection.
2. Note damaging causes and effect of heavy rains.
3. Collect various plant specimens for study.
4. Count and record all varieties of trees found on a trip.
5. Make plaster cast of animal track.
6. Track various animals in the snow.
7. Visit areas of heavy wind damage.
8. Look for evidence of interdependence of nature.

In The Community
1. List ways man depends on nature in his work.
2. Observe poor conservation practices.
3. Visit a bird sanctuary.
4. Observe how man has aided nature in conservation.
5. Observe excavation and study earth strata.
6. Plan an all-day nature outing and a noon cookout.

Beyond The Community
1. Plan a picnic in a park, forest or on a lake front.
2. Visit a saw mill.
3. Plan a trip to a local fish hatchery.
4. Visit a farm to observe planting or harvesting by machinery.
5. Visit a tree nursery.
6. Plan an overnight camp out.

SIXTH GRADE

On The School Ground
1. Practice use of compass.
2. Practice sketching trees and outdoor scenes.
3. Keep a scrapbook on the wildlife found on the school ground.

4. Make weather observations.
5. Write descriptions of interesting observations on the school ground.
6. Study arithmetic ratio by measuring heights by shadow method.
7. Repair badly eroded school grounds.
8. Plant and care for trees or shrubs.
9. Help a primary grade in gathering crafts materials.
10. Practice judging and pacing distances.
11. Plan and cultivate a complete vegetable garden.
12. Draw the school ground to scale.

In The Immediate Neighborhood
1. Take a trip to a nearby wooded area.
2. Make a collection of insects.
3. Study parasite life such as moss and lichen growing on trees.
4. Collect and label leaves from trees.
5. Make a butterfly collection.
6. Study marine life in nearby streams.
7. Observe several tree stumps and their degree of decay.
8. Observe ways in which plants, animals and insects help man.

In The Community
1. Visit a conservation demonstration area.
2. Test soil in various areas with a soil testing kit.
3. Plan an overnight camp-out.
4. Make a rock collection.
5. Visit a water purification plant.
6. Observe dead trees and other decayed matter.
7. Lay out a nature trail.
8. Look for Indian relics.

Beyond The Community
1. Visit a coal mine.
2. Visit a farm to compare modern tools with those of 50 years ago.
3. Visit a strip mine to observe conservation practice.

4. Spend a day at an abandoned farm.
5. Visit a stream, lake or river to test for water pollution.
6. Attend a week at a school camp.

Considering the value received from the relatively in-expensive outdoor classroom, it is hard to see why outdoor education is not universally included in all school programs. In the early beginnings of the movement some schools rushed into outdoor education before the faculty was properly awak-ened to its real purposes and techniques. Some teachers grabbed their books and made for the woods and streams in order to conform to new educational approach and study in the out-of-doors. These teachers reported bad experiences in "outdoor education" and pronounced it as a passing fad, a frill, and a waste of time. Fortunately, many schools in search of activities to supplement and enrich a sound class-room program are discovering the possibilities offered through outdoor education.

Many schools, today, are firmly committed to a sound outdoor education program and are using this valu-able technique in the achievement of the objectives of edu-cation. Rather than jumping blindly into an extended camp-ing experience most schools start with nature hikes, school journeys, school garden activities, school farms, and pro-gressively add programs of outdoor activities as the inter-ests and abilities of the children dictate. Instead of concen-trating on a camping experience and limiting it to a specific grade, a good program of education uses outdoor resources beginning in the kindergarten and extending through all grades.

The nature of outdoor education and camping programs conducted throughout the country indicates a great deal of progress toward an enlightened philosophy and better under-standing of the purposes of outdoor education. The findings of scientific research and psychological testing on the na-ture of learning is reflected in the changing concept of the philosophy and purposes of outdoor education.

Due to the broad scope of teaching possibilities in the out-of-doors, it is difficult, if not impossible to classify teaching materials into logical areas of learning. There are, however, certain major areas of learning under which most outdoor education experiences may be grouped. It must be emphasized, again, that there can be no hard and fast classification as each area is closely related and interrelated and certain activities may fall under two or even more areas, and often may cut across the entire camp program. The complexity, relatedness, and interrelatedness of programs in outdoor education can better be realized by children and teachers as they study life in context and do their own research and classification rather than memorize the ready-made materials which others have compiled.

The major areas of learning in outdoor education, and particularly camping, contribute most to democratic group living, healthful outdoor living, conservation education, and leisure time skills. [2]

DEMOCRATIC GROUP LIVING

President Woodrow Wilson, speaking before a group of school administrators, said, "I urge that teachers and other school officers of the nation increase materially the time and attention devoted to instruction bearing directly upon problems of community and national life." President Wilson knew, as many other scholars before and after, that a democracy cannot flourish unless the schools accept the responsibility of developing political and social intelligence necessary to practice self-government.

To participate efficiently and wisely in a democratic society, children must have an understanding of political and social structures and the democratic process of government. They must experience rich and varied social contacts and be able to follow directions as well as give directions. They must be able to work and play in groups and have a sincere respect for the rights of others regardless of race, color, or creed. Children should not graduate from school and be considered as useful citizens unless they have expe-

[2]William H. Freeberg and Loren E. Taylor, Philosophy of Outdoor Education Minneapolis: Burgess Publishing Company, 1961. Chapters 7, 8, 9, and 10.

rience in democratic group living. Reading about democracy, studying the history of our struggle for democracy and memorizing important codes, declarations, and documents is not enough. Children learn democracy by living it.

A school camp is an ideal laboratory for practice in democratic group living and human relations. Concepts of democracy learned in the textbook are put into practice as the children accept responsibilities and engage in self-government. In a camp setting children learn many concepts so important to living in a democracy that cannot be efficiently learned in the classroom. In a decentralized camp program the essentials to democratic living such as cooperation, tolerance, leadership, "followship," loyalty, fellowship, respect for others, love of God, and a sense of responsibility are necessary to each child if they are to enjoy their experience at camp. The teacher's job is to help children acquire rich and varied experiences and to interpret their real meaning in terms of citizenship and intelligent group living.

In a good school camp, children are given as much responsibility as they can handle. The camp community engages in self-government; problems are discussed and solved by the children. As a result of living in small decentralized groups, managing their own affairs individually and together, representing their groups at all-camp councils, and participating in planning and evaluating their program, children get firsthand experience and know what living in a democracy really means.

A few of the more obvious experiences in the area of human relations and democratic living which are valuable for children are:

1. Group planning, discussions, and evaluations of the activities of the day--and the week.
2. Committee work in which each participates as a leader, a follower, and a member of a work project, field trip, campfire program, or other activity.
3. Experiences in cooperative learning between person and person, group and group, group and

counselor, group and teacher, and counselor and teacher that come about in the social interchange of group living.

4. Participation in a representative form of government as an individual of one group meeting with representatives of other groups in discussion, planning, and evaluation of outdoor education projects and activities.

5. Opportunities for growth in social behavior that come with experience in eating, working, sleeping, and living together. Learning to share at meals and learning table grace and manners while eating three times a day in small groups. Sharing showers, tools, and other necessities for successful living and learning experiences.

6. Opportunities to live in different social situations with teachers, counselors, and other children.

7. Assuming duties necessary for living as a group in the out-of-doors such as acting as host, caring for guests, managing the post office, camp store, bank, keeping the cabin clean, acting as table setter, hoppers, cleaners, sweepers, and many other purposeful and desirable work experiences.

8. Respecting the rights of others at quiet time, bedtime, study time, on the trail and in all activities involving groups living together.

9. Respecting and caring for property of the camp, of others, and personal property.

10. Learning the need for self-discipline and group-discipline.

11. Developing a love for God and nature. Living and experiencing the moral and spiritual values that are the heritage of all mankind.

12. Leaving the camp in as good, if not better, condition for future campers.

HEALTHFUL OUTDOOR LIVING

The school camp is an ideal setting for teaching health

habits and proper health attitudes. By living twenty-four hours a day in an informal and relaxed atmosphere which is free from class routine, schedules, whistles and bells both children and teachers enjoy better mental health.

The well-administered school camp provides innumerable opportunities to practice desirable health habits; well-balanced meals; periods of relaxation and rest; programs of hiking and healthful exercise; planning and preparation of meals; coping with the weather; meeting the problems of sanitation; exposure to plenty of sunshine and fresh air; physical examinations and their purpose; undertaking and protection against poisonous weeds, insects, and snakes; and other day-to-day experiences that call for self-preservation in various ways.

In a camp setting health and safety problems become something real, something that must be dealt with, and something that needs immediate attention. It is not a subject for study or memorization in order to prepare for later life. It is a here and now proposition which can best be learned by making it a part of the child's basic habits, behavior, and living patterns.

An additional advantage of the camp setting is that the teacher is with her pupils both night and day. The health instruction which may or may not be put to practice at home after school hours can be properly supervised by the teacher and properly practiced by the children while at camp.

A few of the most obvious opportunities to practice healthful living in the school camp include:

1. Health examinations and check-ups by the nurse are educational experiences in a friendly atmosphere which makes each child more conscious of his health and its importance.

2. Outdoor living exposes children to a healthy balance of work and recreation in the out-of-doors.

3. Living together twenty-four hours a day offers a controlled environment for observance and correcting health habits of children concerned with personal hygiene, eating, planning balanced meals, sanitation, correct dress for the weather, keeping living quarters clean and tidy, practice

safety, and in all phases of safe and enjoyable outdoor living.

4. Outdoor education through camping introduces children to well-balanced meals each day at regularly scheduled hours in a controlled environment which provides many inherent learning possibilities.

5. Outdoor education provides an informal and relaxed atmosphere which is conducive to good mental health.

6. Activities in outdoor education provide opportunities for experience in the safe use of tools and implements.

7. The natural hazards such as poison ivy, poisonous snakes and dangerous cliffs provide firsthand experience in the development of health and safety procedures. It also develops positive attitudes towards nature's way of doing things.

8. Waterfront activities offer opportunities to learn to swim, to handle a boat, and many other positive approaches to sane procedures of safety around and in the water.

CONSERVATION EDUCATION

Conservation of natural resources has been the concern of private organizations and governmental agencies for many years. In spite of the efforts of such groups through publications, education, and legislation little headway has been made in stopping the exploitation, plunder and waste of the nation's valuable resources. Many conservationists have become alarmed at the poor attitude of the American people toward the conservation of natural resources. The leaders in this field have turned to the public schools for practical results.

In their first attempts, the schools taught conservation education in a traditional manner just as they taught all other subjects, in the only way they knew how--from the textbooks and in the classroom. Conservation units were introduced in science and geography and children learned and memorized through the question-answer, and examination routine. While the teacher was teaching from the book, the school ground, local farms, and city parks may have been eroding and washing away and children's behavior and attitudes toward conservation practice in many cases remained unchanged. It was hard for the teacher to combine conservation theory with conservation practice; it was hard for children to relate their textbook learning to everyday life. It was more important for the student to get a good grade in conservation education on the weekly test than it was to provide experiences which would allow students to put knowledge into practice. Then, too, this knowledge was to be stored for the future; perhaps when the student grew into adulthood, he could put his concepts into actual practice.

Today, good teachers realize that children learn by doing, by getting firsthand experience working on the school ground, in the community, and in a school camp. They associate learning with doing through conservation activities and practices. Important concepts develop into meaningful attitudes; appreciations are developed; and conservation becomes a part of their philosophy of life.

Conservation education is truly the concern of the public schools. Although private, semi-private and governmental agencies have made accomplishments in conservation education and in the promotion of good conservation practices, the major responsibility of mass education in this area rests with our schools.

The public schools are responsible in a democratic society for teaching skills of self-government and teaching duties of citizenship. They are also equally responsible for developing concepts, attitudes and appreciations concerning conservation of resources. Conservation as a way of life is fundamental to American Democracy. The very survival of the nation depends upon principles of conservation. Democracy is based on freedom from want, and freedom from want is concomitant with plenty. Secondly, the care and management of our nation's resources is the concern of every citizen. Wanton carelessness and waste reflects a selfishness, greed, and a disrespect for others which is not in keeping with our democratic ideals.

The basic understandings concerning our natural environment and the conservation of our natural environment is a main purpose of the camp program. Everywhere and everything in the natural environment is a basis for a good lesson in science or nature study. The camp setting is an ideal place to show the intricate interrelationships between soil, water, air, plants, wildlife, and man himself.

Among the many projects and practices involving conservation education in a camp setting the following may be included:

1. Selection of overnight camp sites so that plant life and forest growth will not be extensively damaged.
2. Use of good forestry practice in gathering of firewood.
3. Using good forestry practices in selection of wood for construction purposes.
4. Correct procedures in extinguishing fires.
5. Use lashing techniques where trees are involved in camp construction so that nails are not driven into trees.
6. Set up a weather station and learn how to operate it. Study the effect of weather on animals and plants.
7. Plant, cultivate, and harvest garden produce.
8. Construction of check-dams and other mechanical means to prevent serious erosion of soil.
9. Lay out nature trails or riding trails using conservation practices.
10. Study the source of the camp water supply.
11. Practice in use of the compass and map-making.
12. Explore the camp area to determine extent and type of action needed to help nature regain her balance.

LEISURE TIME EDUCATION

The golden age of leisure which has been the dream of mankind through long centuries of hard work is now a reality. The average American citizen has over 3,000

hours of leisure a year. This sudden introduction of an
abundance of leisure time into the American social structure
has brought many perplexing problems for all American citizens. Instead of enjoying leisure time and using it wisely,
too many people are living a leisure-time life of boredom,
physical degeneration, promiscuity, apathy, time-wasting
activities, and mental stagnation.

In an age when education for leisure is fully as important as education for a profession or a trade the schools
have failed. Past civilizations according to sociologists
have failed because of their inability to cope with leisure
time. Many such civilizations have left their records for
all to study but only a few scholarly sociologists seem to
have grasped the full meaning of their lesson and they are
powerless to get the attention of their contemporaries.

Educators, as early as 1918, realized the growing
problem of how children spent their leisure hours and made
the "worthy use of leisure time" one of the Seven Cardinal
Principles of Education. Unfortunately, actual teaching of
skills in recreation did not materialize. America has had
a history of being adverse to change and the "three R's" had
a firm grip on the school curriculum. The fourth R--recrea-
tion--is still waiting on the outside except in the most up-to-
date schools.

Although American society is moving from a world of
long hours of work to a world of an abundance of leisure
time the public schools are still preparing graduates for
the former society. Now is the time for educators to take
a new look at the school program and give more attention to
one of the major problems of modern society--educating
youth for leisure time.

Recreation should be an integral part of education.
The schools have a twofold responsibility to the children
and to every citizen of the community to (1) place emphasis
on the avocational aspects of all school subjects for leisure
time use, and (2) to provide a variety of recreational opportunities for children and adults of all ages.

Reading is taught in schools as a subject. It should
also be stressed that reading is a basic recreative art.
Teaching children to read is only one small task of the

schools in modern society. They should be taught to want to read and should know what to read.

The second responsibility of the school, in cooperation with other community educational and recreational agencies and institutions, is to provide abundant recreational opportunities for all ages. The public schools should be available to community groups twelve months out of the year and twelve to fifteen hours each day. In addition to athletics and sports, schools should offer opportunities in dance, music, art, nature lore, hobbies and collections, dramatics, reading clubs, swimming and waterfront activities, camping, gardening, and adult education.

Outdoor education, particularly school camping, provides a wonderful laboratory for teaching carry-over recreational skills which may lead to hobbies and leisure time pursuits which children can enjoy the rest of their life. Some of the recreational skills which may be developed in a good school camp are:

1. Development of wholesome attitudes and skills in recreation primarily through the use of nature and natural resources.
2. Participation in cookouts and other activities which require fire building and skills in campcraft.
3. Participation in activities which may result in lifelong hobbies such as hiking, rock collection, bird watching, outing clubs, and nature craft.
4. Development of swimming, boating, fishing, and other aquatic recreational skills.
5. Participation in social recreation skills in the evening and around the campfire such as folk and square dancing, group singing, campfire ceremonies, dramatic presentations, storytelling, and quiet informal activities.
6. Outdoor education can help satisfy the needs for adventure and activity that modern society is making more and more difficult for children to experience.

Selected References

DeWitt, R. T., "Camping Education - A Philosophy,"
    National Elementary Principal, February, 1949.

Freeberg, William H. and Taylor, Loren E., *Philosophy
    of Outdoor Education,* Minneapolis: Burgess Pub-
    lishing Company, 1961.

Hammerman, Donald, "What! Teach Outside the Class-
    room?" *Journal of Health-Physical Education-
    Recreation,* November, 1954.

Harrison, Paul E., "Education Goes Outdoors," *Journal
    of the American Association for Health-Physical
    Education Recreation,* December, 1953.

Irwin, Frank L., *The Theory of Camping An Introduction
    To Camping In Education,* New York: A. S. Barnes,
    1950.

Lee, J. Murray and Lee, Dorris May, *The Child and His
    Curriculum,* New York: Appleton-Century-Crofts,
    Inc., 1950.

Lee, J. Murray and Lee, Dorris May, *The Child and His
    Development,* New York: Appleton-Century-Crofts,
    Inc., 1950.

Manley, Helen and Drury, M. F., *Education Through
    School Camping,* St. Louis: The C. V. Mosby
    Company, 1952.

Michaelis, John U., *Social Studies For Children In a
    Democracy,* Englewood Cliffs, N. J.: Prentice-
    Hall, 1956.

Nash, Jay B., "Why A School Camping Program," *The
    Journal of Educational Sociology,* May, 1950.

Sharp, L. B., "Outside the Classroom" Reprinted from
    The Educational Forum, May, 1943.

Sharp, L. B., "Why Outdoor and Camping Education,"
    Journal of Educational Sociology, January, 1948.

Sharp, L. B., "The Public School Camp," April, 1940,
    Camping Magazine, Second printing.

Vinal, William Gouls, "Let's Take Camping Back to
    Nature," *Youth Leaders Digest,* March, 1951.

Part 2 — Types of Outdoor Education Programs

Thus then to man the voice of nature spake—
Go, from the creatures thy instructions take;
Learn from the birds what food the thickets yield,
Learn from the beasts the physic of the field;
Thy arts of building from the bee receive;
Learn of the mole to plow, the worm to weave;
Learn of the little nautilus to sail,
Spread the thin oar, and catch the driving gale.

—Alexander Pope

There is agreement among educators that one of the primary goals of education is to help youth become effective, participating citizens in home, school, and community; and that schools are organized to help youth take their place in community living.

It must be recognized that there are many ways through which the objectives of education may be achieved. However, it does not seem logical that youth who study government in high school never get a chance to visit a session of the city council; or that youth spend hours studying about people and things that are thousands of miles away and still lack knowledge of their local community; or that the science teacher teaches conservation via blackboard and textbook completely ignoring the problem in the community.

Too much instruction takes place in abstract and unreal settings within the confines of the classroom. In too many cases, teachers organize school experiences entirely apart from any firsthand experience within the community in which the student lives.

How can youth know and understand the community without ever having a chance to observe it firsthand?

The justification of outdoor education programs rests on certain basic tenets of modern educational philosophy. These are:

1. The modern curriculum is developmental, based on real experiences that meet the needs of children and change their behavior pattern toward good citizenship and individual fulfillment.

2. Education is aimed at a common core of learning necessary for each individual in a democratic society. This does not mean identical education for everyone, for in a democracy education must develop diversity and spontaneity.

3. The modern school is concerned with the growth and development of the whole child in all areas of his living.

4. Knowledge is but the first step in real education; there must be added understanding through expression or experience in order to make knowledge more real.

Philosophers and educators have said that schools are organized to help youth take their places effectively in community living. Yet, in too many cases, school experiences are organized within the confines of the four walls of the classroom. It is becoming increasingly recognized that education cannot be completed merely by the use of the printed or spoken word. For words are mere substitutes for things, movements, and phenomena in the child's environment. In the out-of-doors appropriate learnings can take place more naturally, more efficiently and more effectively.

The major purpose of the school curriculum in the schools today is to provide the child with many kinds of experience through which he may learn actively, in contrast to the traditional recitation and memorization type of curriculum which treats the child as a passive receptacle to be filled with facts, knowledge, and information.

Outdoor education programs may vary from a field trip or hike of relatively short duration to an extended experience at a resident school camp. The degree to which the out-of-doors may be used for specific learning assignments depends upon the area in which the school is located, and the resources available in this area. The extent to which the resources will be used depends upon the background and training of the teacher.

A creative teacher with a background, or at least an

understanding, in outdoor education can enrich practically any school subject or area of learning in the curriculum simply by taking the class into the realm of reality through direct experience in the out-of-doors. Although an extended camping experience may be the ultimate goal of the school program, a good program in outdoor education may be had at very little expense by the maximum use of the community resources. Often times a complete laboratory of learning exists just outside the classroom. Where can one teach nature, for instance, better than in a natural setting? Why should the teacher turn his back to the window of the classroom and teach plant life or soil formation from books, charts or the blackboard? Classroom learning at best is vicarious. It may become more meaningful when it is supplemented by other sensory experiences. Learning is seeing, feeling, hearing, and smelling. Just outside the classroom is the world of reality. Outside the classroom are the homes of the children, their neighbors and friends; their community with all its aspects of government, services, transportation, communication, and industry; and to a varying degree, depending upon the locale, a world of nature. The amount, variety, and extent of natural resources will, of course, vary from community to community depending upon the geographic location of the school. The city school will have available an entirely different laboratory than the rural school. Both the city and rural school will probably want extended experience so that they may widen their knowledge of each other's community life. Children in a California school may visit an orange grove or an irrigation project. Children in an Illinois school may visit the historic Mississippi River or the birthplace of Abraham Lincoln. Children in a New England school may visit the rock bound coast where our pilgrim fathers landed, a large tobacco farm of the fertile valleys of Connecticut, or an old whaling port long since inactive. Children of every school regardless of location may study units on birds, trees, plants, conservation, animals, and other aspects indigenous to their own environment.

Although the scope of outdoor education is as "wide as all outdoors," it is not a unit separate from the class-

room. It is as much an integral part of the whole educational process as anything that goes on within the classroom.
Outdoor education is not to be regarded as a vacation or an
escape from the classroom. It is not an interruption of the
educational process but a continuation--a planned part of
the school curriculum. Outdoor education and classroom
activities may be integrated in such a way that outdoor experience can vitalize and improve classroom instruction and
classroom instruction can give impetus and meaning to further experience in the out-of-doors.

Many schools and agencies are offering desirable
learning experiences in one or more of the variants of outdoor education, but a far larger number have not awakened
to, or at least are not taking advantage of, the potential offered by this approach to teaching and learning. Outdoor
education, although practiced and preached from the beginning of our educational process by leading philosophers and
educators, is still in the pioneer stage. Recently, however,
it has acquired a new emphasis. An increasing number of
school systems are expanding existing programs or have
started new programs in outdoor education.

The better programs of outdoor education now in existence are carefully planned, thoroughly organized, directly related to the school curriculum, and are directed by a
competent staff. It is not hard for school systems inaugurating outdoor education programs to justify their investment as long as they are planned and developed according
to local needs. With wise administration and trained leaders outdoor education is ready to make a valuable contribution to the learning process of both children and adults.

Public schools and other community agencies promoting outdoor education may do so in one or more of several ways. The most common practices or prevalent types
of desirable learning experiences in the out-of-doors,
listed in order of their simplicity, inexpensiveness, and
probable availability are school journeys, the school garden, the school sanctuary, the park school plan, the school
farm, the school forest, and the school camp. These
forms of outdoor education may overlap each other and
are not necessarily an entity within themselves.

The extended camp is the ultimate goal of outdoor education for every school. Not only may the students gain experience in nature trips, gardening, farming, forestry, and other conservation activities, but more important, extended camping experience offers an opportunity for children and teachers to live together as a group in the out-of-doors twenty-four hours a day. Modern education requires that the teacher know the needs and interests of her students. This face-to-face relationship in the informality of an outdoor setting aids the teacher in knowing her children more thoroughly and more completely than is ever possible in a classroom where they are together in a formal setting only six hours a day.

Experience in outdoor education is available to every school child in the country. Schools that cannot find, or finance, a suitable resident camping site many introduce youngsters to the outdoors through field trips, nature walks, day camps, school gardens, school farms, or school forests. The degree to which a school uses one or more of the types of outdoor education depends upon the leadership and academic background of its faculty.

Chapter 4

SCHOOL JOURNEYS

A school journey, field trip, hike, tour and excursion are terms used by educators to designate educational experiences outside the classroom. Any planned experience outside the classroom which is used to introduce a new unit or area of study or which is used to supplement the study of a subject and is undertaken by a teacher and her class or a segment of her class is considered a school journey. The field trip or hike is usually considered a more limited journey by foot in the immediate school neighborhood; it may vary from a fifteen minute "look and see" trip by a kindergarten class to a specific, objective journey lasting up to a half day or even a full day depending upon the educational objectives to be achieved.

The tour or excursion are terms commonly used by educators for ventures outside the immediate community made by some mode of transportation other than walking. They usually involve an all-day journey or a journey of several days or even several weeks. Many educators are bothered by the word "excursion" as it connotes pleasure and fun or is suggestive of a pleasant sight-seeing expedition. However, a well-planned excursion can be educational as well as fun and may be justified as worthwhile by either or both of these objectives, especially in the modern era where recreation is considered an equal component to education.

The school journey may or may not be an outdoor education experience in the strictest sense of its definition. The authors, however, are not interested in drawing a fine line between experiences that should be classified as outdoor education and experiences which should be classified as community studies. A well-planned journey to a stream, a forest, a farm or a field may be good outdoor education, but a trip to the post office, fire station, factory, museum, or a session of congress may be equally worthwhile. It is not the promotion of outdoor education that is important, but the concept of extending the classroom in every conceivable way in order to give children firsthand experience with nature, people, and community life.

There must be a good reason for planning experiences outside the classroom. It must be worthwhile educationally, must add to or enrich the experiences of the classroom. Uger found from his experience in New York City that journeys from the classroom are made for one or more of the following reasons:

1. To gain firsthand knowledge.
2. To verify a fact (checking).
3. To settle a pro and con argument.
4. To make a comparison.
5. To make observations.
6. To stimulate interest in a unit of work.
7. To develop an interest and appreciation of work.
8. To make a survey of an industry or a process.
9. To explore a place, and
10. To have fun and adventure. [1]

DEVELOPMENT AND SCOPE OF THE SCHOOL JOURNEY

Although the United States has been slow to make use of field trips and tours for educational purposes, they have been used almost as long as education has existed.

Greek peripatetic teachers took their students to the market place and open fields long before the Birth of Christ. Many Greek scholars traveled abroad to gain knowledge of

[1] Charles Uger, "Excursions Need Direction." School Executive, March, 1941, pp. 15-17.

One of the highlights in the conservation program for Thurston County school children
was a visit to the Webster Forest Nursery of the Department of Natural Resources.
Above, Rex Eide from the Industrial Forestry Association's Col. W. B. Greeley Forest
Nursery of Nisqually, talked to a group of sixth graders as they viewed seedling beds
at the Webster Nursery.

Photo Courtesy of Washington State Department of Natural Resources

School children learn to identify and appreciate a tree at Camp Riley, Bradford Woods,
Indiana. Bradford Woods, which is also the home of the American Camping association, is operated by the University of Indiana.

Photo Courtesy of Reynold Carlson

other cultures. Italy became a mecca for travelers seeking her culture during the Renaissance.

Many teachers of the eighteenth and nineteenth centuries, including Pestalozzi, Rousseau, and Froebel made extensive use of direct learning through field trips.

Field trips and educational tours have been used much more extensively in other countries than in the United States. American educators visiting Europe are amazed at how extensively and freely education is conducted on busy streets, in museums and galleries, and in the woods and along the countryside. As early as 1911, a school journey association was founded in England embracing four types of journeys: (1) The junior school journey in which younger children visited public buildings, institutions, and other places of interest, (2) The walking journey to near-by parks, (3) High school tours in their homeland to study history, geography, and the social culture of their own country, and (4) The extended journey, sometimes across the channel to other countries of Europe.

Germany, Sweden, Italy, Russia, France, Poland, Holland, Belgium, and Japan use field trips in the education of their youth. In these countries school journeys have been used for several decades in connection with practically every subject-matter area. Students study not only their homeland, but they journey to surrounding countries. A firsthand study is made of foreign culture through encountering their problems, observing how they live and what they do, and examining their culture through visits to the museums, art galleries, historic and literary shrines.

In the middle thirties it was a common sight to see a teacher and twenty to twenty-five children with notebooks and pencils traveling the countryside or studying in the cities.

School journeys in Europe are increasing. Many of the journeys are conducted with the aid of travel service agencies. In 1960, the School Travel Service of Enfield, England, assisted over 600 schools on conducted tours throughout the continent of Europe.

Until recently the United States has not made extensive use of the school journey as a technique for instruction. An early exception was Benjamin Franklin who was probably the first American to make use of the field trip as a means for boys to study methods of farming on neighboring plantations.

There are several reasons why teachers in the United States were slow to leave their classroom on journeys and tours for educational purposes. Teachers in this country have always been book orientated and schools have always been book reading schools. Teachers' colleges and colleges of education have not stressed the value of firsthand experience and education outside the classroom. Knowledge was classified and organized into subject-matter areas which were departmentalized and isolated in compartments. School programs thus became inflexible and organized around a schedule which became somewhat sacred and could not be broken. A "businesslike efficiency" of schedules, recitation, study periods, term examinations and other mechanical and formalized routines became the trademark of American schools.

It became much simpler for a teacher to stick to educational routine than to take a chance on trying something new. Informal instruction and cooperative planning necessary for outdoor education is often too challenging. This is especially true for teachers whose own learning does not include experiences outside the classroom.

In spite of the fact that early educators advocated school journeys for many decades the slow acceptance of their extensive use may be summarized as follows:

1. A lack of good transportation facilities and good roads retarded the use of school journeys, especially extensive tours, for many years.

2. The traditional belief in America is that education takes place within the four walls of the classroom and from books. Students should concern themselves with books and activities in the classroom and not be concerned with life in the community. The typical reaction has been that anything outside the classroom is a waste of time and money.

3. It is easier to teach from textbooks and in the classroom. Formal instruction in a classroom atmosphere

in which children are trained in proper procedures is much easier and presents fewer discipline problems. Children engaged in informal learning in the out-of-doors are more natural and are less inhibited.

4. Administrators and teachers, themselves subject-matter and classroom orientated, have not been aware of the great instructional potentials of the school journey.

5. Administrators have had a sacred regard for class schedules. If the student is gone for over an hour, other teachers and other classes are involved. Thus, the school journey interferes with the regularly scheduled school program.

6. The school journey, if used extensively, creates problems for the administrator in keeping records, arranging for insurance and other clerical work, and sometimes obtaining substitute teachers or volunteer parents.

7. Teachers were reluctant to assume the added responsibility for supervising children outside the relatively safe confines of the classroom. Lack of specific knowledge and experience regarding liability and insurance laws retarded educational experiences outside the classroom.

Since World War II a great deal of importance has been added to the field trip or school journey in every section of the United States and on every grade level from kindergarten through college. Colleges of education are offering methods courses and workshops in community resources and field trips. Many state departments of public instruction and city school systems are publishing guides to community resources and manuals for planning and conducting field trips.

There are several factors which have encouraged the more extensive use of school journeys in recent years. The most important ones are:

1. A sincere desire on the part of administrators and teachers to provide more meaningful and enriched instructional experience for their students.

2. A desire on the part of the parents and interested citizens of the community to provide better instructional

programs for their children.

3. Many parents have served in the armed services and have traveled extensively to work in defense plants. Through this travel and their own experiences they have become convinced of the educational value of travel.

4. American people love to travel. Man is by nature an outdoorsman. It is sound education to capitalize upon the inherent desire of the students.

5. Cheap and efficient means of transportation and good roads are available to practically every school. Consolidation of America's schools has given teachers access to school buses which can become mobile classrooms.

6. Many communities have organized youth days, clean-up days, education days, and other special days in which schools are invited to participate. Children become mayor and councilmen for a day, help in clean-up or safety compaigns, and become involved in community life in many other ways.

Today, school programs in nature and outdoor living are provided in some form in most American communities. Teachers are taking advantage of the museum, zoos, parks, rivers, streams, woods, historic sites, natural and scenic beauty, and other points which may supplement the activities of the classroom. No classroom, regardless of grade level, need be denied opportunities for direct experience in the out-of-doors. A school journey is a procedure which may be used on all levels of learning to study objects and materials in their natural setting. School journeys are used by teachers who recognize that certain learning experiences in the out-of-doors can contribute to specific lesson objectives. The artificiality of the classroom may be vitalized by studying real things in real situations. There is nothing artificial or abstract about learning in the out-of-doors. The real situation becomes the learning situation. Children studying a unit on farming visit a real farm. A sixth grade class studying plant life goes to the school ground or nearby park and studies real plants. A high school chemistry class studying sanitation or chemical elements in water visits the sanitation or the water department.

Long journeys or tours involving considerable time
and transportation usually are given most publicity, but not
all good trips need to be so extensive. In the immediate
vicinity of the classroom are plants, trees, rock formations,
or other aspects of nature that can be studied firsthand in
connection with a unit of study. Trips that begin in the immediate neighborhood and extend their scope gradually to
points of a greater distance are excellent means of fostering understanding and interest in nature and at the same
time providing informal group work and acquainting children
with their environment.

Too often, teachers and leaders of children teach
from the textbook and neglect opportunities just outside the
classroom door. In an earnest desire to provide better
education for their pupils, teachers often place too much
faith in book learning. A good example is found too often
in the science class where the teacher studies various
leaves inside the classroom out of contact with trees and
their natural surroundings. Opportunities to work in community activities and in close contact with nature and actu-
ality are available to every teacher alert to the possibilities of vitalizing textbook materials in the out-of-doors.

Short journeys to implement topics or units directly
related to class studies have proven to be an effective technique of teaching in all sections of the country and on all
grade levels. A journey may be used to stimulate interest,
to motivate further study and at the same time provide a
basis for better understanding of the classroom activities.
Journeys may be used to introduce a unit of work, to further
develop a unit, or to summarize a unit of work. Interpretation of the environment through concrete firsthand experiences on trips and tours is essential in establishing meaning and relationships. A rock collection in the classroom
has little or no meaning to children. It is a rare bird, indeed, that will build her nest on a shelf in the rear of a
classroom. A pickled frog or snake in a jar as a science
exhibit loses its functional value. It has no need for food
or protection and thus loses the very aspects of life which
make it a frog or a snake. Therefore, there can be very
little meaning.

Through the school journey the classroom can be enlarged to encompass life as it is lived; instruction can make seeing and hearing realistic and exciting avenues for learning.

VALUES OF THE SCHOOL JOURNEY

Modern educators faced with the problems of making learning more real and meaningful find that the tremendous advantages of school journeys far outweigh the disadvantages. With proper preparation and planning, going outside the classroom is a most effective teaching technique. Some of the more prevalent values of school journeys listed by educators in all parts of the country are:

1. THE SCHOOL JOURNEY ENRICHES THE CURRICULUM WITH REAL EXPERIENCES

School journeys provide an opportunity to supplement, interpret, and enrich the school curriculum.

Every subject-matter area in the curriculum can be given a breath of life through firsthand experience with reality. Bookish, abstract and artificial experience which sometimes characterize classroom teaching can be made more meaningful and more interesting if it is related to reality--to concrete and basic experiences of the child's life.

By studying subjects in their natural setting or as they function children have greater interest, learn faster, have better understanding and retain what they learn longer.

Pearlstein[2] points out that a group of children in New York City took several walks through the streets of their neighborhood to see the many interesting activities carried on there. They watched men building homes, schools and stores, and men repairing streets. They saw steam shovels and fire hydrants and learned the purpose and use of each.

---

[2]Sandra Pearlstein, "An Experimental Approach to Teaching," High Points, January, 1961, pp. 70-72.

From the vantage point of a nearby bridge, the children observed the Manhattan skyline and watched cars, buses, and trains pass on their way to another borough. Because they saw with their own eyes the extensiveness of Manhattan--the river beside it and the land across the river--they were more able, in the classroom, to understand the size of their borough, the fact that it is an island, and its place in the larger city structure.

2. THE SCHOOL JOURNEY PROVIDES OPPORTUNITIES TO CLARIFY VERBALIZATION AND BOOKISH INSTRUCTION THROUGH CONCRETE EVIDENCE AND REAL EXPERIENCING

Classroom instruction, today, suffers because it deals so much with second-handed knowledge. Students spend too much time reading about things or looking at pictures and too little time with real things. Knowledge derived from the printed page too often becomes superficial. Children need to get acquainted with as well as to know about things. Most of the world's greatest writers experienced what they wrote. It is hard to be creative without experience for creative expression is built on experience. A one-sided education from books and the printed page excludes spontaneity and freshness; about all that can result is more verbalization. Concrete evidence and real experience clarifies verbalization and allows for better understanding and therefore greater growth and creativity.

William Cullen Bryant had to live near and visit forests many times before he could write, "The Groves Were God's First Temples."

Joyce Kilmer's poem Trees take on new meaning and a new appreciation and understanding is gained if the poem is recited and discussed under a large and rugged tree rather than in the classroom.

Four outstanding artists were called together and asked to draw a little-known African animal. None of the artists had ever seen the animal and they were asked to draw the animal as they visualized it from a dictionary description. Needless to say, the artists had four entirely different conceptions of the animal. Dictionary definitions or printed descriptions cannot quite clarify things as they really are. At best they are a poor substitute.

3. THE SCHOOL JOURNEY PROVIDES AN OPPORTUNITY FOR CHILDREN TO BECOME ACQUAINTED WITH THEIR ENVIRONMENT

Concomitant with an increase in academic learning school journeys bring about a sense of identification with the community. As Fraser points out, the school journey is an "effective procedure to bring the individual into contact with his culture which is his birthright."[3] His relationship and feeling of belonging to the community is strengthened and his sense of responsibility as a citizen is widened and deepened.

Through participation in community activities such as serving on the safety patrol, organizing a clean-city campaign, running the city government for a day, assisting in improvement projects, and serving as guides for civic functions, students become more intimately acquainted with their community in all its aspects. They come in direct contact with people, things, living conditions, movement, occupations, and recreation in an educational climate.

School journeys to farms and rural areas, woods, and open fields and wilderness areas bring children close to the simple priorities of life that once was the environment of all men. It teaches them, as no textbook can, that mankind is still dependent on the soil even though this may be somewhat camouflaged by man-made machines and industrial development. Although man has mastered the air and sails the seven seas both on the surface and under it with his war craft, he still returns to the land which nourishes him. School journeys may return children closer to, and give them a greater appreciation for, their common heritage.

---

[3] James Fraser, Outcomes of a Study Excursion, New York: Bureau of Publication, Columbia University, 1939, p. 79

4. THE SCHOOL JOURNEY PROVIDES AN OPPORTUNITY FOR CHILDREN TO DEVELOP A BETTER UNDERSTANDING OF THE PRINCIPLES OF DEMOCRACY

The school journey provides students with firsthand experience in planning, managing, and conducting their own affairs. In planning a journey, organization and assignment of responsibility are necessary. Students and teacher work together on the same team each accepting responsibility in planning and carrying out a learning experience outside the classroom.

The teacher and the pupils know that everyone must cooperate to make the journey a success. In this way responsibility is significant and real and not artificial or contrived. Through group planning with the teacher every member of the class is involved in the solution of problems arising from individual and group participation in a natural social situation.

Committees appointed to look after transportation, permissions, lunches, safety, and other procedures and arrangements make the school journey a cooperative enterprise in which the teacher, pupils, parents and interested citizens participate together.

Assignments on a school journey must be made clear and certain. Failure to carry them out can then be reflected swiftly and directly to the student or students responsible.

Cooperation, respect for others, and group planning are experiences which are more than preparation for democracy--it is democracy in action.

5. THE SCHOOL JOURNEY PROVIDES GREATER OPPORTUNITY FOR TEACHERS TO PUT INTO PRACTICE WELL-ESTABLISHED TEACHING TECHNIQUES --OBSERVATION, INVESTIGATION, COOPERATION, INTEGRATION, INFORMALITY, CREATIVITY, AND ACTIVE PARTICIPATION.

The school journey offers teachers an opportunity in many cases to get away from second and third-hand information of the printed word. It makes learning more interesting and motivates children to close observation and investigation of nature's phenomena. Observation is used as a scientific, teaching technique for transmitting information. All of the senses are used to make discoveries about the objects or things being observed. Students are encouraged to discuss the distinguishing characteristics of the things they observe. Through further investigation in the out-of-doors children are led to reasoning, interpreting, associating, and seeing relationships.

The school journey offers many opportunities for meaningful, cooperative experiences for students. Each child is given an assignment with the knowledge that failure to carry out his part of the project may result in failure for the entire group.

Furthermore, learning is an active, on-going process. The informality of the out-of-doors is a better climate for active participation and creativity on the part of both the teacher and the pupils.

Outside the restraining walls of the classroom children see life as an integrated whole, not as isolated areas for study. They learn in an informal way without bells, schedules, and formal lesson plans.

All the above-mentioned factors make for more self-dependence and allows for more individual expression and thus creates more creative thought and action.

6. THE SCHOOL JOURNEY BROADENS INTEREST IN WORTHWHILE LEISURE-TIME PURSUITS

Although too many teachers still cling to the belief that "if it is fun it isn't worthwhile," today's society demands an education that reaches beyond the formal and dogmatic dictates of the tomb to a live and vivacious cultural growth that can only come through individuality and creativity.

Educators need to ponder the fact that the cultural growth of a nation is attained through man's recreation and during his leisure time!

Since most of man's leisure-time hobbies and activities are determined in childhood, school journeys may develop interest in nature activities, the art gallery, scenic spots, literary and historical shrines, the museum and in other places which satisfy their interest and curiosity.

7. THE SCHOOL JOURNEY DEVELOPS MORE WORTH-
WHILE ATTITUDES AND BETTER UNDERSTANDING
BETWEEN STUDENTS AND TEACHER

It is impossible to really get acquainted with a child
in a classroom. Sitting in his seat and obeying the rules and
formal regulations imposed upon him, the child is not natural.

Outside the classroom in an informal learning situation children are natural and the teacher can get a better
insight and understanding of their behavior.

It is good, too, for the children to discover that their
teacher is human, that she can laugh and be fun, that she
can wear informal clothes, and that she can teach informal-
ly in the out-of-doors.

8. THE SCHOOL JOURNEY STIMULATES DISCUSSION
AND NARRATION BY PROVIDING "CLOSE-TO-LIFE"
EXPERIENCES

Motivation is an important factor in the learning process. The experiences that come from close contact with
nature and the community are alive and action-packed. It
is easy to talk about action and excitement. Textbooks lack
motivation and are too often dry and uninteresting as they
are too far removed from the child's experience.

Children will talk and children will write if they can
talk and write about things which are alive and interesting.
They like to tell or write about things they have seen or
heard. Children love to tell of their experience and the
school journey may open new avenues and provide new experiences.

9. THE SCHOOL JOURNEY CAPITALIZES ON MAN'S
URGE FOR TRAVEL AND ADVENTURE

Man likes to explore, to wander, and to be "on the go."
He wants to experience new things, to be in new surroundings, and to meet new people.

The creative teacher seeks ways to use the migratory instinct for worthwhile educational ends and the school journey is one way.

SURVEY OF COMMUNITY RESOURCES FOR EDUCATION

A school administrator alert to the educational possibilities of the school journey has a three-fold task.

First, he has to educate his teachers through general meetings, committee assignments, and in-service workshops as to the instructional possibilities of learning outside the classroom. Since the teacher is in direct control of the students the success of the journey will depend upon her skill in utilizing, planning, and conducting it.

Discussions of the values of the school journey and reports from teachers with mutual suggestions and general ideas for planning, conducting and evaluating the journey will be a big step in making the instructional program more meaningful and effective.

The second task of the school administrator is to educate the parents and citizens of the community to the instructional benefits and educational possibilities which the community can offer the school.

Through parent groups, parent teacher associations, civic associations, and service clubs, administrators and teachers may break down the traditional opposition to education outside the classroom.

The use of parents as assistants on school journeys and having children report to them about their experience on such trips help to stimulate interest and support for this type of education.

The Board of Education in Madison, Wisconsin, put the community behind the schools by adopting the following resolution as early as 1943: "In order to provide the most effective teaching environment, field trips and excursions outside the classrooms and school buildings and grounds under the supervision of members of the school staff are considered by the Board of Education as an extension of the classroom and an integral part of the ecucational program."

In giving further interpretation to this resolution the superintendent of schools said, "The purpose of this resolution is to remove any possible doubt regarding the fact that local study is a legitimate part of the educational program and will be recognized as such by the administration and the Board of Education. In the case of injury to a child, it protects the teachers from any charge that the trip was not in the line of duty and was not a part of the regular school program."

The third job of the school administrator is to instigate and implement a survey of the community for instructional possibilities and resources for education.

This may be done by committee assignment or by the faculty working together as a whole. One person should be appointed to organize and file the materials. The file should be kept up to date by adding new materials and journey ideas as well as deleting journeys which for some reason prove no longer effective. This can be done very efficiently by having the teacher turn in an evaluation and report on each journey she takes.

Only journeys which are legitimate and worthwhile educationally should be selected. Pertinent materials and information regarding each trip should be included. The following information should be included with each suggested journey: (1) relation to the curriculum; (2) value in terms of the contribution it will make to children's previous experiences, needs, and interests; (5) cost of transportation; (6) time it will take; and (7) number of assistants required.

PLANNING THE SCHOOL JOURNEY

The school journey is not to be regarded as an escape from the classroom or a break from the dull routine of learning; it must be the most efficient technique for learning a particular aspect of the curriculum or it should not be taken.

The school journey in order to be worthwhile as a successful teaching technique must be planned just as any other learning activity must be planned. Its success depends upon unity of purpose, keen interest, participation of the students, and careful planning for these three requisites.

Planning a school journey isn't difficult; it can be as simple or as elaborate as suits the circumstances and objectives sought. It does, however, involve something more than hastily deciding on a trip and leading a group of childre into the out-of-doors. The one thing that distinguishes a school journey from a pleasure jaunt is that in the former a real educational purpose exists and much planning is involved to achieve the objectives of the journey.

The length of the school journey both in time and distance will vary with the age of the group and the purpose of the trip. For very young children journeys closely related to their daily life experience should be selected. As the children grow older they may be guided into more detailed study of community activities and natural surroundings which may implement the school curriculum. No trip should be so long that the children are physically exhausted or mentally bored. The children should conclude the trip wanting to see more rather than wishing they had seen less.

TEACHER PREPARATION

One of the pre-planning chores of the teacher is getting the necessary permissions for the trip. In order that the principal knows where his teachers are and the type of activity they are conducting, most school administrators require teachers to obtain permission for the journey a few days ahead of time. In many cases, depending upon the destination of the journey, permission must be obtained from the owners, officials or caretakers.

The third permission should come from the parents of the children. Such permissions are obtained by sending permit slips home by the children a week ahead of the planned journey for signature by the parents. Most schools have a set form for this such as the form used by Grosse Pointe (Wisconsin) School District:

Permit For Excursions

_____, my minor

child (or ward) has my permission to go to

_____ on _____
                                       date

    In consideration of the benefits involved,

The Grosse Pointe School District, its Board of

Education and all its agents and employees are

hereby released and discharged from any and all

liability as a result of said minor making said

trip.

_____
Signature of Parent or Guardian

Dated_____ day of_____, 19_____

    The question of teacher liability arises in connection
with school journeys, but carefully planned and well-organ-
ized trips cause few problems. In most states, the liability
of teachers or other representatives of school boards usually is recognized only when actual negligence is proven. Au-
thorized, supervised school journeys are generally regarded
as being comparable to schoolground or classroom activities.
    Some state legal codes have special restrictions that
should be checked by the teachers. The school principal
will usually have materials from the state administrative
officer giving details about special regulations for school
journeys. In some locations, teachers are considered
negligent if they do not have first-aid kits containing snake
bite serum. In order to be safe, the teacher should check
on legislation concerning school journeys.
    Today many schools have some type of liability in-

surance to protect their teachers. Teachers must keep in mind that the parent's permission blank does not relieve the teacher or school of a possible liability suit.

The teacher should make the journey and study the area before taking the children. She will need to know the most desirable route and the best means of transportation to the destination. Also the teacher will need to know more about the needs and requirements for planning the journey in regards to safety, health, comfort and courtesy.

If the owners or guide is conducting the tour the teacher will want to discuss with him the objectives of the trip, age and comprehension level of the children, number in the group, time of arrival, points to be discussed, and other matters pertinent to the educational aspects of the trip.

The teacher should select the pupil groups, group leaders, parent assistants if any, and review the purposes and plan of the entire journey. Everyone who is in this group may contribute a great deal to the success of the trip if they are properly briefed. Knowing the objectives and route of the journey, they can guide student observation and help to interpret the guide's statements. If children are allowed to help formulate the rules of conduct they will help maintain them. Since school journeys involve relations between the school and the public, the adult helper becomes very important. Not only can they contribute to making a school journey a success, they can also see a well-planned educational technique in operation.

In cities where the destination is within walking distance the teacher should ask the police to assist in traffic. The police are usually happy to render this service if the request is made ahead of time.

Methods of transportation depend upon the distance and the practice of particular localities. Frequently, parents are glad to furnish cars and to serve as adult leaders at the same time. Transportation by bus often proves more practical because it keeps the group together and affords the teacher an easier and more unified control of their activities and behavior.

In any event several precautions should be observed: (1) make sure private cars used on a school journey are adequately covered by insurance, (2) plan the route and the itinerary for the journey, (3) avoid any unplanned stops or deviation from the planned route, and (4) establish check points if the groups are to be separated.

PREPARING THE CHILDREN

Since involvement is the key to success in any learning process the teacher should strive to get every member of the class participating in the planning, conducting, and evaluating of the school journey.

The need and general purpose of the journey should develop naturally out of the classroom experience and the children need to see the relation of the trip to the problem or topic under discussion.

In planning sessions with the pupils the teacher may want them to formulate questions to be asked, list particular points to be observed, gather data, brochures, maps, and other educational aids, and appoint committees for accepting these and other responsibilities. Committees may be appointed to work on transportation, finance, courtesy, safety, bulletin board, refreshments, and other assignments which will vary with each particular journey.

The committee members, with guidance from the teacher, should work out all details with their classmates several days before the journey. The day before the trip the final rules of conduct, safety measures and other committee reports should be made clear to the class.

The class may enlist a few of their parents to help with management and responsibility on the journey. They will also want to discuss what clothes they should wear, rules for safety and courtesy, walking and seating arrangements, provision for lunch, toilet facilities and other measures deemed necessary for the success of the journey.

Rules which a committee on safety may work out with their classmates for final presentation to the class just before the trip may include:

1. Stay with your buddy at all times.
2. Keep close to the rest of the group.

3. Hold the wire for your buddy when going under a fence so he won't get scratched or tear his clothes.
4. When walking on the highway, keep in line and walk on the left side of the road.
5. No one is to get ahead of Richard who will lead the group.
6. No one will walk behind Miss Jones who will bring up the rear.
7. In case of insect bites, cuts or bruises report to Johnny who is in charge of the first-aid kit.
8. Always walk, do not run.
9. Do not stray away from the group even during rest periods.
10. Do not push, shove, or show any manner of disrespect for a classmate.

GUIDE FOR THE PLANNING OF FIELD TRIPS[4]

First Considerations

_____ Is it the best procedure for the purposes of the group?

_____ Is this experience appropriate for the children?

_____ Have adequate backgrounds, needs, and purposes been developed?

_____ Are related materials available--films, books, pictures?

_____ Are there profitable follow-up activities?

_____ Are physical conditions satisfactory--weather, safety conditions in places to be visited?

_____ Will it strengthen the school-community relations?

Preliminary Arrangements

_____ Has administrative approval been given?

_____ Has the teacher made a preliminary visit?

[4]John U. Michaelis, Social Studies for Children in a Democracy, Englewood Cliffs, N. J.: Prentice-Hall, 1956, pp. 220-222

_____ Has the approval of parents been secured?
_____ What number may be adequately accommodated?
_____ Are eating and toilet arrangements satisfactory?
_____ Has the time schedule been prepared?
_____ Has the guide been advised on problems, needs, and maturity of the group?
_____ Have travel arrangements and expenses been arranged?
_____ Are assistants needed to help supervise the group?
_____ Has a list been made of the names, telephone numbers, and addresses of those children who are going?
_____ Others:_____

Teacher-Pupil Planning

_____ Are questions prepared and understood?
_____ Are recording procedures and assignments clear?
_____ Are reporting procedures and assignments clear?
_____ Have behavior standards been developed?
_____ Have safety precautions been considered?
_____ Have the time schedule, travel arrangements, and expenses been clarified?
_____ Have significant side interests been noted?
_____ Has attention been given to adequacy of dress?
_____ Are monitorial assignments clear?
_____ Others:_____

Follow-up Plans

_____ Do next experiences follow naturally?
_____ What findings are to be reported?
_____ What summaries and records should be made?
_____ Is attention given to the development of charts, maps, diagrams, murals, models, scrapbooks, construction, dramatic play, and floor layouts?

_____ Are assembly programs, newspaper articles, exhibits, or displays appropriate?

_____ May findings be shared with other classes?

_____ Are procedures in mind to discover and clarify misconceptions?

_____ Are interesting sidelights to be considered?

_____ Are letters of appreciation and samples of follow-up work to be sent?

_____ How is behavior of the children to be evaluated?

_____ How are recording and reporting procedures to be evaluated?

_____ Others:_____

CONDUCTING THE SCHOOL JOURNEY

The techniques employed on the school journey will, of course, vary with the age and experience of the children, the objectives sought, and the length and nature of the trip.

If the teacher has done a good job of organizing and pre-planning, the journey should be orderly and efficient.

Great stress should be placed on safety consciousness. When children have discussed the hazards of the journey and made their own rules, they are more certain to obey them.

While on the journey the teacher has an opportunity to promote good habits of conduct, courtesy and respect for others, and practice in safety procedures.

When walking there should be an adult leader in front and at the rear of the class. They should not be allowed to run because of the danger involved. The class should stop at intersections to get assistance in crossing the street from police or from the adult leaders.

The children should be kept in the groupings decided upon in order to promote safety, make the journey more effective, and for the sake of carrying out a plan.

The teacher should see that all children have a chance to see and hear, to ask questions, and to participate. The children should not be fatigued either mentally or physically by expecting them to see and learn too much at one time.

Teachers and guides should use good educational

procedures in presenting phenomena--that is, give the children a chance to discuss and ask questions rather than try to explain every detail to them. Children should be encouraged to take notes and gather materials for further discussion on their return to the classroom.

The school journey should not be over-planned so as to destroy the spark of adventure and creativity. There should be time for free exploration, informal discussion on their own, and relaxation.

On all-day journeys a lunch may be had at a restaurant in which case reservations should be made ahead of time. When choosing a restaurant, the teacher will want to talk to someone who can recommend a reputable one. The teacher should visit the restaurant ahead of time to make final arrangements for seating and feeding the class. It would be an added educational experience to chose an eating place with atmosphere, perhaps one children do not always get a chance to patronize such as a Chinese, Italian, French or other nationality restaurant.

In many cases, especially in the out-of-doors, children take lunches with them and eat together in some pre-arranged scenic spot. After picnic lunches the children should thoroughly clean the area so as not to litter the landscape. Here is a wonderful opportunity to aid children in building constructive habits of good citizenship.

At departure time when children begin their return trip to the school the teacher should carefully check roll, have the courtesy committee thank the host or guides, and see that all children are in their respective cars or bus. Plenty of time should be allowed for the return trip so that children will not be late for the regular school dismissal.

A SAMPLE PLAN FOR A FIELD TRIP

Saving The Soil

The sixth grade has read and discussed "The Changing Earth, " and are working on a project concerning soil conservation.

Concepts to be developed:

1. Erosion causes loss of valuable top soil.
2. Many forces cause erosion.
3. Man is learning to prevent erosion.

Questions to be answered:

1. What are the results of erosion?
2. What forces cause erosion?
3. What conditions aid these forces of erosion?
4. What practices prevent erosion?

Activities for research and observation:

1. Compare the depth of top soil at the top of a hill with that of the valley below.
2. Find other effects of soil erosion and list them.
3. Show examples of forces at work or the results of their work: wind, water, freeze, and thawing.
4. Observe good and poor practices in soil conservation.
5. Observe small gullies, mark their extent, and re-visit them after a heavy rain.
6. Observe fields with good cover crops, then visit a field without the cover crop.

Follow-up activities for the classroom:

1. Fill a box with loose dirt. Blow at the dust and observe flying dust. Pour water over the loose dirt and observe the results.
2. Read pamphlets and literature of the local Soil Conservation Service Bureau.
3. Visit the library for further readings in soil conservation.
4. Bring in newspaper and magazine clippings which deal with soil conservation.

SUGGESTIONS TO ASSURE SUCCESS IN SCHOOL JOURNEYS

1.   Educate the public, the school board, and the faculty through parent-teacher associations to the potential of trips and tours as a technique in education.

2.   Begin with short, simple trips and work up to longer tours.

3.   Plan trips and tours which are commensurate to and within the comprehension of the particular grade level involved.

4.   Make a survey of worthwhile experiences which may be gained through field trips and tours in the community.

5.   Anticipate problems and plan for every eventuality to assure complete success of the field trip in terms of objectives, arrangements, expense, time, organization, conduct, transportation, public relations, and safety.

6.   Involve the entire class in planning, organizing, and conducting the trip or tour.

7.   Obtain other teachers, parents, or friends for careful supervision of the trip.

8.   Follow-up the trip or tour with further integrating activities both in class and in the community.

9.   Public relations with agencies, industries, and other community institutions visited should be appreciative and cordial.

FOLLOW-UP AND EVALUATION OF THE SCHOOL JOURNEY

Successful school journeys usually include both a careful follow-up in the classroom and teacher-student evaluations of the experience for future use.

Discussion of behavior of the group (both good and bad), and suggestions from the students themselves as to how their behavior and courtesy could be improved on their next journey should be included in an immediate follow-up. The teacher should discuss with the children whether or not they lived up to their agreement about rules of conduct. This is the time to discuss safety precautions that were not observed by the students. After an honest evaluation, the children should determine if they are ready to take another trip or if they need more help and discussion before trying another.

Pictures, charts, pictorial records, booklets, and other materials collected on the journey may be placed together for display on tables and bulletin boards. This display can serve as a focal point for discussion among the students and with the teacher the various things they saw and learned. The teacher will give more time to particular points that should be stressed.

The teacher should include in her plans varied related activities of educational significance as: thank you notes to all those who helped the class, newspaper write-ups, written reports, and assignment of committees for further investigation, for caring for collected specimens, and for talks and dramatizations.

One of the most important phases of the follow-up is the actual evaluation of the journey itself. The teacher will want to discuss with the students such questions as: Did the trip fulfill its purpose? Could the same purpose have been achieved by other techniques? Did the class get the answers to the questions prepared? Was the trip worth the time, money, and effort? Were new interests developed? What things did you like best? What things did you like least? When we turn in the report to the office should we recommend the journey to other classes?

TEACHER'S EVALUATION OF THE TRIP

1. Did the trip serve the purpose for which it was planned?

_____

2. List a few of the new activities which resulted from taking this trip.

   a. _____   c. _____

   b. _____   d. _____

3. How well did this trip succeed as a planned educational experience?

   a. ————————————————————————————————

   b. ————————————————————————————————

4. What effects did this trip have on the pupils?

   a. ————————————————————————————————

   b. ————————————————————————————————

5. An informative account of what you saw and learned from the entire trip would be appreciated.

   ————————————————————————————————————

   ————————————————————————————————————

   ————————————————————————————————————

   ————————————————————————————————————

   ————————————————————————————————————

   ————————————————————————————————————

Rate Value of Trip   Very High ——— Good———
                          Satisfactory ——— Poor———

————————————————   ————————————————————
Date of Report   Signature of Teacher

                     (Return to the Principal's Office)

THE CAMP TRIP AND TOUR PROGRAM

Trips and tours may be made from any vantage point and by any organization interested in enriching the lives of children and adults by studying their surrounding environment or capturing the pioneering spirit which was once their heritage. In addition to schools, the Youth Hostels Association, camps, churches, the Young Men's Christian Association, the Young Women's Christian Association, recreation departments, and outing and nature lore clubs are a few of the many organizations and groups that use trips and tours to further their educational program.

A good resident camp has a trip and tour program to broaden and extend the regular camp program in order to allow for a greater variety of educational experiences both for the campers and the counselors. These trips and tours may vary from one day to one week and it may be desirable to extend the trips and tours program to several weeks and include visits to all the states and national recreational, historical, and educational places of interest. The trips and tours may be in the form of hiking, cycling, burro trips, horse back riding, canoeing, boating, motor caravans, and tent or trailer camping by automobile.

Many camps in order to get the campers out "on their own" and away from the comforts of a resident camp have a very complete and comprehensive tripping program under the supervision of a competent Supervisor of Trips and Tours.

The Trips and Tours Supervisor is responsible to the Camp Director either directly or indirectly. His duties may include:

1. Coordinate all trips out of camp within the total program.
2. Being responsible to Director for exact location of all trips.
3. Locate possible trip sites.
4. Set up regulations for trips.
5. Check qualifications of groups preparing to leave on trips.

6. Supervise trips out of camp.
7. Being in charge of all camp equipment (tents, cook-out equipment) not charged out to the units.
8. Keep records of all trips.
9. Work with Waterfront Director on planning canoe trips.
10. Work in liaison with neighboring camps concerning trips.
11. Act as receptionist to any visiting camp groups.
12. Schedule sites for use of visiting camp groups.
13. Work with kitchen on cook-outs and trail packs.
14. Turn in and post a daily trip activity report.
15. Attend all possible Unit Leader's meetings.
16. Hold conferences with the Camp Director as needed.
17. Help with pre-camp training, give on-the-job training to others when requested.
18. Instruct in campcrafting and tripping skills to patrols or whole units when time permits and when scheduled by the Unit Leader.

Minne-Wonka Lodge near Three Lakes, Wisconsin, under the direction of Mr. and Mrs. Leslie Lyons has a code on Trip Tips which follows:

1. No crabbing, or griping, or grousing, or complaining. But report any real illness or accident to your counselor at once.
2. Take your share of responsibility for preparation for the trip. Learn how trips are planned.
3. Know where you are going and take responsibility for getting there. (Don't just be a passenger.) Keep yourself informed as to your location and direction. See map, and know your direction.
4. At camp site, organize the work of camping but be willing to do a little more than your share. Don't "drag your feet."
5. Be eager to learn as much as possible. No matter how long you camp, you'll never learn all there is to learn about campcraft; nor about

canoeing; nor about nature. <u>Be</u> <u>Alert!</u> <u>Avoid</u> <u>ac-</u>
<u>cidents</u>.

6. Treat other people you may meet with proper respect no matter how they look or talk. Do not hail
strangers either on the lake or on the road. Conduct yourself so as not to attract special attention.
Real courtesy knows no border lines. Both you
and your camp are judged by your courtesy.

7. In general, although there are exceptions, <u>quiet-</u>
<u>ness</u> is a distinct asset. You will see more wild
life and run less risk of disturbing others。 Henry
Wellington Wack says: "only fools and asses bray
in the forest, " and he might have added "or on the
lakes. "

8. Food supplies on a trip, (especially on a canoe
trip) become very important and should be guarded
with every possible care. This is because lost or
spoiled food frequently cannot be replaced. This
is true to an extent of <u>all</u> equipment. Do not go
on a trip if you are not willing to eat the kind of
food available for trips.

9. Watch your "<u>footwork</u>" around the cooking fire.
Never step over fire, food or utensils, walk
<u>around</u>. This one thing spots the dub camper
more quickly than anything else. Your footwork
is a very essential part of your campcraft.

10. Don't let your enthusiasm die down. When things
don't break just right, you don't have to be a
Pollyanna to stay with it and see things through
without a grouch. Can you "take it, " and <u>smile</u>?

There are several travel camps operated in the United
States and many of them have been conducted every summer
for several years.

One of the most unique mobile camps is the Trailer
Travel Camp conducted by the Outdoor Education Associa-
tion with its home base at the National Youth Leadership
Camp on the shores of Little Grassy Lake near Carbondale,
Illinois.

The Trailer Travel Camp pulls a trailer which is

designed to accommodate ten to twelve campers and four
staff members. The unit is pulled behind a car or station
wagon and is designed to provide all necessary facilities
with an occasional time out on the road to replenish the food
supplies.

The travel itinerary is planned by the group prior to
departure from the base camp. The itinerary is mimeographed for distribution to parents with mail stops indicated.

The camp sites are 150 to 200 miles apart and are
usually in State or National Parks, and forests.

When the group arrives at camp the trailer is unpacked.
Canvas tops are rolled out with poles and stakes to make a
large and roomy shelter. One side of the trailer is the
chuck wagon with a kitchen completely equipped for outdoor
cooking; the other side is the program side and includes a
library, laboratory, workshop, and office with pertinent
supplies and equipment. From the center section of the
trailer large equipment, bed rolls, and other camp para-
phernalia are stored.

Dr. L. B. Sharp, Director of the Outdoor Education
Association, says the modern trailer is a substitute for the
old conestoga wagons of the Oregon Trail days. Substituting the trailer for the wagon, the automobile for the horse
results in the trailer travel camp. Dr. Sharp points out
that, "exploration learning is the basis of our program.
This means really seeing what we look at as well as going
to see."

"Our approach," says Dr. Sharp, "is semi-scientific.
We want to get acquainted with people, their history, and
how they live, as well as with nature's work and wonders."

The Trips and Tours Program at the Camps operated
by the Recreation and Outdoor Education Department of
Southern Illinois University are designed to care for the
younger and more inexperienced campers as well as those
who have returned for their third or fourth summer of
camping.

Inexperienced children stay relatively close to the
base camp for at least a week. They live in small units
isolated in the woods where they learn skills in campcraft
and living in the out-of-doors. When they adjust to camp

life and learn skills necessary for camping, they begin
leaving camp with trip packs for cook-outs, overnight camp
outs, and soon are making more extended trips across the
lake by canoe or barge.

Older campers with more experienced counselors
plan trips by canoe from Grassy Lake to Crab Orchard Lake
to the Muddy River and down the Mississippi. Sometimes
they go by car to the Current River in Missouri and start
their long canoe trip down the swift and clear waters of
this beautiful river.

Western Treks are being worked out for the next camp
ing session with camp-outs on the way to Cody, Wyoming.
Here they will make headquarters for trips to visit scenic
and historical sites including a two-day pack trip into the
mountains.

Selected References

Atyeo, H. C. *The Excursion as a Teaching Technique*
New York: Bureau of Publication, Teachers College,
Columbia University, 1939.

Blanc, Sam. S. "Vitalizing the Classroom--Field Trips
and Excursions," *School Science and Mathematics,*
November 1952.

Blough, Glenn O., Schwartz, Julius, and Huggett, Albert J.
Elementary School Science and How To Teach It.
New York: The Dryden Press, 1958.

Brown, S. *They See For Themselves* New York: Harper
and Brothers, 1945.

Bullington, Robert A. "Winter Field Experiences for
Biology Teachers," *The American Biology Teacher,*
January 1959.

Dale, Edgar *Audio-Visual Methods In Teaching* New York:
The Dryden Press, 1955.

Frasser, James Anderson *Outcomes of a Study Excursion*
New York: Bureau of Publications, Teachers College
Columbia University, 1939.

Haake, B. F. "Guides For Successful Field Trips,"
Elementary School Journal January, 1952.

Harrold J. P. "Using the Community As a Laboratory, "
    American Biology Teacher October, 1952
Hoban, Charles F., Charles F., Jr. and Zisman, Samuel B.
    Visualizing The Curriculum New York: The Cordon
    Company, 1937.
Lynd, Helen Merrel, *Field Work In College Education* New
    York: Columbia University Press, 1945.
Maddux, Grace C. "Techniques and Values of Field Trips, "
    School Science and Mathematics January, 1950.
McKown, Harry C. and Roberts, Alvin B. *Audio-Visual*
    Aids To Instruction New York: McGraw-Hill Book
    Company, 1949.
Michaelis, John U. *Social Studies For Children In A*
    Democracy Englewood Cliffs, N. J.: Prentice-Hall, 1956.
Sands, Lester B. *Audio-Visual Procedures In Teaching*
    New York: Ronald Press Company, 1956.
Weaver, David A. "Excursions In A Metropolitan Center, "
    The National Elementary Principal Thirteenth Year-
    book, Washington, D. C.: National Education Associa-
    tion, 1934.
Wehrle, M. F., "Bringing The Farm To The City, "
    American Childhood June, 1953.
Wolf, Ise H. "Success for Your Field Trip, " *Practical*
    Home Economics February, 1950.

Chapter 5

THE SCHOOL GARDEN

The school garden is one of the oldest and most common forms of outdoor education. Gardening itself is one of the oldest arts. The pyramids reveal garden scenes in the ancient tombs of the Egyptian kings leaving ample evidence that men were raising grain and vegetables in the valley of the Nile thousands of years before Christ. The Bible, world literature, historical documents, old almanacs, and old garden books attest to the age and universality of gardening. The early settlers brought a knowledge of gardening as an aid to eking out a livelihood in a new country. Today, people of all ages in every part of the world work in gardens both for economic and recreational reasons.

SCOPE OF SCHOOL GARDEN PROGRAMS

There is nothing fundamentally new in the school gardening program. Many schools throughout the United States have used some form of gardening as a teaching device since the turn of the century. The modern concept of education with its child-centered curriculum and emphasis on "learning by doing" gave impetus to school gardening activities. The school garden has been popular in European countries much longer and much more extensively than in the United States.

During World War II gardening in the United States was probably at its most productive peak due to the impetus of the Victory Garden campaign. Gardens flourished across the entire nation for obvious economic reasons and were sponsored by home, school, and community groups. Many schools and clubs have continued a program of gardening activities since World War II because of the sheer joy of working together in a worthwhile cooperative venture and because of the many obvious educational and recreational values. Educators throughout the country while promoting the Victory Garden for economic and patriotic reasons found that well planned and properly supervised activities in gardening can enrich and vitalize the school curriculum.

The need for elementary school instruction in gardening is more real today than several generations ago. It is also needed more for city children than for those attending rural schools. Urban life has robbed city children of garden experience; it has deprived them of contact with the earth; and they are seriously handicapped because of a distorted and artificial picture painted by textbook learning alone. It is worth the effort of an interested teacher to provide whatever experiences possible in gardening to all children possible.

School gardens range from window boxes, potted plants, or a small plot of soil on the school yard to several acres of ground conveniently reserved throughout the city for school gardens. Too often garden activities have been confined to a plot of ground for growing flowers and vegetables on or near the school yard. School gardening programs should be broad enough to include activities in landscaping and caring for the lawns, shrubs, and flower beds of the entire school area. With the cooperation of the school custodian children may develop valuable attitudes and appreciations for beauty and outdoor living through experiences in pruning, mulching, mowing, and firsthand experience with plants and shrubs.

No school is too small and no faculty is too specialized to provide a plot of ground and leadership necessary for garden activities. School gardens are found in every state of the union and on every grade level. The kindergarten and primary grades may observe germination of seeds and work at simple garden care while upper grades may study soil, fertilization, plant life, irrigation, weather, conservation and the interdependence of nature. High school classes may try out their knowledge of soil preparation, chemistry, or botany.

Although the school garden is still of value to the one-teacher rural school, it should be used to a much greater extent in the schools located in large cities where children have less opportunity to observe and work with plant life.

Many of the large cities of necessity confine their gardening to indoor activities in seed germination and flowering plants while others are fortunate enough to have plots of ground set aside on the school yard or at the home of one or more of the children living near the school.

New York, Cleveland, Minneapolis, and Los Angeles are among the many cities which sponsor outstanding programs in school gardening. The state of Hawaii is an excellent example of school gardening conducted on a state wide basis.

The gardening program in the New York City schools is related to the study of living things and is included as one of the seven areas of their science curriculum.

"In the garden more grows than the gardener sows" according to an old proverb. Here children gather tomatoes that they planted from seed, transplanted and cultivated. The garden activities is part of the camp program operated by the Recreation and Outdoor Education Department, Southern Illinois University.

Outdoor and indoor gardening projects are developed and conducted under the guidance and with the assistance of the Supervisor of School Gardens.

Teachers use a handbook, Living Things, published by the Board of Education to guide their instruction in gardening activities. Some of the areas of study are plants and animals around us, the needs of plants and animals, getting new plants, living things need other living things, and how our senses help us.

Teachers may call on the office of Elementary Science and School Gardens for assistance and guidance in their gardening projects. An annual inventory and garden supply form is used for teachers to order their supplies and request any other help including an assigned helper or teacher for a summer garden program.

The Cleveland (Ohio) Public Schools has had a gardening program since 1904. The Division of School Gardens is an Auxiliary Agency in the Cleveland School System under the direction of the Assistant Superintendent of Special Schools and Activities and a Garden Supervisor. Its purpose is to aid teachers and pupils in conducting educationally desirable and effective experience in gardening.

Cleveland has twenty-three acres of school gardens. Thirteen acres are used for over 3,000 individual children's plots and ten acres for general instruction for both pupils and adults. There are six greenhouse buildings or separate classrooms for gardening on the various garden tracts.

In 1960, nearly 15,000 students from all grade levels in 156 Cleveland public schools participated in the school gardening program.

The school garden program enlists the aid and cooperation not only of the Garden Division of the Cleveland Public Schools but of the entire school staff, the Housing Division, and the Parent Teachers Association.

The garden program is helped throughout the year by a Saturday morning television show called "Down To Earth." Teachers and garden specialists discuss such topics as

Picture Page
for Third Grade Planting Kit

1 DIGGING AND FERTILIZING THE GROUND OF THE PLANTING PLACES

THE LUMP TEST FOR SOIL CONDITION

TOO WET

READY TO WORK

DIG EACH FURROW FULL WIDTH OF THE GARDEN

SCATTER FERTILIZER EVENLY AND LIGHTLY

HOE FORWARD

2 PLANTING GREEN BEAN SEEDS

SPACING OF LARGE SEEDS

BEAN

1½" - 2" DEEP

HOW TO HOLD SEEDS FOR PLANTING

3 PLANTING ZINNIA SEEDS

PLANT ABOUT 4 SEEDS TO AN INCH

HOE HANDLE

OR YOU CAN SCATTER SEEDS IN A FLOWER BED

⅛" - ¼" DEEP

4 PLANTING GLADIOLUS CORMS (BULBS)

SPACE 6 INCHES APART

4 TO 5 INCHES DEEP

5 PLANTING THE TOMATO PLANT

SLIGHTLY OVERSIZE HOLE

SET PLANT A LITTLE DEEPER THAN IT FORMERLY GREW

PRESS SOIL DOWN FIRMLY

SET PLANTS 3 FEET APART

6 GROWING THE PLANTS (CARE)

SEEDLINGS BEFORE THINNING

AFTER THINNING

HOW TO CULTIVATE WITH A HOE

SHALLOW SLICING ACTION

CLEVELAND PUBLIC SCHOOLS *Division of School Gardens*

growing tomatoes, weed control, plant diseases, harvesting vegetables, flower arrangements, fall ground improvement, and the garden show.

The annual School Garden Exhibit sponsored by the Division of School Gardens is a garden science project for all grades and all schools of Cleveland. Posters are distributed showing the date and place of exhibit and children are taught the correct procedures in exhibiting by use of a slide film "The School Garden Exhibit."

Each classroom is assigned an area of wall, table or floor space for an exhibit of a class project pertaining to plants or gardens. Prizes are awarded for winning exhibits and certificates of achievement are awarded children earning recognition for outstanding work.

The garden exhibits are used not only to teach points of quality in garden products but also to stress traits of character such as punctuality, following orders as directed, honesty, and being good winners and losers.

The Minneapolis Public Schools' Junior Garden Program, like many other school garden programs, was started in 1944 as a World War II victory garden and is still in existence today. The tremendous success of the program is due to the energetic three-way cooperation of the public schools, the homes of participating children, and the Parent-Teachers Association.

This Junior Garden Program is carried on with children from the kindergarten throughout the eighth grade. Experience indicates that it is most effective with the children in grades three through six. The program begins in the spring of each year, with an auditorium presentation in each school by qualified personnel from the office of the Consultant in Science. During this presentation the children have the project explained to them and see slides which suggest procedures in gardening and what vegetables and flowers may be grown. Usually a few kodachromes of the previous year's gardens are also projected. At this session the school's P.T.A. Garden Chairman is introduced to the children.

With her own group each teacher discusses gardening, the types and sizes of gardens and the problems connected

with the work of a garden. Children who are interested in
having a garden at home receive the form letter to sign and
the sheet of instructions to take home. If a child reports
back that his parents say that he can have a garden, the pink
enrollment form is sent home for complete information and
the parent's or guardian's signature. Teachers send these
completed enrollment forms to the school office where they
are mailed to the Consultant in Science. In the Consultant's
office, alphabetical lists of enrollees by schools are typed
in quintuplicate, a Minneapolis Junior Garden Club membership card (billfold size) is sent to each enrollee, and he receives a copy of the Minneapolis Junior Gardener's Handbook which is especially developed for this program.

The recreation Chairman of each building- P. T. A. and
the principal of each school must be contacted to secure a
Garden Chairman who is personally sold on the project.
The Science Consultant's office sends all pink enrollment
slips, each stapled to a white "grading sheet, " to the Garden Chairman of each school along with a carbon copy of
the list of enrollees and a letter of summer directions.
During the third week of June the Garden Chairman with at
least two other interested persons visits each garden. On
this first visit the contacts of the judging team with parents
and child (1) encourages the child in producing a good garden, (2) explains the grading sheet and its purpose, and (3)
develops a better understanding among all of the gardeners
and acquaints them with the benefits of the program. At the
close of each garden visit, the visitors' scores are totaled
on the grading sheet.

During the third week of July the Garden Chairman and
assistants make a second visit to each garden which fosters
even better public relations. By this time there is ample
evidence of each child's efforts and accomplishments which
are used in reporting to the child and his parents. After all
gardens are visited a second time and totals are recorded
on each grading sheet, the three best gardens in each district are recommended for final judging in the city-wide
awards competition. All forms, grading sheets and enrollment blanks, are returned to the Science Consultant's office.
A special judging team is sent out from this office to visit

and judge all gardens recommended for the final city-wide awards.

In the city-wide competition each child who follows through on his garden activities and receives a score of at least sixty per cent is presented a "green hand" button. Other awards of certificates and ribbons are made for various achievements and accomplishments. At the close of the 1958 season with an enrollment of 1,765 gardens, there were seven city-wide first awards, fifteen city-wide second awards, and twenty-five city-wide honorable mention awards given. In most cases an auditorium program was held in each school for the presentation of awards to their gardeners. Many schools held garden fairs during which time children could exhibit the produce of their gardens. Over 1,750 children participated in the garden program.

The Junior Garden Program closes in the fall with a half-day trip to the Northrup, King and Company's experimental plots near Minneapolis. Each school is permitted to choose two of their best gardeners to send on this trip. After a guided tour through the plots, the children are given treats plus pumpkins and flowers to take home.

The Los Angeles City School Districts provide gardening experience in the junior high school. The program carries over into the community and offers exceptional opportunities for home landscaping and maintenance and production of flowers and vegetables. The recreational possibilities of home gardening, so valuable in urban communities, are emphasized in all courses.

The junior high school pupil is given an opportunity on an assigned plot of ground to lay it out, prepare, plant, maintain, and harvest a crop by using approved skills and techniques.

The pupil is given an opportunity to see the completion of the growth cycle of a plant and can appreciate what takes place from the time the seed is put in the ground until the plant matures.

Supplemental instruction within the classroom is given on such topics as safe use and care of tools, classification of vegetables, importance of rotation, soil needs and preparation, maintenance of indoor plantings, common nursery practices, and plant identification.

Teacher committees prepared a publication, Instructional Guide For Gardening, to serve a threefold need for gardening instruction in the junior high school:

1. To maintain a basic framework for consistency of the gardening courses offered in all junior high schools.
2. To establish minimum standards of achievement which may reasonably be expected of all pupils.
3. To provide the opportunity for each youth to gain desirable skills, knowledge, and attitudes in the field of agriculture so that he may make the most of himself as an individual and make his greatest contribution to society.

Gardening has long been recognized in the schools of Hawaii as a very important means of motivating students in the whole range of school subjects.

"In a perfectly natural way," says Superintendent Clayton Chamberlin, "gardening contributes to the other fields of teaching and learning tending to integrate the learning process and to make it effective. Its value as a subject or as an end in itself becomes apparent when we consider the importance of gardening, avocationally and culturally, in Hawaii today."

The Department of Public Instruction in Honolulu has prepared suggested learning activities and teaching aids for teachers using gardening as a means of promoting education. This publication, A Guide To Elementary School Gardening in Hawaii, gives teachers help in planning the garden, preparing the soil for planting, fertilizing, planting, irrigating, thinning, spacing, transplanting, weeding, cultivating, controlling insects and related pests, controlling plant diseases, harvesting and the education implications, administrative policies, and evaluation procedures for such activities.

TYPES OF GARDENS

There are several types of gardens and all types have more or less educational value according to the purpose of the garden program, the amount of time spent on them, and the degree of skill both in gardening and working with children possessed by the teacher.

The most common types of gardens found in school programs are the indoor garden, the rock garden, the flower garden, the vegetable garden, and a garden that combines two or more of these types.

The indoor garden may range from a few flowering plants to an elaborate display of plants and vegetables beautifully arranged in pots, pans, and window boxes. Children may experiment with germination of various kinds of seeds by planting them in boxes of soil. They may through fertilization and proper care grow plants and vegetables from the seed to maturity. Experiments with different kinds of soil may be carried on inside the classroom by filling pots with varieties of soil, planting seed in each pot, and carefully observing the results.

A lack of school owned acreage or space on the school ground for an outdoor garden hampers many crowded city schools in conducting a good program in gardening activities. However, a resourceful teacher may improvise and provide opportunity for growing and observing many kinds of plants without benefit of a plot of ground.

Children may learn many concepts about plant life in the classroom. Some of the more obvious are: plants need water, soil, light, and proper temperature; plants require space in which to grow; the common plants seen in classrooms have leaves, stems, roots, and sometimes flowers; a seed contains a baby plant; and plants grow toward the light.

Suggested topics on indoor gardening for study may include:

Can we sprout seeds from our Halloween pumpkin?
Can we sprout seeds from a sunflower?

What care must we give a plant?
What are the requirements needed for a plant to grow?
Will plants grow in any soil?
What soil is best?
Can plants grow in water alone?
Can branches cut from a tree or bush grow?
What seed can we use to make a window garden?
How can we make our plant bulbs grow?
How can we make a terrarium--a little world of
   living things?

The rock garden is usually planned on a natural slope where rocks are plentiful and their arrangement provides beauty and at the same time prevents soil erosion. Children may with their teacher look over the garden site, discuss and submit plans for making the garden, and have an opportunity for creativity in designing irregular paths, pools, cascades, waterfalls, rock stairways, and variety in grass, flower, and rock arrangement. Children may find help in garden magazines and library books on what type plants are suitable for shade and porous soil.

The flower garden offers opportunity to develop appreciation of harmony and design in color. It also beautifies the school ground or the home and gives the children experience in working with a variety of flowering plants. Although flowers may be planted in other type gardens, most flower gardens are planned as an integral part of the school plant and are surrounded by a low hedge, sidewalks, and lawns.

The vegetable garden is the most common type of school garden, probably because of its universality and practical value. Man required food as a basic necessity and beauty after his hunger was satisfied.

A school district with enough land available for a vegetable garden is fortunate in that many more children throughout the school system experience the educational benefits of gardening.

Many schools offer experience in all types of gardening. Seeds are germinated in hotbeds or the classroom for transplanting in the outdoor garden when the season is right.

Flowering plants and even a rock garden may become part of the scheme of a large vegetable garden. Regardless of the type and extent of school gardening, there should be a sound and comprehensive plan which relates the activities of the children to a purposeful well-designed curriculum.

EDUCATIONAL VALUES OF SCHOOL GARDENS

There is an old proverb that goes, "In the garden more grows than the gardener sows." Growing of radishes and lettuce is not the purpose of a school gardening program; the vegetables and flowers raised are incidental. Of greater importance are the desirable habits, attitudes, and appreciations developed, the knowledge gained, the interests and skills acquired, and the recreation enjoyed.

No activity can better enrich and vitalize the curriculum more than the school garden. In the real school garden the child learns at firsthand not only a great variety of natural objects but also myriads of natural phenomena. He learns to appreciate and enjoy nature; he learns the cycle of plant life and the intricate balance of nature. In battling garden enemies and, at the same time, working with the friendly elements of nature, the child learns science in a meaningful and interesting way. He learns to understand and to appreciate the out-of-doors, the interrelatedness of nature, and the beauty and mystery of growing plant life. His textbooks come alive with concepts which he can use, and his experience with nature motivates him to further reading--reading for a purpose.

Arithmetic becomes more than a pencil and paper game when children are faced with real problems such as plot planning, sorting, buying, counting, and other basic skills which are necessary in gardening activities.

Garden activities may easily be projected into nutrition and health, social studies, art, and language arts.

Gardens can lead to a powerful stimulus to better nutrition. The school should encourage children to check their diets as to number of calories needed and the vitamin and calorie content of the different vegetables. The child

who has observed the care needed by growing plants--good
soil, regular watering, sunshine, air, cultivation--begins
to develop a sense of appreciation and respect for the health
care involved in his own growth and development.

Social studies come alive as children improve their
leisure time in the promotion of a worthy hobby and in the
beautification and development of gardens and lawns, as
they learn to know and work with community agencies, and
as they learn of the importance of crops.

Language arts are strengthened in a real and meaningful way as the children read, catalogue, follow and give
directions, keep a diary, write of experiences and commu-
nicate with others.

Some of the outstanding results which can come from
school gardens are:

1. School will be more interesting.
2. The children, parents, and teachers will have a
   feeling of pride in their accomplishment.
3. A feeling of interdependence between the school
   and community can be established.
4. The quality of school lunches and food habits of
   the children can be improved.
5. The school environment, both inside and out, can
   be more attractive.
6. School gardens can result in children growing
   either vegetables or flowers at home.
7. Valuable techniques and skills in gardening can
   be learned and practiced.
8. The need for careful planning and wise management can be understood.
9. A knowledge of resource people and of materials
   will be acquired.
10. Interest in beautifying and improving the land-
    scape could carry over into the home and commu-
    nity projects.

It is hard to understand how many biology teachers in
large city school systems teach the intricacies of biology

from a textbook when most of their pupils have never seen
a radish grow or a flower unfold. Teachers today must be
devoted to the individual child and must dedicate themselves
to meet his needs, interests, and abilities for better social
adjustment, emotional stability, and healthful living. Among
the most obvious contributions of the school garden to education are the changes brought about in the child through
his experience in garden activities.

They may be listed as follows:

Interests --
In outdoor life
In worthwhile activity
In association with garden activities
In living and growing plants
In production of food
In the work of Luther Burbank
In research in Horticulture

Habits --
Of observation
Of recording
Of work
Of neatness and orderliness
Of responsibility
Of dependability

Knowledges --
Of the soil, fertility, and plant care
Of the interdependence of nature
Of the "balance of nature"
Of the struggle for existence
Of the importance of soil to men
Of the propagation of plants and animals
Of flowers and vegetables
Of the use and care of tools
Of the importance of good food and proper care
Of the cycle of life
Of the science of horticulture
Of the value of air, moisture and sunlight
Of the value of exercise and fresh air

Abilities --
To use tools
To plan, execute, and evaluate activities
To interpret natural conditions
To adapt to the environment
To work and cooperate with others
To make social adjustments
To provide food from growing plants

Attitudes --
Of respect for the rights of others
Of the joy of sharing
Of patience
Of sympathetic understanding of nature
Of pride in a job well done

Appreciations --
For the joy of discovery
For the phenomena of growth
For the mysteries of nature
For the meaning of life
For the beauty in nature
For healthful outdoor activity
For doing things with the hands

YEAR AROUND ACTIVITIES IN GARDENING

Successful school gardens involve so many details of facilities, equipment, management, and operation that the inexperienced teacher can hardly be expected to foresee them all. To insure a successful gardening program there must be a capable person in charge. A person with all the qualifications of a good teacher who has a knowledge of and practical experience in gardening is most likely to conduct a successful program in gardening.

Garden activities provide natural motivation for classroom activities. Correlations are possible with art, music, reading, oral and written expression, social studies, arithmetic, and every area of the school curriculum.

Many people think of gardening as a spring activity,

but in reality good gardening practices require year around activity. The activities include planning the garden, preparing the soil, planting the seed, cultivating the garden, and harvesting the produce.

PLANNING THE GARDEN

Begin and keep a diary of garden activities
Selection and measuring of garden plot
Removing rocks, ash piles, unsightly shrubs or worthless trees
Making soil tests
Examine magazines, books, and seed catalogues for information as to planting, soil, and climate requirements
List plants that seem desirable
List seed for indoor planting and transplanting
List bulbs which are perennial
List bulbs to be stored and re-set each year
List vocabulary of new words
Write seed companies for their catalogues
Study units on weather, season change, soil and plant life
Learn the growing habits of plants
Draw a master plan of the garden to scale with placement of plants
Subscribe to good garden magazines such as Horticulture, House and Garden and Better Homes and Gardens
Decide what tools are needed and have them ready
Prepare an assignment sheet for each individual or committee
Order seed needed for the garden
Make the garden plan for discussion and adoption-- note shady spots, decide on flower beds and borders
Take field trips to local nursery and greenhouse

PREPARING THE SOIL

Level off land according to plan
Cut all brush and weeds
Rake the ground and pick up rocks and glass
Test the soil to see if fertilizers are needed
Add rich manure or fertilizers
Spade or plow the garden
Rake or disk the garden to break the clods
Study the contour and take steps necessary to prevent erosion

PLANTING THE SEED

Plant seed for transplanting early indoors or in hot-beds
Make a row marker with two stakes and a string the length of the garden rows
Plant the seed according to placement on master plan and sowing time
Use edge of hoe or garden plow to make rows
Drop seed cover and pat earth firmly
Transplant plants as weather permits
Lay out borders and paths

CARING FOR THE GARDEN

Feed plants regularly with plant food
Cultivate plants
Irrigate or water if the rain fails
Prevent and control insects and diseases when first seen
Provide for summer care of garden by parents or committee of children
Observe the growth of plants
Know the garden enemies - insects and worms
Know the garden friends - snakes, toads, birds

HARVESTING THE GARDEN

Gather produce as it matures and ripens

Arrange committees to sell produce, give it to needy
organizations, or take it to parents or school
cafeteria

Collect, clean, and oil all garden tools and store in
a safe, dry place

SUGGESTIONS FOR CONDUCTING A SCHOOL GARDEN

1. The type and scope of a school gardening program
will vary with the locality, the soil, the climate, the resource people available, and the age of the children who
participate.

2. There are three methods by which gardening experiences can be effectively organized within the school
program:

 a. Classroom lesson units in science such as the
care of house plants, making new plants from
old, and sprouting seed.

 b. Home-School garden projects in cooperation
with parents. The projects are planned in
school and supervised by school personnel
in cooperation with the parents.

 c. School garden plots or tracts in which pupils
grow gardens on property controlled-by-the-
school and under teacher guidance at all times.

3. Before introducing children to a school garden program, the school administrators should make an over all
educational plan for the project from its inception. Cooperation of parents and staff must be sought and partnerships
worked out with parents, custodians, and other interested
community spirited citizens. Committees of teachers,
administrators, and parents should work out the over-all
objectives, the plans for procedure, the type and quality
of leadership available, and in-service instruction necessary to guarantee desirable learning experiences.

4. Gardening for most pupils will be their first

responsibility for a practical experience based on scientific facts. The garden must not be an imposed task, but one that calls on the pupil's own interest and thinking. Teachers must put children on their own--guide rather than lead--let them experiment, help them to secure and use scientific information from books, resource people, and other reliable sources. State agricultural colleges in forty-five states publish bulletins on gardening. Garden clubs may be of help. The vocational agriculture teacher and the local county agricultural agent are possible resource people.

5. Gardening is a long term process not a three month proposition. Activities related to gardening can be charted by the children for each of the four seasons: fall, winter, spring, and summer.

6. The school garden program should be regarded as a laboratory for every grade level and for every subject-matter area in the school. It is not to be regarded as a panacea for all educational ills, but neither is it to be regarded as a frill or a fad.

7. A school garden should be publicized to the parents and the community so that the educational value can be seen by all concerned with the education of their children.

8. The necessary seed and gardening supplies should be provided by the school just as basketball suits or football shoes are provided the relatively few who make the team. Charges for seed, if charges are made, should be nominal.

9. A qualified teacher--one skilled in working with children and one skilled in garden procedures--should be available for instruction in gardening. In-service workshops where all teachers are taught gardening by available resource people in the school or community is a worthwhile means of strengthening a school garden program.

10. A school garden exhibit or other device which recognizes the accomplishments and shows the products of the work of such accomplishment offers children an opportunity to exercise initiative in planning exhibits, encourages wider participation in school gardens, and gives recognition to outstanding gardeners for work well done.

A SAMPLE INSTRUCTIONAL UNIT IN GARDENING[1]

PLANTING

A. Objectives

To have pupils become familiar with the following problems:
(1) What are seeds and what is their purpose?, (2) What happens when seeds grow?, and (3) How can we grow plants from seeds in our gardens?

B. Information

1. What are Seeds and What is Their Purpose?

Seeds develop from flowers when they are "fertilized," or when the male and female cells unite. Seeds are usually formed within a fruit which protects them. Nature's purpose in developing seeds is to provide for continuing and extending the plants which produce them. Seeds are often used as food for man and animals. Seeds vary in size, shape, and color.

A seed is the part of a plant that contains the "embryo" of the future plant. The essential parts of an embryo plant found within a seed coat are: (a) the plumule or true leaf, (b) the hypocotyl or root, (c) the cotyledons or seed leaves which contain food for the early development of the embryo.

2. What Happens When Seeds Grow?

The beginning of growth in a seed is called germination. Moisture, warmth, air, and darkness are required for normal germination of most seeds. Some kinds of garden seeds germinate in a few days, while others take as long as three weeks or more.

[1]Agricultural Education and Elementary Education Department. A Guide To Elementary School Gardening In Hawaii, Honolulu: Department of Public Instruction, 1953.

The following steps are noticeable when seeds germinate: (a) Swelling of the seed, (b) bursting of the seed coat, (c) appearance and downward growth of the embryo root, (d) lengthening of the stem as it pushes toward the surface, taking the seed leaves or cotyledons (in most seeds), (e) cotyledons turn green as soon as they are exposed to the light and function as leaves.

Only live or viable seeds will germinate. Seeds kept in a refrigerator will germinate better (higher percentage of germination) than those kept at ordinary room temperatures. Germination tests may be carried on to determine whether seeds are worth planting or not.

3. How Can We Grow Plants From Seeds In Our Gardens?

Good seed is essential to successful gardening. Seeds planted too deeply, or in ground that is packed too hard, or in ground that is water-soaked, cannot germinate, because air cannot get to them. Seeds that come up with thick seed leaves such as beans and radishes should not be covered more than five times their thickness. Seeds that do not push their seed leaves to the surface such as peas and corn may be covered ten times their thickness. Seeds should be planted deeper in a loose, sandy soil than in a soil that is clayey.

4. Parts of Flowers and Plants

a. The function of the flowers
Flowers form seeds which are necessary for reproduction.

b. The function of the stem
The stem serves as a means of communication between the leaves and the roots.

c. The function of the leaves
(1) Leaves take in carbon dioxide from the air and energy from the sun.

  (2) The leaf is the workshop where carbon dioxide from the air and water from the soil are converted into starch, which in turn is required in the making of all other substances.

 d. <u>The function of the roots</u>
  (1) Roots hold the plants in position.
  (2) Roots take water from the ground. This water contains plant food.

5. Cross Pollination

  Cross-pollination is the process in which the pollen grains (male) of one flower are placed on the stigma (female) of another flower.

  Each pollen so placed on the stigma will fertilize an ovule in the ovary, forming a seed.

6. Testing Seeds For Germination

 a. Materials Needed
  (1) Two pie baking plates
  (2) White blotting paper
  (3) Clean sand
  (4) Seeds
  (5) Forceps

 b. Procedure
  (1) Place a layer of clean, wet sand a half inch deep in the bottom of one plate to assure a uniform supply of moisture.
  (2) Cut two circular pieces of blotting paper to fit above the layer of sand and moisten them.
  (3) Count out a certain number of seeds, picking them at random without selecting any particular size, shape, or color.
  (4) Space the seeds evenly over the blotting paper.
  (5) Cover the seeds with the other piece of blotting paper.
  (6) Cover with the second paper.
  (7) When seeds start germinating, remove them

with a pair of forceps and keep a record of
the number germinated.
(8) Determine the percentage of germination.
Seeds should show at least a fifty per cent
germination.

Small seeds like lettuce and carrots should be covered
one-eighth to one-fourth inch; medium seeds such as beets
and radishes from one-half to three-fourths inch; and large
seeds like beans, peas, and corn from one and one-half to
two inches.

The use of seed-protectant chemicals such as Semesan and copper oxide (Yellow Cuprocide) will prevent a
common disease called camping-off. Damping-off is a
term applied to failure of plant seedlings to develop as a
result of attack from small organisms present in the soil
and at the soil surface. These organisms may attack the
seedlings before they come out or after they come out on
the soil surface. An unmistakable sign of seedlings affected
with damping-off is the small diameter of the plant stem
near the soil surface. The apparently healthy-looking seedlings may suddenly topple over and a water-soaked appearance of the stem near the soil surface may be noted.

Treat broccoli, cabbage, radish, and turnip seeds
with Semesan.

Treat celery, lettuce, and tomato seeds with copper
oxide.

Treat beet, carrot, chard, eggplant, bean, kohlrabi,
and green pepper seeds with either Semesan or copper
oxide.

Method of seed treatment: Place seeds to be planted
in a glass jar and add a small amount of Semesan or copper
oxide (depending upon the kind of seeds to be treated), using
a wooden spoon. Cover the container tightly and shake the
jar until the seeds are thoroughly coated with the fine powder. Plant the seeds. Pour excess powder back into the
container.

Method of seedling treatment: Dissolve one table-
spoon of Semesan or one and one-half teaspoonfuls of Yellow

Cuprocide in a gallon of water. Sprinkle the solution over
the seedlings in a sprinkling can.

Seeds need moisture for germination. For this reason, the planted beds should be properly watered. The re-
volving type of sprinklers with a fine-nozzle adjustment is
ideal for this purpose.

C. Suggested Learning Activities

1. Put the problem, "What are Seeds and What is their
   Purpose," on the blackboard and discuss it with
   pupils.

2. Have pupils bring to class different kinds of flowers.
   Have them become familiar with the male and female
   parts of flowers such as hibiscus, papaya, and beans.

3. Using a hibiscus flower, separate the male parts
   from the female parts.

   a. Female parts (pistil)
      (1) Stigma
      (2) Style
      (3) Ovary

   b. Male parts (stamen)
      (1) Filament
      (2) Another sac
      (3) Pollen

   c. Cut a cross-section of the ovary to locate the
      undeveloped seeds (ovules).

4. Draw a diagram of the pistil of the hibiscus flower
   on blackboard and explain how the pollen reaches
   the ovary and fertilizes the ovule or undeveloped
   seed.

5. Have pupils list the various ways in which a flower
   may be fertilized. Examples: bees, butterflies,
   and other insects, wind, man.

6. Have pupils collect samples of the various kinds of seeds including those of vegetables, fruits, flowers, and other ornamentals.

7. In order to obtain a clear relationship between the fruit (ovary) and the seed (ovule), have pupils bring to class several kinds of fruits; cut and study them. In the same manner, have them study such vegetables as tomato, eggplant, corn, beans, soybean, etc.

8. Give each pupil a lima bean seed which has been soaked overnight in water and have them make the following observations:

   a. Remove the skin (seed coat) which is located around the edge of the bean. What purpose does the seed coat serve?

   b. Open up the two halves. These are called cotyledons (seed leaves) and contain a storage of food to nourish the embryo plant in the early stages of growth.

   c. On one of the cotyledons will be found another structure. Reproduce this on blackboard, showing the plumule or true leaf and the hypocoty or root.

9. Have pupils make a list of seeds which are used as food. Examples: beans, peas, soybeans, peanuts, macadamia nuts, etc.

10. Have pupils organize into groups and prepare a report on the following simple experiments:

    a. How to make seeds sprout

       (1) Put different kinds of seeds on wet sawdust, sand, earth, blotting paper, cloth, or sponge

       (2) After the seeds are soaked, they must not lie in water, nor must they be allowed to become dry.

     (3) Keep soaked seeds covered with a piece of glass or an inverted tumbler.

b. Will seeds germinate without air?

     (1) Take a small bottle or a jar and put some damp blotting paper on the bottom of it.

     (2) Fill the bottle or jar three-quarters full of soaked seeds and close the container tightly.

     (3) Place a few other seeds of the same kind and similarly soaked in a second container with damp blotting paper on the bottom. Cover this container loosely to prevent evaporation but allow access of air.

     (4) Place the containers side by side so that they will have the same conditions of heat and light.

     (5) Watch and compare results daily.

c. How to test seeds

     (1) Place a layer of clean, wet sand a half inch deep in the bottom of one pie plate to assure a uniform supply of moisture.

     (2) Cut two circular pieces of blotting paper to fit above the layer of sand and moisten them.

     (3) Count out a certain number of seeds, picking them at random without selecting any particular size, shape, or color. Use forceps for picking up small seeds.

     (4) Space the seeds evenly over the paper. Cover the seeds with the other piece of paper.

     (5) Cover with the second pie plate.

     (6) When seeds start germinating, remove them with a pair of forceps and keep a record of the number germinated.

(7) Determine the percentage of germination. Seeds should show at least a fifty per cent germination.

d. How do beans come up?

(1) Plant some beans in soil or sand at least one inch deep. Observe the processes of growth carefully.

(a) What becomes of the cotyledons or seed leaves?

(b) Make two or three drawings showing the different stages of this early growth of beans.

e. How do squash, pumpkin, and melon come up?

(1) Plant these seeds in soil or sand and observe how they come up. Compare them with each other and with the beans.

(a) What becomes of the cotyledons?

(b) Watch them for a week after they are up and see if the cotyledons meet the same fate as those in the beans.

(c) Make a few drawings.

f. How do peas come up?

(1) Plant some peas in soil or sand and when they come up make the following observations:

(a) Does the tip point straight up as it comes out of the ground?

(b) Do the seed leaves come out of the ground? What happens to them? Dig up a plant and see.

g. How does corn come up?

(1) Plant some corn and observe the same points as in the preceding experiment.

(a) How many seed leaves are there?

(b) Do these seed leaves come above the ground?

(c) Does the plant come out of the ground pointing straight up or is it arched over?

h. Is sunlight necessary for germination? Is it necessary for plant growth?

(1) Prepare two gallon cans and plant several kernels of corn in each. Keep one of them in good light and keep the other in a dark place, or invert a box over it so as to darken it.

(a) Do the seeds that are kept in the dark come up as soon as those that are kept in light?

(b) Watch them for a few weeks after they are up. What is the effect of darkness on growing plants?

i. Should various kinds of seeds be planted at the same depth?

(1) Take seeds of corn, beans, peas, cucumber, and radish. Plant a few of each kind an inch deep, and a few of each kind two, three, four, five inches deep. Observe results.

(a) Which came up first?

(b) Did all the seeds come up?

(c) Which grew the most vigorously?

11. Demonstrate the use of a seed protectant either in a packet or in a jar with cover.

Put a small amount of Semesan, Yellow Cuprocide, or any other seed protectant (Arasan, Spergon, etc.) over the seeds, fold over the packet or cover the jar and shake until seeds are thoroughly coated.

a. For small-seeded crops such as carrots and lettuce, it is wise to plant three or four times the quantity required for a perfect stand. This is done to offset the possible poor stands due to cutworms, damping-off, weak seedlings, poor germination, etc.

b. For crops such as beans, corn, and soybeans, it is well to plant only a very few more or no more than are actually needed for the desired stands.

c. Beet and chard should not be planted too thickly because each so-called seed is capable of producing two or more plants.

d. Seeds of such root crops as carrot, radish, turnip, and beet may be scattered laterally over three or four inches of furrow. This practice provides more space for young plants to grow, more plants per linear foot of row can be left standing, and thinning will be facilitated.

e. There is no need for pouring seeds into the soil in extra large quantities. This practice results in unnecessary waste of seeds, tedious work in thinning, and oftentimes a complete loss from damping-off.

13. Problems

a. One hundred bush beans, Bountiful, were tested for germination and eighty of them came up. What was the percentage of germination?

b. Eighty corn seeds, U.S.D.A. #34, were tested and seventy of them came up. What was the percentage of germination?

D. Teaching Aids

1. Audio-Visual Library

a. Movie films

(1) Mysteries of Plant Life--sound, color,

eighteen minutes. This film shows hibiscus and other flowers opening and closing. It shows seeds germinating and sprouting on blotting paper.

(2) Fresh From the Garden--sound, color, twenty minutes. This is one of the finest garden films available.

(3) Grow Your Own--sound, b/w, twenty minutes. This film gives a humorous presentation of good gardening. It shows the DON'TS of home gardening that may mar the success of beginners.

(4) The Life of Plants--sound, b/w, thirteen minutes. This film shows by time-elapse photography the growth of a seed from the time it falls to the ground until it has developed into a fullgrown plant.

2. Audio-Visual Center, Oahu Schools

a. Movie films

(1) Plant Growth--sound, b/w, ten minutes, MF 520. This film shows the growth of plants. The pea is used as an example, and the film presents the complete life history from sprouting of the seed to the dispersal of the ripened seeds in the mature plant. The processes of pollination and fertilization are clearly shown by means of photography and by animated diagrams.

(2) Seed Dispersal--sound, b/w, eleven minutes, MF 521. This film shows ways by which seeds of plants are scattered in order to insure the propagation of the species. The methods illustrated include dispersal by the wind, transportation by animals, and forceful propulsion from the seed case. It shows the germination of seeds under various con-

ditions and the struggle for survival in the plant world.

(3) Planting Our Garden--sound, color, eleven minutes. This film portrays the activities of a family in planting a vegetable garden. Explains the process of seed germination and development, and the conditions that various seeds must have in order to grow.

Selected References

Beattie, W. R., *Useful and Ornamental Gourds*, Farmer's Bulletin, No. 1849, Washington, D. C.: United States Department of Agriculture, 1940.

Board of Education, *Science, Grades K-6, Living Things*, New York: Board of Education, 1959.

Boswell, Victor, *Growing Vegetables In Town and City*, Home and Garden Bulletin, No. 7, Washington, D. C.: United States Department of Agriculture, 1951.

Department of Public Instruction, *A Guide to Elementary School Gardening In Hawaii*, Honolulu: State Department of Public Instruction, 1953.

Division of Instructional Services, *Instructional Guide For Gardening*, Los Angeles: City School Districts, 1955.

Emsweller, S. L., *Growing Annual Flowering Plants*, Farmer's Bulletin, No. 1171, Washington, D. C.: United States Department of Agriculture, 1950.

Fairbrother, Nan, *Men and Gardens*, New York: Alfred A. Knopf, 1956.

Foley, Daniel J., *Vegetable Gardening In Color*, New York: The Macmillan Company, 1943.

Hellyer, A. G. L., *The Amateur Gardener*, New York: Translantic Arts Incorporated, 1954.

Rockwell, F. F., *Around The Year In The Garden*, New York: The Macmillan Company, 1939.

Shoemaker, James S., *Practical Horticulture*, New York: John Wiley and Sons, 1955.

167

Taylor, Norman, *The Guide To Garden Flowers, Their Identity and Culture,* Boston: Houghton Mifflin Company, 1958.

Wilder, Louise Beebe, *What Happens In My Garden,* New York: The Macmillan Company, 1935.

Wright, Richardson, *The Practical Book of Outdoor Flowers,* Philadelphia: J. B. Lippincott Company, 1924.

Chapter 6

THE SCHOOL
FARM

The story of man may be written in terms of his epic struggle with tilling the soil. Almost from the beginning of recorded history, ancient literature reveals that men were practicing manuring, liming and crop rotation. Homer in his Odyssey tells of a dog "lying on a heap of dung with which the thralls were want to manure the land." Many years before Christ the Romans had developed many good handbooks on the science of farming. Columella's Husbandry written A.D. 60 made suggestions that are considered good even today.

The Bible refers to farming activities on many occasions. In Deuteronomy is found the passage "And I will send grass in thy fields for thy cattle that thou mayest eat and be full." Children may enjoy searching the Bible for other references to farming. Every child should know how farming has developed from the crude stick dragged across the soil to the labor saving machinery of a modern-day farm. The lore, skills, and experiences of two hundred generations of men has developed farming to its highest level of productivity in all history. Every child should know the history of the development and importance of farming in the growth of the United States. Then, as today, agriculture was, and is, the foundation of American life and culture. The manner in which the colonist cleared the fields of virgin forests to eke out a living in the wilderness is an interesting chapter in American History. Only a generation ago, almost every farmer led a hard life, working from dawn to dusk. Today, thanks to the scientific experiments,

The Newark Valley (N.Y.) High School is built on 146 acres of land. Unlimited opportunities for firsthand experiences with nature are available to the entire student body. In the foreground is a load of poles gathered by the Future Farmers of the Agriculture department.

A group of handicapped children visit the School Farm of the Tyler (Texas) Public Schools. Here children become acquainted firsthand with farm animals and farm life under the leadership of James E. Dudley.

Photo courtesy of George Donaldson

theories and research in all aspects of living, farming has become a large business.

SCOPE OF SCHOOL FARMS

Although field trips and class visits have been made to farms for many years, the idea of a school-owned farm is a relatively new innovation in education. Many organizations, including schools, have realized the value of farm experience for city children and have provided various farm activities for several years. In highly industrialized cities children have often been sent to live on a farm for as long as a week. Many children see their first cows, pigs, and other animals and get firsthand experience feeding the animals and doing farm chores. Some city schools have worked out an exchange program whereby city children are exchanged for children of a rural school for one week, thereby providing a good experience for all children concerned.

Although school farms are a relatively new technique in learning, they are by no means unique. Many agriculture departments of high schools have owned and operated farms for years.

Almost two hundred high schools in California teach agriculture and close to fifty of these schools own their own farm. The size of the tracts owned vary from a few acres adjoining the school ground up to 120 acres.

The Kern County Union High School Future Farmers of America operate a 180-acre farm near Bakersfield, California. The boys have developed outstanding herds of cattle and hogs and conduct experiments with poultry, grain and all phases of farm activity. They have built dormitories for week-end occupancy, constructed hog houses and other farm buildings and have learned agriculture through firsthand, real and meaningful experience.

The ninth grade children have a small vegetable garden and elementary school grades frequently take trips to the school farm to study farm life.

The Bristol County Agricultural High School in Southeastern Massachusetts owns a 235-acre farm which is used as an instructional laboratory. The Williamsport school district in Pennsylvania operates a 750-acre farm which was willed to the school district.

Many high schools in every state of the Union either own or rent a farm to make textbook and blackboard agriculture practical. School farms offer the agriculture classes a laboratory to put into practice the theories and ideas which are discussed in class. Experiments in crop rotations, fertilization, conservation, and many other farm practices make class activities more meaningful to the boys involved.

The weakness of most school farms is not in their philosophy or method of teaching, but in the fact that they are limited to students taking courses in agriculture. Every child from kindergarten through high school could benefit from experience on a school farm. Many schools, especially in the city, give children no experience whatever in the outdoors, then require a course in botany, chemistry, or zoology in high school. Without the proper background these very interesting courses too often fail to challenge many good students and become difficult, meaningless and most unpopular.

The school farms of Battle Creek, Michigan, and Tyler, Texas, are two examples of how a farm may be used as a valuable laboratory of learning for children of all grade levels.

The school farm of the Battle Creek public schools, located four miles outside the city limits, has provided gardening and farm experience for all children of the Battle Creek Schools for the past 15 years. Each of the 15 schools in the district has a plot of ground for gardening by fifth and sixth graders. A Junior Garden Club of approximately 100 children continue work in their garden plots during the summer months.

Although the facilities and farm staff are used primarily by the fifth and sixth grades, any grade level or community group may use the farm as an outdoor laboratory. A shelter lodge and picnic area have been constructed for use by school and civic groups. Requests for use must be submitted a week in advance.

The school farm is a part of the Willard Trust Fund

and is operated by the Board of Education in cooperation with the Security National Bank.

The operation of the farm is primarily devoted to education. However, some cash crops are raised which contribute to the general upkeep of the farm.

Each spring the farm staff attempts to stock the farm with a wide variety of fowl, a few rabbits, and sheep. Activities include planting pines, spruce, and other trees, shrubbery and hedge rows for wildlife development, gardening, cropping, use of cold frames for starting plants, bee keeping, and feeding and caring of farm animals.

Over six hundred fifth and sixth grade children are transported to and from the farm each year.

Teachers organize their instructional material in the spring so that in early spring a unit on weather and its influence upon farming is introduced. A little later children hear a talk by the farm director and see slides of previous activities and accomplishments. They are given the size of their plots and begin planning and preparations for planting. Around the first of May actual planting begins. Picnics given for the parents serve a two-fold purpose of providing experience for children in planning the picnic and at the same time showing the parents the value of school farm activities.

Younger children make field trips to the farm to study animals, garden, poultry and other aspects of farm life. High school biology classes have a perfect laboratory for firsthand study of birds, plants, animals, insects and other areas of biology.

The Tyler, Texas, school farm is another outstanding example of getting the most out of an investment in outdoor education. In 1950, a group of educators realized that although most city youngsters were only two generations removed from the farm, they needed more knowledge of conservation and the importance of farm life in the struggle for food, clothing and shelter. A complete school farm was established as an outdoor laboratory.

The 160-acre farm managed by a former vocational agriculture teacher, boasts of a registered dairy herd, beef cattle, rabbits, laying flock, a farm shop, grown crops and a well-rounded pasture program.

While the farm is self-sustaining, its chief purpose is to furnish the Tyler public school system a laboratory for teaching conservation and appreciation for rural life.

During the school year children feed the cows, hogs and chickens. They watch the farmer cultivate the crops and learn farm life by assisting him with the many chores. They become acquainted with feeding pens, hay crops, legumes, fence repair, and other activities and problems of farm life. The farm manager often stops the tractor or whatever work he is doing to give the visiting class a lecture on how clover builds the soil, or whatever farm task may be at hand when they arrive.

Many schools have initiated a good farm program without ownership of a farm. Often times it is possible to find a retired farmer interested in children who will cooperate with the school in offering his farm and services for an outdoor education laboratory.

SUGGESTIONS FOR OPERATING THE SCHOOL FARM

School systems interested in starting a farm program will find no set pattern to follow. Each program will be unique in many respects as it should be adapted to the needs of the particular community. The school farm should have a farm family living on the farm to operate the farm weekends and during vacation and to assist teachers in their educational activities throughout the school year.

The farm family must be chosen with great care so that complete cooperation with school children and teachers may be assured when they visit the farm. He should have a genuine love for farm life, for working the soil and planting varieties of field crops, garden vegetables, fruit trees, and flowers. His enthusiasm should be equally great for farm animals, poultry, and above all for eager and enthusiastic children who will ask all kinds of questions which require patience and understanding. The farm director must have a sincere love for children and must realize his job is to keep the farm operating as efficiently as possible; that the school farm is for educational purposes; and that profits though desirable are secondary to the educational objectives.

Since the school farm is primarily operated for educational purposes it should provide as wide a variety as possible in the amount and kinds of plants, animals, and machinery

Children should have an opportunity to see fields of corn, pasture land, hay crops, beans, and other crops native to the area.

The farm garden should grow every possible vegetable and flower both common and unusual. Colorful Indian corn, flowers, popcorn, and gourds should be available for children to take back to the classroom. They should have opportunities to assist in planting, cultivating and harvesting garden products and be able to gather apples, cherries, plums, peaches, grapes and other delicious fruits from the trees, shrubs, and vines.

In addition, the farm should have available every conceivable farm animal and variety of breeds in poultry and rabbits possible. Baby farm animals such as calves, lambs, pigs, dogs, and kittens create great interest among children and provide motivation for education in growth and development of animals, how they serve man, and the wonderful story of the procreation of man and all life.

Instead of having one breed of poultry the farm should have a few poultry of several breeds so that the children may see and enjoy the variety. The farm should have a few turkeys, ducks, geese and guinea. In addition a variety of colors of rabbits would be of interest, especially to younger children.

The school farm should have all the various types of machinery necessary for modern farming. Children should see how the ground is prepared, how crops are planted and harvested and how modern machinery helps the farmer perform these and many other tasks more efficiently.

The school farm director should also be alert to the educational possibilities of machinery used in earlier days. To have a threshing engine and separator in good repair on the farm and to hold an occasional threshing every two or three years would not only prove exciting to the children, but would bring out the older folks for a nostalgic look and deeper interest in what the school farm is trying to accomplish.

A team of horses to pull the hayrides and on occasion break the garden with a horse-drawn plow would demonstrate farming techniques of the past as well as provide a recreational pastime enjoyed by boys and girls of a hundred years ago.

THE SCHOOL FARM AND THE CURRICULUM

The school farm is another opportunity for schools to provide a rich and meaningful laboratory of learning. The curriculum receives added vitality when real observation and real work supplements the lecture and the blackboard.

A school farm offers all the experiences and all the educational values of a school garden and, in addition, has other values to offer. Farming includes many more areas beside gardening and offers students an opportunity to gain experience and understanding in broad concepts related to the importance of the farm to modern society and the part farming has played in the advancement of civilization. Educational values of the school farm will be similar to those of the school journey, the school garden, and the school forest. It is another opportunity for the schools to provide the modern generation a chance to work in the soil, see farming done with horsedrawn tools and watch the work of modern machinery.

The program can begin on the primary level where children may take field trips to the farm. The program may extend through the high school where students may conduct special farm projects. Several good activities and exercises which may be used in connection with a school farm have been planned for various grade levels by curriculum committees throughout the nation. The teacher will, of course, have to work up farm units to fit her own particular situation regarding the background of her children and the availability of educational experiences provided by the particular farm.

UNIT OF WORK ON THE FARM[1]

Children who grow up in an urban society need help to gain a feeling of stability which comes from close and realistic experiences with the out-of-doors. The unit--"The Farm"--should help provide such first-hand experiences for the children of Pasadena if it is to be successful as a teaching aid.

We hope that the teachers who use this unit will find it helpful in stimulating the development of concepts concerning the out-of-doors and rural life in America.

Willard E. Goslin
Superintendent of Schools

I. General Purposes

A. To provide a series of related experiences in order to give each child an awareness of his place in a well-balanced school program.

B. To provide an opportunity for each child to learn to work and play democratically in a group, both as a leader and as a follower.

C. To help the child become more intelligently self-directive in solving his own problems.

D. To help develop within the child responsibility toward himself and others.

E. To help each child to feel secure within himself, so that he may become a happy, wholesome individual.

F. To provide opportunity for the child to participate in all types of functional experiences and in the use of all types of materials.

G. To provide an opportunity for the child to express himself creatively.

---

[1]Prepared by a Joint Committee of Elementary Teachers, Supervisors, and Curriculum Coordinators of the Pasadena City Schools, Pasadena, California.

II. Specific Purposes

    A. To provide the child with experiences and activities that increase the understanding of farm life and its relationship to his own life.

    B. To help the child understand how farm life has changed due to modern developments, such as electricity, machinery, specialization of work in a modern industrial society, and modes of living today.

    C. To understand the responsibilities of family life on a farm in contrast to family life in the city.

    D. To help the child develop an appreciation and an awareness of the value of farm life.

    E. To help the child understand how food reaches his home from the farms.

    F. To develop an interest in the relationship between conserving natural resources and farm life.

    G. To bring about an understanding of and an appreciation for the natural sciences in an agricultural environment.

    H. To provide an opportunity to participate in purposeful reading, arithmetic, and language arts experiences as related to farm life.

    I. To provide many opportunities for first-hand experiences, such as using and experimenting with materials, taking excursions, and using audio-visual materials.

    J. To stimulate creative expression through art, music, rhythms, stories, and poems.

    K. To understand the need for safe and healthful living on the farm.

III. Initiation of the Unit

    The environment should be stimulating and challenging. The room is a combination laboratory-workshop and a pleasant living space for many kinds of activities and experiences. Extend the classroom experiences and activities outdoors whenever possible. Some suggested ways to initiate the unit are:

A. Through a stimulating environment that may include:

1. Attractive pictures of farm life. Sometimes a thought-provoking question as a caption under a picture may be added.
2. An attractive library center featuring interesting books on farm life and activities.
3. A center of artistic interest in the room that may feature flowers, greenery, weeds, seed pods, animal figurines, pictures, grains, and fruit branches.
4. Many centers of interest to stimulate expression as areas for:
   a. Wood and tools   d. Attractive reading games
   b. Clay   e. Art
   c. Natural science   f. Music
5. Small trucks, boxes, wooden animals, and people.

B. Through neighborhood walks to:

1. Observe different types of soil, trees, and flowers.
2. Homes of children who might have ducks, chickens, a pony, pigeons, or goats.
3. A dairy or truck farm.

C. Through children's experiences and contributions such as:

1. Discussions of farm life fostered by:
   a. Experiences on farms.
   b. Newspaper and magazine articles and pictures.
   c. Exhibits of farm products such as corn, seed packets, and fruits.
2. Dramatic play of farm life.
3. Books, pictures, and records about farm life.

D. Through other related activities such as:

1. The showing of slides or films followed by a discussion and second showing.
2. A brief review of phases of market life that might include:
   a. Discussion of:
      (1) How the retail market obtains food from wholesale markets, dairies, bakeries, and canneries.
   b. Drawing pictures of food enroute to wholesale market from the farms.
   c. Singing market songs.
   d. Seeing a film that has been a part of the market experiences

3. Make such charts with the group as:
   a. Questions to determine what we want to learn about the farm. Statements of summary may be added under the questions as the study progresses, as:
   Why is a farm so important?
      (1) It provides us with food.
      (2) It provides leather for shoes, wool for clothing.
      (3) Special farms might give us rubber for tires, and so forth.
   What kinds of farms do you know about?
      (1) Dairy farms   (4) Citrus groves
      (2) Poultry ranches (5) Cattle ranch
      (3) Walnut groves   (6) General farm
                               (many animals,
                               trees, plants)
   What will we have on our farm?
      Cows, horses, sheep, chickens, pigs, dogs, cats.
      Vegetables.
      Fruit trees and nut trees.
      Buildings.
   Will our farm be one of long ago or a modern one?
      A modern, progressive farm.

What would a farmer of long ago do?
He would plow with a horse.
He would check fences on horseback.
He would go to town in a horse and buggy.
What would a modern farmer do?
He would plow with a tractor.
He might check his fences with a plane.
He would go to town by automobile.
He would spray and dust his fields with a
plane or helicopter, and so forth.
   b. Begin a chart of words especially pertaining
to a study of farm life that will help in writing.

E. Suggested room arrangements.

F. Suggested programs.

IV. Development of the Unit

The order in which attention is directed to various activities is not in any sequential arrangement. Each section is interwoven into the other in actual use with groups. The order is not of great importance as long as there is interest and transition from one experience to another. A group might give more emphasis to one phase than another, but should develop all phases to some extent.

A. TO FIND OUT ABOUT FARMS

   1. To Find Out Types of Farms

Content
General farm contrasted with special farm as to:
(1) Crops, (2) How worked, (3) Animals
Special farms: (1) Citrus groves, (2) Fox farm, (3)
Chicken farm, (4) Dairy farm, (5) Cotton farm,
(6) Cattle ranch, (7) Walnut groves
Reasons why certain farms must be located in certain
areas, as: (1) Apples in north, (2) Oranges in south

Experiences Involved
- Discuss types of farms
- See films of farm life
- Discuss personal experiences relating to farm life
- Read stories and poems of farm life
- Draw or paint various aspects of farm life
- Write simple stories of the farmer and his family
- Make charts
- Write letters to children living on farms
- Sing songs of farm life, as:
  - "Mary Had a Little Lamb"
  - "Farmer in the Dell"
  - "Familiar Friends"
  - "My Little Brown Hen"
- Take trips to farm

2. To Find Out the Types of Foods Raised on Farms

Content
- General farms produce: (1) Wheat, (2) Cattle, (3) Chickens, (4) Corn, (5) Beans, (6) Ducks, (7) Turkeys, (8) Sheep, (9) Vegetables, (10) Fruits. Special farms, as: (1) Citrus grove, (2) Poultry ranch, (3) Dairy farm, (4) Walnut grove, (5) Fruit and berry farm, (6) Truck garden

Experiences Involved
- Show film of foods raised on farm, as: "Tomatoes from Farm to Market"
- Read stories and poems
- Finger paint designs from plant life
- Draw or paint pictures of:
  - Foods growing on farms
  - Farmer at work in the fields
  - Picking fruits and vegetables
- Sing songs, as:
  - "Farmyard Song"
  - "The Cow"
  - "The Butter Song"
  - "How They Grow"

Model clay fruits and vegetables

Use maps: (1) To show where foods are produced, (2) To show where cattle are raised

Use outline maps: (1) To make picture maps, (2) To show agricultural areas

Make various foods, as: (1) Vegetable soup, (2) Dried foods, (3) Jelly

Have dramatic play, as: The farmer taking produce to market; Activities of producing foods as: (1) Plowing, (2) Planting seed, (3) Cultivating; Children doing farm work: (1) Gathering eggs, (2) Feeding chickens, (3) Feeding calves

Make charts of fruits and vegetables

Play classification games, as: (1) Wordo, (2) Book games

3. To Find Out the Types of Animals Raised on Farm

Content

Animals for food: (1) Rabbits, (2) Sheep, (3) Cows, (4) Pigs, (5) Poultry, (6) Others

Animals for clothing: (1) Cows, (2) Sheep, (3) Rabbits, (4) Fox, (5) Others

Work animals: (1) Horses, (2) Mules

Other animals: (1) Dogs, (2) Cats

Care and protection of animals and fowl: (1) Housing, (2) Food, (3) Protection from disease

Experiences Involved

Discuss: (1) Types of animals, (2) Care of animals

Show animal films

Draw or paint pictures including farm animals

Model clay animals

Sing songs:

"I'm a Duck"

"Five Fat Turkeys"

"The Cow"

"The Little Red Calf"

Make informational charts about different breeds of pigs, chickens, cows, and horses

Take walks and trips to see different kinds of animals
Play rhythms of animals
Do research to find: (1) Characteristics of animals and
   fowl, (2) Special kinds of foods for animals
Set a hen and hatch baby chicks

4. To Find Out Kinds of Machinery on Farms and
   Their Use

Content

Hoe	Tractor	Threshing Machine
Spade	Harrow	Airplane or Helicopter
Rake	Disc	Milking Machine
Shovel	Plow	Separator
Combine		

Experiences Involved
   Show pictures of farm implements
   Make charts of types of farm implements
   Write to an implement company asking for pictures of
      machinery
   Write thank-you notes for these pictures
   If possible, go to see farm machines
   Have rhythms of farm machines
   Walks to see tractors in action
   Draw or paint pictures of farm implements in action

B. TO UNDERSTAND HOW OTHER PEOPLE HELP THE
   FARMER

1. To Find Out the Relationship of Specialized Workers
   to the Farmer

Content
   Work of:

Veterinarian	Train workers
Government inspectors	Mechanics
Farm laborers	Doctors
Truck drivers	Postman

Experiences Involved

Have discussion, as: (1) The need for the services of
these people, (2) The work of these persons in relatio
to farming

Show films and slides of specialized workers on the farm

Create stories, as: (1) How the veterinarian saved my
pony, (2) The seeds the postman brought

Read stories and poems

Paint or draw these helpers at work

Sing songs:
"Country Road"
"Team Work"

Have dramatic play

Make pipestem cleaner dolls of the veterinarian, laborer
truck driver, and so forth

Create songs about such topics, as: (1) Workers, (2)
Rural free delivery

Make charts, as: (1) Specialized workers on the farm,
(2) Services of the government inspector

2. To Find Out About Organizations That Assist
Farmers

Content

Future Farmers, an organization in high school to learn
of farming

4H Clubs, for young people to interest them in learning
to meet needs; 4H Club fairs

U. S. Department of Agriculture, gives service through
farm agents, literature, and so forth

Grange, for adults: (1) National organization with
branches in each community, (2) Informational meetings, (3) Social meeting, (4) Has insurance for farm
buildings and equipment

Experiences Involved

Discuss: (1) Farm organizations, (2) How the government aids the farmer

Invite someone in to tell of the work of 4H Clubs

Write to U. S. Dept. of Agriculture for literature and

pictures that would enrich understanding of farm life
Might have an exhibit of vegetables raised in gardens
Organize a farm club and utilize subject matter as topics
to discuss at meetings

3. To Find Out How Farmers Assist Each Other With
Their Work

Content
Loaning or hiring out farm
equipment
Exchange of products
How farmers of long ago
helped each other

Exchange of laborers
Cooperatives
How farmers of today help
each other

Experiences Involved
Draw pictures of large farm implements
Discuss meaning of cooperative idea
Have dramatic play, as: (1) Exchange of products, (2)
Exchange of laborers, (3) How to use borrowed equip-
ment, (4) Quilting bee, (5) House or barn raising

C. TO UNDERSTAND HOW THE FARMER MEETS HIS
BASIC NEEDS

1. To Find Out How a Farm is Housed and to Build
a Farm

Content
Types of farms
Plan a farm to build
Possibilities for construction: (1) House, (2) Barn,
(3) Garage, (4) Silo, (5) Windmill, (6) Sheds, (7)
Fences, (8) People, (9) Trucks, (10) Haywagon,
(11) Animals, (12) Troughs, (13) Doghouse, (14)
Trees, (15) Corrals, (16) Fields, (17) Gas tanks
for mechanized farm, (18) Powerhouse for electrical
equipment
Aircraft in relation to farm life

Experiences Involved

Review kinds of farms through discussion, to aid in planning our farm

Make charts, as: (1) Things we need on our farm, (2) Material needed for the construction, (3) General layout of the farm, (4) Working groups or committees

Do research to gain information with: (1) Books, (2) Pictures, (3) Films, (4) Magazines, (5) Newspapers

Draw farm buildings

Make clay or papier-mâche animals, fruits, and vegetables as pumpkins, squash, tomatoes, and melons for farm fields

Animals on the farm

Play reading games, as: (1) Wordo, (2) Book games

Discuss and illustrate when needed: (1) Technique of using materials and tools stressing safety, (2) Problems of proportion in relation to construction

Discuss and record on a chart: (1) Ways of working with materials, (2) Our work plans

Construct the items listed on the chart "Things we need on our farm"

Make background for a farm set-up using poster paint, chalk, water color, crayon, or combination of these

Plant grass, wheat, oats, rye, or alfalfa in a shallow metal pan to be used as fields of grain for the farm

Evaluate work frequently to raise standards

Sing Songs, as:

"From Wheat to Bread"

"The Farmer Grows the Corn"

"Down in the Garden"

2. To Find Out How the Farmer Feeds His Family

Content

Products from the farm, as: (1) Milk products, (2) Eggs, (3) Poultry and meats, (4) Vegetables, (5) Fruits and nuts

Products from market, as: (1) Soap products, (2) Bread, (3) Flour and cereals, (4) Sugar and spices, (5) Coffee, (6) Tea, (7) Cocoa

Experiences Involved
Discuss which products are grown on the farm and how
they are prepared for use by the family
Have dramatic play as: (1) Milking cows, (2) Gathering
eggs, (3) Picking vegetables, (4) Making butter and
ice cream
Prepare and cook some vegetable such as peas
Raise an herb garden
Plan an exhibit of foods raised on farm, purchased in the
city
Read grocery ads in newspaper for prices
Discuss why certain foods must be purchased at market,
such as flour
Taste and identify spices
Make list of items to be purchased in town to make cocoa
Draw or paint such pictures as: (1) Farmer's wife gath-
ering, preparing, and cooking foods; (2) Farmer going
to town for supplies by plane, truck, auto
Sing songs, as:
"We Farmers Go to Market"
"My Pumpkins Are Ripe"
"Working on the Farm"
"Wake Up, Sleepy Head"

3.   To Find Out How the Farmer Clothes His Family

Content
Interchange of materials from farm to city, and, later,
from city to farm
Contrast modern method of obtaining clothing to that of
years ago
Products from farms that are used in wearing apparel,
as: (1) Cotton, (2) Leather, (3) Wool, (4) Linen

Experiences Involved
Discuss why the farmer does not directly use wool for
clothes, leather for shoes, and so forth
Make comparison of early day farm life with modern
mode of living
Have an exhibit of raw and finished products of wool,
skins, cotton, linen

Learn how to arrange an exhibit artistically
Sing songs, as:
"From Sheep to Sweater"
"Mary Contrary"
Use catalogs to select clothing
Use films and other visual aids to enlarge understanding
of obtaining clothing
Illustrate songs
Make a list of clothing to be purchased for winter use,
summer use, and school use
Illustrate these lists of clothing
Make reports on processing of wool, leather, cotton
Write original stories and illustrate, as: (1) My wool
dress, (2) The travels of a shoe
Dress pipestem dolls for unit set-up

D. TO UNDERSTAND WHY THE FARMER MUST PRODUCE GOOD CROPS

1. To Find Out About Producing Good Crops

Content
Soil: (1) Types, (2) Fertilization and fumigating,
(3) Conservation
Water: (1) Irrigation, (2) Cover crops to prevent
erosion
Weather conditions as they affect the crops: (1) Rain,
(2) Temperatures and smudging, (3) Fog, (4) Sunshine,
(5) Dewpoint
Seed selections and care
Control of harmful pests: (1) Insects, (2) Birds, (3)
Animals
Care of orchards, groves, and crops by: (1) Spraying,
(2) Dusting, (3) Fumigating
Conservation of birds, insects, reptiles, and animals
that benefit the farmer
Use of modern machinery in the care of crops, as:
(1) Airplanes, (2) Helicopters, (3) Tractors

Experiences Involved

 Discuss: (1) Types of soil, (2) Crops that can best be grown in different types of soil, (3) New methods of dusting and spraying, (4) Planting cover crops by plane, (5) Checking fences, irrigation, and ditches by plane

 Bring magazines and newspaper clippings about modern care of crops to: (1) Share with the class, (2) Make an interesting bulletin board arrangement, (3) Create charts to learn about layout and art composition in charts

 Compare scientific and non-scientific feeding of crops

 Take walks: (1) To find varieties of soils, (2) To identify varieties of fruit and nut trees

 Have exhibits of: (1) Soils, (2) Fruits, (3) Grains, (4) Nuts

 Create and illustrate stories about farmers caring for crops

 Take bird walks

 Plant a garden and care for it

 Experiment with: (1) Planting seeds in various types of soil, (2) Soilless garden, (3) Plants grown in shade and sun, (4) Eggshell garden

 Observe how sunlight, vitamins, fertilizer, moisture, and air affect plant life

 Read science stories on topics related to producing good crops and make reports

  2. To Find Out Why the Market Demands Good Products

Content

 Reasons for markets

 Why people go into the market business

 Selection of products for marketing

 Buying and selling produce at the market

 Spoilage as a factor with fresh fruits and vegetables

Experiences Involved

 Discuss: (1) Care of products to be marketed, (2) Methods of marketing crops

Review what the group knows of wholesale markets and
care of produce

See films

Dramatic play of: (1) Marketing potatoes, (2) Selling at
a roadside stand

E. TO UNDERSTAND WHAT THE FARMER DOES WITH HIS PRODUCTS

1. To Find Out How Grain and Legume Crops are Harvested

Content

Farm machinery used: (1) Care and use, (2) Safety

Farm labor: (1) How secured, (2) Housing and feeding,
(3) Health

Weather conditions: (1) Wind affecting harvest, (2) Moisture, (3) Temperature, (4) Transportation

Storage and preservation of crops by using: (1) Grain
elevators, (2) Hay barns, (3) Corn cribs, (4) Silos

Processing of these crops, as: (1) Wheat to flour or
breakfast food, (2) Beans to mills to be packaged
or canned, (3) Corn to "Fritos," "Post Toasties,"
Starch

Experiences Involved

Make information charts, as: (1) Types of grain and
legume crops, (2) Story of wheat to bread, (3) Exhibit
charts

Use design and new media for decorating charts

Dramatic play, as: (1) Harvesting grains, (2) Transportation of grain to elevator hay barn, (3) Daily routine
of a farm laborer

Chew grains to distinguish flavors

Cook cereal, bake cookies, pop corn

Write creative stories that may be assembled in a book
and illustrate these stories

Play singing games, as:
"Oats, Peas, Beans"
"Farmer in the Dell"
"Let Me Show You How the Farmer"

Create number games and stories
Sing songs, as:
"Mister Farmer"
"Oats and Beans"
"Farmer in the Dell"

2. To Find Out How Fruits and Vegetables Are
Preserved for Use

Content
Canning at home: (1) How food is prepared, (2) Process
of canning, (3) Safety
Cannery process: (1) Selling, (2) Transportation
Drying and dehydrating of fruits and vegetables: (1) Preparation (2) Cleanliness, (3) Use of sulphur, (4) Protection from insects, (5) Weather effect, (6) Packaging,
(7) Use
Freezing: (1) Home vs. commercial, (2) Values, (3)
Preparation of food for freezing, (4) Use of frozen
foods

Experiences Involved
Discuss safe methods of canning
Create and illustrate stories about canning
Cook dried fruits, make jelly, can fruit or vegetables
Make vegetable soup from dehydrated vegetables
Make charts or booklets, as: (1) Directions for pre-
paring food for canning, (2) Recipes, (3) Classifica-
tion of fruits and vegetables

3. To find Out How Milk is Processed

Content
Dairy cattle: (1) Care, (2) Feeding
Dairies: (1) Barns, (2) Machinery used there
People who work at the dairy
Kinds of milk: (1) Pasteurized, (2) Raw, (3) Evaporated,
(4) Condensed, (5) Dried
Use of milk
Milk as a food

Government inspection of milk
By-products of milk: (1) Butter, (2) Cheese, (3) Ice Cream

Experiences Involved
Review work of the dairy farmer
Make butter, make cheese
Take a trip to a dairy
Write stories about the dairy
Sing songs, as:
"Butter Song"
"Milk"
"Take Your Choice"
"The Milk Train"
Make chart stories about the baby animals that drink milk
See films on dairying activities
Construct a dairy barn
Model clay animals
Make informational charts, as: (1) Kinds of Milk, (2) Use of milk, (3) By-products of milk

4. To Find Out About the Care of Cattle, Sheep, Hogs, and Poultry To Be Marketed

Content
Feeding, shelter, health inspection
Service of veterinarian: (1) Importance of weight, (2) Cleanliness of shelter and feeding utensils
Protection by sprays, shots, and so forth
Driving cattle to market in early days in comparison to taking them by truck or rail today
How other animals reach the market

Experiences Involved
Discuss such topics as: (1) Similarity in kinds of food used for animals and people, (2) Reasons for shelter for some animals, (3) Pastures for cattle and sheep
Compare weights of types of cattle, sheep, and hogs
Dramatic play: (1) Rounding up cattle, (2) Feeding time for animals, (3) Cleaning of barns, stalls, coops, pens

Create rhythms of animals in action
Use film "Rhythms in Nature"

V. Anticipated Outcomes of the Unit

   A. Culminating Activities

These activities may indicate how deep and meaningful the experiences in farm life have been to the
group. These activities need not always come at
the end of the unit but may culminate a phase of it.
These activities may be given in the classroom or
assembly room for the group's own enjoyment, or
for other classes or parents. Such activities are:

1. Simple plays that originate in the dramatic play
of farm life and incorporate the results of various
activities worked out in the unit, such as murals,
stage properties, songs, poems, stories, rhythms,
dances, games, and such charts as:
a. A Day at the Farm   c. A Quilting Party
b. Getting Ready for the   d. A 4H Club Meeting
County Fair

2. Simple rhythmic dramatizations with songs, orchestrations, rhythmic accompaniments, or
original songs, dances, and games as:
a. Activities in the construction of buildings and
of the workmen around a farm
b. Activities on the farm in daily living or on
unusual occasions such as harvesting

3. A program of songs, orchestrations, stories,
games, and bodily rhythms given by individuals
or the group.

4. An "Open House" to show such work done during
the study of Farm Life as pictures, stories,
songs, charts, construction, and books.

5. The dramatizing of stories about life on the farm.

6. Making a movie roll to show information gained,
activities on the farm, or to illustrate a well-
liked story of farm life.

7. Developing an informative program, using audio-

visual aids, charts, and short informal talks.

8. Creating a class book of stories, informational material, charts, and pictures to show information gained.

9. Share the butter, ice cream, jelly, cheese, or other food prepared with parents, another class, or received as gifts.

B. Basic Understandings
The child should evidence:

1. An increased understanding of his relationship to the farmer.

2. A broader understanding of farm life and what people in agricultural areas contribute toward better ways of living.

3. A better understanding of the need for adequate food, clothing, shelter, and leisure-time activities on the farm.

4. An understanding of the harmonious inter-relationship necessary among all persons in order to have a desirable world.

5. A better understanding of how and why rules, regulations, and laws are made.

6. A better understanding of the various services rendered to rural communities through transportation and communications facilities, workers, and modern scientific developments.

7. An understanding of the needs for health and safety regulations in farm life, and for personal health and safety habits.

8. A better understanding of the need for each person to be an effective citizen of a community.

9. An increased understanding of the things of nature the effect of it upon the ways of living, and of the advances man has made in controlling it.

10. A broadening understanding of an ever widening community life.

11. An understanding and appreciation of beauty found on the farm and in the farm way of life.

C. Appreciations and Attitudes
The child should evidence:

1. Reasonable growth in the attitudes desirable

for effective social living and in personality adjustment as shown by:
- a. A desire to bear his own share of responsibility
- b. An appreciation of work done by various persons in relation to farm living
- c. Attitudes essential to working effectively with others including:
  - (1) Willingness to follow work rules formulated by the group
  - (2) Respect for the rights of others
  - (3) Willingness to do his share of the work
  - (4) Care in the use of materials
  - (5) Taking turns when working with a group
  - (6) Giving and taking constructive criticism
2. Growth in a feeling of inner security in self-expression through art, music, rhythms, dances, and language.
3. Appreciation of any respect for health and safety regulations.
4. An increased, intelligent curiosity toward an environment just beyond our own community.
5. Increased growth in a courteous attitude toward all people.

D. Skills and Techniques

The child should evidence increased proficiency in
1. Techniques of democratic life, as:
   - a. Setting up plans and working effectively toward their solution
   - b. Using freedom while engaging in worth-while activities
   - c. Working independently and in groups in an effective manner
   - d. Using initiative and "followship"
   - e. Facing and solving problems
   - f. Evaluating his own work
2. Ability to read and understand books, magazines, newspapers, charts, pictures, and so forth, in order to extend information and enrich experiences.

196

3. Ability to go to the source for information if possible, as going to a farm, interviewing people, performing experiments, planting a garden, and so forth.
4. Ability to express himself orally or in writing.
5. Ability to spell words needed.
6. Ability to write legibly and neatly.
7. Ability to use an increasing vocabulary, to speak clearly, and give information in an interesting manner when communicating with others.
8. Ability to use number concepts and fundamentals, and to solve problems in a functional manner.
9. Ability to use tools in order to meet needs that arise.
10. Ability to express ideas through fine and industrial arts, music, bodily rhythms, and language.
11. Ability to do critical thinking and study.
12. Beginning research techniques.

Selected References

Ako, F. C., "Relation of the School Farm to the Instructional Program in Hawaii," *Agriculture Education Magazine,* March, 1945.

Ballard, D. W., "School Farm," *Agriculture Education Magazine,* September, 1960.

Bathurst, Effie G. and Hill, Wilhelmina, *Conservation Experiences for Children,* (Bulletin No. 16) Washington, D.C.: U. S. Department of Health Education and Welfare, 1957.

Boylston, E. R., "First Grade Studies the Farm," *School Arts,* June, 1940.

Couper, G. P., "California's School Farm," *Country Gentleman,* February, 1946.

Eckelberry, R. H., "School Farms offer Educational Opportunity," *Educational Research Bulletin,* September, 1949.

Julian, K. L., "Life on a Farm" *Instructor,* April, 1939.

Markland, D. and Dunser, A., "Art and the Farm," *American Childhood,* November, 1953.

Tooke, J. R., "Farm in the Classroom" *School,* June, 1940.

Walters, H., "Peter and Peggy Visit the Farm: A Unit for Primary Grades," *Instructor,* November, 1938.

Chapter 7

THE SCHOOL FOREST

Before white man came to America, forests extended practically unbroken from the Atlantic Ocean to the Mississippi River. The Rocky Mountains and the Pacific Coast region were covered extensively with a heavy stand of beautiful giant trees. Approximately one-half of the United States was covered with timber with only the Great Plains area practically void of trees.

The Indians who numbered not more than one million were swallowed up by the mighty forest so that their total modification of the natural forest was practically negligible. With few exceptions they lived on the land for generations with little or no disturbance of nature's wonderful balance of natural resources.

When the early settlers landed on American shores they immediately began their plunder against the greatest forest ever inherited by man. The virgin forests were both a curse and blessing to pioneer life. On the one hand they occupied the soil needed for cultivation and buildings while on the other they furnished materials for building log cabins, stockades, sheds, tools, and for furniture. Fuel as well as many of the necessities of colonial days came from the forests.

As the population increased on the American continent forests were destroyed to make way for farm land. The demand for food became the greatest single factor in the destruction of forest lands. It is estimated by the United States Forestry Service that approximately 300,000,000 acres of virgin timber were completely destroyed. Just before the turn of the century far-seeing citizens began to see the ill effects of poor practices in forestry. Forests became more valuable in the industrial age. Markets for lumber and forest products rapidly expanded. The quantity and quality of lumber was becoming more difficult to obtain. Not only was timber becoming scarce, but rich farm land was being washed down the streams and rivers by the tons. Problems relating to watersheds and soil conservation were found to be directly related to forestry practices. American people were beginning to realize the meaning of the old Chinese proverb "to rule the mountain is to rule the river." The attitude of many thinking Americans were recently summed up by the Honorable Martin L. Davey speaking in the House of Representatives:

> Men and women of America, we cut down the great forests that blessed this country. We allow the remnants to be burned over and the vegetation destroyed. The rains pour down water, and instead of being held in check by the loose and porous soil in the network of roots, it rushes down over the hillsides and carries with it the fertile soil, leaving in its wake barren hills and deep ravines.
>
> Thus we have alternating floods and droughts. The fertile soil is gone, the product of hundreds of years of Nature's providence. The little springs that come from water held in check, and that feed the lakes and streams must gradually diminish, and I greatly fear, cease to exist in large part.
>
> This question of reforestation is of monumental importance. America cannot continue to exist as a virile, forward-moving nation unless we protect what we have and start to build up that which we have so ruthlessly destroyed. We cannot afford to be a nation of vandals much longer. America must reforest, or America must drink the bitter dregs of national decline and impotency.

Although a few thinking men in government, private agencies, and educational institutions began to see the importance of stopping the shameful waste of resources and the need for conservation education, it was hard to obtain constructive results. This was a new and unexpected area of education and the machinery for instituting it was not

200

Sunlight filters through the canopy of a fine stand of second growth Douglas fir as a group of Lewis County youngsters stroll down a forest road. In settings such as this, thousands of Washington school children are learning the reasons for conservation and wise management of the state's natural resources. This photo was taken on the 550-acre Ed Haase tree farm near Napavine, where the Lewis County conservation education programs are held.

Photo Courtesy of Washington State Department of Natural Resources established or even readily accepted. There was much indifference and complacency on the part of the public.

Small conservation groups were organized, a division of Forestry was established, and a great deal of legislation was passed. A few far-seeing educators introduced courses in conservation or added units to existing courses, but the textbook approach with emphasis on knowledge and facts made little progress toward checking the waste and exploitation of the nation's natural resources. Poor conservation practices continued. These early efforts to save resources tended to focus on badly exploited resources--forests, soil, water. Little was done toward the important cause of such waste or the correction of the cause by development of correct attitudes, habits, and appreciations for the God-given resources.

Belatedly, the problem of conservation became the concern of the public schools. Educators began to realize that just as the schools were charged with the responsibility of teaching the skills of self-government and the duties of good citizenship, they were equally responsible for the development of correct concepts, attitudes, and appreciations in the conservation of the natural resources. A good citizen in a democratic society must also have an unselfish attitude and a deep appreciation for the soil, the rivers, the wildlife, and the people which determines the degree of success enjoyed by his country. The success of the school or any other agency engaged in the uplifting and betterment of humanity is predicated upon the abundance of natural resources of its society. A country barren of natural life-sustaining resources cannot expect to foster a democratic and responsible society regardless of education.

DEVELOPMENT AND SCOPE OF SCHOOL FORESTS

School forests developed as the need for good forestry practices became evident. Since forests contribute greatly to the welfare of a nation and its citizenry, educators have found ways and means of providing firsthand experiences that enable children to understand the importance of forests in relation to their country's present and future needs. It is important that children realize that the welfare of the American people depends upon wise and efficient conservation practices. Many schools provide children with experiences in raising seedlings, planting trees and keeping trees in a healthy condition on the school ground, in the city parks and in their own back yard. Schools located near State and National forests quite frequently cooperate with forestry agencies in helping with forestry practices or they may be assigned areas for reforestation. Many other schools own and operate their own school forest. Nevada County, Arkansas, for example, provides a school forest for every school.

School forests afford children a broader and longer lasting experience with conservation than the more limited experiences on the school yard. Greater variations in activities for children of all ages are possible with school-owned forest plots.

A survey completed in 1960 by the authors to determine the extent and variety of outdoor education programs in the United States revealed many good school forests and their number and scope is ever increasing. Outstanding forestry programs involving public school children are found in over one-half the states of the United States; and such programs are expanding within these states and are being started in other states.

Although school forests are found in many states, a few states are gaining nation-wide attention through their cooperative efforts on a state level.

SCHOOL FORESTS IN WISCONSIN

The idea of using school owned forests as a technique in education has spread throughout the state of Wisconsin.

By 1948, some 300 school forests were owned and operated by Wisconsin Public Schools and the number has been steadily increased by the addition of new school forests each year.

School owned forests are particularly numerous in the central and northern part of the state since the land

The Florida Board of Forestry operate 60 school forests averaging in size from 35 to 40 acres. These programs are carried out through district Information and Education Foresters.

Photo Courtesy of Morris W. McClure

is rapidly being abandoned by farms because of poor soil. Schools are encouraged to take over such areas for school forests.

Trees For Tomorrow, Inc., organized in 1944, is another reason for Wisconsin's great interest in school forests. This is a non-profit, semi-public organization which is backed by the many pulp wood mills and is dedicated to the advancement of reforestation in Wisconsin.

Trees For Tomorrow carries on a widely varied program in forestry of which education is one of the major objectives. Public schools are given assistance in acquiring land, mapping and establishing school forests. Much land has been donated to the various public schools and seedlings are distributed free to schools, community agencies, and landowners interested in reforestation. Each year, Trees For Tomorrow present five five-hundred dollar forestry fellowships to students showing outstanding interest and ability in forestry.

A conservation camp is maintained by Trees For Tomorrow at Eagle River, Wisconsin. The camp is run on a non-profit basis and is available for use by schools, 4-H Clubs, college classes, conservation departments, foresters and other groups that are interested in conservation. The nine state colleges and the Milwaukee Conservation alliance use the camp for summer session workshops and the Institute of Paper Chemistry also uses its facilities for research and study.

Although some criticism is leveled at the work of Trees For Tomorrow on the basis that the member paper mills are using schools to promote their selfish interests, the paper mill executives point out that the prosperity of Wisconsin is very closely tied up with the prosperity of the paper industry and their work not only helps their paper mills, but also helps the state of Wisconsin through increased paper production. Most school men as well as public spirited citizens agree that the activities sponsored by Trees For Tomorrow are worthwhile both economically and educationally and provide an excellent means for school, community, and industry to cooperate for the material benefit of all.

The Merrill High School of Merrill, Wisconsin, is a typical example of how a school forest may be started with good leadership and little cash outlay. At this school a school forest committee was formed which consisted of the superintendent, three teachers, and four children from the junior high school. The school forest committee is responsible for the conservation program.

In 1943, the Forestry Club of Merrill High School was formed with an enrollment of about fifty students. The purpose of the club was to study forestry in its various phases and to acquaint the students with the importance of forests and the conservation of our natural resources.

As the need for a school forest became evident, land became available. Through the work of the superintendent, former graduates, Trees of Tomorrow, and Wisconsin Public Service, a total of 765 acres of land was acquired and is now known as the Nels P. Eujue Memorial Forest named in honor of a pioneer woodsman during Merrill's booming sawmill days.

The land is an ideal site for an outdoor laboratory and

school forest. The topography is varied, the plant species are varied, and altogether it provides a suitable site as well as suitable farm for all types of resource studies.

A forest management plan has been worked out with the help of the Trees For Tomorrow foresters, and is carried on by the school's conservation teachers. The plan includes tree planting, thinning, harvesting and marketing of the forest products. Although high school students cut several cords of pulp wood and some saw logs, most of the timber is cut on a contractual basis by local woodsmen. The harvest provides the school with a fair amount of revenue with which to improve their forest land and build facilities for overnight camping.

The school forest may be used by any teacher in the Merrill school system and projects and units are developed throughout all grades.

Another example of a school forest in Wisconsin is the one conducted by the Wausau High School on a 400 acre tract of land owned by the school. The school forest was started in 1942 when 120 acres of tax delinquent land was deeded to the school by the county. Adjoining cut-over timber land was donated later by Trees For Tomorrow and an interested citizen.

The forest is used by all classes and clubs in the school. In 1948, eighty acres were transferred to the junior high school. The Industrial Arts Department helped move, and improve, an old barracks to the forest, constructed a fireplace and provided a place for other educational activities. The biology classes mapped and laid out a trail along the Wisconsin River. Grade school children use the area for field trips and help in spring tree planting and other conservation practices.

Wisconsin State College at Stevens Point offers a major in conservation education. The department has five full-time staff members and offers twenty-five different conservation courses. The department works on numerous tracts of land including the 160 acre tract owned by the Portage County chapter of the Izaak Walton League.

The Conservation Department is designed for the preparation of teachers who will teach conservation in the public schools. There is no attempt to specialize in any one phase of conservation such as forestry or soil but rather the students are given a more general education stressing regional problems as they relate to the entire field of conservation and stressing the methods of teaching conservation to children.

Field experience and "learning by doing" is put into practice so that the students receive a practical as well as a theoretical preparation.

Trips are made to the various tracts of land for tree identification, thinning, improvement cutting and other conservation practices. The effect of thinning on growth increments is studied over a period of time. All students are required to get practice in tree planting and to observe and operate the planting machine.

In all the courses offered--soil conservation, general forestry, wildlife management, general biology--efficient land use is stressed. Since reforestation is being stressed so strongly in the area, each biology student is required to plant 100 trees.

SCHOOL FORESTS IN MICHIGAN

In 1931, the Michigan State Legislature provided for county, township, city, village, and school forests. This act has enabled over 600 school districts to acquire some 65,000 acres of state land.

One of the outstanding school forests in Michigan is operated by the Felch Public Schools in Dickinson County. The Felch School Forest began in 1929 when 80 acres was granted to the school by private land companies. Since that time, the Conservation Department donated 80 acres. The school bought 120 acres and through other purchases and donations, the school now owns 320 acres containing an average, to better than average, stand of timber of twenty or more varieties of trees.

The school forest affords educational and recreational opportunities for the entire school system as well as visiting groups from neighboring schools and community agencies.

Every child and teacher plants seedlings in the school forest. By 1958, the school administration reported over 150,000 trees planted. In addition, the teachers use the forest to supplement classroom teaching in connection with studies in conservation study of precipitation in the area, rise and fall of water in the river, study of fish, and marine life, building and contributing to a museum of natural science, study of birds, identification and study of twenty-eight different types of Michigan rocks, study of soil and experience in land management and usage are activities used in the Felch Public Schools by teachers of all grade levels and in every subject field.

SCHOOL FORESTS IN OHIO

The state of Ohio is performing an outstanding educational function in getting school children involved in conservation practice through school forests. Two relatively new laws, added to those with which school leaders are familiar, make acquisition and operation of outdoor laboratories legally possible in Ohio. Boards of education have the legal right to acquire, hold, or sell property, and to receive money for educational purposes (Ohio Revised Code, Section 3313.17). Boards of education may accept bequests (RC 3313.44), hence may accept lands offered as gifts and develop forests on them. In a 1947 survey 50 per cent of Ohio's high schools reported ownership of unused lands. Only 12 per cent of the 387 areas reported were of less than one acre while one hundred sixty-three unused tracts were at least five acres in extent. City high schools owned 320 idle acres. The areas of idle land then owned by high schools alone totaled more than 7,500 acres. [1]

In 1952, the governor of Ohio, Frank S. Lansche, set a goal of 10,000,000 trees to be planted during the year. The biology class of Perry high school became interested in this project and sent out mimeographed invitations for

---

[1] Carl S. Johnson, "School Forests in Ohio," Unpublished MA thesis, Ohio State University, 1947.

a meeting to Garden Clubs, Boy Scouts, Girl Scouts, Boards of Education, American Legion, nurserymen, and other interested people in the community.

As a result of this meeting a school forest was established with over 5,000 trees planted. Each spring the schools leave their classrooms for a week to devote time to the school forest.

Another project sponsored by the Perryville High School was called "Trees For Every Student." Each student in the Perryville school system from grades one through twelve was given a tree seedling, with complete planting instructions, to take home and plant in his yard.

Schools interested in starting a school forest receives much help from the Ohio Forestry Association, Inc. This organization has published a little pamphlet prepared by Dr. Carl Johnson of the Conservation Department, Ohio State University, and is entitled, Planning School Forests.

Included in the pamphlet is a discussion of the importance of conservation, the possibilities and benefits of school forests, and an outline of the steps necessary to start and maintain a school forest. *Planning School Forests* was jointly underwritten by the Rausanberger Foundation and may be obtained from the Ohio Forestry Association, Southern Hotel, Columbus 15, Ohio, at a price of 25¢ a copy.

The Ohio State Department of Education recommends the school forest program and lends its support to the increasing interest and acceptance of this valuable teaching technique.

Demonstrational woodland areas which may serve as patterns for school forests are operated by Ohio State University, Ohio University, and Antioch College.

Antioch College leases part of their 900 acre outdoor laboratory, Glen Helen, to the Yellow Springs schools for a school forest.

SCHOOL FORESTS IN OTHER STATES

New York State has many good school forests in operation and a great deal of emphasis is placed on the wise use of resources at all grade levels. The New York State Department of Education, and other state agencies work together in stressing conservation at all levels as a responsibility of good citizenship.

The Newark Valley (New York) High School was built on a 146 acre tract in 1931. The land was bought by the school board for educational purposes and has been used most effectively. The land lies behind the high school and the entire student body participates in the management and care of the acreage. Since 1937, the agriculture students have managed the forest. The older trees are now thirty years old and require pruning, thinning and other forest management operations. The forest through the sale of Christmas trees, post and other salable forest products is a source of revenue for the Future Farmers of America Club and provides stock materials for the shop classes.

At one time the high school boys erected a building for weekend and overnight camping. Biology classes use the forest occasionally and it is available because of its proximity to the school to any class for even one class session at a time.

The Steelville Public Schools of Steelville, Missouri, in 1948 purchased 250 acres of land upon passage of a bill by the Missouri State Legislature that permitted public schools to own such property. The school planted much of the cleared land in evergreen trees and the remainder is covered with a second growth stand of natural hardwood most of which is oak.

The forest is used by conservation and biology classes. The course in conservation is made as practical as possible through discussion of local problems relating to the management of the school forest. Students are transported to the school forest by bus where they are taught conservation practices, good forestry methods, and other knowledges and practices which can be taught more effectively outside the classroom.

The state of Florida has fifty-five school forests ranging in size from 2 to 640 acres. Land owned by the state due to delinquent taxes is under the supervision of the Florida Board of Forests and Parks. Much of this land is deeded to local Future Farmers of America Clubs for as long as the club practices good forestry and land managemen

Leon High School of Tallahassee has an 80 acre forest which students have thinned, cleared, and replanted under the supervision of the Agriculture Department. Fire lanes have been laid out at intervals in the forest and quite a bit of turpentine has been marketed as well as some pulp wood.

The school forest is used primarily as a demonstration area for practice in tree farming. The tree farm program is sponsored by the Florida Forest Service and the State Chamber of Commerce. Their primary objective is to guarantee a continuous growth of forest crops. Each year students will get experience in facing trees for turpentine gum, cutting pulp wood, planting trees and thinning trees as well as experience in protecting the forests from fire and receiving first-hand practices in conservation. In addition to conservation experience, the members of the Future Farmers of America Chapter receive practical experience in business as they receive seventy-five percent of the net cash return from the forest products.

The state of Minnesota through the cooperation of its various educational and governmental agencies is strengthening its conservation program by involving thousands of school children in the protection and wise use of the states natural resources.

Minneapolis school children have at times collected tree seeds, taking them to their schools where state officials gather them for the forestry department. Hundreds of bushels of oak, ash, brasswood, elm and evergreen seeds have been collected. Many concomitant learnings occur as the result of direct experiences in this program. Some of these learnings include the kinds and types of seeds collected, the phenomena of nature's cycle concerning trees, a new method for identifying trees, and a strengthening of concepts and attitudes concerning conservation.

Severe forest fires in 1933, 1939, and 1945 destroyed over 355,000 acres of Oregon forest land--some virgin timber over 4000 years old.

The State Department of Forestry is cooperating with local communities and the Portland public schools in reforesting the burned-over areas.

The area is located fifty miles from Portland and is known as the Tillamook Burn Replanting Project. Every high school in the city of Portland is assigned a 40 acre plot to reforest. The State Department of Forestry furnishes the trees, the tools, and a forester to supervise the students. The school furnishes the transportation and the teachers always accompany their class.

Children from elementary schools are brought in to assist high school students. Their experiences in tree planting either lead to or conclude units on conservation which involve extensive study and research as well as practical experience in conservation practices. Students who are involved in the Tillamook Burn Replanting Project have all experienced real conservation in a useful and meaningful way. They are contributing to the beauty and economic value of forests, learning how to care for them, and they are learning the ill effects of carelessness which results in forest fires. They are also gaining firsthand direct experiences with many aspects of their natural environment.

The fifth and sixth grades of Harmony Elementary School in the Mount Baker School District, Washington, have their own Christmas tree plot. The parents assist the teachers and children in planting. There is a tree planted for each child and several trees are planted to replace non-survivals.

The school children of Seattle take field trips to privately owned forests in order to see logging practices. They also visit the giant trees which are some 800 years old. Foresters provide them with practical experiences in planting Douglas Fir seedlings on strips of land which were cleared for reseeding.

The Beckley Public Schools of Beckley, West Virginia each year bring in specialists from the State Conservation Commission to demonstrate to students and interested parents the correct procedures in tree planting. Seedlings are furnished free. All demonstrations are made for hand planting so that planting will be encouraged at home and in the community as well as at the school.

The American Forest Products Industries, Inc. in

West Virginia cooperates with the schools, the 4-H Clubs, Future Farmers of America, Boy Scouts and other interested agencies and institutions for a three-fold purpose; (1) keeping West Virginia green, (2) encouraging the development of tree farms, and (3) carrying on the "Green Thumb Program" which is a Christmas tree project especially planned for the strip mines.

THE SCHOOL FOREST AND THE CURRICULUM

The general objectives of the study of forestry in the public schools have been well stated by Haley:[2]

1. An appreciation of the usefulness and the aesthetic revelation of trees and life itself.
2. An increased recognition of various common trees.
3. An appreciation of literature, poems, and music that concerns trees and/or has been inspired by natural phenomena.
4. An enlarged vocabulary and understanding of science (terminology, methodology, etc.)
5. An appreciation for the need of conservation and a recognition of the role he can play.
6. A more alert and inclusive sense of observation.
7. Increased socialization in group endeavors.
8. Increased skill in purposeful reading and writing.
9. An appreciation for the need of purposeful living.
10. A fuller comprehension of the totality of the world lived in.

The United States Forest Service offers the following suggestions for integrating forestry in the modern curriculum:[3]

ELEMENTARY LEVEL

Influence upon life in the home, school, and community.

---

[2] Tenison F. Haley, "Trees: An Experience Unit of Work For Junior High Schools," Curriculum Bulletin, Eugene, Oregon: School of Education, University of Oregon, 1962, p. 6

[3] United States Forestry Service, Department of Agriculture, Washington 25, D.C.: "Suggestions For Integrating Forestry In The Modern Curriculum," 1952. Other kits and conservation packets are available on request.

Making a home:

> Things in the home from the forest.
>
> Home life in forest lands.
>
> Effects of abundance or scarcity of forests upon the way houses are built.
>
> Improving home grounds through tree planting and care.

Earning a living:

> How the pilgrims, Indians, and pioneers used the forest and western range lands.
>
> What the woodsman does and how he lives.
>
> Forest industries give work to many men, both rural and urban.
>
> What the farmer uses and sells from his wood lot.

Performing the responsibilities of citizenship:

> Our manners in the woods.
>
> How we can prevent forest fires.
>
> How we can protect our forests from insects and diseases.
>
> How the forest ranger protects the forest.
>
> Helping with the community or school forest.
>
> How planting new forests helps the community.

Conserving and improving material conditions:

> Caring for and protecting plants and wildlife about the home and in the community.
>
> Presence of trees improves home environment.
>
> Forest homes and communities endangered by forest fires.
>
> Tree planting stops erosion and muddy water.

Expressing spiritual, aesthetic, and emotional impulses:

> Use of trees and shrubs in beautifying home and school grounds.
>
> Telling others how forests serve us.
>
> The lessons we learn from the forests.

Engaging in recreation:

> Kinds of forest recreation appealing to children.

JUNIOR HIGH SCHOOL LEVEL

> Adaptation of the individual to his physical and social environment.

Relation of forests to the environment.

Making a home:
>The importance of forests in the housing needs in this and other countries.
>
>Comparison of uses of forest products in the colonial and modern home.
>
>The varied uses of the different woods.

Earn living:
>Making more efficient use of forest products. Elimination of waste.
>
>How different parts of our country and other countries use their forests.
>
>How forests affect transportation, communication, trade, industry, and agriculture.
>
>How different industries developed in or near the forest.
>
>How forests determine where certain industries may develop.
>
>The importance and uses of the standing forest.

Performing the responsibilities of citizenship:
>Some great leaders who have helped establish conservation policies with regard to our forests.
>
>The agencies of government that manage our forests and range lands.
>
>How forests aid in the development of other natural resources.
>
>The duty of the citizen toward forest conservation.

Conserving and improving material conditions:
>How forest fires are started and controlled.
>
>Destructive practices in the use of forests and ranges.
>
>Technical advances in lumbering and effects on the forest.
>
>Research in forest use and its application to industry and community stability.
>
>What may be done to improve forest and range use.
>
>How reforestation and other forest improvement work is carried out.
>
>Importance of soil to plant growth and to clean waters.

Expressing spiritual, aesthetic, and emotional impulses:
>Architectural uses of wood.

Methods of finishing wood to bring out its beauty.
Preserving and creating beauty in the forest environ-
ment.
Inspiration from and enjoyment of the natural beauty
of forests.
The effects of forests in music, literature, and art.
Engaging in recreation:
Improving forest areas for recreation to make avail-
able to more people in all parts of the country.
Establishing community forests.
The development of the sylvan theatre.
Healthfulness and adventure of forest recreation.
Advantages of forest camps for young people.

SENIOR HIGH SCHOOL LEVEL

Understanding, controlling and improving group relationships and trends in modern society.

Making a home:
Improvement of living conditions through adaptation
of forest products for construction, insulation, and
beautification.
Improving home environment-protection-beautification.
The relation of forests to housing and the possibilities
of pre-fabrication of wooden houses.
Earning a living:
Stabilization of employment in forest work and forest
industries by proper management (Conservation) of
the forests.
Changes in forest labor conditions.
Using the land for its best use.
Greater utilization of forest products, not substitu-
tion, means greater possibilities for conservation.
The problem of the people on submarginal lands best
fitted for forest production.
Performing the responsibilities of citizenship:
Developing and utilizing our forest and range resources
for the greatest good to the greatest number of peo-
ple.
Cooperation between Federal government, state and

private forest landowners in forest protection, tree
planting, forest management and forestry extension.
National security and prosperity depend upon wise use
of the natural resources.
Forests in our national defense program.
National and State forest.
The place of research and planning in regard to con-
servation of natural resources.
Reforesting devastated forest areas and submarginal
farm lands.
Prevention of wasteful exploitation.
Conserving and improving material conditions:
The interdependence of natural resources, and espe-
cially the importance of forests in the conservation
of soil, water, and wildlife.
Scientific use of forest resources in harmony with the
balance of nature.
Protection and use of watersheds.
Irrigation, hydroelectric power, and navigability of
streams maintained by forested and well grassed
watersheds.
Forest highways, purposes and values.
Tempering winds and cold by establishing shelterbelts,
relieving strain of monotonous landscape.
Expressing spiritual, aesthetic, and emotional impulses:
The maintenance of national and state forests as a
part of extra-ordinary scenic areas.
National and State Parks.
The maintenance of primeval areas in forests without
human use or interference, except to protect from
fire, to enjoy and to be traversed only by foot,
horseback, or canoe.
Forests as living memorials.

FACTORS IN GOOD SCHOOL FOREST PROGRAMS[4]

School forest programs which result in the achievement

[4]Carl S. Johnson, Planning School Forests Laboratories For Outdoor Education, Columbus:
Ohio Forestry Association, 1955.

of the basic objectives of conservation laboratories will have some characteristics in common. Of course, all the desirable qualities may not be exhibited by any one program. Ways and means will vary with circumstances. Nevertheless, the experience of several schools in Ohio and greater numbers in other states (notably Wisconsin and Michigan)-- plus a consideration of the principles of effective teaching-- indicates some factors essential to all good school forest programs.

1. OWNERSHIP

The forest site should be owned by the school, or if absolute ownership is not feasible, the land should be controlled by the school's governing body--the school board-- on a long-term and renewable lease. The school must be able to control the management of the forest, and all returns must accrue to the school. If leased, the cumulative rent, if any, for the time required for plantations to reach maturity should not exceed purchase price plus interest for the same period. Suburban plots might be exceptions; as previously admitted, school forests may not be "economical" on a commercial-forest basis.

Ownership is most desirable because the school should be responsible for the management of its forest, its farm, or other outdoor laboratory. Responsibility is essential for long-range operations and for the inclusion of all phases of land-resource operations. Ownership is often requisite for harvesting forest products and for obtaining the returns from such harvesting. Harvesting and marketing the products of land use are essential to resource-use education. Good conservation education should show realistically that conservation pays.

2. SIZE

The school forest should be of sufficient size so that true forest conditions can be produced and maintained. It is believed that anything less than one acre is unsuitable, though smaller areas--perhaps designed as forest plantings--may be managed for Christmas trees, as wildlife areas, or as

arborea. At least four acres in a compact shape are necessary to produce true forest conditions on most sites in Ohio.

Much greater area is necessary for commercially
economical management, though farm woodlots of even ten
acres can show profits to their owners. The more intensive
the management the smaller the area necessary for economic
practicability. Christmas tree plantations, for instance, can
be profitable on less than an acre.

3. CAPACITY

The minimum size for school forests, however, is also
conditioned by an educational consideration. They must be
large enough so that many students can work in them. They
should be large enough to provide succeeding generations
of students opportunity to engage in all phases of forest
management. Furthermore, the larger the area the greater
is the variety of conditions, the broader is the range of activity, and the less serious is the conflict between multiple
uses. For these several reasons--forest conditions, operational practicability, opportunities for succeeding classes,
and space for many uses--it is believed that ten acres is
about the minimum size for a good school forest.

4. ACCESSIBILITY

The school's outdoor laboratory must be accessible.
Ideally it adjoins the school grounds. With class periods
short and most high school time-schedules not flexible, ten
minutes walking distance may hinder use of a school forest.

However, suitable tracts do not commonly adjoin the
school grounds, so provisions for readily reaching the
school forest must be made. If the school forest is more
than ten minutes' walking time from the school, transportation should be provided. Double periods of flexible time-
schedules will be helpful for outdoor education regardness
of the distance between a school and its forest.

But, though flexible scheduling and adequate transportation are helpful, they are not a completely satisfactory
substitute, for having the forest near the school. A school
forest developed in conjunction with a school camp may be

the most practical solution for many city schools.

5. CONTINUITY OF LEADERSHIP

The direction of a school forest program should be the responsibility of a committee or board so constituted that continuity is assured. No one person should be solely responsible for it; all too often where one person has started a school forest, work in it ended with his departure. School forests are long-range projects, and continuity of leadership is absolutely essential to programs which must last many years.

It is believed that membership on such committees should be constituted largely by office rather than by name. The school administrator, its biology teacher, and the vocational agriculture teacher, if any, should be members. Others may be appointed either by office or name: an elementary teacher, a school board member, student representatives, a community representative, and a technical consultant. The latter may be the farm forester, or a farm planner.

6. MASTER PLAN

The long-range plan for development and use of the school forest should be a matter of written record. This plan is, of course, tentative and subject to modification, but there should be specific indication as to what may be done in each of the early years, and in more general terms, what may be done thereafter.

The operational plans ought to be supplemented with maps, showing plots to be planted in each year of the reforestation cycle, and areas in which improvement cuttings are to be made.

The technical consultants can be of great assistance in developing plans, but it must be borne in mind that the main objectives of a school forest are educational. Professional foresters or farm planners may not be aware of the opportunities or limitations which will be obvious to teachers. Planning must therefore be a cooperative process.

The work of planting, culling and cutting is planned for many years ahead. If, for example, only an acre is to be planted, the plan would call for setting out only 200 trees each year for six years, followed by Christmas tree harvests in successive seasons, and then replanting.

A larger tract will give more student-generations experience in planting. If a student can learn the process by planting ten trees, why should future students be deprived of the same opportunity? On larger tracts, thinning for Christmas trees could follow planting by from six to ten years. Still later thinnings will yield poles, Christmas greens and finally saw timber. Each successive class for which a role is planned should have work to do.

The area may also provide for experiences in other aspects of conservation. Water control structures may be needed, for example, and wildlife resources should be developed. Here again, plans should be so modified as to spread the experiences over as many years as feasible.

7. CONTINUOUS PLANNING

Planning should also be a continuing process. The basic plan should not be so detailed as to discourage revision, addition and refinement. The people who are being educated, teachers as well as students, should share the responsibility for evaluating and modifying the basic plans, the final decisions resting with the school authorities.

Resource technicians, namely, farm foresters, farm planners, wildlife management agents, conservation engineers, and county agriculture agents, should be consulted. These are the same technicians from whom managers of farms and forests seek advice. The farm planners of Soil Conservation Districts have helped many schools prepare their basic plans. Indeed, many school forest committees cooperate with Soil Conservation Districts as do farmers. But good farm planners do not make or revise farm plans for farmers, and good technical consultants will not make plans for the school, nor will a good school ask them to do so. They will do the planning together--that is, with each other's help.

8. MULTIPLE USES

In accordance with good land-use principles, school forests, like all forests, should be managed for as many uses as are feasible and reasonably compatible. School forests are primarily managed for educational purposes but, since multiple-use is a conservation principle which should be taught, they must be managed for all those purposes. This should be made evident in the general plan. Forests not only yield timber products; at the same time they protect watersheds and wildlife, and provide opportunities for education and recreation.

Since some conflicts between uses are inevitable and are more frquent as the size of the area decreases or the range of uses expands, the general plan may suggest some sort of zoning. For educational purposes, however, it is more desirable that the plan suggest means for discussing conflicts as they arise instead of laying down an elaborate code at the outset.

9. STUDENT PARTICIPATION

When students share in the planning, it is then their own work they do when the plan is executed. Then, too, it is their school forest and they need practice in planning as well as in working. This implies more student participation in planning than just the opportunity given the student representative on the school forest committee.

Too often school forest programs--as well as other phases of school activity--are planned for instead of with the students. Too often student participation begins after the planning has been completed.

Student participation in school forest activities should be well distributed through the school. Girls as well as boys should do their share. Elementary students can plant trees, gather seed, use nature trails, rake fire breaks, identify and measure trees. The good school forest is not an exclusive project of Vocational Agriculture classes, the FFA chapter, or even biology classes. Each grade level may have some part in the program.

All students should make some use of the forest each

year and most, if not all, teachers should have educational missions there. Observation, recreation, or tasks such as gathering leaves or seeds for collections or decorations, observing spring flowers, animal homes, or animal tracks in snow, watching the felling and bucking of a tree into logs and fuelwood, are among the great variety of activities for which a trip to the school forest may be made. In addition to learning about the biotic resources, the school forest provides opportunity for both observations and activities on soil and water conservation.

Teachers of subjects closely related to conservation should make regular use of the area. Activity should become progressively more challenging and purposeful as students mature. Students should keep their interest even after their 12 years of school.

10. RECORD KEEPING

A school forest is a living, changing laboratory. Change occurs continuously whether the forest is well or poorly managed or not managed at all. Plants grow and plants die. Future students should have some way of knowing what changes have occurred and also what has been done to the forest. Adequate records should be kept.

The records should show all management operations and all expenditures and returns. Cash outlay, gifts and donations, whether of money, material or work, will be entered in the books. Returns should show products used as well as those sold. They might also assign value to less tangible benefits, such as recreation and education. Names of individuals who were responsible or made major contributions should be recorded. Groups which did work should be listed. The value of discovery by a student that his parents once planted the trees on "Plot 9" may be surprisingly great.

The records should include maps and photographs. The basic map may be an aerial photo obtainable from farm planners or county agents. In several counties, soil survey reports provide excellent aerial photos. Students ought to do some of the mapping and they can also make large maps from air photos.

Pictures will be especially valuable for educational purposes. The long-range plan should provide for the establishment of "picture points"--permanently marked points from which pictures will be taken at regular intervals--and for the taking and filing of pictures of activities and progress each year. The maps, pictures, and records may also contribute research data for a later time. The records should be brought up to date at least once each year and students should have a part in keeping them.

11. EARNINGS

Economic returns from forest products, whether sold or used by the school, should be of visible benefit to all students. Students should have the opportunity to help plan use of returns. Only when students visualize returns can we feel certain they can realize that good forest management pays.

Most returns will probably be re-invested in outdoor laboratory development. Several schools in Wisconsin are constructing school camps from school forest returns. One Ohio school owns a tree planter as the product of school forest program returns--though tree planters are not recommended for school forests for they deprive students of a needed opportunity. Another has sold firewood and logs to buy fire-fighting equipment for its forest. Students themselves recommended that returns from sale of fuel, wood and posts be used to acquire more abandoned land for the enlargement of one Ohio school forest. Part of the Christmas tree festival returns will go into the fund for the senior class trip at another school.

12. FIRE AND GRAZING

Pasturing cattle and growing trees are not compatible uses of hardwood forests. School forest programs must help forest owners realize that woods should not be grazed. Hence, school forests must emphasize the protection of forests from grazing as well as from destructive fire, a known enemy. Fences and multiflora rose hedges will afford protection from cattle. Access roads, fire breaks, coupled with training in fire control and eternal vigilance will help keep out fire.

Insects and disease each year ruin more timber than does fire. Less is known about combatting these enemies of forests economically, but advanced classes in biology and Vocational Agriculture should acquire some grasp of this problem by trying to control insects and disease in the school forest.

13. COMMUNITY RELATIONS

Ideally the forest is so located that the whole community will readily be able to observe it. Community cooperation should be encouraged. Fathers could help some at adult activities such as felling trees, or furnishing tractors for building a farm pond in the school forest or for contour furrowing prior to tree planting. At Yellow Springs, Ohio, parents buy Christmas trees from the school forest. One school planned a picnic area; others with relatively large forests could do likewise. Organizations have often provide planting stock. At Danville, Ohio, a civic club provided the land; in Wisconsin, Trees For Tomorrow donated land. These are some ways by which the community is involved in the program, and involvement is the most effective way to become informed.

Passers-by as well as the community may be told that a school has an outdoor laboratory for conservation by an attractive and durable school forest sign. A 2' x 2' two-faced steel sign, framed for hanging, is available from the Ohio Forestry Association. It is given to schools which develop school forest programs which meet certain standard The criteria for such recognition and the procedure for obtaining it are described later.

14. REPLANTING

The success of all school forest ventures should be assured by persistent efforts to make up for failure or mistakes. If a dry summer causes death of some of one spring' plantings, the vacant spots should be filled the next spring.

Failure to do this may result in students concluding that reforestation is not effective. Failure to try again has had
this effect at several Ohio schools. On the other hand,
failures have been turned to advantages. At one Ohio school
a village laborer cut 500 trees the school had planted that
spring on village well-land. The ire of the children plus
good strategy by the local school executive resulted in wider
participation the following year. The village council furnished a thousand trees, farmers furnished plows and tractors, and more students participated than would have if the
earlier planting had not "failed."

Selected References

Adams, M. L., "Fifth Graders Reforest," *Progressive
Education,* December, 1940.

Bannerman, G. W., "Trees For Tomorrow," *National
Education Association Journal,* April, 1959.

Boettcher, E. H., "Projecting The School Forest Into The
Classroom," *National Association Secondary School
Principal's Bulletin,* April, 1956.

Clemons, Roger, "Forestry Goes To High School," *California Journal of Secondary Education,* February, 1952.

Duthie, G. A., "Forestry and the Public Schools," *Journal
of Geography,* May, 1937.

Garrett, H. P., "School Forests and Their Possibilities,"
Ohio Schools, September, 1947.

Jackson, Jim, "Trees on the School Ground," *School and
Community,* January, 1960.

Johnson, Carl S., *Planning School Forests,* Columbus,
Ohio: Ohio Forestry Association, 1955.

Kitching, E., "Conservation: A 7th Grade Unit on Florida's
Forests," *Clearing House,* September, 1939.

Mattoon, Wilbur R. and Shinn, Erwin H., *Forestry For 4-H
Clubs* (miscellaneous publication 395) Washington,
D.C.: U. S. Department of Agriculture, 1950.

Morrill, M. B. And Seeber, C., "To Teach Conservation
These Schools Use Forest Lands," *Nations Schools,*
June, 1953.

Stanley, Robert, "A Tree For Every Student, " *Science Teacher,* April, 1954.

Wheeler, H. N., "Forest Conservation: Its Importance To Youth and Its Place in the Curriculum" *National Education Association Procedures,* 1940.

Whittle, C. A., "Cooperative School Programs In Forestry and Wildlife, " *Agricultural Education Magazine,* August, 1940.

Wisconsin Conservation Department, *School Forests a Handbook* (circular 387, publication 614) Madison: Wisconsin Conservation Department, 1950.

Chapter 8

THE SCHOOL CAMP

Educators were slow to recognize the educational potential of school camping. Church and agency leaders and private camp directors were concerning themselves with the educational significance of camping long before school men became concerned with education outside the classroom.

In recent years, however, educators in increasing numbers are realizing the educational significance of camping and many administrators throughout the United States are making it an integral part of the school program. Over the past ten years educational literature contains an increasing amount and variety of materials which discuss camping in terms of philosophy, leadership, campsite development and layout, administrative problems, and programming. A compilation and study of many articles reveals the excellence of the material in terms of proposed standards and in terms of guides to the successful conduct of a school camp. The literature also contains information on the techniques employed to integrate textbook learning with firsthand, direct experience with nature and the out-of-doors. There are some predictions that school camping will expand rapidly as an important adjunct to the school program. This point of view was expressed in an article as early as 1947 in a national magazine:

> All signs suggest that the extension of public-school camping will be the next major development in American education. This, say the educators, is as it should be if we really care about eliminating the great disparity

in educational opportunity for children of high-income
and low-income families.[1]

One of the strongest statements made in support of
school camping was made in a publication prepared for the
American Youth Commission in 1941:

> To the educators of the future a major mystery of the
> development of their profession in the first half of
> the Twentieth Century will surely be the slowness with
> which camping was adopted as a functional part of the
> system.[2]

Many educators believe that an experience in camping
such as has been offered in the summer months by private
agencies should be made available to all children. In a dem
ocratic society camping should not be a privilege of the rela
tively few children whose parents are able to afford the pric
or a privilege for those at the other end of the scale who
qualify for camping through welfare or public health agencie
The logical agency to offer camping experience to all
children is the public school. School programs should only
serve to supplement the fine experiences now provided by
private and agency camps. This idea is expressed by
Sharman:

> The public school is the agency that should assume the
> major part of the burden of organizing and operating
> camps. The objectives of camping are primarily educa-
> tional and recreational and, therefore, fall appropri-
> ately in the sphere of the responsibilities of school
> boards. It is certain that the schools must accept
> promptly this new responsibility. Otherwise society
> will create some new public agency to handle the prob-
> lem of camping that would probably not be as well
> qualified as the school. Many critics of the public
> schools believe that educators and school boards have

[1]Amy Porter, "Open Air Schools," Colliers, March 1, 1947.

[2]Gilbert Wrenn and D. L. Harley, Time on Their Hands: A Report on Leisure,
Recreation and Young People, American Council of Education, Washington, D.C.,
1941, p. 81.

been too slow to recognize changed social conditions and to adapt the school program to meet the new demands being made on it.[3]

Many educators, especially in rural areas, quickly endorse school camping programs for children coming from large metropolitan areas. "Why, some city children have never seen a cow," they will tell you. Outdoor education and school camping is much more than merely "seeing a cow" or, in fact, seeing any new phenomena. It is a technique of teaching and a way of learning which is just as important to a child from a rural environment as to a child from the city. Grubb comments on the values of camping experiences to children of rural areas:

> Children and young people from isolated rural sections need camping as much as children from the city. The social values from camping are many, and much is lost to the farm boy or girl who serves a long apprenticeship during the summer months without an opportunity to make wide acquaintances and broaden their interests and abilities by acquiring various new skills and purposes which are vital to them at this stage.[4]

Porter points out, too, that experiences in camping are needed by all children regardless of rural or urban background. She says:

> It isn't only the tenement children of big cities who miss these meaningful experiences. Battle Creek, Michigan, is a country town when compared to New York City or Chicago, yet in a recent check-up twenty-eight of the thirty-one children from Battle Creek stated that never before had they gone for a walk in the woods.[5]

Camping, today, is advocated by so many different groups and organizations and for so many different purposes

[3]Jackson R. Sharman, "Camping, A School Responsibility," Phi Delta Kappan, 21:116-117, December, 1938.
[4]Gena Grubb, "Camping Is Education," Journal of Health, Physical Education and Recreation, May, 1943, p. 226.
[5]Amy Porter, "Open Air Schools," Colliers, March 1, 1947.

that it is difficult to describe its scope or enumerate its values. Camping programs are sponsored today by social agencies, churches, municipal recreation departments, by local, state, and national governmental agencies, by municipal and state boards of health, by boards of education of public schools, by private schools, by state departments of education and conservation, by colleges and universities, and by various other public and private groups.

It must be recognized that many values are derived by boys and girls attending various camps sponsored by public and private agencies and organizations. However, this chapter is limited to a discussion of camping sponsored by schools for the primary purpose of extending the education of children through nature and the use of the outdoor laboratory.

Furthermore, the authors are primarily interested in the true definition of camping. Much is done today in the name of camping which is not camping even in the broadest definition of the term. In 1956 a committee of the American Camping Association adopted the following definition of camping:

> Organized resident camping is an experience in group living in a natural environment. It is a sustained experience under the supervision of trained leadership. . . .camping provides a creative educational experience in cooperative group living in the out-of-doors. It utilizes the resources of the natural surroundings to contribute significantly to mental, physical, social, and spiritual growth.

The word camping should signify a nature-centered program. It should mean a program conducted in the woods or forests and in a setting that has a minimum amount of artificial development. A camping program is most valuable when its primary purpose is to take individuals to the woods, forests, streams, and hills for a rich and rewarding experience with nature. Planned camp activities which are closely associated with nature and which provide the individual with opportunities to know himself, to understand his environment, and to respect his fellow men are vitally important. Other kinds of highly organized activities unrelated to the natural environment which are conducted in camp programs are of questionable value. They are more significant and may be better enjoyed back on the playground.

It makes as much sense to conduct a garden program in the gymnasium as it does to conduct a basketball game at camp.

DEVELOPMENT AND SCOPE OF SCHOOL CAMPING

A review of educational literature shows that a precedent has been set for school camping and the roots of camping--even for educational purposes--reach far back into history.

The history of organized camping for educational purposes is largely a history of outstanding scholars of the past --men who possessed the pioneer spirit and the vision of bringing back those values which come from living close to nature and in the great out-of-doors.

Many educators of the past, and more and more the outstanding educators of today, are seeking ways of making methods of education more real and meaningful by going to nature in order to improve learning.

Thamus, an early Egyptian king, warned that the discovery of writing "will aid not wisdom but reminiscence." He was afraid that his subjects would become divorced from reality and hieroglyphics would become more and more a substitute for real things. He warned that emphasis on the written word as the sole means of learning would make students "hearers of many things" but learners of very little.

Early Greek philosophers suggested that children leave their books to learn from nature. Socrates advocated a vacation for school children so that they "might acquire some education."

Comenius, often referred to as the father of modern educational theory, insisted that all learning must come through the senses and advocated open space to walk and play in and gardens where children "may feast their eyes on trees, flowers, and plants."

Outdoor education is a year-around activity at the Glen Helen Outdoor Education Center of Antioch College. Here children are searching for evidence of "life in the forest" in winter.

Photo Courtesy of Jean Sanford

Pestalozzi in his <u>Diary</u> beseeched teachers to lead the child "out into nature, teach him on the hilltops and in the valleys."

Grundtvig, the Danish poet and statesman, shocked his contemporaries by establishing the Folk Schools so that children may engage in "learning for living." The Folk Schools and Peoples Colleges laid the foundation for the cooperative movement in the Scandinavian countries. School teachers, then and now, may be seen throughout the countryside as they seek education outside the classrooms in the Scandinavian countries.

These are only a few of the expressions and thoughts of the many early educators who advocated a more direct and realistic way of learning. To their names may be added Pythagoras, Democritus, Plato, Aristotle, Erasmus, Rousseau, Basedow, Frobel, Spencer, and more recently John Dewey, Ralph Waldo Emerson, George Bernard Shaw, and Alfred Lord Whitehead only to mention a few.

John Dewey's philosophy that education is life and education is experience brought education in close relationship to the changing culture of the day. He attempted to narrow the educational gap between what is going on in the world and what children study in school. His basic tenets that education is life, we learn by doing, education is experience and his concept of educating the "whole child" placed the burden of education not only on schools but on many agencies such as the home, church, recreation department, and other neighborhood and community agencies. The community as well as the school became responsible for the education of youth. Thus, Dewey convinced the world that "a book cannot be substituted for civilization."

Alfred North Whitehead in his books Adventures in Ideas and The Aims of Education regards books as sources of information to be used for practical application to real life situations. They are not materials to be memorized for their own sake. Whitehead defines education as "the acquisition of the art of the utilization of knowledge." He states in The Aims of Education that the solution is to "eradicate the fatal disconnection of subjects which kill the vitality of our modern curriculum... There is only one subject matter for education, and that is life in all its manifestations."

These and the many other proponents of outdoor education would like to see school camps become a permanent part of the nation's educational system on a year around basis. They contend that something more than book learning is needed in the schools of today in order to make each child more aware of things real and more able to live with them. Every child in America needs the benefit of experience offered in a good school camp.

Other countries saw the benefits of camping as an educational asset around the turn of the century. The German Youth Movement in 1898 exerted a significant influence upon the education of that country. The Youth Movement with emphasis on wandering over the countryside and outdoor living was a revolt against the intellectual and bookish approach to education employed by the schools. Groups of young people with self-elected leaders made extensive trips on foot or by bicycle cooking their own meals and living in the open spaces. Although the Youth Movement was checked by the advent of World War I, it made its contribution to the revision of the static, German school curriculum.

Young historians collect and analyze artifacts at the Lorado Taft Field Campus of Northern Illinois University. All students majoring in elementary education participate in outdoor education sometime during their freshman and junior year. This experience is culminated in their senior student-teacher assignment as they bring their class to Lorado Taft.

Photo courtesy of Don Hammerman

The Youth Movement was revived in 1936 by Hitler as a tool of the Nazi party. Every boy and girl had to belong to one of the youth organizations, all of which stressed German ideology and preparation for military service. The youth of Germany spent many days camping out in the open. Thousands of boys were sent to foreign countries each year. Had the Youth Movement been for educational rather than military purposes, Germany could have set a good example for other nations in enriching the education of her youth by studying firsthand not only her own culture but the cultures of surrounding foreign countries. It seems logical to assume that if a totalitarian nation can use camping as a tool for capturing the minds of youth and bending their thoughts to the objectives of the German state, then it can become an equally effective instrument for teaching children to live effectively in a democracy.

Since the days of the Spartans, government leaders have realized that in order to perpetuate their political ideology, no matter what it might be, they must first capture the youth of a nation and indoctrinate them and control their thinking, keeping them healthy and fit to do the duties and work ascribed by the national leaders.

The Youth Movement appeared in Russia as early as 1910 and by 1917 numbered about 50,000 boys and girls. During the beginning years of the Soviet government, the Youth Movement continued, but it was gradually replaced by Communist youth organizations. The emphasis on outdoor living and camping continued but as in Germany, the educational and recreational objectives were supplanted by the militaristic goals of the Soviet government.

Indoctrination to a way of life is most successful in building attitudes and behavior patterns in our youth. The youth of America must be given many opportunities for experiences in our democratic form of government. A school camp program under proper supervision will provide many experiences in democratic group living. Our democratic form of government has withstood the test for centuries. It can be strengthened only through proper instruction for our youth.

SCHOOL CAMPING IN THE UNITED STATES

In the last decade, school camping has made significant progress in many states and in widely scattered sections of the United States. Over 300 school districts are conducting at least a day camp and many are conducting resident camps for two days to two weeks duration.

There is some controversy in determining which of the earliest camps was the first organized as a project in education. Most studies dealing with school camping give Frederick Williams Gunn, the founder of the Gunnery School for Boys in Washington, Connecticut, credit for establishing the first school camp. In the summer of 1861 Mr. and Mrs. Gunn took the entire student body of Gunnery School on a camping venture for two weeks. Mary Gunn Brinsmade gives an account of the first school camp:

> The school year was divided into two parts--the summer term from the middle of May to the end of September, and the winter term from the middle of November to the end of March.

When the Civil War began, the boys were eager to be
soldiers, to march, and especially to sleep in tents.
They were given opportunity to roll up in blankets and
sleep outdoors on the ground, and sometimes the whole
school would camp for a night or two in this way at a
lovely lake nearby. In the summer of 1861, Mr. and
Mrs. Gunn took the whole school on a hike, or gypsy
trip, as it was called, about four miles to Milford,
on the Sound, near New Haven. This trip took two days.
The tents, baggage, supplies, etc., were carried in a
large market wagon. There were also a few comfortable
carriages and two donkeys, but many walked much, and
some of the boys all of the way. Camp was established
on the beach at Welch's Point and named Camp Comfort.
Here two happy weeks were spent boating, sailing, fishing, and tramping. This proved such a helpful and delightful experience that Mr. Gunn repeated it in the
years of 1863 and 1865. Old boys came back to join the
merry troop, and with friends of the school, some of
them ladies, made up a party of sixty or more in the
following trips.

At a later period this seaside jaunt gave place
to a Gunnery Camp at Point Beautiful on Lake Waramaug,
seven miles from the school, and for twelve years the
school spent two weeks in August camping in this pic-
turesque and delightful spot. The Gunnery was one of
the latest schools to adopt the long summer vacation
and this change eliminated the summer camp.

In 1893, Judge Clark established the Keewaydin Camps
and gave credit to his old schoolmaster for the origin of
the camping idea. Judge Clark writes:

In 1872, the year of my birth, Mr. Frederick William
Gunn, the Master of the Gunnery School in Washington,
Connecticut, came to the conclusion that the summer
vacation was too long for the average school boy. Mr.
Gunn thought it would be better to have the boys occu-
pied during the summer time; and so in that year he
established the Gunnery Camp on the shores of Lake
Waramaug in Washington, Conn., and took practically
all of his pupils with him to this camp for the summer.
It was a regular camp, in which the time was spent, not
in studies, but in recreation and general training.
This camp was continued for many years. In the fall

of 1880, when I was eight years old, I became a pupil
of Mr. Gunn's at the Gunnery school. Mr. Gunn died a
few years afterwards and the Gunnery Camp was discontinued at the time of his death.

Although one of the earliest camps, if not the very
first one, was established for educational purposes, the public schools have been very slow to accept the values of school
camping.

One of the first public school ventures in camping was
in 1912 when the Board of Education in Dubuque, Iowa, cooperated with the visiting Nurse Association in establishing
a summer camp for malnourished school children.

In 1917, J. Madison Taylor of Temple University proposed that "each state provide, as part of its education system, a vacation camp for boys." He proposed a program
for thirteen to fifteen year old boys in the out-of-doors and
in a camping environment which would aid the boys in knowledges, skills, and appreciations in health, growth, character, teamwork, patriotic citizenship, group spirit, leadership, nature, and the development of knowledge and skill.

In 1919, the Chicago Public Schools established a
camp for normal boys in cooperation with the War Department and the Association of Business Men. It was primarily
an R. O. T. C. camp but activities such as sports, lectures,
campfire programs, and crafts were included in the program. The camp, known as Camp Roosevelt, was directed
by Major F. L. Beals.

In 1925, the Irvington Health Camp was established at
Irvington, New Jersey, and was partially financed and supported by the Board of Education. The camp, still in existence, has a recreational program for one-hundred under-
nourished and underprivileged children between the ages of
seven and fourteen who spend four weeks at camp.

Clear Creek Camp of the Los Angeles City School
System has provided school camp programs supported by
the public schools beginning as early as 1925. Each year
educators of the Los Angeles School System, impressed
with the educational values of camping, improve and expand
camping opportunities for their children. Outdoor education

study groups and curriculum committees have developed
valuable guides for conducting school camping programs.

By the early 1930's, at least seven cities in the United
States had camps maintained or directed by Boards of Edu-
cation. The cities are Chicago, Dallas, Dearborn, Jersey
City, and LaCrosse, Oshkosh, and West Allis, Wisconsin.

One of the most noteworthy projects in school camping
is the community school camp program organized by the
Kellogg Foundation in the communities of Lakeview, Otsego,
and Decatur, Michigan. Each community organized a camp
committee composed of parents, teachers, and campers to
work out the purposes and details of the camp sessions.
During the precamp period, counselors and teachers worked
with the students in preparation for a two-week camp session. The program was planned in terms of developing work
experience, healthful living, leisure pursuits, and social
living.

New York City, with backing from Superintendent
Jansen, has conducted camp programs for public school
children for several years. Dr. L. B. Sharp, working
closely with school personnel of New York City, conducted
an experiment in school camping which proved the educational value of camping in a scientific study with two control
groups. Dr. Sharp wrote of the story of New York City's
research in outdoor education in his book, Extending Education Through School Camping. [6]

Many other school systems in all parts of the United
States are seeing the educational value of outdoor education
programs. The states of Michigan, California, Illinois,
Texas, New Jersey, Wisconsin, and Indiana are leading
the way toward getting children out of the classroom for
firsthand and meaningful experience in the out-of-doors.
Michigan, with over a hundred school districts participating
in school camping, has over three times that number engaging in field trips, day camps, school forests, and a variety of other outdoor education activities.

Educational literature contains an increasing volume
of materials on the value of camping experience. Numerous

[6] This book may be purchased from the Outdoor Education Association, Inc.,
800 South Illinois Avenue, Carbondale, Illinois.

educational leaders have advocated the establishment of camping programs as a part of the public school system and there are some predictions that the movement will expand rapidly.

Colleges and universities are operating camps for developing leaders in outdoor education, providing laboratories for many subject matter areas, and providing facilities for the development of true concepts of democratic group living, conservation education, healthful outdoor living, and leisure-time education.

The large financial expenditure required for the purchase of a camp site has been a deterrent for many schools in inaugurating a school camp program. Outright purchase, however, is not always necessary.

The Tappan Junior High School (in Michigan) Parent-Teacher Association joined with other community groups to purchase a camp site. The Lion's Club purchased a camp site for the schools in St. Charles, Michigan. Carbondale, DuQuoin, Marion, and other school school systems in Southern Illinois use the camp facilities of Southern Illinois University. Iron County, Michigan, took over the old C. C. C. barracks for their camp program. New Britain, Connecticut, rents a camp from a church organization. Private camp and community agency camps are used by many school systems throughout the United States.

Several schools have purchased their own school site or have had such a site donated by some public-spirited citizen. There are also examples such as in Calhoun County, Michigan, and Pillar Rock County, Washington, where several school districts combine in a joint ownership of a camp site.

VALUES OF SCHOOL CAMPING

The increased emphasis on school camping in the last decade has been one of the major and most promising frontiers of curriculum improvement. Schools have been criticized for maintaining a static curriculum in a changing and dynamic society. Outdoor education, especially school camping, offers a plan to breathe life into a rigid and static school program.

The school camp provides an ideal setting for small group living twenty-four hours a day. It is a perfect laboratory for human relations where children live in close relationship with each other and with other groups all faced (some for the first time) with the management of their own affairs. They plan their program, make the rules, plan the menus, and learn to accept as well as delegate responsibilities. Children are given an opportunity to learn many things firsthand through direct contact. They get at the source just as their teachers did. In this way learning becomes interesting and children derive real and meaningful concepts.

THE SCHOOL CAMP PROGRAM

In a modern school the learning of the three R's is an important part of the educational program. However, the school program is considered in a much broader context than merely the acquisition of subject matter facts and knowledges. The school curriculum includes everything that happens to the child while at school. Educators realize that learning is possible not only in the classroom through textbooks but in every activity sponsored by the school. The cafeteria, the library, the gymnasium, a nature hike, experience in a school forest, a school garden, or in a school camp all add to the child's education and affects his behavior.

The program at camp is everything that happens to the child, everything that brings about a change in his behavior. Since the child is in camp twenty-four hours a day the camp becomes an ideal laboratory for learning from firsthand experience with nature and with classmates and teachers. The child has a chance to accept and carry out responsibilities; to live close to nature and feel the interdependence of all living things in his environment; "to be on his own"; to meet challenges and problems in primitive living; to engage in functional and critical thinking; and to develop himself through creative self expression and action.

EVOLUTION OF THE MODERN CAMP PROGRAM

The modern concept of programs in education and the modern concept of camping in education is the result of social and economic changes in our American way of life which has stimulated necessary reforms in our educational system.

The modern concept of school camping has evolved through at least four stages. All four phases are still in use and all have undergone change and improvement. The four stages involve:

1. Classroom instruction in an outdoor setting

Some of the beginning attempts at outdoor education programs were hastily done, poorly planned, lacked purpose, and were not educationally sound. Outdoor education had many different meanings to school administrators and teachers. Many schools who made early attempts at outdoor programs merely transplanted their class, their books, their formal methods, their schedules, and their controlled learning to an outdoor setting. There was little reason to meet out-of-doors for this type of program and it was hurriedly transplanted back to the formal classroom. Thus, some schools felt that they had attempted an outdoor education program. Outdoor education was a new method of education that school administrators felt should be introduced immediately into their school system in order to keep abreast of the times.

There are many parallel situations in American educational reform that have been met with the same lack of vision, planning, and proper educational interpretations. In John Dewey's attack on the "listening school, " he showed cause why schools should also be concerned with "learning by doing" and "learning through activity. " Many school administrators hurriedly changed and modified their programs without giving adequate interpretations to the philosophy or principles of education that were being proposed. The school administrators were most interested in being classified as progressive schools.

Most of these early attempts in outdoor education were disappointing because they were based on conformity and were conducted merely to get credit for conducting outdoor education programs. Most of these programs have been discontinued or have been improved.

2. School instruction to improve outdoor experience

Considerable progress was made when teachers began planning and orienting the child for his prospective experience out of the classroom. When subject-matter courses in the classroom needed further interpretation and explanation a field trip or a hike to the woods was suggested. Before the trip was made there were extensive plans made by both teacher and students to get maximum benefit from the experience. Discussion centered around safety, self-discipline, purposes of trip, observations to be made, collections of materials or data, uses of trip for future classroom needs, and other needs and uses for the experience. This same procedure also is involved in extended outdoor education experiences. An announcement to the class that a school camp experience is planned is not only cause for great excitement but is cause for serious pre-camp plannings and learnings by teacher and pupils. Much of the planning which could be carried on at camp is done as a pre-camp curriculum experience in the classroom. When the teacher announces to her class that they are going on a camping trip, she has immediately awakened new pupil interest and enthusiasm. Immediately they begin to ask questions and set the stage for cooperative planning and group work in all subject areas. Answers to such questions as, What shall we do at camp?, Where will we go?, What shall we wear?, provides unlimited opportunity for plans, discussions, study groups, committee work, library research, resource personnel, and endless other projects and material collections. All this work is culminated in the actual camping experience. The better the planning which occurs in the classroom the greater the degree of success the teacher may experience in the camp situation.

3. Integration of school instruction and outdoor experience

A later development in outdoor education was the integration of classroom programs with experience in the out-of-doors. The school curriculum includes outdoor education which begins in the classroom, continues in the out-of-doors setting, with a follow-up in the classroom. Thus, integration of classroom activities with outdoor experience may become a year around process involving all types of outdoor experience but building up to an extended camping experience. All classroom teachings and all learning situations in the classroom need not be and are not associated with planned outdoor education experiences. The teachings and learnings which occur in the classroom are more meaningful when they can be associated with the child's experiences. If there is a noted lack of experiences on the part of the child in areas relating to the subject matter being taught, it is well to provide such experiences. However, many learning experiences in the classroom still involve drill and formalized teaching.

In terms of the outdoor education program the school year may become a pre-camp, in camp, and post-camp experience. Pre-camp orientation stimulates and motivates children in planning activities; in camp experiences provide an opportunity for learning activities in an outdoor setting, and post-camp activities bring the child back to the classroom with a broader concept and understanding of the knowledges and skills learned and a great desire to learn more through further study. Outdoor activities offer unlimited possibilities for relating abstract textbook learning to real firsthand experience. Experience in the classroom motivates learning at camp, learning at camp and activities in camp interpret knowledge and stimulate further learning when the group returns to the classroom.

4. Vitalizing class instruction through outdoor experience

The most recent trend in outdoor education concerns the idea of utilizing the out-of-doors to supplement, interpret, vitalize, and further motivate school instruction. Educators and parents are becoming more convinced that a larger portion of the curricula content of public schools can be learned most effectively through direct experience in the out-of-doors. The modern curriculum is developmental, based on real experiences that contribute to the growth and development of the whole child in all areas of his living. The modern school through programs in outdoor education assures greater appreciation and understanding for educational concepts that are based on scientific fact. Furthermore, there is enough concrete evidence to make the basic assumption that direct learning is faster, and is retained longer than facts learned in an isolated and artificial setting.

Educators have partially failed in their attempt to classify and organize areas of learning into logical subject matter fields. When facts are presented or skills taught, they should not be pulled out of context through a unit or series of events. Knowledge is not an end in itself but an aid to further understanding. Relationship between one subject and another, one fact and another, or one experience and another can best be taught or explained as a correlated and integrated whole rather than in isolated parts. It is impossible to isolate the various facets of life to fit a course of study and still retain its full meaning. Fields of study, and life itself for that matter, cannot be independently learned. All life and all learning is integrated and interrelated. The school curriculum with its logical organization of subject matter makes it difficult, even for the brighter students, to learn materials in isolation and then re-organize and relate these learnings to his own experience. Associations and relationships are learned faster and better if the cause and effect relationship are presented simultaneously. The public schools have been criticized because too often their graduates leave school with an accumulation of isolated facts and skills without the wisdom to organize and use them. It takes more than years of schooling and a diploma to become educated. Education is the process in which man strives to organize knowledge and experience in a way that has meaning for him. The degree to which a student is educated is the degree to which he is able to organize his knowledge and experience in a meaningful fashion.

The changing concept of education, which places the child rather than the curriculum as the focal point of education, has placed emphasis upon meeting the needs and interest of children. One of these needs has become the enrichment of classroom experience in order to give meaning to the abstract and isolated facts and knowledges. Knowledge is no longer taught for knowledge sake. School subjects are not ends in themselves. Knowledge, skills, and experience are means to gaining attitudes, understandings, and appreciations.

In recent years curriculum committees have experimented in many ways to find more effective methods of teaching various subjects. Two of the most prevalent trends in curriculum reconstruction are the unit or horizontal method, and the fusion or integration of courses, more commonly known as core-curriculum.

The unit method of teaching organizes learning around problems rather than subject-matter and brings to bear all subject-matter areas upon the solution of these problems. The justification of the unit method rests on the tenet that students' problems in human relations and daily living do not fall into isolated subject-matter areas. Problems cannot be assigned to a single discipline. Such problems must be considered from many angles before a solution is possible. The unit method of instruction cuts across many subject lines. Functional knowledge is applied to the problems of youth and each area of study may contribute relevant materials for the possible solution of these problems.

The core-curriculum as it is most commonly practiced is the fusion of two or more subject areas together in order to better teach relationships. It also transcends or cuts across subject lines. Subjects such as geography, economics, history, government, and civics, for example, may all be combined and taught as Social Studies.

Another technique of integrating and correlating all learning is outdoor education. Outdoor education transcends both the unit method of teaching and the core-curriculum grouping. It can be used to vitalize and enrich learning regardless of the philosophy of education or technique of teaching employed, whether a vertical watertight subject-matter approach or the core-curriculum and unit approach. Outdoor education, however, is not to be regarded as a cure-all for all the ills of education. It cannot be claimed that outdoor education can be a substitute for teaching all the knowledge and skills that children should be taught. It can only serve as a valuable tool for supplementing many activities of the classroom, for supplementing and vitalizing textbooks, and for enriching the total life of the child.

Education in the out-of-doors is more than the teaching of conservation and nature; it is an object lesson in the intricate relationship of man and his environment. Outdoor education as a technique in teaching attempts to discover certain significant relationships through established facts and forces that make up nature and crystalize them in a clear and comprehensive picture. Outdoor education is teaching by the whole method as opposed to the part method usually employed in the classroom. The classroom, at best, deals with segments of learning classified according to subject area, teaches these subjects in an artificial setting, and hopes that the students will be able to reassemble and relate their learnings to life experience. Outdoor education involves not only the organization of knowledge and experience but also the planning, presentation, and evaluation of the learning activities, materials, and experience. The experience is usually organized around a point of interest related to the students own day-by-day experience. In this way the student sees the experience as a part of his ongoing life and not as a formal subject or course of study.

Outdoor education is a controlled laboratory of learning. Program planning is not easy since outdoor education by nature is complex and expert planning is necessary to integrate its many educational offerings.

EDUCATION THROUGH CAMPING

The outdoor education program should attain its maximum goals through the school camp program. The school camp should be located in a natural setting where a minimum amount of man-made intrusions or developments have occurred. Classes should be organized as much as possible on a decentralized basis, particularly for living purposes. The small group approach to living and learning in the out-of-doors is most desirable. It is also important that the living arrangements and the living accommodations are in accordance with the most desirable health, safety, and sanitary practices. In a camp situation these practices may vary considerably from home and school conditions and still meet desirable health standards.

There are a number of other factors which must be considered to obtain maximum results from the school camp program. Land should be available to the school for their own use in developing programs such as forests, gardens, and nature centers. Formalized and modernistic structures and conveniences in a natural camp environment tend to formalize the camp programs. Large dormitories and centralized facilities often cause facilities to dictate programs. Well-planned school camp programs will enable the physical layout of the camp to conform and meet the educational objectives of outdoor education.

The leadership team representing the school or the classroom should understand and practice the informal approach and the democratic approach necessary for successful teaching in a camp environment.

School camp programs vary in length from day camps, to overnight camps, and to the extended or resident camp. Many schools wisely start out with day camp programs and work up to the resident camp as the teachers and children become acquainted with the more informal techniques of outdoor education.

THE DAY CAMP

One of the most promising practices in integrating outdoor education with classroom activities is that of the school day camp program.

Day camping is group living during the daylight hours in the out-of-doors. The day camp counselors share the responsibility for the children with the parents as the children return home for the evening meal, a night's sleep, and breakfast. The children usually gather at a vantage point--the school, church, or recreation center, are transported or hike to a suitable site, and return to the vantage point for dismissal. The day camp usually includes only the noon meal which can be a sack lunch prepared and taken from the home or a cook-out over a campfire. On special occasions the campers may remain late to prepare an evening meal and a campfire program before returning home. On this occasion they usually invite their parents.

The Girl Scouts are generally credited with starting the day camp movement since they were, if not the first, the most enthusiastic and universal users of this type of camping. Today, day camps are sponsored by the Girl Scouts, the Boy Scouts, the Young Women's Christian Association, the Young Men's Christian Association, churches, schools, recreation departments and many other agencies and institutions. It is estimated that well over a million boys and girls engage in day camp activities each year.

Many cities set aside certain desirable sites in their parks for day camping by the various groups and organizations of the city who are interested in camping activities. Schools or other groups located near state and national parks or forests are fortunate in having ideal settings for camping. Some schools enlist the cooperation of farmers to use their wooded area or creek banks for outdoor education. An increasing number of schools, becoming alarmed at the disappearing wilderness lands, are buying their own camp sites and developing them for optimum use as outdoor education laboratories.

Regardless of how, or from whom, the camp site is obtained, all potentialities should be carefully explored for the spot most ideally suited for camping and outdoor experiences.

Besides offering possibilities for outdoor activities the camp should meet high standards of health and safety. In 1954 the American Camping Association compiled a mimeographed booklet on Day Camp Standards which is available for those interested in starting a day camp program. The following criteria should be considered in the selection of a site for day camping in order to assure high standards and maximum educational opportunity:

1. The camp site should be accessible. It may be within walking distance and should not be so far away that more than one hour is required to transport the children to and from camp. The camp must be accessible to medical assistance at all times and, if possible, should have a telephone at the site or nearby.

2. The camp site should have adequate sanitary facilities. Although children may carry drinking water, a good pure water supply at the camp site is an obvious advantage. Toilet facilities or sanitary latrines are an obvious necessity. Cleanliness and good drainage or disposal plumbing, of course, are important. Facilities for disposing of leftover food, garbage, and paper or trash need to be provided at the site.

3. The camp should, as much as possible, be in a wilderness setting away from sight or evidence of man-made structures or industrial activity. Plenty of shade and natural beauty such as hillsides, brooks, lakesides, and plant life is highly desirable. The camp should be fairly secluded and free from distractions such as railroads, highways, and public activities.

4. Adequate provisions should be made for inclement weather. If buildings are not available, simple shelter roofs with open sides may serve the purpose very adequately.

5. The camp site should be free from sink holes, swamp lands, poisonous plants, dead branches, and other unnecessary hazards.

6. The camp site should have proximity to facilities for program enrichment such as waterfront, an open playing field, a council ring or campfire area, a variety of plant life, trees, animals, and other natural phenomena.

7. It is highly desirable to have the camp site in an area rich in recreational, historic, scenic, and folklore possibilities.

Although a teacher is expected to guide twenty-five to thirty children in a classroom, she will need help with this number in the out-of-doors program. Some experienced

helpers may be obtained from a nearby college or university,
from the high school, or from capable parents and other com
petent adults.

The camp program will depend upon the site, the circumstances, the facilities, and the leadership available, and
the objectives of the camp. The program requires a great
deal of preparation and planning. It should allow for flexibil
ity and free play. Much of the value of the program will be
gained during the unplanned free activity periods. The camp
program should be built basically on out-of-doors living and
on nature study. Experiences which cannot be gained in the
classroom and on the playground should be emphasized. Day
camping should offer experiences in pioneering, building
fires and outdoor cooking, use of an axe, preparing a camp
site, living in the woods, preparation and eating of food,
sanitary practices, nature crafts and games, informal
games, hiking, and conservation practices. No two day
camps will follow the same program. Each program must
be designed to fit the needs of the children, the leadership,
and the camp location.

The teacher should not become a slave to a schedule
and should allow children an opportunity to assist in planning
the day's activities. Following are two examples of day
camp programs carried out by two different classes in
schools of Southern Illinois.

Day Camp Program (I)

9:00	Arrive at camp
9:00 - 9:30	Organize for activity
9:30 - 11:30	Group activities (30 minutes each activity) Nature hike Arts and crafts Conservation Camp craft
11:30 - 12:30	Build fire and prepare meal
12:30 - 1:30	Free period

1:30 - 3:30	Group activities
	Nature hikes
	Arts and crafts
	Conservation
	Camp craft
3:30	Leave camp

Day Camp Program (II)

9:00	Arrive at camp
9:00 - 9:30	Arrange personal belongings and prepare for day's activities
9:30 - 10:30	Hiking activities
10:30 - 11:00	Rest period
11:00 - 12:30	Prepare and eat meal
12:30 - 1:00	Clean-up period
1:00 - 1:30	Arts and crafts
1:30 - 2:00	Informal games
2:00 - 2:30	Camp craft
2:30 - 3:15	Special activities (swimming, Indian lore, etc.)
3:15 - 3:30	Prepare to break camp
3:30	Leave camp

THE OVERNIGHT CAMP

The overnight camp, as its name implies, is camping overnight. Overnight camping should be an outgrowth of day camping for those students whose outdoor skills have advanced to the point where they are ready for a more extended experience in living away from home. The overnight camp offers a progression of experience for older campers and stimulates interest in day camping if used as an incentive to further learning.

Overnight camping experience involves additional problems concerning such things as preparing a camp kit, locating a site, checking the water supply, making provisions for latrine construction, making provisions for sleeping facilities, consideration for protection against fire and poisonous plants, and a well-developed plan for subject-matter learnings. The more problems and the more primitive the camp, the greater the challenge becomes. As a result, more educational and social experiences become an inherent part of the program. Facing problems that concern the well-being, comfort, and happiness of all campers, each individual is required to do his share and accept responsibilities in a democratic group experience.

The overnight camp can offer the same program possibilities found in a day camp such as nature study, conservation, group living, health and safety practices, manners and morals, wildlife study, arts and crafts, and observation of many things in their natural environment. The overnight camp, in addition, has obvious advantages over the day camp. The program need not be so hurried, as two days and one night may be utilized rather than one day. In addition, more experience is available as four or five meals are prepared rather than one; selection of site, preparation of latrines, provision of pure drinking water, preparation of shelters or living quarters for the night is necessary. Astronomy and nocturnal life, bird watches, and night time observations of nature are possible. A campfire program may be added which includes singing, skits, stories, and informal type activities.

THE RESIDENT CAMP

The resident camp is designed for an extended experirience in the out-of-doors. Children are taken during the regular school year for a period of a week, and sometimes longer, to the school camp site.

School camps throughout the country are provided for children from the fourth grade through the eighth with the sixth grade the most universally chosen for the camp experience. Although the sixth grade is not considered sacred, it does offer two distinct advantages. In the first place the sixth grade is, in most cases, the last grade in which one teacher is in control. Beginning with the seventh grade, children usually move from room to room and have special area teachers. The junior high school schedule would involve more teachers and disrupt the school program to a greater extent.

Another reason for choosing the sixth grade is that their maturation level seems more ideal for an outdoor education experience. They are at a stage just before the boy-girl interest and are full of imagination and curiosity, and are ready to explore.

In most school districts offering a camp program every child in the sixth grade from all schools in the district are given a camp experience for a full school week. By continuing this experience each year, every boy and girl in the district is assured of a week at camp.

Often if facilities allow, two or more sixth grades from different schools go to camp the same week. The classroom teacher accompanies the class to the camp and spends the week with them in educational activities that were planned back in the classroom.

Teachers are assisted, of course, with an adequate number of capable counselors; or in some school systems the camp is already staffed with a camp director, counselors, a program director, and research personnel.

The most successful camp seems to be the decentralized plan in which the children are divided into small groups for activities and come together as a whole unit only for meals and group activities such as campfires. The class arrives in camp Monday morning and departs Friday afternoon.

The program at camp involves firsthand experience with nature. One of the greatest weaknesses in American education is the lack of understanding and the lack of recognition given to the value of using nature itself for understanding and enjoyment of life. Those who know the needs, interests, and characteristics of youth have seen them "blossom out" as they unload from the bus and "head for the woods." To our youth, camping means adventure, exploration, discoveries, challenges, fun, new experiences, and new learnings. The camp leader's job is to recognize these inherent characteristics of youth and to wisely use them and direct their experiences into successful enjoyment and appreciation of nature. Too often camp sites are cluttered with athletic fields, baseball bats, volleyball nets, tennis racquets, and other paraphenalia which can be used more safely and wisely at the school plant.

Children in the woods should be more concerned with cooperative adventures in those things not possible at school. The camp program consists of nature study, wildlife study, conservation, rocks and minerals study, laying out nature trails, building bridges, practice in camp craft and outdoor skills, and direct experience in subject-matter learnings. The extended camp experience also offers to teacher and pupil alike intimate contact with each other in an informal environment which gives them an opportunity to learn and live together as they establish common interests and close companionship, which is not possible in a classroom.

Selected References

Allen, H. K., *Camps and Their Modern Administration,* New York: The Woman's Press, 1947.

Burns, Gerald P., *Program of the Modern Camp,* Englewood Cliffs, N. J.: Prentice-Hall, 1954.

Clarke, James Mitchell, *Public School Camping,* Palo Alto, California: Stanford University Press, 1951.

Department of Public Instruction, *School Experiences in Camp,* Bulletin No. 420, Lansing, Michigan: Department of Public Instruction, 1948.

Dimock, H. S., *Administration of the Modern Camp,* New York: Association Press, 1948.

Dimock, Hedley S., and Hendry, Charles E., *Camping and Character,* New York: Association Press, 1929.

Educational Policies Commission, *Education For All American Youth: A Further Look,* Washington, D. C.: National Education Association, 1952.

Irwin, Frank L., *The Theory of Camping,* New York: A. S. Barnes, 1950.

Jobe, M. L. , *The Handbook of Day Camping,* New York: Association Press, 1949.

Macmillan, Dorothy Lou, *School Camping and Outdoor Education,* Dubuque, Iowa: Wm. C. Brown Company, 1956.

Mason, B. S. , *Camping Education,* New York: The McCall Company, 1930.

National Association of Secondary School Principals, "Camping and Outdoor Education, " Bulletin No. 147, Washington, D. C. : National Education Association, 1947.

National Society for the Study of Education, *Adopting The Secondary School Program to the Needs of Youth,* 52nd Yearbook, Chicago: University of Chicago Press, 1952.

Western New York School Study Council, *Education Beyond Four Walls* Mimeographed Bulletin, Buffalo: University of Buffalo, 1959.

Chapter 9

THE PARK - SCHOOL PLAN

The local park has always been a significant part of American community life. Historically it has had different meaning to the local people and it has a varied concept for being.

In England many of the parks were set aside for the wealthy, the royal family and the nobility. The first city parks of London were open only to privileged classes and admission was charged.

This concept of parks was early introduced into America, but its acceptance and success was short lived and gave way to our democratic approval to the use of public facilities.

The American population has up until recently been considered primarily rural. Farming and living from the soil was the primary means of a livelihood for the masses.

As America became steadily an urban population, there was a strong desire on the part of the people for open spaces. Many feel that this is one cause for the development of our park and forest programs at the local level. As people moved from the farms to the city, they not only longed for the green spaces, but they had also acquired knowledge and appreciations for natural areas and places of aesthetic beauty. The city park in many cases gave some satisfaction to the new city dwellers.

Many parks, including our national park program, were acquired because of necessity.

Many of our natural areas of beauty and areas with geological and historical significance were fast disappearing. Timber was being cut, areas were being mined, unsuitable land was being farmed, and there was a general deterioration of once priceless natural areas. It was purely a matter of good conservation practices that caused many local, state, and federal parks to be created.

Today the provision of parks for the satisfaction and enjoyment of all citizens is a recognized responsibility of the city, state, and national government. Cities carefully plan their parks and provide facilities that can be shared as equally as possible among all citizens.

City planners, educators, park administrators and recreation leaders are in general agreement on the make-up of an ideal city park. More and more city park planners are setting aside acreage for natural refuges, outdoor education centers and sanctuaries.

The park often provides a large enough area which is needed for students to see and understand the interdependence of plant and animal life. They begin to understand how many animals cannot survive without plants and how plant life is dependent upon animal life for existence. Here in the park the students will observe the beauties of nature. They will also see how cruel nature can be. They will have a better understanding of life as they see how weaker animals serve as food for the stronger animals. They will see how small plants give way to the larger plants; and they will comprehend how the perpetuation of life is more important than the individual.

The operation and supervision of city parks is usually carried on by a separate department of the city government under the direction of a park commission or park superintendent.

The growth of cooperative action on the part of school and park authorities in the acquisition, planning, construction and maintenance of areas for school and community education and recreation is a striking and significant development in recent years. The removal of real and imaginary obstacles that for many years deterred such cooperation and the resolution of jurisdictional differences between school and park authorities represent a drastic and desirable advance in relationships and practice.

The park-school concept received a great deal of impetus as a result of the National Facilities Conference which was held at Jackson's Mill, West Virginia, in December, 1946. National leaders in the fields of school administration physical education, health, and parks and recreation were called together to discuss problems of land and facilities associated with public schools. This conference was made possible through the sponsorship of the Athletic Institute, Inc.

In May, 1956, a second conference was held and a more clear view of the park-school concept was formulated. They expressed their views as follows:

> The park-school as conceived in this report, is a facil ity which combines a park, a school, a playground and/o a play field, and single recreation facilities into a single functional unit for education, recreation, and other community activities. The concept is greater tha just a grouping of these facilities on a single site. I is a unit, the wholeness of which is its essential char acteristic. It is a plant functionally designed to house and make possible an integrated program of education, recreation, and community activities suitable to the geographic area it serves. In addition to the econ omy it represents in land use, construction, and operation, it represents a wholeness of environment in which integrated living in education, recreation, and community life takes place.
>
> The functional concept of this facility is in keeping with the current educational thought which is focused upon developing individuals capable of carrying their responsibilities as citizens in a democratic society. The concept further recognizes that the day-by-day experiences of children and youth of school age which take place outside the school are also educational program as many of the more formally organized classroom activities. The park-school, therefore; is designed as a facility in which it is possible to integrate both school and community experiences into one over-all program of community education. In no sense does this concept imply that this cooperative program should be under the administration and direction of school people alone. Rather, it should be a living experience in democratic cooperation which is

so essential to life in our society.

Possibly the concept of the park-school program, which leads to the designation of the park-school as the basic functional facility, can best be expressed by suggesting that this program should be related to the idea of a "community curriculum" of education-recreation which is developed and directed through joint effort of the agencies and organizations actually concerned with meeting the needs of children and youth.[1]

The day has passed for the park director who measures his achievements in terms of shrubs, trees, and turf with little regard to the human element. Education of both children and adults in modern society is the concern of all. The educator who sees education as a process only to be exercised in the classroom is rapidly disappearing. The modern educator supports recreation and cooperates with recreation authorities in teaching leisure-time skills. Modern schools see recreation as a vital and important part of their education program and integrate leisure time activities with the academic curriculum.

Failure to use park authorities in planning school buildings and reviewing plans to provide facilities for wide community use is a waste of taxpayers money and a serious handicap to the cultural achievements of the community.

Cooperative school-park action follows no uniform pattern, but has been achieved in many ways. Formal agreements endorsing the general principle of cooperation in the acquisition and improvement of properties have been reached by school and park authorities in several cities. In other such agreements have related only to specific properties. Officially appointed coordinating committees in some cities review all proposals for new areas and facilities, and recommend to the respective authorities procedures that will bring maximum benefits to all. Informal arrangements whereby school and park area plans are reviewed regularly and in their early stages by park and school personnel, joint employment of a landscape architect by the two departments

[1] The Athletic Institute, Inc., Planning Facilities For Health, Physical Education, and Recreation, by Participants in National Facilities Conference, Revised Edition, Chicago, Illinois, 1956, p. 4.

and agreements for leasing school properties to the park
department and vice versa.

The City of San Diego and the San Diego Unified Schoo
District entered into a contractual agreement for operation
of a Recreation program for the citizens of the community.

To clarify and expand policies pursuant to the agreement a contract was drawn up between the city and the schoc
district. The contract reads as follows:

> WHEREAS, the City of San Diego, through its Park and
>   Recreation Department and the San Diego Unified
>   School District are mutually interested in and con-
>   cerned with the provision of adequate facilities
>   for the recreation and physical well-being of the
>   people of the City of San Diego; and
> WHEREAS, the San Diego Unified School District has cer
>   tain play areas, toilets, auditoriums, gymnasiums
>   and other educational facilities under their juris-
>   diction, suitable for a community recreation pro-
>   gram, and the City, in its Park and Recreation
>   Department has in its employ certain employees well
>   qualified to supervise, direct and conduct such a
>   community recreation program; and
> WHEREAS, for the many years past, the City of San Dieg
>   and the San Diego Unified School District have main
>   tained a cooperative working arrangement whereunder
>   many school grounds and facilities have been and ar
>   being used by the two authorities for general recre
>   ational purposes, thus affording to the community
>   greatly increased recreational opportunities at
>   costs much below what would otherwise be necessary;
>   NOW THEREFORE,
> In order to continue and improve the cooperative ef-
>   forts of the San Diego Park and Recreation Depart-
>   ment and the San Diego Unified School District.
> IT IS HEREBY MUTUALLY AGREED BETWEEN the said San
>   Diego Unified School District hereinafter known
>   as the "District" and the City of San Diego, for
>   and on behalf of its Department of Parks and Recre-
>   ation hereinafter designated as the "City," that:
> The District will make available to the City for com-
>   munity recreation activities:
>   a. All permanently operated playground areas which
>   are suitable for community recreation activitie

these areas are to be selected by the Park and Recreation Director of the City of San Diego and approved by the Manager of the City and the Superintendent of the District.

c. The use of such selected school facilities shall be in accordance with the regular procedures of the School District in granting permits for use of school facilities as provided for by laws of California and the rules and regulations of the Board of Education.

d. Schedules shall be established for said use of selected school facilities by designated representatives of the Superintendent of Schools and the City Manager.

IT IS FURTHER AGREED that when an admission charge is made to cover expenses only for a community recreation event in a selected school facility other than the Russ Auditorium, there shall be no rental fee charged to the City.

IT IS HEREBY AGREED that in the event the City shall schedule a community recreation event in the Russ Auditorium and an admission charge is made to cover expenses only, then the District shall charge the City the minimum rental fee as established by the District.

IT IS HEREBY AGREED that a schedule of dates for the use of the School District facilities will be worked out in advance; that this schedule will be so arranged as to avoid any conflict between the school and the Park and Recreation Department use; that in the scheduling of said facilities, school events and programs shall have the first priority and the recreation program established by the Park and Recreation Department shall have second priority and any other events by other groups or agencies shall have third priority.

IT IS FURTHER UNDERSTOOD AND AGREED that this schedule may be changed at the request of either party by the mutual consent of the other.

The City through its employees in the City Park and Recreation Department agrees to provide adequate personnel to supervise the recreation activities which take place after school hours and during holiday and vacation periods at the above selected areas.

It shall be permissible where such activities are beneficial to both school and recreation programs to allow the working hours of the City personnel to be integrated with school hours. In the event such activities are conducted during school hours with school children, the employee of the Park and Recreation Department shall be subject to the administrative authority and supervision of the principal of the school.

IT IS HEREBY UNDERSTOOD that the personnel employed by the City of San Diego in its Parks and Recreation Department shall be under the supervision of the City Park and Recreation Department except as outlined above.

IT IS UNDERSTOOD AND AGREED that school principals are expected to and will advise in the planning and administering of a recreation program to be conducted by the City Park and Recreation Department, on or in the facilities under said principals' jurisdiction.

IT IS RECOGNIZED that school properties and facilities are intended primarily for school purposes and for the benefit of children of school age. It is therefore agreed that, in planning programs and scheduling activities on school grounds, the recreational needs and opportunities of such children will be well provided for and adequately protected.

IT IS FURTHER AGREED that in the event any dispute or difference arises as a result of the recreation program being conducted on the sites jointly used and selected as above outlined or as to the use of school district facility, then, in that event, said dispute or difference shall be settled and arbitrated by appealing to the respective department heads of the School District and the City, in accordance with regular heretofore established procedures.

IT IS FURTHER AGREED that the City Park and Recreation Department will furnish and supply all expendable materials necessary for carrying on a community recreation program for all ages.

IT IS FURTHER UNDERSTOOD AND AGREED that the School District will install and maintain all fences, play apparatus and facilities necessary for its school program and that said equipment, apparatus and facilities may be used by said Park and Recreation Department for community recreation purposes.

IT IS FURTHER UNDERSTOOD AND AGREED that the City Park
and Recreation Department with the approval of the
school board will furnish and supply all the facilities and equipment necessary for the community recreation program which are not included as a requirement for the school program and that, in that event,
the facilities and equipment so furnished may be
used by the school district for school purposes.

IT IS FURTHER AGREED that the School District will provide all the custodial services for auditorium,
gymnasiums, toilets and other indoor facilities
of any school plant used by the City Park and
Recreation Department.

The School District further agrees that it will prepare and maintain the school play areas for regular
school activities and that in the event said school
play areas are used by the City Park and Recreation
Department will prepare and maintain said school
play areas for said recreation activities.

IT IS HEREBY FURTHER AGREED that the City, for and on
behalf of the Park and Recreation Department shall
be responsible for any and all damages to school
property which may be incurred as a proximate result
of any recreation activity being conducted by the
City Park and Recreation Department.

The School District further agrees to inform the proper
officers of the City whenever new school sites are
to be selected so that the City may purchase adjoining property for the location of additional recreational facilities in event the City desires to do
so.

IN WITNESS WHEREOF, The City of San Diego has caused
this agreement to be executed by its City Manager
pursuant to Resolution No. 89539 of the Council of
said City, and the San Diego Unified School District
has caused this agreement to be executed by its
Superintendent and the President of the Governing
Board of the San Diego Unified School District,
San Diego County, State of California, pursuant
to resolution of said governing board, this 7th
day of September, 1948.[2]

                    THE CITY OF SAN DIEGO

[2]State of California Recreation Commission, Public Recreation and Parks in California,
Publication 56-4, 1947, pp. 42-54.

The Jackson County (Missouri) Authorities was allocated approximately 30 acres on Lake Jacomo for development of a Nature Education Center and Wildlife Sanctuary.

The Nature Education Center and Wildlife Sanctuary is intended to serve as the nucleus for an education program providing:

1) Teacher and youth group leader training
2) School class lectures
3) Professional group guidance

In addition, the Nature Center and Wildlife Sanctuary will be organized to provide for and encourage the informal education of family groups and other casual park visitors.

Benefits to be derived from this endeavor are two-fold:

1) Enjoyment of, and appreciation for, the natural environment, which provides the setting for all park activities, will be increased. This is desirable because an appreciation of natural phenomenon must be acquired by most urban residents.
2) Nature education will assure improved consideration for the natural elements--trees, wildflowers, birds and animals; and, as a result, conservation for future generations will be voluntary. An important ramification of this consideration will be an increasing sympathy toward future expansion of park facilities to accommodate our expanding population.

Although cooperation between park, recreation, school and other community authorities is important in every aspect of education and recreation, the authors are concerned primarily in the school-park cooperation in the use of outdoor park areas to supplement the school classroom in instruction related to nature and the out-of-doors. Park administrators are becoming more concerned about human relations and educational techniques as well as the management of the physical aspects of parks. Educational use of parks is a rapid growing trend. The increased demand for multi-purpose use of park facilities to allow for the greatest public good has been a major factor in closer cooperation between park departments and school systems throughout

The Tennessee Conservation Department provide children firsthand and practical experience in conservation on school grounds throughout the state.

Tennessee Conservation Department Photo

the country. In this age of diminishing wilderness lands, rising population, and increasing automation it is imperative that park and school systems explore ways and means of cooperating for the mutual benefit and increased service to the communities which they serve.

The modern trend toward the "Community School" is most appropriate to meet the needs of children in a nation that is fast losing its rural heritage. In such a school the entire community becomes a laboratory for education and recreation for people of all ages and this includes the school building itself. Education cannot afford to be limited to children from age six to eighteen.

The community school reaches out into the community for resources and instructional material to supplement the curriculum with firsthand direct contacts with life. The parks, being available to all people of the community, provide natural laboratories for education. Parks can help the schools in providing human satisfaction and rich education opportunities for the children of the community.

Park directors are quick to realize that the develop-

ment, extension, protection, and wise use of park properties is contingent upon a well-educated citizenry. This new
idea of park-school cooperation in educational ventures
should develop better citizens and should develop better
community solidarity.

Park superintendents today in many cities are employing naturalists and other specialists to conduct educational
projects in cooperation with the schools. Some of the cooperative experiences sponsored by park departments for the
schools include nature trail development, conservation
demonstrations, observation and study of plants, animals,
and soil, horticultural and landscaping activities, school
forests and arboretums, school gardens and farms, wildlife
sanctuaries, amphitheaters and outdoor classrooms, facilities for day and sometimes extended camping experiences
and picnic areas and recreational courts, areas and facilities.

The Conservation Department of the Cook County Forest Preserve District has an outstanding program in outdoor
education for both public schools and adults which was started
in 1945. The Forest Preserve's Conservation Department
has improved both the quantity and quality of natural science
and outdoor education in the public schools. They accomplished this chiefly through public relations and leadership
education. As a result of their work more and more schools
are hiring competent naturalist-teachers. The chief methods
of stimulating interest in outdoor education is through the
publication of a weekly nature bulletin, lectures and movies
on outdoor education to school assemblies, teacher education courses in cooperation with Chicago Teachers College,
demonstration lessons, field trips, pilot studies in the out-
of-doors and day camping.

It is estimated that during the year 1961, the personnel of the Cook County Forest Preserve provided services
for approximately 250,000 children and adults. There are
no means of estimating the numbers reached through the
weekly radio and television programs, and the newspaper
articles which originate from the department.

The park-school plan in Geneva, Illinois, is a good
example of what can happen when a community plans to-

gether for maximum efficiency with minimum cost. The new Geneva Community High School and Civic Center built in 1958 was a fulfillment of the plans and labors of citizens of the Geneva community. The two facilities are united by a common purpose and are joined by a common wall.

In 1954, the Board of Education of the Geneva Community School Unit District asked the University of Chicago to make a survey of the present and future needs of the school district. The new high school-civic center building is a result of the survey. The Civic Center, forming one wing of the new structure, is owned and operated by the Geneva park district. It is available, along with all park facilities, to the high school each day of the school year. It is used after school, evenings, and vacation periods by all organizations. Advanced arrangements are usually made with the park board.

The park-school cooperative plan is made possible in Illinois by legislation passed by the General Assembly in 1955.

> SECTION 1. Whenever the territories of any two or more municipalities in the State of Illinois comprise the same or partly the same territory, the municipalities concerned have the power jointly to purchase land and to construct buildings and all necessary appurtenances within their common corporate limits, and to own, operate and maintain the land and buildings jointly with one another for their joint municipal purposes, on terms and conditions to be agreed upon by the municipalities. Such municipalities have the power to exercise the right of eminent domain formity with the provisions of the constitution and statutes of the state for the acquirement of property, advantageous or desirable for joint municipal purposes.
>
> 2. The purpose of Section 1 is for the benefit of municipalities with common territory and whose building needs can be most efficiently and economically handled by joint buildings for the several municipalities. Section 1 shall be liberally construed to give effect to these purposes.

McClellan Community and Field Community Consolidated Schools in Mt. Vernon, Illinois, are the first elementary schools in the state to cooperate with the Division of Conservation Education, Office of Public Instruction, in tree planting projects.

Photo Courtesy Delo Photo Craft

Glencoe, Illinois, designed their school-park areas for maximum amount of joint use. The landscape plan of the central park-school grouped the school facilities adjacent to the park. The park has been developed for instruction in nature and outdoor education. Areas are designed for school gardens, tree and ornamental planting and nature hikes.

One of the outstanding programs in the United States in which school resources and community resources have been coordinated is found in Flint, Michigan. All of the schools in Flint are considered community schools. A community school is defined as--"a school whose total staff considers that a child is the product of not just the classroom but of his total environment--home, family, recreation, friends, church, the entire community. Therefore, the school, to do the job of educating that child properly, must have an influence on all of these; must help folks to make their community the best community possible."[3]

The two main factors which stimulated the development of the community school concept in Flint, Michigan, were a civic minded group of citizens and financial support from the Charles S. Mott Foundation fund.

[3]Flint Public Schools, Answers to Questions Most Frequently Asked by Visitor to Flint's Community Schools, Flint, Michigan: 9-1-59-V25-SB20, Rev., p. 5.

Many citizens in Flint assumed a dedicated interest in
the educational and social welfare of all its people. They
made a great deal of progress toward improvement of the educational system in the community and were given a tremendous impetus through the establishment and cooperation of
the Mott Foundation.

The Mott Foundation Project is--"A program in community improvement, cooperating with the Flint Board of
Education, whereby the Mott Foundation Program acts as
pioneer for the Board of Education in trying out needed service programs and services for which public funds are not
now available."

The purpose of the Mott Foundation program "is a
'grass roots' long range program of community improvement. It attempts: (1) to make possible the maximum utilization of school buildings and school facilities, as well as
other community resources--personal, material, and organizational; and (2) to act as a 'pilot project' to try out and
to demonstrate to the local Board of Education and to other
communities the possibilities of what may be accomplished;
and (3) by demonstrating what can be done to stimulate constructive influences not only in this community, but eventually in other parts of the state, the nation, and the world."

The fundamental philosophy governing the Mott Foundation is that the program "is committed to the philosophy of
investing its financial resources not in additional buildings
but in the individual by expanding and improving family recreational and educational services and opportunities for the
entire community. Through cooperative effort and a better
understanding of the problems of family and community living, it is hoped Flint may become an increasingly better
place in which to live.

With this type of philosophical approach to education,
one would expect outdoor education to play an important
part in the total education program for the Flint community.

One of the first contributions of the Mott Foundation
program was to establish an education camp. The following
is from the camp brochure:

Mott Camp offers an adventure in living together.
Here in an outdoor setting uncluttered by civilization's attendant social and economic barriers, hundreds of boys and girls from Flint's Community Schools

each year enjoy special programs for special needs,
all guided by a common principle: democratic living.
It is the principle which from the beginning has made
America strong and from which our future strength must
come.

It's regular camping program begins immediately
following the end of the school year in June and closes
just after Labor Day. During the school months the
camp serves as an outdoor "laboratory" for nature study
and as a winter playground for groups of students and
adults.

Camp counselors are students from area colleges.
They are specially selected for their ability to work
with young people and to establish high democratic
standards. For their work at camp it is possible to
receive credit towards their education degrees. Many
later become teachers in Flint's schools.

The Flint educational program has broken the barrier
between the school and the community. The education program and the educational resources of this community have
become centralized and integrated.

Students now range in age from 5 to 90. All students
study community problems, accumulated knowledge in textbooks, literature, nature, and themselves.

In 1958 Flint, Michigan regarded themselves as a
"Mecca of the nation's educators who are seeking new techniques."

Thousands of educators have flocked to Flint to study
and observe the community-school approach to education.

Roseville, Michigan, was one community which quickly accepted and followed the educational pattern established
in Flint, Michigan.

Outdoor education programs are an important and integral part of the community-school approach to education.

There are many educational systems in the United
States which are attempting to fulfill the aims of the community-school educational philosophy. Some schools conduct
cooperative programs with specialized segments of their
community. Many school districts are working cooperatively with other community agencies in developing outdoor education programs.

Detroit, Michigan, is a city which practices close cooperation between the school and park authorities. They
share the cost of a community center which is used by the

school while it is in session and by the park during the time school is not in session. Many teachers are employed for twelve-month periods to work for the park department during the school vacation period. The parks are used for gardening programs and other outdoor education activities throughout the year.

There are many other cities throughout the United States which could be cited for having outstanding park-school programs. Among these cities can be listed Cleveland, Ohio; Columbus, Ohio; Pontiac, Michigan; Rockford, Illinois; Oakland, California; San Diego, California; and Richmond, California.

NATURE AREAS, SCHOOL SANCTUARIES AND OUTDOOR CLASSROOMS

Isaiah knew the value of solitude and the need for areas where man could associate with nature when he sounded his warning centuries ago in his book of the Bible (Isaiah 5:8) "Woe unto them that join house to house, that lay field to field, till there be no place that they may be placed alone in the midst of the earth!"

Modern day educators are alarmed at the fast disappearance of our natural areas and resources in America. They are recognizing the growing concern over man's destruction and waste of his national heritage. Many school administrators are acquiring land for outdoor classrooms in available areas for educational purposes. Galbreath states that:

> Due to the elimination of natural areas by ever-expanding super-highways, suburbia, and industry, there is developing a greater need, in every school and especially in the big high school, for an outdoor laboratory, readily accessible the year round, and dedicated permanently to the study of outdoor biology, where the wise use of natural resources may be studied first hand through scientific and educational investigation.[4]

According to Webster's New World Dictionary, "a sanctuary is a place where animals or birds are sheltered for breeding purposes, and may not be hunted or otherwise molested." Any natural area providing homes for a variety

[4] J. W. Galbreath, "The Value of a Nature Area in Teaching Biology and Conservation," Illinois Educational Press Bulletin, March, 1960, p. 20.

of birds, insects, snakes, and mammals and which may be used to present an educational experience to school children would be an invaluable addition to school property.

Such a reservation may be located adjacent to the school yard as a large wooded site, a grove of trees, or a field of hay or grass. However, there is no need to limit education to the immediate area around the school building. Sanctuaries or natural areas could be located several miles away and be reached by school buses. It must be recognized that larger sites are needed to provide protection and propagation for larger species of wild game. The school sanctuary may be a part of the educational center of the community and thus be located in community parks, or at municipal, private, church or public camp areas. Even a grown-over vacant city lot may provide a storehouse of living things for study. Reynold Carlson states:

> I have for over two years watched a neglected fifty foot lot in a metropolitan area. Here I have observed 28 species of birds, including one ring-necked pheasant; 5 trees, 8 shrubs; and herbaceous plants, not all yet identified, running into the scores. Two snakes, mice, cottontail rabbits, and hundreds of species of insects have been seen there. Through a magnifying glass, I have watched the young aphids being born alive, and the pupae of the lady-bird beetles feeding on the aphids. The drama of life goes on in intensity even in this unsightly, weed filled "vacant" lot.[5]

Schools have potential sanctuaries and nature areas all around them and they need only to locate and develop such an area, into a living classroom.

If facilities are really limited and not even a vacant lot is available, the classroom itself may serve as a sanctuary. The children should be encouraged to bring in pet hamsters, cocoons, fireflies, pollywogs and other interesting phenomena found in their neighborhood for the class members to share with their classmates. Terrariums of small plants and animals or aquariums may in the broadest sense of the word, be considered indoor sanctuaries. Therefore, the possibilities of a school sanctuary open new avenues of learning and understanding in nature study for the children.

[5]Reynold E. Carlson, "Enriching The School Curriculum" The Bulletin of the National Association of Secondary School Principals, May, 1947, p. 127.

What does the school sanctuary contribute to the education of the child? The main purpose served by the school sanctuary is to acquaint pupils with the various plants and animals living in their environment and to give firsthand experiences with them. Through observation and frequent study of these animals, children gain new understandings of life about them. In a school sanctuary the children may identify a variety of birds, insects, and other kinds of life in their natural habitat. They may also study their life habits, their homes, diets, noises, birth processses, and means of locomotion. These and other activities in the school sanctuary may contribute to their knowledge and appreciation of their surroundings. For instance, the children enjoy following animal trails, stalking animals, making plaster casts from animal trails, and feeding the animals. Bird feeders and special foliage may even be used to attract particular birds, insects, or animals, and records may be kept of their patronage of food stations and habits.

These activities may then be coordinated and integrated with the core curriculum areas. For instance in science, the class may study animal cunning and how nature protects animals. They may study the life of an ant or the metamorphasis of a butterfly. The topic of bird migration and wildlife surveys may be used in arithmetic for constructing graphs, reading tables and counting species. Flight patterns, effect of climate and eating habits would concern geography. English may be stimulated by writing poems and accounts of animals, birds and nature. Thus, the natural area or sanctuary can be used to supplement all areas of subject-matter.

Mowier sums up the wide use and great value of nature areas in the following statement:

> Poets of all times and places, most painters and sculptors, the majority of great writers, many abstract thinkers, the greatest scientists have avowed an intimate need of nature. In some of them the thirst for natural things, for the full sky, landscapes, trees, flowers, wild animals, the tang of the autumn wind, the tumbling seas and tranquil lakes, has been an obsession. They have truly fed upon nature in all of its aspects. The implication is clear that severed

from nature, man's imagination and inquiring mind would diminish, perhaps wither utterly.[6]

In Natick, Massachusetts, there is a good example of community effort in establishing a natural area or sanctuary. Natick organized a group of civic leaders, teachers, scout leaders, students and parents to develop a 100 acre city-owned tract into a Natural Science Park. The group organized itself into committees to do research on plants, animals, Indian lore, ecology and other such headings and wrote pocket manuals on the wildlife of the area. Their manuals were then sold to finance the cost of printing. The group made a motion picture showing committees at work and field trip techniques which is available from the American Humane Education Society, 181 Longwood Avenue, Boston 15, Massachusetts.

The campus of Natick High School has a small lake, wooded bluffs of mixed hardwood and softwood species, a natural amphitheater said to be formed by the melting ice of the glacier age, grassy areas, and beautiful natural classrooms with scenic beauty around the lake.

Such a setting provides an ideal outdoor art studio; a wonderful laboratory for study of aquatic life; and a classroom for landscaping, weather stations, bird life and insect study, conservation, nature trails and other learning experiences in the out-of-doors.

The West Lafayette (Indiana) High School has its own outdoor laboratory of 2.8 acres just across the street from the school. Although the land was by no means a sanctuary --it was an unsightly vacant area full of debris and neighborhood junk heap--it has been converted into a beautiful wood land. The entire project was completed by student committees. The biology classes removed the cans and dead trees, burned the paper, and helped in restoring the area to an outdoor education classroom. Student committees secured seedlings from the state nursery and planted the area in a variety of trees, built bird houses and bird feeding stations, made brush-pile protections for wildlife and applied their classroom learning in conservation to practical use. Such activities as identification of trees and shrubs, study of the types and habits of birds and animals and identification and study of insects make the land acquisition a classroom for

[6]Edgar Ansel Mowier, "Sawdust, Seaweed and Synthetics," Saturday Review, December 8, 1956.

nature study close enough to be used by any teacher during a class period.

The John Marshall High School building in Cleveland, Ohio, is built in the form of an "E" with two areas formed between the wings of the building. These two areas have been developed by the conservation classes as an educational project.

One of these plots has been made into a wildlife area. Plants which will provide food and cover for small mammals and birds have been introduced and a heavy cover of small trees and shrubs has been encouraged. Bird feeders have been built and several pairs of birds have nested in the area.

The second area has been developed into a formal garden. Trees and shrubs have been planted around three sides which are bounded by the building. A small bed of roses, two evergreens, and a bird bath are located at the center of the area, while the rest of the ground is covered with a well-tended lawn.

These areas have been established and are used principally by the students in conservation classes. These classes have labeled the trees and shrubs so that the areas can be better used by other students. The conservation students also use these areas in comparing the types of plants and animals which will live in these areas, the type of soil that it formed, and the ability of the soil to retain water.

The state of Maryland is promoting game refuges and sanctuaries throughout the state under the sponsorship of the Department of Game and Inland Fish.

Under this program a landowner may lease from five to twenty-five acres of land from the Department of Game and Inland Fish for a period of five years with option to renew.

The Izaak Walton League has been active in promoting this program by trying to interest individual landowners and organizations in sponsoring a refuge. Resource people from conservation service and the various state departments are available for help in planning the refuge.

The purpose of the refuges is to provide food and protection for small game animals. The refuges, thus, will help to maintain the population of small game in the surrounding countryside.

The Richard Montgomery High School of Rockville, Maryland, sponsors a refuge of twenty-five acres just a mile and a half from their school. Classes from the school are involved in soil preparation, seeding and planting food for wildlife, preparing brush piles and cover for small game maintaining bird feeding stations, operating a tree nursery, and providing maximum soil erosion control.

The Colesville (Maryland) Elementary School sponsors a refuge of ten acres just a few hundred yards from their school ground.

The fifth and sixth grade pupils under adult supervision maintain the refuge. The refuge has a nature trail, a farm pond, feeding stations, and provides opportunities for planting, wildlife study, field trips, nature work and experiences in conservation.

One of the most renowned sanctuary and outdoor education centers is Glen Helen, a 920 acre tract which adjoins Antioch College in Yellow Springs, Ohio. A large portion of the Glen Helen outdoor education center is left to be undisturbed; left completely to nature as a wilderness area. Other sections include nature trails and facilities for outdoor education activities.

The Glen Helen area is used by classes at Antioch College--biology classes for plant and animal life; engineering classes for map making and surveying; art classes for landscape painting; and physical education which has substituted nature hikes and more functional exercises for some of the formal and traditional physical activities.

In addition, area schools have access to the outdoor educational center for use in various educational activities.

The campus of Principia College in Elsah, Illinois, is located on the east bank of the Mississippi River on a 2,100 acre tract. About 1,400 acres of the tract is in timber, some land is cultivated and some is left in a natural state. A large portion of the land is devoted to a game reserve. The college has been engaged in a tree planting program and has acquired samples of most tree planting species of the United States.

A one-room cabin with fireplace and overlooking the river is available for use by both students and faculty.

The area is used most intensely by the biology department. Botany and zoology students study plant and animal life. Several field trips are taken in winter months for identifying animal tracts in the snow, identifying winter birds and making animal and bird census studies. In addition to classroom requirements each student is assigned an outside project such as a weekly bird list, a bird feeding station, bird banding, plaster cast of animal tracts and collection and care of live laboratory specimens.

A general forestry course is offered by the university in the fall where students learn to identify native trees, forestry surveying, tree planting, crusing and marketing and forest management.

The geology classes have a natural laboratory to study the several rock layers exposed in the bluffs along the river. The Mississippi River offers opportunities to study bedding, weathering, erosion and fossils.

There is a very definite trend throughout the United States in various governmental agencies towards a revision of administrative policies governing land use. A large number of Federal agencies now own or control almost one-third of the land in the United States. These lands are managed primarily for conservation and recreational uses. The new trend involves a more concentrated effort in their so-called interpretation programs. This program involves public education on a mass scale towards interpreting the uses for which the land has been acquired. It also involves mass education on proper use and respect for the lands made available for recreation and education.

One of the most effective education programs that can be accomplished by Federal, state and local governmental agencies is through cooperative programs with the public schools.

Many Federal, state and local agencies who are involved in land management have negotiated for cooperative land use with many school districts. The primary purpose for this land use is conservation education, specialized education, and recreation.

Some of the Federal agencies most closely involved in "land for educational use" include the Federal Fish and Wildlife Service, the U. S. Forest Service, the U. S. Corps of Army Engineers, and the National Park Service. At the state level are the State Park Department, State Conservation Departments, State Departments of Public Instruction, and State Agricultural Departments. At the local level are found many city parks, park districts, county forests, and other special district agencies.

Southern Illinois University has contracts for "Educational land use" with the following agencies: The Federal Fish and Wildlife Service, the U. S. Forest Service, the State Department of Conservation, the State Park Department, the Carbondale Park District, and the City of Carbondale.

At one stage in our history (Northwest Ordinance Act - 1783) many public schools were blessed with an abundance of land. Most of this land that was once owned by the schools has long disappeared. Today most schools are starved for land.

It would be well for schools to abandon their closed corporation type of administration. There should be extensive cooperative education with all community, state, and federal agencies who are willing and capable of improving learning for all students.

Selected References

American Association of Health, Physical Education and Recreation, *Outdoor Education For American Youth*, Washington, D. C.: National Education Association, 1957.

Johnston, Verna, *Natural Areas For Schools*, Sacramento: State Department of Natural Resources.

Michigan State University and American Institute of Park Executives *Outdoor Education Through Park-School Programs*, Park Management Series, Bulletin 8, Wheeling, W. Virginia: American Institute of Park Executives.

Recreation Commission, *Public Recreation and Parks in California*, Sacramento: California Recreation Commission, 1947.

The Mott Foundation Program of the Flint, Michigan, Public Schools, *The Flint County Schools*.

Part 3

Outdoor Education and the School Curriculum

But how shall nature be taught;
how shall we guide a child to see
this story as it lies within all growing things?
Not just by precepts, certainly,
or through some formal lessons printed on a page
are such truths learned.
These things are personal.
They must be seen and felt,
not preached about or memorized.

A vase of flowers within a classroom's space,
some autumn leaves arranged upon an altar,
or paintings hung upon the walls
which take one out-of-doors, to look at them.
But better still, an exploration in the fields,
one taken hand in hand with friendly teachers [1]
who have seen, as Moses saw, the burning bush.

—Charles M. Laymon

Good teachers do not teach arithmetic, history, English, or science; they teach children. This statement implies that a good teacher must know more than subject matter, for knowledge is by no means the most important goal of education. In addition to knowing subject matter, a good teacher knows and understands children, knows how to teach, and knows the philosophy and objectives of education. Having a good command of subject matter, although important, does not guarantee that a person will be a good teacher. Some of the poorest teachers are often excellent scholars. How often have we heard, "he knows his subject but he can't get it across!"?

It is imperative that teachers have a good background in child growth and development; that they know the teaching principles and techniques of modern education; and they know the purposes of education in a democratic society.

In order to assure that every teacher knows and understands how their particular subject contributes to the broad general objectives of education it is essential that

[1] *International Journal of Religious Education*, September, 1957, p. 3.

they are involved in formulating objectives and planning these activities.

A faculty that is involved in planning the total curriculum of a school is able to see the relationship of one subject to another and have a better perspective of the total picture of education.

Too many schools have culture so tightly compartmentalized in blocks of subject matter, and too many teachers are so academically entrenched in their own specialty that they see little value in many other subjects of the curriculum. They give little consideration to the modern practice of leaving the classroom for educational purposes. Thus, many teachers who are not involved in planning outdoor education programs look upon school gardens, school forests, school camping and other types of education outside the classroom as a waste of time. Unless all the staff is involved in discussions and planning, teachers cannot be expected to understand or support activities that help interpret subject matter by way of practice and firsthand experience. They need to ask themselves: How can we give expression to knowledge and thereby make it more meaningful? How can we convert knowledge to wisdom?

Reiser states that "the modern university is so often departmentalized that there is no longer any significance to what the university is doing." He further states the need for greater emphasis and more science in another field - social studies:

> Consider the plight of society under the impact of science. Surely one of the fundamental difficulties of our world is that while the scientists are racing toward their specializations, they are failing to do their part in the recreation of social institutions to protect mankind from the harmful use of scientific knowledge. If, as the advertisement informs us, we should "thank science for the miracle drugs of modern medicine," by the same logic we should also "thank science for hydrogen bombs and fallouts and the techniques of biological warfare." Scientists have not greatly helped the world to humanize science and socialize technology. But most tragic of all, scientists have not done what is possible toward integrating

the bodies of knowledge created by science into a unified interpretation of man, his place in nature, and
his potentialities for creating the good society. Instead, they are entombing us in dark and meaningless
catacombs of learning. Scientific knowledge must now
be implified and integrated; through a supreme effort
the vast stores of unified and applied knowledge (mis-
applied) principles must be integrated into a meaningful philosophical synthesis.[2]

Robert Hutchins, in The Higher Learning In America,
complains of too much departmentalization in higher education. He deserves greater credit for spotting the problem
than for his proposal for the solution. His observation is
well taken but the "Great Books" program was hardly the
answer to solving the problem. He states that:

> The modern university may be compared with an encyclo-
> pedia. The encyclopedia contains many truths. It may
> consist of nothing else. But its unity is in much the
> same case. It has departments running from art to
> zoology; but neither the students nor the professors
> know what is the relation of one departmental truth
> to another, or what the relation of one departmental
> truth to those in the domain of another department
> may be.
>   If this indictment is sound, the modern univer-
> sity has little reason for being, except for the ig-
> noble purpose of turning out specialists who are en-
> tombing themselves (and the rest of us) in their dark
> and meaningless catacombs of knowledge.

Ideally, when facts are presented or skills taught they
should not be separated or isolated from the context of a
unit or series of events; subject compartments should be
ignored. In practice, however, this is most difficult.
    With the invention of the printing press and the advent
of scientific thinking, events and phenomena have been
classified and logically filed in textbooks and moved to
libraries and classrooms. Think of the valuable experiences and education that was gained by the scholars as they

[2]Oliver L. Reiser, The Integration of Human Knowledge, Boston: Porter Sargent
Publisher, 1958, p. 3.

gathered data and classified knowledge for use in the class-room! Then think of the plight of the modern day student who must learn this same knowledge second, third or fourth-hand from the printed page. Education has become over the centuries a dull and dry process. The fun of exploration and experimentation has been taken away. The chief requirement for a student of today to graduate from the public schools and colleges is to be able to read and memorize.

Rather than going outside to learn firsthand from na-ture, it has become more convenient to teach from the text-book in a formal atmosphere. It has become more conveni-ent to teach en masse and teach the same thing to every pupil in a particular grade. Convenience has caused the education process to take the whole apart, divide it into separate subjects and teach each one of them as something as an end in itself. The history teacher is not concerned about English and the English teacher is not interested in the progress her students are making in history. It is the failure of students in putting these separate compartments back together in a sensible whole as they were in the begin-ning that accounts for so many graduates who have plenty of knowledge but not enough wisdom to be regarded as truly educated. The late Alfred North Whitehead states that: "Education is the acquisition of the art of the utilization of knowledge." The use to which the student puts his knowl-edge is as important as the knowledge itself.

One of the chief values of outdoor education is its unique contribution to every subject area in the curriculum. The creative teacher has a tool in outdoor education which can vitalize, enrich, interpret, and give meaning and under-standing to her particular area of study or subject matter. Bookish abstractions become concrete and practical con-cepts. The printed page becomes meaningful as what is read about becomes real experience. Firsthand and direct experience with things real stimulate children to read fur-ther about what they discover for themselves. Furthermore outdoor education helps the teacher to show how her subject matter is an integrated part of the whole and is not an iso-lated area. By learning from nature, children see the rela-tionships and interrelatedness of one subject area to another of man to nature and man's dependence on nature for his existence.

The modern school curricula is under attack from all sides. Much of this criticism is just and many educators themselves are concerned with the seemingly unpreparedness of the public school graduates. The chief criticism of the school curricula are:

1. The curriculum is too remote from the students' daily life outside the school. Schools do not give enough consideration to the everyday living of the pupils. Too, frequently the school maintains an academic atmosphere so remote from actual life that students can see no connection between it, the home, and the community. The schools also fail to articulate other agencies which are serving youth.

2. The curriculum is not sufficiently adjusted to modern life. Too many phases of courses of study are unrelated to the lives pupils live. The problems given them to solve in school are not the same as those they encounter in their daily lives. They are asked to write on subjects which are impractical, and to engage in activities which have little or no carry over value.

3. The curriculum does not reflect the ambitions, drives, and interests of pupils. It often ignores the most urgent desires of youth save those of the more academically minded students.

4. The curriculum is not sufficiently adapted to the individual differences of the pupils. Pupils are often treated as groups, as the college-preparatory group or the vocational group, rather than as individuals, and no provisions are made to meet the needs and interests of all youth.

5. The curriculum has not kept pace with the latest developments in psychology and education. Through the medium of research, the most desirable practices are determined and evaluated, but educational practice lags far behind the discovery of new truths. For example, it is doubtful that the chief psychological theories on which the traditional curriculum was based can be used to justify the existence of courses of little worth in and of themselves. No longer can the average child be expected to apply the facts taught in the classroom

284

to life situations without assistance, for transfer does not take place automatically by the mira-
culous process of studying something hard, uninteresting, and unrelated to life.

6. The present curriculum gives too little attention
to emotional and social attitudes and to mental
hygiene. In many cases, these play a more important part in the development of youth than do their
intellectual interests and vocational intentions.

7. The traditional curriculum has failed to produce
integration. Life adjustment problems do not come
in little subject-matter packages. It would be
almost an impossibility for one to find a problem
involving one subject only for its solution. If
pupils are to be taught to solve problems which
are worthwhile to them and are to develop integrated personalities, it cannot be done by dividing the phases into small parts, isolating and
presenting phases for use when needed. Pupils'
ability to do this would involve a great ability
to transfer materials learned in one situation to
another and also to organize the materials for use.

8. Schools have not placed enough emphasis on the
development of moral and spiritual values. This
does not mean that religion should be taught directly, although some advocate it, but that indirectly, through the medium of the entire school
program, greater emphasis should be placed on
developing higher values, better attitudes, and
moral character.

9. Citizenship has not been stressed or taught properly. This means, not that it has not been accepted as an abstraction, but rather that it has
not been taught so that the development of appropriate attitudes and skills which will be practiced is the ultimate aim. The same criticism
has been voiced about the teaching of democracy.[3]

In an attempt to meet the criticisms of education, educators are searching for ways and means of making the curriculum more useful and meaningful to the students. In this
search many have turned to the community and to activities

[3]Bent, Rudyard K. and Kronenberg, Henry H., _Principles of Secondary Education_,
(New York: McGraw-Hill Book Company, Inc., 1955) pp. 247-248.

and life outside the classroom. Outdoor education as a technique for program enrichment is now being recognized by leaders in education as a vital and important force for education.

The opportunities for teaching in the out-of-doors is not the heritage of any one specific subject matter teacher. Outdoor education transcends subject matter divisions. It may be used by all teachers in all subjects. It is not to be used just for the sake of keeping up with the modern trend in education. If it has no contribution to make to a specific learning unit it obviously should not be used. The skilled teacher will use the outdoors just as he or she uses audio-visual aids, reference materials, or any other aids to learning--when it is needed or when it can make a contribution to the unit of study. It behooves every teacher to explore the educational possibilities offered in the out-of-doors. Today, more than any other period in history, with the practice of compulsory education, with stress on democratic living and with the modern philosophy of education for living, the creative classroom teacher is constantly in search for activities and techniques for making learning real and meaningful to the students.

Chapter 10

SOCIAL STUDIES

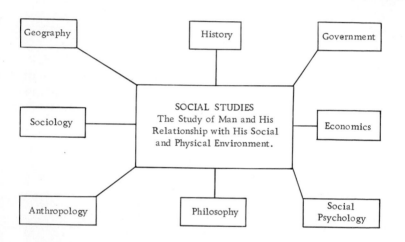

Social studies are the study of man and his relationships with his social and physical environment. To understand and evaluate social studies in relation to the whole
curriculum, it is necessary to interpret the role it plays
in the entire educational process. Rugg and Kreuger see
the social studies as, "all those activities and materials
which are needed for an understanding of modern civilization and their historical development. They form a broad
department which is coordinate with the natural and physical
sciences, the creative arts and the language arts of reading,
literature, writing, etc. Thus the social studies comprise

Children at the Southern Illinois University camps gain experience in constructing their own shelters. Erecting a teepee under the guidance of an adult counselor involves communication, arithmetic, social living, health and physical activity.

the intellectual care of the entire school curriculum. "[1]

Social Studies in its broadest sense represents a body of instructional materials which promotes human relationships. It draws from many areas which were traditionally taught as geography, history, economics, civics, sociology, anthropology, social psychology, and philosophy. Today, in the elementary school where subject-matter barriers are of less consequence, the instructional materials are organized around the social needs and interests of the children. The social studies program is one of the focal points around which the experience of children are organized.

In more advanced grades or as the student increases his skill in relating one subject area with another, the social studies materials are classified and organized into logical areas of study; students usually choose only one such area as a major on the college level. There is a trend, however, to fuse all subjects relating to man and his relations with man and his environment into one interrelated whole. Educators have tended to eliminate subject-matter lines in the social studies to give students a more realistic approach to the complex problems of modern society. Solutions to the problems of today require an understanding of the many facets of learning and an understanding of the cause-effect relationship which cuts across all subject-matter areas. Geography, government, history, sociology, economics and similarly designated subjects are too closely related and have too many interacting forces to be taught successfully as an entity.

An examination of several good teaching guides reveals general agreement on the definition and purposes of the social studies. Typical definitions are found in curriculum guides used in the California schools:

> The social studies are those studies that provide understandings of the physical environment and its effects upon man's ways of living, of the basic needs of man and the activities in which he engages to meet his

---

[1]Rugg, H. O. and Kreuger, Louise. The Social Studies In The Elementary School. A Tentative Course of Study.

needs, and of the institutions man has developed to perpetuate his way of life.[2]

The social studies are the knowledge, activities, and skills required of an individual to be effective as a person and as a member of groups. The social studies pertain to the relations of human beings--men, women, children--to one another and to the physical environment in which they live, work, and play.[3]

The report of the Commission on Social Studies contains four pertinent statements with regard to the nature and function of social studies:

1. The social sciences take as their province the entire range of human history, from the earliest times down to the latest movement, and the widest reaches of contemporary society, from the life and customs of the most remote peoples to the social practices and cultural possessions of the immediate neighborhood.

2. The social sciences thus embrace the traditional disciplines which are concerned directly with man and society, including history, economics, politics, sociology, geography, anthropology, and psychology. Each of these disciplines possesses an intrinsic nature and a core of substantial data and inferences, and yet all are intimately interrelated in their several approaches to a common goal - the knowledge of man and society.

3. Without wishing to emphasize what has been called "the conventional boundaries" between the several social disciplines - boundaries which have never been treated as rigid and which of late have been increasingly and very profitably cut across - the Commission repudiates the notion that any general or comprehensive social science has been created which transcends the disciplines themselves. Each of these branches of scholarship furnishes a distinctive point of view from which materials are surveyed and brought into an organization of knowledge; each contributes in

[2] _The Social Studies Program for the Schools of California_. Sacramento: State Department of Education, 1948, p. 3.
[3] _Teaching Guide, Social Studies, Kindergarten through Grade Six_. San Francisco: Public Schools, 1947, p. 11.

its own way to general human insight into the world of man and society.

4. The main function of the social sciences is the acquisition of accurate knowledge of, and informed insight into, man and society; that of social science instruction is the transmission of such knowledge and insight, with attendant skills and loyalties, to the individuals composing society.[4]

OBJECTIVES OF SOCIAL STUDIES[5]

Knowledges and Understandings

1. Growing understanding of the American heritage, including a knowledge of the historical development of the United States, an understanding of the principles which have fostered our way of life, and a grasp of the methods by which Americans have solved their social and economic problems.
2. Increasing knowledge of our form of government and the laws and freedoms under which we live.
3. Increasing knowledge of the geographical environment in which men live, both in this country and in other countries and areas of the world, and increasing understanding of the growing interdependence of men everywhere in development and use of human and natural resources.
4. Increasing understanding of the cultures of various people of the world and the relationship of those cultures to our own (social institutions, religion, arts, government, resources, ways of making a living, family life, and the like).
5. Increasing understanding of social concepts, generalizations, and principles through which men seek to control experience. Such concepts, generalizations, and principles may be illustrated from several points of view. In the field of science, for example, the principle of contour plowing is em-

[4]Conclusions and Recommendations, Report of the Commission on Social Studies, Charles Scribner's Sons, pp. 6-7.

[5]Denver Public Schools. "The Social Studies Program of the Denver Public Schools," Denver, Colorado: Department of Instruction, 1954, pp. 3-4. Used by permission.

ployed in the conservation of soil and water on sloping land; in social science we extend the concept of environment adaptation to include the principle that the movement of peoples is usually in the direction of increased food, water supply, or vocational advantage. In sociological matters one may use to advantage the principle that giving equal opportunity to all individuals is basic to the development of a democratic society.

Values and Ideals

1. Growing faith in the democratic way of life; respect for the dignity and worth of individual personality; joint thinking and action in the solution of common problems; use of intelligence in guiding behavior.
2. Growing respect for the ideals of fair play and generous behavior, the ideals of human brotherhood.
3. Growing desire to be an active citizen of school, community, state, nation, and world.
4. Growing sense of responsibility for the welfare of others and a willingness to sacrifice for the common good.
5. Loyalty to basic institutions of our country; democratic family; government under laws of the people, by the people, and for the people; free public education.
6. Loyalty to basic traditions of freedom, as expressed in the Bill of Rights.

Skills and Habits

1. Growing skills in cooperative planning and action in school and community.
2. Growing skills in solving human problems by use of the scientific method--identifying problems, finding facts and feelings, setting up possible solutions, trying out various suggestions, choosing the most likely, evaluating results, recognizing new problems.
3. Growing awareness of the feelings and problems of others.
4. Growing respect for self and for others.
5. Growing recognition that for every privilege we enjoy, there is an accompanying responsibility to self and to society.

6. Growing recognition of unresolved issues in many aspects of human relationships and the faith that these issues may be solved through democratic processes. Such issues are seen in the tension between East and West in international relations, problems of fair employment practice, states rights equal opportunities in education, housing, and intergroup relations.

SOCIAL STUDIES SEQUENCE

The content of the social studies is designed to fit the maturation level of the child. In the primary grades the social studies sequence consists almost entirely of firsthand experiences. The children explore their environment, learn about the activities in the school and of people immediately around them.

As the child matures and his interest develops his awareness is extended to broader community life. His previous experience plus his newly acquired skill in reading enables him to enlarge his understanding of the environment. Before he leaves the elementary school, the child knows of his state, his nation and the world community.

A good example of using the experience of children as a focal point for presenting social studies and for utilizing the principle of widening horizons as a basis for grade placement is found in Philadelphia. [6]

Kindergarten and Grade I

Living at Home and in School

1. Having fun together
2. My home
3. How mother helps us
4. How can we help at home?
5. People who help us in school
6. Caring for ourselves
7. Exploring our school

---

[6] A Guide to Social Studies in the Elementary School. Philadelphia Public Schools, Curriculum Office, 1950.

8. Caring for our pets
9. When company comes
10. Let's be safe
11. Let's get ready for (the coming season)

Grade II

Living in the Neighborhood

1. Let's be good neighbors
2. How do we have fun in our neighborhood?
3. Many people help us in our neighborhood
4. Plants and animals live in our neighborhood zoo
5. How can my family help my neighbors?
6. Helpers who come to our door
7. Signs in our neighborhood
8. Finding out about our neighborhood
9. Celebrating holidays in our neighborhood
10. Workers for health and safety

Grade III

The Wider Community

1. We need the farmer
2. Food from the sea
3. Many people help to build our homes
4. How do we get our clothes?
5. Where does our grocer get his products?
6. Wires and pipes join my house to the world
7. Plants and animals give us many things
8. People work and play together in our community

Grade IV

Living in our City

1. Everyone shares in city planning
2. Having fun in Philadelphia
3. Highways, waterways, and airways in Philadelphia
4. How Philadelphians are fed
5. The communities in our city
6. How do Philadelphians earn a living?
7. Philadelphia--birthplace of our nation
8. Being good neighbors in Philadelphia
9. Going to school in our city

Grade V

Life in Our State and Union

1. People in Pennsylvania live in big cities, in small towns, and on farms
2. Pennsylvania today and in colonial times
3. How inventions have changed American life
4. The United States--a nation of neighbors from all parts of the world
5. The sections of our nation are interdependent
6. Life in American river valleys
7. Let's make democracy work
8. Spending a vacation in the United States
9. Our nation's natural resources help the world

Grade VI

Living in the World

1. Nations exchange goods and ideas
2. People need houses the world over
3. The United Nations builds its first home
4. Are we good world neighbors?
5. The airplane brings people closer together
6. Protecting and sharing the world's treasures
7. We are a world family
8. Our debt to the past
9. People everywhere celebrate holidays

PRESENT TRENDS IN SOCIAL STUDIES[7]

An examination of several curriculum guides in social studies shows several distinct trends. These trends are well formulated as following:

Toward increased:

1. Understanding and utilization of the potentialities of the individual
2. Respect for the uniqueness of the individual personality

[7] Kalamazoo Public Schools, Comprehensive Curriculum Guide For Elementary Teachers, Kalamazoo: Department of Instruction and Guidance, 1959, pp. 9-10.

3. Use of needs and interests of the learner in planning the curriculum
4. Emphasis on good human relations in the home, school, community, commonwealth, nation and world
5. Understanding and appreciation of the principles, practices, and ideals of democracy
6. Cooperative planning of teachers and pupils on major objectives and daily procedures
7. Practical experience in democratic procedures and cooperative living
8. Understanding of world organization and cooperation
9. Consideration of practical civic, economic, and and social situations
10. Ability to adjust to life situations
11. Individual responsibility and adjustment to desirable change
12. Understanding and improving of present day living through the study of our historical heritage
13. Functional use of skills
14. Use of a variety of materials and methods
15. Use of facts for critical thinking and problem solving
16. Use of community resources for curriculum development
17. Organization of the curriculum into large themes or units
18. Integration, correlation, and continuity of subject matter
19. Postponement of vocational training and college preparatory courses

THE TEACHING OF SOCIAL STUDIES

Social studies are concerned with the interaction and interdependence among men, the adjustment between man and his environment and the relationship of man and his community to the rest of the world and to the universe.

296

In the past, teachers have taught book knowledge in classes
such as history, civics and geography with little or no effort
to relate them one to another. If a student could memorize
and relate dates of historical events, name the states and
capitols in prescribed order, and repeat the pledge of allegiance, the preamble to the constitution and the bill of
rights, he was considered a good social studies student.

Education was a preparation for life and was concerned with acquiring the tools for living later. As Kelly
so aptly puts it:

The child . . . "works by himself, at a desk, so
much alone as though he were not surrounded by many
other social beings. Of course we have some trouble keeping him from being social, and to the extent that he is social, we regard him as an undesirable student. The one
who pays the least attention to the fact that he is surrounded
by other social beings is the one we value most. Particularly undesirable is the one who either gives help to or receives help from another social being."[8]

In recent years teachers have become increasingly
aware that a classification of social studies into special
fields such as geography, civics, history and economics
left much to be desired in the teaching of many important
phases of social living. Social living relates to the whole
of current social process and not to small isolated segments.
It is impossible for children to live democratically or have
an intelligent appreciation of the broad area of human relations in modern society with a segmented and textbookish
approach. Isolated knowledge and facts which are designed
to foster a democratic way of life have too often become
more important than the end for which it is taught. Small
wonder that graduates of our public schools have such an
apathetic attitude and so little interest in government. How
can we say our social studies curriculum has been effective
when a 50 per cent turnout of eligible voters at the polls in
an important national election is considered a good turnout?

Today, educators realize that a child may remember
facts and even understand all things necessary to receive

[8]Earl C. Kelley, Education For What Is Real, New York: Harper and Brothers, 1947,
p. 19.

Children find evidence of geological history at Glen Helen Outdoor Education Center of Antioch College, Yellow Springs, Ohio.

Photo Courtesy of Jean Sanford

good marks in social studies and still be a social misfit in the classroom and on the playground. Educators are beginning to ask of what use is knowledge if it does not change the lives of children to make them happier and more capable of desirable social living. Education is beginning to mean changed behavior and not high marks on report cards.

With this approach social studies is concerned not only with a textbook and its content, but with the student and his understanding of his social world--his home, community, nation, world, universe, and past history. All of these things have a bearing on his present social, economic, and political improvement. With this concept the teacher begins with the child and not the textbook. The textbook becomes a means--and only one of many--to an end, to imbue the pupils with a sense of community responsibility and an awareness of the world in which they live so that they may lead useful lives as parents and citizens.

Social studies, in the modern school curriculum,

stresses care and life-situation programs with increased consideration of man's social development as a whole. Thus, a social studies program is presented, not in segmented subjects, but as a whole with history, civics, geography, economics, as well as science, art, music and literature interwoven with socialized aspect of the child's behavior.

The schools are working increasingly with the home, the church, the recreation department and all community agencies in helping children in their relations with other children, their parents, and their community. Democratic behavior, good sportsmanship and acceptance of responsibility (sharing, leading, following) are the ends to which knowledge of the social studies is put to use.

The social studies room in the modern-day school has been converted from a recitation room into an activity room where children learn by doing rather than merely repeating facts. Children learn best to work together if the teacher guides them into actual group experiences. They learn democracy, not by studying about it, but by living it. Educators have learned that some of the children's best learning occurs when they are actively engaged in discussions and activities. This is not to say that reading from a textbook, working alone, or listening are to be abandoned as educational techniques, but they are to be used along with many other techniques to enhance the teaching and achieve the objectives of social studies.

The curriculum of the social studies recognizes that children are not complete neophytes when they enter school but have much pre-school experience on which to build. By building on these experiences from year to year, the child's understanding of himself, his classmates, and his community is extended. A developmental plan of accepting the child where he is, as he is, starting with the home, then the school, extending to the community, the city, the state, the nation, the world and the universe, is the most acceptable method of teaching cooperation, critical judgment, responsibility, and other fundamentals necessary for wholesome living in a democracy. The developmental curriculum in social studies should be organized on a plan which specifies large areas of study at each year of the child's school experience.

All phases of the child's life should be related and closely interwoven throughout each of the broad areas of study. It is impossible to separate any phase of social living from transportation, communication, food, shelter, clothing, government, arts, and in short, life itself.

The primary grades relate social studies to the home, the school, the community. It shows students their relationship with parents, teachers, classmates, the policeman, milkman and other people in their lives.

Activities, discussions, and reading in the primary grades are centered on life in the home, the school and the community; occupations of the parents; proper respect, care and use of property at home, school and in the community; respect for parents, teachers and each other; how farmers help us live in cities and how the city workers help each other and the farmer; how people lived long ago; comparison of life then and now; and other interests close to the lives of the primary grade student.

The young child is curious about many things and the social studies program cannot be set up in definite prescribed units or according to specialized areas of study. The curriculum in the primary grades is not divided into various isolated areas for here the teacher cannot successfully teach isolated facts. Children cannot relate them either to experience or knowledge. Their interest is wide and their explorations cannot be contained in separate subject matter compartments. Some of our very best teaching in American schools today is found in the primary grades. Furthermore, it is generally agreed that as the child progresses to the upper grades, the caliber of teaching gets progressively worse, this is primarily due to the educational methods employed. Passive education replaces activity. Children are required to conform more to prescribed rules. They read more and see less; they listen more and talk less; they memorize more and originate less; they are tested more and taught less; and they are graded according to their ability not to think but to memorize, not to lead but to follow and not to live democracy but to study about it.

As children grow older their learning horizon is widened and they want to know more about other nations and the people who live there. They become more interested in world people and world affairs. They have watched television programs in the home and now can read of people of other lands. They not only relate the past to the present but become more and more aware of the interdependence of man as he lives on this earth and shares his cultures and knowledge to the improvement of world brotherhood.

By the time children reach junior high school, they should begin to realize their civic advantages and responsibilities. They should be aware of their place and their nation's place in the total world picture. They are ready for a more chronological study of man's history both past and present; the sequence of events leading to present conditions and the geographic and economic influences upon the development of the United States and other countries.

When the student enters high school, he should have developed a basic understanding of his total environment. He should have acquired a good fund of knowledge and understanding in the various areas of social studies, but more important still he should demonstrate that he has learned to be a responsible member of his home, his school and his community--in short, a good citizen of a democratic form of government.

The major function of the social studies and the major responsibility of the entire school is twofold: (1) to educate children for enlightened citizenry, and (2) to convince children that democracy is the best way of life. The school's task is to lay the intellectual and moral foundations for an understanding of what democracy means and what it demands of its citizens.

Every teacher, administrator and staff member of the school system has a joint responsibility of educating all children to live in a democracy. This is not easy. Democracy means so many things to so many people. Too many people go through life demanding their rights as stated in the constitution, but are not willing to give something in return. There are too many political bosses, too many selfish interest groups, too many lobbies and too little interest among the rank and file to correct these and other undemocratic practices.

Although every teacher must teach democracy and must democratically teach, it is the major responsibility of the social studies to build concepts, insights and understandings which will make his rights and obligations correlative ideas. Rickover states that:

> The student will have attained full political maturity when he realizes that he is personally responsible for making democracy work and has no excuse if his country is badly governed; when he overcomes the myopia that afflicts persons who are wholly centered on self; when he attains the long-range vision that lets him see that the national interest is part and parcel of his own personal interest.[9]

Any nation that hopes to perpetuate itself must call upon its school system to indoctrinate its young people with the beliefs which underlie its political philosophy. In the early thirties, the Nazi party in Germany dismissed teachers who were anti-Nazi, and staffed the schools with teachers who could be trusted to teach the political doctrines of Nazism.

Similarly the Communist party in the U.S.S.R. took over the school system and captured the minds of the youth of that nation for communism.

The public schools of the United States is the nearest approach to a classless society that can be found in any part of the world. Each child has as near equality of opportunity as their native endowments and home environments allow. Skill and scholastic ability, and not social status or wealth, are the deciding factors in making the athletic team or in making the honor roll. In spite of an ideal climate for teaching democracy, the schools are not succeeding.

Democracy is losing ground in the battle for free government because its schools are failing to foster patterns of behavior and intelligent self-expression necessary for its survival. As Hightower points out, "Education in America must build within all individuals it touches, a love for the democratic way of life based on the freedom of the individual,

---

[9] H. G. Rickover, "Democracy: The Subject Our Schools Don't Teach," McCalls Magazine, March, 1962, p. 126.

as well as the needs of the social group. The love of this way of life presupposes the assumption of the responsibilities as well as the rights of free men."[10]

SOCIAL STUDIES AND OUTDOOR EDUCATION

Much has already been written in other portions of this book concerning activities and experiences which can be used to foster democratic living by way of outdoor education. Outdoor education provides a very realistic laboratory for teaching social studies. The outdoor education program causes things to happen. It brings the student in contact with nature, with community life, with other children, with objects and things. Reactions occur; attitudes are formed, social relationships occur; observation and investigation take place; and through first-hand direct experiences the educational goals in the social studies field are being accomplished.

When students observe social studies content after reading about it, they learn better and comprehend more. The teacher must work with the pupils, gradually allowing children more freedom to work on their own, on committees, or in groups so that they may realize the value and satisfactions that can come from doing things on their own with a minimum of interference. Experienced teachers will start with short term committee assignments, short hikes and trips on the school ground or nearby park. Later, the teacher will guide her pupils into long term assignments requiring greater skill in working together and in sharing and accepting responsibility.

Classroom recitation and classroom audio-visual aids are a poor substitute for actual learning by travel and observation. Effort should be made to study the earth and its people, rather than to study a book and its contents. School journeys, forests, farms, and other outdoor activities not only provide an effective means of learning history, geo-

[10] Howard W. Hightower, "The School - Its Social Role," Progressive Education, January, 1948.

graphy, economics, and culture of the community, but provide important group experiences in learning to work together, to share responsibilities and to cooperate in carrying out worth-while projects to a successful conclusion. Trips to abandoned farms give vivid illustrations of the changes in modern living and under the guidance of a skilled teacher can lead to worthwhile projects, readings, reports, and discussion of life fifty or a hundred years ago. Likewise, a visit to a modern farm may be used to stress the importance of land management and conservation, changes brought about in farming methods and the place of the farmer in modern society.

Children participating in the government of a camp and assuming civic leadership and responsibility as they develop social skills are learning something about democracy.

The democratic spirit that prevails in a camp run by qualified teachers is the very basis of learning to live with others. Democracy is founded on the premise that man can and will think; education for living in a democratic society needs to teach children to think, give them facts and experiences on which to base their thinking and offer them opportunities to practice skills in human relations. School camping offers a superb opportunity for this phase of education. It serves as a facility as well as a method. The outdoors serve as a laboratory for acquiring knowledge of the universe and self-preservation; it presents opportunities for living with others, for the development of individual responsibility, and for acquiring skills through knowing, thinking, feeling, and doing.

Education is going on constantly in the camp. The classroom is the outdoors and it is a 24-hour a day educational experience and is the most natural method of education.

Among the experiences and opportunities which outdoor education provides the social studies teacher are:

> Developing initiative in making choices
> Identifying oneself with others
> Respecting the rights of others
> Sharing materials, tools and ideas

Solving problems cooperatively
Experiencing success and failure
Sharing responsibilities
Respecting group decisions
Participation in democratic government
Accepting criticism and suggestions graciously
Developing a realization of the individual's relationship to a group
Experiencing leadership
Working with others
Gaining self-reliance, self-control and self-respect
Gaining self-confidence through contributions to group
Learning about renewable and non-renewable natural resources activities
Learning about the depletion of natural resources
Learning about the restoration of natural resources
Learning how the government helps develop, control and protect natural resources
Learning about the agencies which contribute to the wise use of natural resources
Understanding the effect of natural resources upon population distribution
Understanding the effect of natural resources upon the history of civilization
Searching for Indian relics and learning about Indians
Visiting historical sites
Interviewing old settlers
Learning map reading and construction
Countless other activities

Selected References

Association for Childhood Education International, *Social Studies for Children,* Bulletin No. 97, Washington, D. C.: The Association, 1956.

Commission of Secondary School Curriculum, *The Social Studies in General Education,* New York: Progressive Education Association, 1940.

Commission on Social Studies, *Conclusions and Recommendations,* New York: Charles Scribners' Sons, 1936.

Denver Public Schools, *The Social Studies Program of the Denver Public Schools,* Denver: Department of Instruction, 1954.

Educational Policies Commission, *Purposes of Education in American Democracy,* Washington, D. C.: National Education Association, 1938.

Ellsworth, Ruth and Sand, Ole, *Improving the Social Studies Curriculum,* Twenty-sixth Yearbook, Washington, D. C.: National Council for the Social Studies, 1955.

Hamilton, Jean F., "New Trends in the Social Studies Textbooks," *The Grade Teacher,* May, 1952.

Hightower, Howard W., "The School--Its Social Role," *Progressive Education,* January, 1948.

Jarslimek, John, *Social Studies in Elementary Education,* New York: The Macmillan Company, 1959.

Kelley, Earl C., *Education for What is Real,* New York: Harper and Brothers, 1947.

Lee, Murray J. and Lee, Dorris May, *The Child and His Curriculum,* New York: Appleton-Century-Crofts, Inc., 1950.

Michaelis, John U., *Social Studies for Children in a Democracy,* Second Edition, New York: Prentice-Hall, 1956.

Miel, Alice and Brogan, Peggy, *More Than Social Studies: A View of Social Learning in the Elementary School,* Englewood Cliffs, N. J.: Prentice-Hall, 1957.

National Council for the Social Studies, *Education for Democratic Citizenship,* Washington, D. C.: The Council, 1952.

Preston, Ralph C., *Teaching Social Studies in the Elementary School,* Revised Edition, New York: Rinehart and Company, Inc., 1958.

San Francisco Public Schools, *Teaching Guide, Social Studies, Kindergarten Through Grade Six,* San Francisco: Department of Instruction, 1947.

Stratemeyer, Florence B., Forkner, Hamden L., and
    McKim, Margaret G., *Developing a Curriculum for
    Modern Living,* New York: Bureau of Publications,
    Teachers College, Columbia University, 1947.
Tiegs, Ernest W. and Adams, Fay, *Teaching the Social
    Studies--A Guide to Better Citizenship,* Boston: Ginn
    and Company, 1959.

Chapter II

COMMUNICATIONS

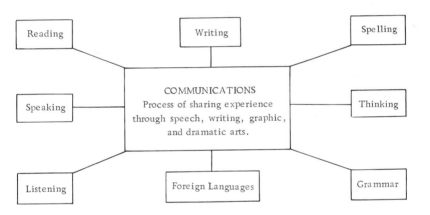

Reading and writing are skills that have been stressed since the beginning of formal education. They were the one and two components of the old traditional school program of "Readin', Ritin', and Rithmetic" which has been known through the years as the "three R's."

In the early colonial schools and, in fact, up until recent years instruction in the language arts was largely devoted to developing the mechanical skills of reading, spelling and writing.

The language art program in the modern school is built on a much broader base. New and faster means of communications must be mastered by man if he is to be able to be a self-sufficient citizen of democracy. The challenge of the telephone, radio, television, motion pictures

brings newer perspectives to education. Language arts
in the modern school are developed in relation to the whole
personality and are inseparable from social, physical and
mental development. In the modern age of mass media in
communication, children must learn more than reading and
writing. They must learn to listen and evaluate critically
what they hear. The ability to think is very closely related
to language arts. Children must learn to read with comprehension and discrimination. They must be able to express
their ideas in writing so that others may read and understand them. In short, the language arts program must (1)
develop the abilities of children to express their ideas and
feelings, and (2) to receive and interpret messages.

Language is the child's principal means of expression
and is used in relation to all his activities both in school and
out. Language is a social instrument. There are at least
three good reasons why the child must have a good command
of the skills of communication:

1. Language is a means of communicating ideas to
   others.
   If a child is incompetent in conveying ideas
   to others either orally or written it is obvious
   that his effectiveness in social living is seriously handicapped. He does not have the means of releasing personal feelings; of developing understanding of others; of sharing ideas with others, and of
   satisfactory participation in social undertakings.

2. Language is a tool for learning.
   Thinking is an active mental process which the
   pupil carries on by means of language--either
   through communication with others or with himself.
   In building on to an idea the pupil verbally re-
   calls his own experience, and establishes relationships and silently makes tentative statements and
   evaluates them. In short, the child must be able
   to express ideas to himself as well as to others
   in order to be able to learn.

3. Skill in language arts fosters security, confidence
   and poise which enhances growth and development.
   Communication of ideas are so closely tied to
   social relationships that a person's cultural or intellectual level is often judged by his language

performance. Failure and insecurity seriously retard his social and emotional development. Skills in language arts, then, are essential for good personality development.

THE LANGUAGE ARTS CURRICULUM

An examination of curriculum guides from cities throughout the nation reveals great uniformity in the philosophy and purposes of instruction in language arts. Lee and Lee list nineteen basic principles which may guide the work of a teacher in the instruction of the language arts:[1]

1. Language is that mode of social behavior whose primary function is communication.
2. No worthwhile language experience takes place without thought.
3. Giving the child rich and varied experience is of first importance. When firsthand experience is impossible, vicarious experience should be provided.
4. Expect child to use his experiences as a basis for thinking, saying, and writing.
5. Expression is a reflection of the general personality pattern.
6. The program of language should center upon content rather than form.
7. Excessive and premature emphasis on formal correctness may prove to be an actual deterrent.
8. Language is learned like any other mode of social behavior.
9. Language must be considered a part of every school activity and not limited to artificial situations during the language period.
10. Language development is best accomplished through a purely functional approach in which expression follows experience in purposeful activity.
11. Artificial stimulation of basic language structure is almost fruitless, for structure appears to be the outgrowth or expression of experience and maturity.

[1]Lee, Murray and Lee, Dorris May, The Child and His Curriculum, (Third Edition) New York: Appleton-Century-Crofts, Inc., 1960, pp. 287-88.

12. Language should be developed in a free and informal atmosphere.
13. Departure from the literary standards does not necessarily lead to the corruption of language.
14. Corrective language work is done individually.
15. Drill work should be in terms of, and as a result of, an established need which is realized by the children as well as the teacher.
16. Good emotional health is fundamental to good speech development.
17. The speech level of the child is most effectively altered by his hearing and recognizing his own speech inadequacies and wanting to change.
18. The speech of the child under natural situations is the measure of his speaking level.
19. Oral language activities have a much more important part in the curriculum than has formerly been accorded them.

With the advent of mass media of communication and the parallel improvement in transportation, children today need more skills for living in a complex world. It is now essential that every child develop his language arts capacities to the fullest extent if he is to meet the responsibilities of world citizenship and live a happy and useful life as a member of his community.

The modern language arts program includes oral and written communication: listening, speaking, reading, writing, and the related skills of handwriting, spelling, punctuation, and correct usage.

LISTENING

In the classroom of fifty years ago, little instruction was given in the art of listening. The teacher implored her pupils to "listen!" but could not realize that listening is a skill that requires much thought and concentration.

Modern inventions in communication; radio, movies, and television--and a more complex social structure have made listening increasingly important. Since one of the purposes of reading is to gather information and since the average person listens to the radio and television more than he reads, it follows that the development of listening

skills cannot be left to chance. Some children will learn
better by listening than they will by reading.

Authorities in the communication arts classify listening skills in four categories--critical, attentive, appreciative and passive.

Critical listening is for the purpose of evaluating or
weighing what is said against the personal experience and
knowledge of the listener. The pupil must learn to evaluate
the speaker's argument or the television commercial in
terms of his own experience. He must learn the difference
between facts and opinions and be able to recognize propaganda, bias, and prejudice. When the listener makes judgments, draws inferences and recognizes pressures, he is
practicing critical thinking. Children need guidance beginning in the kindergarten and continuing on every grade level
through college in developing ability to do critical listening.

Attentive listening is required in conversation and
discussions. Pupils must listen to questions in order to
answer them intelligently. Attentive listening is required
in following directions, getting assignments, announcements,
reports and recitations.

Appreciative listening increases the listeners enjoyment. Music, films, records, television programs, plays,
movies, and poetry reading are activities which encourage
appreciative listening.

Passive listening is involved when sounds although
heard are given little attention unless they demand attention
of the listener. Listening to background music when studying, or listening to two or three different sounds or conver-
sations and tuning in on only parts the listener wants to hear
are examples of passive listening.

A suggested guide for developing listening skills have
been worked out by the public schools of Glencoe, Illinois.
This guide, of course, will have to be modified according
to the previous experience, the needs and the maturity of
the pupils.

Primary Grades
    The child at the primary level learns how to gain
information and appreciation by:
1. Paying courteous, careful attention.
2. Listening attentively to others while waiting his
   turn to speak.
3. Paying careful attention to directions.
4. Giving full attention at assemblies, meetings,
   movies, television and radio programs.
5. Using information gained in listening.
6. Developing some discrimination in selection of
   radio and television programs.

Intermediate Grades
    The child at the intermediate level builds on
these and adds further skills:
1. Listens attentively and with interest to longer
   presentations.
2. Is able to recall and use what he has seen and
   heard.
3. Reacts intelligently to what he hears. Develops
   discrimination, evaluates and constructively cri-
   ticizes.
4. Participates as an active member of the group.
5. Listens with increasing appreciation to music,
   poetry and literature.
6. Grows in wise selection of radio, movie and television programs.

Upper Grades
    The child at upper school level carries these
skills further:
1. Gives full and individual attention to longer
   speeches and group discussions.
2. Reflects on what he hears, relates it to his experiences, analyzes ideas, distinguishes facts
   from emotions, recognizes propaganda, verifies
   statements.
3. Begins to identify himself with the speaker to
   understand motives and purposes.
4. Learns to discriminate in choice of music, radio,
   recordings, television programs and other audio
   and visual experiences.[2]

---

[2] A Curriculum Design For Elementary School Education, Glencoe, Illinois: Board of
Education, 1955, p. 42.

SPEAKING

The traditional language arts subjects--readin' and ritin'--are important but listening and speaking are used in the formative pre-school years. Children learn about 2000 words by the time they reach kindergarten and they have been learned primarily by listening and speaking.

In earlier schools, children were encouraged to work alone and study their lessons "hard". They were allowed little opportunity to talk to each other. Socializing in the classroom was considered a waste of time. The traditional custom of the day was to read silently, sometimes orally, and to recite.

Today, the classroom should provide a wholesome and permissive atmosphere where children are encouraged to talk, to share, to discuss and to plan together. Educators feel that speaking is a vital means of expression and the modern school should provide an environment where language can be stimulating, effective and spontaneous. The school's function is to help each child acquire the skills and attitudes he needs by encouraging him to exchange ideas and express his experience in words.

The entire school program of the modern school offers children experiences which give them something to say and a need for saying it.

Following is a guide for developing speaking skills of elementary school children:

Primary Grades
A relaxed but stimulating classroom situation is especially essential for the primary child to participate orally in activities. If there is such an atmosphere, he learns to share his ideas orally by:
1. Having something worthwhile to talk about.
2. Speaking clearly with good enunciation and pronunciation.
3. Taking part in assemblies, discussing plants, giving directions, making announcements and giving simple reports.
4. Taking turns in speaking.
5. Dictating, dramatizing and telling stories.

Intermediate Grades
    At the intermediate level, the child further
develops the skills of the primary years and adds to
them by learning:
1. How to select content for reporting.
2. How to relate events in correct order.
3. How to organize an oral report from current events,
    reading materials, notes and outlines.
4. How to discriminate between relevant and irrelevant
    materials.
5. How to develop greater confidence and poise in
    speaking situations and to use his voice effective-
    ly.
Upper Grades
    In the upper school, the child grows in all the
skills listed above and adds to them by:
1. Learning to vary methods of reporting by panels,
    skits, dramatics, visual and other aids.
2. Emphasizing the vocabulary of grammar and generali-
    zations or rules.
3. Understanding and using the rules of grammar.
4. Developing better voice control--pitch, quality,
    and enunciation.
5. Speaking effectively in all kinds of situations:
    Making announcements; giving reports and direc-
    tions; summarizing materials; acting as host,
    chairman or guest.
6. Asking for and profiting from suggestions and cri-
    ticisms.
7. Participating in group evaluations.[3]

READING

A commonly accepted definition of reading is "getting
meaning from the printed page." Reading is many-sided in
its scope and is based on the ability to understand the meaning of the printed word. It is a thinking process involving a
variety of complex skills.

To know a word involves three different aspects of
knowing it--the meaning, the sound and the printed form.
By the time a child starts school he knows the meaning and

[3] A Curriculum Design For Elementary School Education, Glencoe, Illinois: Board of
Education, 1955, p. 42.

sound of some 2000 words but to know them in their printed form will be a new adventure.

Reading is rightly considered a tool subject for a large part of a child's success in school (and as an adult later in life) depends upon his ability to get meaning from the printed word.

Research in reading shows that in order to read well a child must have a broad life experience, must be physically and mentally well-adjusted, must have a desire to read, must be able to listen well, must be observant, must develop language skills, and must be able to understand relationships and idea sequences.

With all these prerequisites to learning to read, it is easy to see that each child will not learn to read at the same rate of speed. Teachers must allow for individual differences in their readiness to read. Children will differ in the rate at which they learn to read because of differences in rate of mental development and in background.

The more a child can experience a word the easier it will be for him to add it to his vocabulary. Therefore, it is important to add to the child's pre-school background by providing as many varied experiences as possible both inside and outside the classroom.

Teachers, not only of reading, but teachers of all subjects should have enough background in reading to guide their pupils through their various stages of individual growth in the expansion of their reading skills to include increase in speed; increase in vocabulary and greater understanding of words; increase in locating written information and judging its validity; and reading for pleasure and recreation. Since students vary in maturity, they will pass through the stages at different times.

Progression in reading skills has been outlined by the Glencoe Public School's[4] staff as follows:

Primary Grades
By the end of the primary level (third grade), a child should be able to:

[4]Glencoe Public Schools, A Curriculum Design For Elementary School Education, Glencoe, Illinois: Board of Education, 1955, p. 44.

1. Gain information appropriate to his development of reading skill.
2. Use context clues to recognize new words.
3. Recognize new words through word analysis by:
   a. Applying knowledge of phonics to unlock a word.
   b. Dividing words into syllables.
   c. Recognizing known parts of words.
   d. Noting structure of work: length of word, height of letters.
4. Use punctuation as clues to meaning.
5. Read smoothly in phrases rather than by words.
6. Read to answer specific questions.
7. Find details and follow directions.
8. Begin to read critically and interpret what is read.

Intermediate Grades

The child in the intermediate grade builds on these skills and adds to them as he:
1. Reads for a specific purpose: fun, general or specific information, to verify statements.
2. Begins use of reference materials--dictionary, encyclopedia, periodicals, table of contents, index.
3. Increases vocabulary through wide reading and work study.
4. Uses library facilities with increasing skill.
5. Organizes materials into simple outlines.
6. Uses many sources in search of facts and information.
7. Reads for interpretation.
8. Enjoys reading and becomes more discriminating in his choice of material.

Upper Grades

The pupil in upper school increases and extends these skills:
1. Uses reference and source materials more effectively: dictionary, index, table of contents, footnotes, bibliography, encyclopedia, periodicals, Reader's Guide, atlas, almanac, textbooks.
2. Takes notes, makes outlines, summarizes, and generalizes from a wide variety of sources.
3. Improves skill in oral reading--uses it in an audience situation--gains in poise and use of voice.
4. Learns how to skim materials for information.

5. Increases and extends vocabulary through reading.
6. Gets information from a wide variety of visual materials: graphs, charts, maps, cartoons, slides, pictures, film strips.
7. Shows discrimination in selection of reading materials. Increases variety of reading: Biography, drama, poetry, classical, historical and modern fiction.

WRITING

Handwriting as a tool for recording and conveying thoughts, ideas and experiences is a part of the language arts curriculum. Writing has always been the concern of schools and in early times was the hallmark of literacy.

Earlier schools stressed the mechanization of writing while the schools of today stress writing as a tool of language expression. Writing, today, is taught not as an isolated drill subject with its own special content, but as a tool for all written work the school program may require. This approach--and the same may be said for reading, listening and speaking--makes every teacher a teacher of writing.

The teacher has the difficult task of helping children develop clear and accurate writing skills and at the same time maintain a free and easy expression. Too much emphasis on mechanics stifles the ease of expression and too much freedom from correction results in illegible writing. Since writing is for the purpose of communicating there is a need for consistent and purposeful practice in handwriting in the primary grade level and a concern for correction and improvement in the intermediate and upper grades.

Progression in the writing skills may follow a pattern something like the one below. [5]

Primary Grades
The child in the first grade should dictate his stories and ideas for others to write until he has the skills to write for himself. A child at second and

[5] Glencoe Public Schools, A Curriculum Design For Elementary School Education, Glencoe, Illinois: Board of Education, 1955, p. 45.

third grade level may still have difficulty in putting his ideas down in writing. He too should have the opportunity to dictate until his skills are adequate for writing. When the primary child has acquired these skills, he shares his ideas by:

1. Having something to write about.
2. Recording experiences and ideas in a few sentences.
3. Writing original stories and poems.
4. Learning use of period and question mark.
5. Understanding simple sentence structure.
6. Learning correct form for writing stories, letters and notes.
7. Using correct spelling, increasing vocabulary.
8. Writing neatly and legibly.

Intermediate Grades

The child at the intermediate level improves in these skills and adds to them by:

1. Drawing on a variety of experiences for original stories and poems.
2. Using writing more extensively in school work: reports, experiments, events and information.
3. Learning correct form for various kinds of writing.
4. Developing more technical skills: complete sentences, paragraphs, logical order of ideas, punctuation marks, (periods, question marks, quotation marks, comma, colon, exclamation point) and capitalization.
5. Expressing himself with increasing clarity.
6. Writing clearly and legibly.
7. Working for correct spelling, increased vocabulary.
8. Using dictionary, applying skills of work analysis to spelling.
9. Understanding the use of grammar such as noun, verb, subject, predicate, phrase, and applies it in his writing.

Upper Grades

The pupils in the upper school refine and extend all these skills by:

1. Using wide variety of content from full range of experiences.
2. Developing greater skill in various forms of writing: stories, poems, reports, outlines, letters, announcements, invitations, advertising notices.
3. Using proper form and style for each kind of writing.

4. Showing technical competence in written language, understanding and using the rules of grammar.
5. Continuing to work for correct spelling.
6. Writing rapidly in a neat, legible hand.

LANGUAGE ARTS AND OUTDOOR EDUCATION

One of the problems in teaching the language arts and promoting growth in the art of reading, writing, listening, and speaking is the pupils' lack of interest. In order to encourage children to develop their capacities in the language arts teachers are more and more turning to the out-of-doors and to real life situations.

All writing and all speaking, in fact, all forms of creativity is based on experience. The more experience a student has the broader the base on which he may build further creative expression. The outdoor setting can provide the permissive and inspirational setting needed for self-expression. Talks, essays, and writings based on firsthand experience makes for better compositions than topics assigned from the textbook. Good literature is based on the firsthand experience of great authors. The best novels are lived by the author.

Genuine expression occurs when a child wants someone else to share his experience. The school may extend the child's experience, stimulate his interest, provide opportunity for discussion, and stimulate a desire to write by giving the children an opportunity to engage and share in rich and meaningful activities. This can, of course, be done in the classroom with good books, an interesting history unit, a puppet play, and many other worth-while activities. Nothing, however, creates interest and excitement like a venture outside the classroom. A hike on the schoolground, a trip to the gravel pit, a bird walk, a trip to a farm, working in the garden, beautifying the school grounds or planting a tree--all of these activities provide exciting opportunities to stimulate expression of genuine thought and interest.

In short, language is a major tool of education; as the child progresses in language skill, he also develops in intellectual, social, and emotional capacities. He develops best in all these areas in a rich and varied program of activities.

Children learn words and increase their vocabulary out of the materials of their experience. Classroom practices of memorizing long lists of words out of contexts, defining lists of words in the workbook, filling in blanks in exercises and writing themes on subjects totally unrelated to their experience is a poor approach not only to language art but to all areas of education. The out-of-doors is a classroom which provides most inexpensively a wealth of opportunities for exploration and investigation in the world in which children live. In this type of experience the teacher need not worry about stimulating children in oral or written expression; she can hardly prevent it.

Many trees, shrubs, and other objects in nature have foreign names used in identifications. This is another rich experience in the language arts field still mostly unexplored.

Any attempt to list all the possibilities for enrichment of language arts instruction would be futile. The world is full of excitement and adventure just waiting to be told-- both orally and written.

Some activities in outdoor education which involve the language arts--reading, writing, spelling, punctuation, speaking and conversation--are:

Writing letters to parents and friends

Keeping a camp diary

Taking notes in the fields of special interest

Reading for research in the camp library

Reading for pleasure during leisure time

Telling stories around the campfire

Writing articles for the camp newspaper

Group discussions in planning and evaluating program activities

Labeling and classifying specimens

Creative writing of original plays, essays, and stories

Writing original poems on nature and outdoor life

Participation in dramatizations, skits and stunts

Informal conversation at meal time and cabin time

Make signs for use in garden or farm activities

Telling personal experiences about visits to farm or
school camp
Making announcements, introductions and invitations
Keeping a log of experience or a diary
Learning new words obtained from nature and conser-
vation
Keeping field notes
Writing for a camp newspaper
Listening for sounds in nature
Oral reports to class or committees
Preparing skits and stories for campfire

Selected References

Adams, Fay, Gray, Lillian and Reese, Dora, *Teaching
Children To Read,* New York: Ronald Press Company,
1949.

Applegate, Mauree, *Helping Children Write,* Scranton: International Textbook Company, 1949.

Dawson, Mildred A. and Dingee, Frieda Hayes, *Directing
Learning in the Language Arts,* Minneapolis: Burgess
Publishing Company, 1948.

Gates, Arthur I., *The Improvement of Reading,* New York:
The Macmillan Company, 1947.

Glencoe Public Schools, *A Curriculum Design For Elementary School Education,* Glencoe, Illinois: Board of
Education, 1955.

Lee, Murray J. and Lee, Dorris May, *The Child and His
Curriculum,* New York: Appleton-Century-Crofts,
1960.

Strickland, Ruth G., *The Language Arts in the Elementary
School,* Boston: D. C. Heath and Company, 1951.

Thomas, R. Murray, *Ways of Teaching,* New York:
Longmans, Green and Company, 1955.

Witty, Paul, *Reading In Modern Education,* Boston:
D. C. Heath and Company, 1949.

Chapter 12

MATHEMATICS

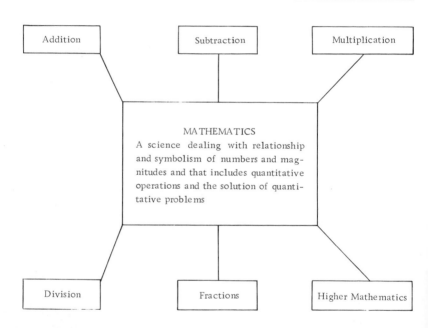

Addition	Subtraction	Multiplication

MATHEMATICS
A science dealing with relationship and symbolism of numbers and magnitudes and that includes quantitative operations and the solution of quantitative problems

Division	Fractions	Higher Mathematics

   The importance of arithmetic has been evident from the beginning of civilization. The Egyptians had "experts" in mathematics who helped with the Pyramids; the Phoenicians used mathematics in their great feats of navigation; and the early Romans were highly advanced in using mathematics for building great roads and buildings, the ruins of which still stand. The practical use of mathematics in everyday life was one of the reasons for the high level of civilization and culture of these early people.

In America just a hundred years ago relatively few persons needed to be an expert in arithmetic. Life was simple and transactions were simple. Children learned what little arithmetic that was needed through direct participation working with their elders in the home, in the field, or at the shop or store. Very few people received instruction beyond the famous "readin', ritin', and rithmetic" level.

Today, in an age of unparalleled scientific and technological development the study of mathematics is as important to man as any other area of study. Not only is vocational success dependent upon the worker's ability to use arithmetic but every adult is called upon to use arithmetic to handle personal economics in the demands of modern living. It would be impossible for a child to reach a proficiency in arithmetic necessary to live in the complex society of today without instruction in the public schools. In the age of science the study of mathematics is essential. As William Vergara points out in the preface of his book, Mathematics In Everyday Things, "without mathematics, the exact sciences would revert to philosophical abstractions; without science, mathematics would remain a profound plaything."

THE ARITHMETIC CURRICULUM

Until recently instruction in arithmetic has stressed rote memorization with little or no real and meaningful learning. If children were unable to learn the mechanical skills and mathematical processes they were labeled as not having a mathematical mind. In reality as Thomas points out, "much of the difficulty with arithmetic that students experience should be blamed more on poor teaching than on a supposedly nonmathematical mind. The major element of this poor instruction has been teaching for rote rather than for meaningful learning."[1]

---

[1] R. Murray Thomas, Ways of Teaching In Elementary Schools New York: Longmans, Green and Company, 1955, p. 279.

Too many schools, even today, present arithmetic as a series of number names purely on the basis of rote memorization with little or no realization of the full meaning of the words. The number exists for children only as so many words. They can count to ten but are unable to identify the number of four or six or eight objects when laid before them. Children are taught abstract terms without an adequate concept of the meaning of these terms. They fail to apply abstract knowledge to concrete situations because they fail to interpret the abstract formula. In too many instances children fail to see a relationship between concrete number and abstract number because the latter has not been developed out of the former in a way which enables them to tie the two together in their thinking.

Educators and specialists in mathematics are taking a good look at both the content and the method of mathematic instruction. Perhaps no other subject has come under great er scrutiny and greater criticism than the teaching of arithmetic. Too many parents remember their arithmetic as being very dull, very difficult or both. Furthermore, they have found very little practical use for much of the abstract formulas which they were required to memorize. The story is told of a student who wondered all his life why he was required to take a course in algebra. Years later his son brought his algebra home work to his father and asked for help.

"Now I know why I had to study algebra," the man exclaimed happily, "I can help my son with his home work."

This story illustrates how mathematics as taught in too many classrooms in America has broken away from the substantive area of its application. The child of today too often sees arithmetic as a pencil and paper activity which is to be performed in the classroom.

Some of the most common criticisms of arithmetic as it is taught today are:

1. Mathematics as taught in the schools today is too much divorced from the needs imposed by society. The abstract subject matter of mathematics is of little use to students and is largely forgotten by the pupil when he leaves school and enters his life work.

2. Too many students approach mathematics with fear and a defeatist attitude. This has been due in the past perhaps to the mathematics teacher's conviction that mathematics is too hard for most students. Who can doubt their sincerity when they themselves were exposed to a mechanical and abstract mathematics curriculum.

3. Children are required to do a great deal of home work and must rely on their parents to aid them. Parents, like the children, are more concerned in getting answers than in stressing meaning.

4. Arithmetic teachers use rote practice and drill to insure accuracy and speed in mathematical computations but such drill comes before and not after the understanding of the process has been achieved.

5. Arithmetic teachers do not take into account the differences in maturity in children. The factor of individual differences in children poses the problem of fitting materials and methods of arithmetic to every child in the classroom including the slow learner as well as the fast learner.

In view of these and other criticisms of the arithmetic program in the public schools it is safe to assume the coming decade will witness major changes in the teaching of arithmetic. Because so many arithmetic teachers in today's schools "learned" arithmetic in a mechanical and meaningless way, they are going to have to reteach themselves a new approach that will assure the development of understanding. Teachers will have to keep up with the latest trends, developments, and research in the field and be ready themselves to experiment in new materials and new approaches which will help tie arithmetic to the everyday experience of the child.

A review of school curriculum guides, textbooks and research reports reveals several basic considerations for teaching arithmetic. These basic considerations should be of help to teachers in guiding children in arithmetic experiences:

1. Emphasis should be placed on developing mathematical concepts rather than on studying specialized areas as algebra or geometry. Mathematics is a system of ideas, relationships and processes, and not a book collection or

memorization of textbook materials and drills. The new approach to teaching arithmetic is to teach in terms of significant and real problems of everyday life--not to pass the final examination but mathematics to use in living.

2. Teachers should emphasize the thought processes rather than rapidity and manipulation. Accuracy and speed is a follow-up to understanding and thinking--not a precedent. The newer concept of teaching arithmetic does not eliminate drill but instead utilizes drill only after understanding of the process has been established.

3. Instruction in arithmetic on any given grade level must take into account individual differences in children and fit materials and methods to each individual member of the class. This can be done by individual assignments, more concrete problem solving situations for less mature students enrichment of program for more mature students and flexible grouping of students for various learning situations.

4. The methods of evaluating pupils' progress in arithmetic should be broader than paper and pencil tests which require exactness of answer with no credit for proper steps in the problem solving situation. In addition to written tests, teachers should evaluate student progress in arithmetic by interviews, oral examinations, and closer scrutiny of a pupil's daily work.

5. The mathematics curriculum of the elementary school should provide for continual development in mathematical ideas. Hence a teacher:

- . . . relates each new idea to previously acquired ideas.
- . . . provides each child with opportunities to discover for himself the ideas of mathematics.
- . . . expects each child to progress toward the formulation of more mature concepts.
- . . . provides each child with a set of unifying ideas around which he may organize his mathematical concepts.

6. The mathematics curriculum of the elementary school should provide situations that develop ways of thinking. Hence a teacher:

. . . provides each child with the opportunity and time
for independent thinking.
. . . chooses situations that give the child sufficient
opportunity to use a learned concept until he
develops competence in its use.
. . . chooses problem situations that are vital because
they are familiar and important in a child's life.
. . . chooses experience that provide opportunity for
each child to progress toward a more mature level
of thinking.

7. The mathematics curriculum of the elementary
school should provide for varying levels of ability, interest,
and achievement. Hence a teacher:

. . . is aware of a child's readiness for a new concept
. . . challenges each child at his own level of attainment.
. . . allows each child to think about problems in his
own way, guiding him to more mature ways of
thinking.
. . . plans so that each child will have both successful and satisfying experiences.[2]

8. Arithmetic concepts should be made more real and
therefore more meaningful. The teacher should develop life
problem situations and real problems involving the daily lives
of the children. While it is probably not possible to find enough
actual problem situations in the children's daily lives due
mainly to limited time, it is necessary to see that the problem solving situations are realistic ones for the children.
If the abstraction is to possess a richness of meaningful
content, the concrete must precede the abstract in breadth,
depth, and variety toward progressive stages of abstraction.

ARITHMETIC AND OUTDOOR EDUCATION

Arithmetic is kept too close to the exercise book. It
originated in the outdoors as an important aspect of man's

[2]Basic Considerations 5, 6, 7, adapted from: Illinois Curriculum Program, Thinking In
The Language of Mathematics, Springfield, Illinois, Superintendent of Public Instruction, 1959, pp. 9-10.

everyday life. The measurement of time, the measurement
of land, the building of pyramids, and other such activities
in the out-of-doors put arithmetic to everyday use.

The child can see geometry in life all about him in
tire treads, in advertisements, in clover leafs, in tree
limbs, in land formation, and in many other outdoor objects.

Mathematics instructors at University School, Southern Illinois University look on as
eighth grade boys apply mathematical principles learned at school to bridge construction at the school camp.

If school instruction is to become more meaningful,
outdoor education must be used to enrich and vary the pupils
concrete experience.

Actually an analysis of different arithmetic concepts
taught at the different grade levels--counting, adding, sub-
tracting, multiplying and dividing--show that they can be
put to practical and purposeful use in outdoor activities. In
the school garden, the school forest, on the school farm,
or at the school camp the teacher may use the out-of-doors
to interpret the abstractions of the textbook and show how
they are embodied in reality in the everyday living of the

children. Through firsthand experience in the out-of-doors
with meaningful projects and activities, mathematical abstractions of the textbook become vital and meaningful in
the everyday life of the children.

In the first grade, children are taught place value and
counting. The teacher has many opportunities to encourage
practice in these skills as the children take hikes on the
school ground, work in the school garden or visit the school
farm.

How many trees on the school ground?
Why are they there?
How did they get there?
How many cows in the field?
How many rows of cabbage in the garden?

It is much more meaningful for a child to count the
spaces in a garden and tell how many tomato plants he needs
than it is to count rectangular strips of paper in the classroom. Relating arithmetic to real life necessities is more
meaningful.

The second grade introduces basic addition and subtraction and here again the child has many possibilities in
which to use these skills; We have an extra person on our
campout; how many buns do we now need? The counselor
will be gone tomorrow; how many pieces of meat will we
need for our table? How many cars do we need for the field
trip for thirty persons?

The third grade introduces the concept of adding and
borrowing. If the child has properly learned place value
(and he certainly will if it is made meaningful for him) adding and borrowing will not be the problem that it is in the
regular classroom. The child can add or subtract number
combinations of cattle in two or more pens; the number of
sticks needed to complete a project in arts and crafts; the
number of children entering or leaving the raft. This also
helps to establish the concept of how an unseen number is
added to a seen number with which a great number of children have difficulty.

Fractions are introduced into the fourth grade and
children of this level should be taught how to add and subtract basic fractions. Although a cardboard pie is usually

330

used in a classroom situation, it is both more meaningful and rewarding to use a real watermelon on a campout. If half of the children are going on a trip and half will stay at camp, how many are going if there are thirty-six in the entire group? Problems such as these arise from daily living and working in a garden, on the farm, or in a camp, and their teaching at the appropriate time makes arithmetic more meaningful and hence more easily retained.

Division and multiplication of fractions are taught in the fifth grade as well as addition and subtraction of decimal fractions. Problems relating to area such as floor space in a tent or the number of people allowed in certain program activities can be answered by using these newfound skills.

The sixth grade includes teaching of multiplication and division of decimals as well as simple percentages. Again any problem requiring a fractional part or a mixed number must be solved at camp.

Besides teaching the basic skills in arithmetic, vari-

Children combine work with recreation as they learn about plant life and garden activities at the camp garden operated by the Recreation and Outdoor Education Department, Southern Illinois University. Arithmetic becomes meaningful as children decide how many rows, how many plants in the row and the total number of plants needed.

ous measurements are taught at various grade levels. The very young can not only be taught how to tell time so that they arrive at meals on time, but also how hot it was at three o'clock today; the direction and pressure of the wind; how many gallons of kool-aid will be needed on an overnight; how many dozens of eggs will be needed for breakfast; how much money is needed for the cookout, the picnic, or to buy garden seed; how many yards of gravel will be needed to build a road to the rifle range once the dimensions have been established; how much plywood is needed to build an addition to the arts and crafts building; how many gallons of milk will be needed for both cereal and for drinking. Problems such as these that arise daily can best be answered when the child is made aware of the mathematical principle involved and is allowed to work out his solution immediately.

The camp program can make arithmetic more meaningful by placing the children in real life situations and have them solve the problems for themselves.

Measurement and distance can be brought into the outdoor program by asking the question, "how far is it to that tree?" This question will bring many reactions from the students. Those who don't know how to estimate a short distance soon learn how to compare a segment of the unknown distance with familiar lengths such as one's own height. In judging distances, the children should be shown just how far 100 yards really is. This can be done by measuring off 100 yards with a tape measure and letting the students count how many steps it takes them to travel this distance. This will always come in handy because there are a lot of games which take place in an area of 100 yards, and the students can actually set up the court of playing area without a tape measure.

What is the size of an acre of ground?
What is the depth of an average farm pond?
What is the height of a building?
What is the power of a tractor?

All of these concepts have more meaning through observations and mathematical experience.

Each student can judge how tall a tree is by using his

or her own shadow. Student (A) who knows how tall he is stands at the base of the object which is to be measured, (lining his shadow up with the shadow of the object to be measured) while student (B) marks the point where his shadow ends. Student (A) then moves up to this mark and the process is continued until his shadow comes to the end of the object's shadow. To find the height of the object, student (A) takes his height times the number of shadow lengths marked off in order to reach the end of the object's shadow, therefore, giving the approximate height of the object.

The students can also determine the distance to the tree or other objects without pacing it.

This brings in another phase of measurement. Recalling classroom work with similar triangles, provides background for the solution of the problem. Judging the width of a river can be solved by using the methods of similar triangles and the pythangorean theorem. All this enables the group to estimate the distance fairly close in relation to the solution obtained by indirect measurements.

Simple geometry, the use of square root, and other classroom learning becomes better understood as children actually see that all these techniques help solve problems which have meaning to them.

The cost of a school trip should be determined by the class previous to the trip. The children will have to start to save money for the trip and maybe for the camp fee. For some this will involve budgeting their allowance and wise planning.

The children should help or take part in the planning of the expenses of food supplies and transportation. This will give them a little insight into the magnitude of the enterprise. Not only can the children benefit from planning the budget, but they can also have a store at camp. To accomplish this, they may also have to set up a small bank which will handle money or checks. This will call for bookkeeping on how many checks a student has written or how many he will be allowed to write in one day. In order to accomplish this, accurate accounts will have to be kept by the people who are in charge of them.

These and other outdoor activities and projects serve

to give functional and concrete experience for the teaching of arithmetic on every grade level from kindergarten through high school. A few additional activities might include:

Plotting a graph of the weather at camp
Determining the age of trees by the stump
Hiking with a compass
Making a scale map of the camp
Operating a stop watch to determine speed of walking
Determining individual scores on the archery range
Planning amount and cost of food for cook-outs
Construction of bridges, stiles, shelters, feeding stations
Pacing distances in hiking
Estimated and measuring distances between trees or buildings
Laying out fields or activity areas
Staking out an acre of ground
Cutting and piling a cord of fireplace wood
Measuring board feet in a piece of lumber or in a building
Measuring the circumference and diameter of a tree
Estimating the board feet in a log
Estimating and measuring dimensions of a building and reporting on per cent of error
Estimating the per cent of slope
Estimating and measuring the height of trees through the measurement of shadows
Determining the distance away of lightning
Estimating and measuring the width of a river or lake
Operating the camp bank
Finding the amount and cost of gravel for a road bed
Counting the average number of trees in an acre
Drawing a scale plan for a garden
Marking out a garden plot
Plotting a graph of the weather at camp
Working in the camp bank or trading post
Building an outdoor fireplace
Cost of seeding or re-sodding a plot

AN EXPERIMENT IN INCREASING THE FUNDAMENTAL KNOWLEDGE OF MATHEMATICS IN AN OUTDOOR EDUCATION PROGRAM[3]

Finding Speed of Walking and Calculating Distances

EQUIPMENT NEEDED

1. Tape measure
2. Several (2-4) stop watches or watches with second hands
3. Pencils
4. 4 x 6 cards

METHOD

Measure and mark off a distance of 200 yards (600 feet). Demonstrate to each participant how a stop watch is operated. Particular attention should be given to the second and minute marking. The participant now walks at a normal pace the measured distance timing himself simultaneously. The results should be placed on the 4" x 6" card. He would again time himself on the return trip and place the result on his 4" x 6" card. The average of the two times will give a result that can be used in calculating miles per hour that he actually walked. Calculations should follow a pattern: Assuming that the average time was 2 min. 47 seconds, the result should be first of all changed to minutes to the nearest hundredth. The 47 divided by 60 (the number of seconds in a minute) gives a result to three decimal places of .783. Since the third decimal place is less than 5 (it is 3 in this example), it is dropped. Had it been 5 or more than 5, one additional figure would have been added to the hundredth place. The result has now become 2.78 minutes. The result just obtained divided into the distance given ($\frac{600 \text{ ft.}}{2.78 \text{ min.}}$) is 215.827 or 215.83 feet per minute at the rate of walking.

[3]Developed by Dr. Clarence Stephens, Vice-President for Operations, Southern Illinois University, Edwardsville Campus

If this result is multiplied by 60 (minutes in an hour) a result of 12949.8 ft. per hour is obtained. If the last answer is divided by 5,280 ft. (12949.8/5280), it is found that the walking rate is 2.45 or 2.5 miles per hour.

From the preceding calculations a speed of 215.83 feet per minute was obtained. By using the figure just found plus the stopwatch, it is possible to find the distance between any two objects. Suppose the distance from the entrance of the camp to the cookhouse is desired. The camper should walk at his pace to the cookhouse keeping an accurate record of the elapsed time. By multiplying feet per minute by the time in minutes (remember that seconds have to be changed to minutes, seconds/60), the distance can be found in feet.

It might be wise to give a prize to that participant who comes closest to the correct answer in the last activity.

Calculations
Mathematical knowledge needed
      1. Multiplication of decimals
      2. Division of decimals
      3. Changing seconds to minutes
      4. Rounding off numbers

BOARD FEET

Finding the Number of Board Feet in the Side and End Walls
of a Small Building

EQUIPMENT NEEDED

      1. Yardsticks
      2. 4" x 6" cards
      3. Pencils

METHOD

The number of board feet in a piece of lumber is always found by multiplying the length in feet by the width in feet by the thickness in inches. Theoretically, a thickness of less than 1" should be counted as 1" whereas in any unit of more than 1" the actual thickness has to be used. Thus a board 8' x 1' x 1/2" would contain 8 board feet (the 1/2" has to be included as 1"). On the other hand, a board 8' x 1' x 1-'/2" would contain 12 board feet (the 1-1/2" is more than 1", so actual thickness is used). However, in this unit for the purpose of simplification, any fractional part of an inch should be changed to the next highest inch. (1-1/2" = 2" or 2-1/4" = 3".) Thus in actual multiplication a board 6' x 4-1/2" x 2-1/4" would become simplified to 6' x 5" x 3". If a calculation of the number of board feet is made for the preceding example, substitution into the formula: board feet = length in feet x width in feet x thickness in inches would give 6' x 5/12 (inches changed to feet x 3 = 7-1/2 board feet. Don't forget to change the width to terms of feet.

As an example, suppose the number of board feet in the original building at the edge of the camp were to be found. The activity could best be initiated by the campers as a group, measuring the length, width, and thickness of the outer walls including the windows. They should check their measurements. Let us say the building is 19' 6" long, 9' 2" wide, 8' 6-1/2" high, and the side walls are 1/4" thick. The number of board feet in each side wall is 19-1/2' x 8-7/12' (6-1/2" changed to 7" x 1" (3/4" changed to 1") = 167.375 or 167.38 to the nearest hundredth. The work in the preceding calculation can best be done by changing the 19-1/2' to 39/2 and the 8-7/12 to 103/12. The total number of board feet in the two outside side walls including windows would be 334.76. Calculations on the end walls should be made in the same manner. Each wall is 9' 2" long, 8' 6-1.2" wide, and 3/4" thick, so substitution into the formula would give 9-1/6' (2" 2/12' = 1/6') x 8-7/12' x 1" or 55/6' x 103/12' x 1" = 76.680 or 76.68. The two end walls including the windows and door, contain 153.36 board feet.

Next the dimensions of the door and windows should be found by the campers. The calculations then involved are as follows:
Door = 32" x 6'8" x 1" = 2-2/3' x 6-2/3' x 1 = 8/3 x 20/3 x 1" = 160/9 = 17.777 or 17.78

Window = 33" x 40" x 1" = 2-3/4" x 3-1/3' x 1" = 11/4 x
  10/3 x 1" = 110/12 = 19. 166 or 9. 17
Window = 30" x 41" x 1" = 2-1/2' x 3-5/12' x 1" = 5/2 x
  41/12 x 1" = 205/24 = 8. 541 or 8. 54
Window = Same as second window   8. 54
Window = Same as second window   8. 54
Window = 29' x 41' x 1" = 2-5/12 x 3-5/12 x 1 = 29/12 x
  41/12 x 1 = 1189/144 = 8. 256 or 8. 27
Board Feet estimated   9. 17
                                    8. 54
                                    8. 54
                                    8. 54
                                    8. 27
                                   _____
                                   60. 84

The result obtained must be subtracted from the total number of board feet in the walls, 153. 36 plus 334. 76 = 488. 12
- 60. 84 = 427. 28 board feet.

In the building to be measured there are seven walls.
The windows are covered therefore their measurements
should be included in the calculations. A thickness of 1"
should be used, because the actual thickness of the plyboard
outer wall is less than 1". There are 3 pairs of equal opposite sides. In these instances, if the number of board
feet in one wall were doubled, the total for two walls would
be obtained. This, of course, includes doors. The east
side of the building would have to be measured separately.
The next result would be found by adding all results together.
The measurements of the doors would have to be made and
the results subtracted to find the total number of board feet
of lumber in the building.

Mathematical Calculations
    1. Multiplication of fractions
    2. Dividing whole numbers
    3. Multiplication of decimals
    4. Addition of decimals

FINDING THE COST OF THE GRAVEL FOR A ROAD INTO LITTLE GRASSY LAKE

EQUIPMENT NEEDED:

1. Tape measure
2. 4" x 6" cards
3. Pencils

METHOD

To find the amount of gravel needed for making an all-weather road into Little Grassy Lake Camp it is necessary to know the length and width of the road as well as the depth of gravel desired. For the purposes of this unit, it is to be assumed that the width suitable for two cars to meet is essential. Since a road 15' wide is ample for the purpose just mentioned, all campers should use that measurement. A depth of gravel of 8" should be used. It will be necessary first of all to find the length of the road. Measurements should begin at the west edge of the parking lot and end at the edge of the blacktop and should be made by the campers working in pairs.

The calculations should be patterned after the following example. If the road had a length of 2,000' and using the other standard dimensions, the volume of rock in cu. ft. needed could be found by substituting into the formual V = lwh (height and depth are the same as follows: V=2000' x 15' x 3' (The eight inches have been changed to 2/3' by dividing 8" by 12") The formula after multiplication would become $V = \frac{60000}{3} = 20000$ cu. ft. If a cancellation process were used, the results would be as follows: V=2000 x $\overset{5}{\cancel{15}}$ x 2/$\cancel{3}$ = 20000 cu. ft. Since there are 40 cu. ft. in a ton, if 20000 is divided by $\underline{40}$ $\frac{(20000)}{40}$ it is found that 500 tons of gravel are needed. The delivery price of gravel at Little Grassy is $2.45 per ton. The total cost would be derived by multiplying the number of tons, 500, by the price per ton, $2.45. The total cost of gravel in the example is $1,225.

It is best in this problem to use only one tape measure and alternate the pairs making the measurements. The other campers could make sure that the work was being done correctly. After obtaining all of the data necessary for working the problem, the campers should work individually in finding their final solution.

Mathematical Calculations
1. Multiplication of whole numbers
2. Multiplication of fractions
3. Division of whole numbers

FIND HEIGHTS OF OBJECTS THROUGH MEASUREMENT OF SHADOWS

EQUIPMENT NEEDED

1. Yardstick or small tape measure
2. Pencil
3. 4" x 6" cards

METHOD

Hold the yardstick so that one end is perpendicular to the horizontal plane of the earth's surface. If the ruler is parallel to the trunk of a nearby tree, it is almost a certainty that it is perpendicular to the horizontal surface. Mark the end point of the shadow and the point that the yardstick touches the ground. Measure the distance between the two points and place the measurement on a diagram as follows:

3'

Shadow

3' 4-1/2"

Caution - Be sure that the yardstick is so placed that its shadow is extended on the same or like slope of ground as for the object whose height is to be found.

Measure the length of the shadow of the object. Place the measurement on a diagram.

h

Shadow

15' 9"

The height of the object can be found by substituting into the following formula:

$$\frac{\text{Height of object}}{\text{Length of shadow of object}} = \frac{\text{Height of yardstick}}{\text{Length of shadow of yardstick}}$$

Thus in the example given the result after substitution becomes:

$$\frac{\text{Height of object}}{15' \ 9''} = \frac{3'}{3' \ 4\text{-}1/2''}$$

Cross multiplication gives:

$$\text{Height of object} = \overset{a}{\frac{3' \times 15' \ 9''}{3' \ 4\text{-}1/2''}} = \overset{b}{\frac{45' \ 27''}{3' \ 4\text{-}1/2''}} = \overset{c}{\frac{47' \ 3''}{3' \ 4\text{-}1/2''}} =$$

d
47-1/4'
3-3/8"

Note for answer d: 47' 3" = 3 4-1/2/12' = 3 9/2 x 1/12 = 3 9/24 = 3 3/8'

e $\dfrac{169/4}{27/8}$ = 169/4 x 8/27 = $\dfrac{1352}{108}$ = 12. 5' = 121 6"

Calculations should be made in finding the heights of at least three varying objects. In finding the second height it would be best to change inches to decimal feet as follows:
4-1/2" = 4. 5" = $\dfrac{4.5'}{12}$ = . 375' or . 38' to the nearest hun-

dredth. Use of decimals or fractions in finding the 3rd height should be dependent on the ability of the students. Use that method with which they have the most difficulty.

Mathematical knowledges necessary
1. Changing a mixed number to an improper fraction
2. Changing a mixed number to a decimal value
3. Multiplication of whole numbers
4. Multiplication of fractions
5. Multiplication of decimals
6. Division of whole numbers
7. Division of fractions
8. Division of decimals

ESTIMATING DISTANCES

EQUIPMENT NEEDED

1. 1 Tape measure
2. 4" x 6" cards
3. Pencils

METHOD

In this unit the counselors should be attempting to increase camper ability in estimating distance. The three units of length with which the children will be working are inches, feet, and yards.

This project should be started by having the campers seat themselves in a semi-circle. It should then be explained to them that many of the people in our modern world have very little concept of lengths and distances. Also in many instances they have no idea as to which unit to use. The leader should then pick up a stick from the ground which is less than 1' in length. Ask them initially which unit of length they would use in describing the stick. Get several concensus from the group that the unit that should be used is inches. Next have them estimate the length and write the result on the 4 x 6 card. This should be followed by getting volunteers from the group to measure the stick. Results should be compared. The procedure described should be used in estimating and measuring the length of a stick that is less than 2' in length. Using the latter stick the group can be asked which other unit of length might be used to describe its length. It should be described in terms of feet. At least two more estimations and measurements involving feet should be made. It is to be remembered that volunteers from the group should make all measurements. To lead the discussion into yards, a comparison between feet and yards should be made on the last object measured. Estimations of and measurements in terms of yards should be made for a short distance between two objects (5-10 yds.) then for a longer distance (15-25 yds.). Student estimations should be compared with measured results in every in-

stance. The teacher should know the length of his normal
stride (procedure as to how to find this will be given later
in this unit) or be able to step approximately a yard. He
should then tell the students that he has a little better method of estimating distances in terms of yards. He should
then walk or stride through the distance between two points
and tell the group his result. Actual measurement should
give a result that does not vary too much from the estima-
tion. The entire group could then walk the distance between
two points and get estimations. Comparisons with actual
measurements will give some results that are somewhat
in error. A determination of the length of the normal step
of each camper should be made. This is done by measuring
off 50 yards, having them count the number of normal steps
needed to walk through the distance, then dividing the number of steps by 50. The result obtained should be checked
by having them repeat the process. They should then all be
asked to walk in the same direction a distance they think is
75 yards. Assuming that the factor previously obtained was
1.2, they would have to take 90 steps (1.2 x 75). A measurement of 75 yards should then be made to check the accuracy of the estimations. The process should be repeated
for a distance of perhaps 45 yards. The last of the abilities
necessary is to be able to find the distance between two objects. This can be found by dividing the number of steps
required by the factor previously obtained. Assuming that
the number of strides needed actually taken is 80 and the
factor is 1.2, the result would be $\frac{80}{1.2}$ of 66.67. This reduced to the nearest tenth would become 66.7 yards. One
distance should be determined and compared with the actual
result. The campers should then estimate a second distance and file the result with the counselor. That camper
who came the nearest to the actual measured result should
be recognized at the group meeting the last afternoon.

Mathematical Calculations
1. Multiplication of decimals
2. Division of decimals
3. Rounding off numbers

WORKING WITH FRACTIONS

EQUIPMENT NEEDED

1. Bow
2. Arrow
3. Target
4. Pencil
5. 4" x 6" cards

METHOD

In this activity it would be best to have two targets. Other equipment needed should be such that 4 - 5 participants could fire in rotation or simultaneously at the target. Three shooting areas need to be marked off as follows:

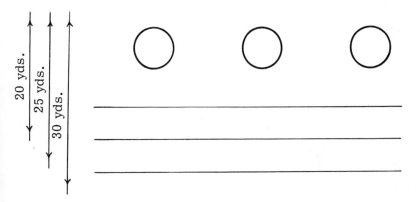

Each participant will shoot 12 arrows at each of the 3 ranges beginning at A and ending with C. Scoring would be as is indicated on the target circle.

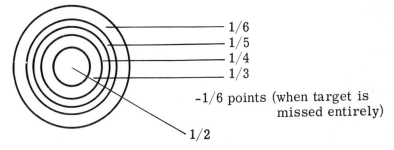

The score should be computed for each range before moving to the next. The total score would be the sum of the scores obtained on ranges A, B, and C.

Mathematical calculations involved
1. Adding of fractions
2. Multiplication of fractions
3. Subtraction of fractions

Selected References

Brueckner, Leo J. and Grossnickle, Foster E., *Making Arithmetic Meaningful,* Philadelphia: John C. Winston Company, 1953.

Hickerson, J. Allen, *Guiding Children's Arithmetic Experiences,* New York: Prentice-Hall, 1952.

National Society For The Study of Education, *The Teaching of Arithmetic,* Chicago: N. S. S. E., 1951.

Superintendent of Public Instruction, *Thinking in the Language of Mathematics,* Springfield of Illinois: Superintendent of Public Instruction, 1959.

Thomas, R. Murray, *Ways of Teaching in Elementary Schools,* New York: Longmans, Green and Company, 1955.

Wilson, Guy W., *Teaching the New Arithmetic,* New York: McGraw-Hill, 1951.

Chapter 13

SCIENCE

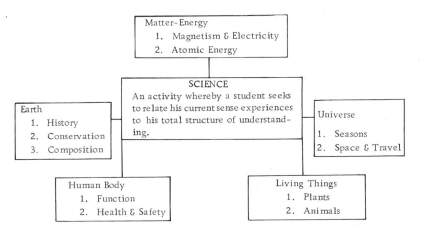

Matter-Energy
1. Magnetism & Electricity
2. Atomic Energy

SCIENCE
An activity whereby a student seeks to relate his current sense experiences to his total structure of understanding.

Earth
1. History
2. Conservation
3. Composition

Universe
1. Seasons
2. Space & Travel

Human Body
1. Function
2. Health & Safety

Living Things
1. Plants
2. Animals

Science can be one of the most exciting and challenging areas in the school curriculum if it is properly taught. The biological and physical environment of the child, the world in which he lives, is a laboratory for exploring the wonders of science and provides the thrills of discovery. Science is all around him and the teacher has a natural starting point for many good lesson plans in following his interests and helping him answer his questions: What is a star? What is thunder? What causes lightning? Why do we have fog? If the teacher does not capture the child's interest and satisfy his curiosity by helping him answer his questions and solve his problems, the student will usually direct his interests elsewhere.

The march of science is of growing importance to every citizen. It was surprising to note the apathy found in the schools during the pre-sputnik days. It is a sad commentary on our public schools and the men and women who run them that science had to receive its recent impetus due to the successful launching of Russian rockets. Science is important; it is unique as a technique of learning with its reliance on observation, experimentation, and investigation. All senses (seeing, hearing, smelling, feeling, tasting) are put to use in collecting scientific data.

The educational value of science goes far beyond the advantage of being ahead of Russia or of what the wise use of science may contribute to modern living. The president's Science Advisory Committee in 1959 points up some of the educational values in the following statement:

> The student of science quickly learns that all scholars seek the truth and that they must be critical and honest with each other. The study of science may offer to the young student his first and possibly his best early opportunity for learning how easy it is to make mistakes and how hard it is to advance knowledge. It may also provide the simplest early experience of the supreme virtue of intellectual honesty.
>
> Then, too, we must be aware of the humanizing aspects of science. The beauty and order of nature which science reveals are as moving in their way as great paintings or fine drama. The vast reaches of the universe now being examined by the modern astronomer are as inspiring as great music. The fact that the laws of science span all national and ideological boundaries makes science the universal language, a link between nations, and a real potential force for peace.
>
> Americans diminish their capacity as citizens, give up an early strengthening intellectual experience, and forego great pleasure, excitement and adventure when they neglect to study science.
>
> The study of science thus enhances the education of _every_ citizen, in addition to providing the neces-

sary basis for the education of the future professional scientist, engineer and technologist. For all these reasons we believe it is appropriate and necessary that the American educational system give due recognition to instruction in mathematics, science and technology.

The teaching of science, or any other subject for that matter can be a waste of time if the teacher does not understand science or does not understand children. Too often teachers specializing in science are eager to make accomplished scientists of all the students and place too much emphasis on the textbook and the memorization of scientific data--most of which, may be obsolete by the time the pupil graduates. Pupils can often pass classroom tests and yet be unaware of the application of science to gain insight into the methods and concepts of science so that he can understand the world in which he lives.

The best materials and facilities for the study of science are those found in the child's immediate environ-

Children have an inherent fascination for pond life. Cook County Forest Preserve naturalists conduct field trips for over 30,000 day camp children each year.

Courtesy of Roland F. Eisenbeis

ment. No vicarious experience is as effective as direct experience. No textbook, or pamphlet, or flat picture, or slide, or movie can take the place of actually seeing the problem of conservation and the phenomena of nature as it exists in the immediate environment.

To use these local educational resources, extensive field trips and excursions need not be undertaken. Too often possibilities are overlooked on the schoolground or in the backyard. A nearby gully or roadside cut, an eroded pathway cut across the corner of the playfield, an overgrazed hillside, or a nearby creek or river bed will be more effective than any written or pictured account. Assuming that the teacher has developed a fundamental point of view about nature, these simple and familiar illustrations can do more to develop awareness of the social and economic problems involved than any amount of lecturing or reading.

The purpose of the science curriculum is not to start boys and girls on the road to becoming scientists but rather to enable them through science instruction to develop an understanding of science and to live an effective and happy life in a world where science plays so important a part.

Science is ever-changing; new ideas are being added and old ideas revised in practically all areas of human knowledge. For this reason it is more important to develop scientific attitudes, skills, appreciations and interests than to insist on memorization of scientific facts and data which may not be valid by the time the semester examination is given. Sir James Jean points out that science is more than knowledge when he states:

> The raw material of every science must always be an accumulation of facts. . .But, as Poincare remarked, an accumulation of facts is no more a science than a heap of stones is a house. When we set to work. . . to create a science we must first coordinate and synthesize the accumulated piles of facts. It is then usually found that a great number of separate facts can be summed up in a much smaller number of general laws. . .These express the pattern of events for which we are searching.[1]

[1] Sir James Jeans, Physics and Philosophy, New York: Cambridge University Press, 1943, p. 8.

The teacher may through science instruction, especially in the use of observation, investigation, and experimentation, develop a scientific attitude and a habit of critical thinking that will carry over in the student's studies and activities. The North Carolina Public Schools in their bulletin Science For The Elementary School have developed what is meant by scientific attitude and critical thinking which should be helpful to all teachers.

> The Scientific Attitude--The ability and intent to think clearly and logically. These include:
> 1. A curiosity about the world in which we live.
> 2. A belief that every happening has a cause.
> 3. A refusal to accept statements as facts unless there is sufficient proof.
> 4. A desire to observe carefully.
> 5. A refusal to draw conclusions until enough evidence is available.
> 6. A respect for the opinions of others and a willingness to change our opinions in light of new facts.
>
> Then the teacher and children work together "to find out how and why things happen," as soil erosion in the yard, or to produce a situation for a purpose, as to produce mold on bread, the scientific attitude is at work.
>
> > --they plan.
> > --they search for facts.
> > --they try out.
> > --they check what they find and see.
> > --they apply these facts to their own uses.
> > --they draw some conclusions.
>
> How far they go into either of these depends upon the subject and upon the teacher's values of its worth-whileness.
>
> Critical thinking--Often the child does not show promising critical thinking attitudes because he does not know what it is. He has heard the teacher say many times, "Now you must think," or "Now think hard." To "think hard" to him may be to try to recall a fact. In critical thinking he does recall. But he weighs facts and draws conclusions. It may not have occurred to him that he is using a critical thinking approach, for example, when he is doing these things:

1. looks for more facts.
2. reorganizes the facts that he has.
3. withholds judgment.
4. does not rely upon guessing.
5. rejects superstitions.
6. comes to know the difference in facts and opinions.
7. accepts more than one way of approaching a problem.
8. questions his own ideas.
9. discounts varieties of fortune telling.
10. discredits magic as science.
11. being aware that there is more to learn later on the subject.[2]

There is a common misconception that if a course is difficult it has great value. All too often science professors in college in an effort to add status to their department give the impression that science students must be more brilliant than scholars in other areas of study. It is obvious, of course, that great minds are needed in other areas of study. Great minds are needed in all areas of human endeavor and especially in the area of human and social relations. Science, although important to a good liberal education, will not solve all our problems.

Good teachers whether on the college level or in the beginning grades teach science as they find it--exciting, adventurous and challenging. Too many teachers try to play the role of the "answer man" or try to find all the answers in the book.

Considering what research has revealed to the modern teacher concerning the laws of learning and education, it is not only alarming and hard to understand but it is inexcusable and disgraceful that so many teachers teach science each year without once leaving the classroom.

THE OBJECTIVES OF SCIENCE EDUCATION

The science curriculum will strengthen and implement in every way possible the major objectives of general educa-

[2] State Superintendent of Public Instruction, Science For The Elementary School, Raleigh: North Carolina Public Schools, 1952.

The "Little Red Schoolhouse" Nature Center is enjoyed by young and old alike. In 1962 over 132,000 visitors came to see the exhibits and walk the self-guiding nature trails.

Courtesy of Roland F. Eisenbeis

tion. The objectives of science instruction vary from school to school both in scope and somewhat in purpose. However, an examination of many different lists of objectives formulated by committees of teachers throughout the country shows many objectives in common.

Every aspect of the science program contributes in some way to the achievement of the science objectives and to the broad general objectives of general education.

The major objectives of science education recommended by the National Society for the Study of Education, [3] although general, cover most of the frequently stated objectives of science instruction. These objectives provide for:

1. Growth in the functional understanding of scientific facts that are part of the environments children live in at

[3]National Society for the Study of Education, Science Education in American Schools, (Forty-Sixth Yearbook) Chicago: University of Chicago Press, 1947, pp. 28-29.

home, in school and elsewhere.

2. Growth in the development of an understanding of scientific concepts and principles that function in children's experiences and help to explain them.

3. Growth in the use of basic instrumental skills involved in the location of scientific data.

4. Growth in the ability to use the problem-solving skills involved in the methods of science.

5. Growth in the assumption of such scientific attitudes as open-mindedness, intellectual honesty, suspended judgment, sustained effort and respect for human dignity.

The objectives of science instruction formulated by the Chicago Public Schools[4] fall under three main categories:

Social objectives in science instruction
  Protecting life and health
  Meeting vocational responsibilities
  Enjoying wholesome leisure
  Satisfying spiritual and aesthetic needs
  Using the tools of communication effectively
  Developing economic competence
  Improving family living
  Building human relationships
  Practicing American citizenship

Achievement objectives in science instruction
  To stimulate systematic thinking and action regarding the preservation of bodily health
  To derive spiritual and aesthetic satisfactions from observation of nature's ways and wonders
  To discover and appreciate the role of science in the conservation of natural resources
  To acquire ability to use ways of science in meeting individual and group problems
  To appreciate the vocational and leisure implications of scientific inventions and discoveries
  To appraise the potentialities of science for improving man's productive and economic status
  To apply science principles and knowledge in consumer activity
  To realize how today's physical and social world is being changed through scientific developments in transportation and communication

[4] Chicago Public School, Teaching Guide For Science, Pre-School Through Junior College, 1955, p. 4.

To acquire and use an adequate science vocabulary

To utilize the physical resources of the school, home, and community as a laboratory for observing natural phenomena and physical adaptations.

Pupil-personality objectives of science instruction

To develop and maintain emotional stability

To develop critical thinking at child's developmental level

To develop a sense of security

To develop self-direction

To develop an acceptance of realistic standards

To develop cooperative attitudes

To develop a sense of responsibility

To develop social effectiveness

To develop creative satisfactions

To develop reasonable acceptance of authority at child's developmental level.

TRENDS IN THE TEACHING OF SCIENCE[5]

A number of very promising trends are becoming firmly established in the teaching of science. With these few trends, we are pointing to the direction in which we are moving in our science program.

1. There is definitely an increased emphasis on science as an integral part of the school program, either as a separate subject or in combination with social studies or some other area.

2. Many state, city and county units are developing or have completed more or less definite courses of study or curriculum guides to enrich the study of science. Such course outlines help to ensure a sequence of subject matter from grade to grade through the entire school experience.

3. Science experiences are being built around the solving of problems which are significant to pupils rather than on the answering of unimportant questions that stress the recall of unrelated scientific facts.

[5]Department of Instruction and Guidance, Comprehensive Curriculum Guide For Elementary Teachers, Kalamazoo, Michigan: Kalamazoo Public Schools, 1949, p. iii.

4. There is growing emphasis on practical science for the daily life activities of pupils with less requirement for notebook drawings, for filling in cookbook type manuals, and for other time-consuming activities in favor of more practical everyday useable materials.

5. Effort is being made to use actual experiences whenever possible to make the learning in science more meaningful. In other words, there is more doing on the part of children and less reading and hearing about science. These experiences include, among other things, experimenting and observing real applications of scientific principles.

6. Persistent effort is being made to fit the science offerings and the learning methods to the needs, interests, and abilities of the learners.

7. Much stress is laid on using community resources in order to bring science to life.

8. Administrators, teachers, and pupils are working together to an increasing extent to plan and carry out an effective program.

9. Increasing effort is being made to determine exactly how science can most effectively make its unique contribution to the development of children and fit into the total learning situation.

10. There is a greater degree of flexibility in selection of content for science experiences. This permits selection of content in keeping with broader goals and objectives.

11. There is promising development in terms of making scientific attitudes, scientific method, appreciations of science, and logical reasoning functional in the daily thinking and activity of pupils in connection with personal problems.

12. There is far greater emphasis on science experiences which have value for leisure home activities and for vocational or avocational consideration.

13. There is growing emphasis on science which can be valuable for all youth, adaptable for the slow learner as well as for the fast learner.

Teachers who feel strongly that this is the right way to teach science point out that science is so closely interwoven into the pattern of every day living that it is impossible to separate it into an isolated area of study. Others claim that in integrating science instruction with other subjects, too little emphasis is placed on important scientific concepts. They contend that too many teachers confuse science with technology and teach the results of science rather than the exciting intellectual scientific process.

Another disadvantage to integrating science with other subjects is that many important areas of science may not be presented, especially if it does not fall into units of study stressed in the other subject areas. Furthermore, teachers with a good background in science see science as vitally important in the education of children and ask why not integrate the other subjects with science.

Some elementary schools depend upon the daily interests and activities of children to direct their instruction in science. Incidental science experiences are introduced as the children observe certain phenomena in nature, and ask questions about happenings involving nature. The teacher seizes upon this teachable moment to discuss and guide children to further investigation and development of the why, what, when, how and where of science experience.

The incidental method of teaching science leaves the selection of science activities entirely to the children. The pupils make their selection by the interest they display and the problems they bring to class. Many authorities are concerned that this method is not adequate. Following children's interests is not enough; teachers must also consider their needs. Teachers will have to broaden the children's horizons by introducing science topics and facts which children will not find in their limited experience. Education is not only the organization and reorganization of experience but also the extension of experience. The teacher must see that the child grows by extending his experience to include a variety of scientific concepts and facts.

The third method of science instruction is the planned science sequence in which a set amount of time is regularly devoted to the study of science the same as certain other school subjects. The amount of time devoted to science instruction varies from school to school but with the recent Russian success in rocket and space science, society is putting pressure on educators to increase the time devoted to the teaching of science.

Usually the planned sequence for science instruction involves the use of a textbook and follows a pre-set outline or content of study. Although the textbook can provide certain obvious advantages, especially for inexperienced teachers, it may also have a stifling effect on the study of science. Improperly used science textbooks, as in any other subject, may enslave the teacher to set and prescribed content with little or no relationship to life at hand. Thomas makes an excellent reference to what can happen in this respect.

> Rather than serving the children and helping them become interested, efficient investigators of their world, the text may come to rule the class and often prevent rather than promote useful learning. One morning early in November the seventh graders chattered about the early-winter freeze and snowfall that had descended on the community the night before. Tony said that his father's car "froze up and split the block." Jean said, "Our milk was frozen this morning. It was the funniest thing. The bottle tops were pushed way up by a kind of icy neck of cream." Carl said, "My dad had to shovel a big drift away from the garage door before he could get the car out. I wonder how much snow fell." Frances asked, "How cold is it today? Will the ice on the pond behind school be thick enough for skating? By the way, how thick does it have to get before they let us skate?" All of this talk had to stop when the bell rang, for the teacher announced:
>
> "Class, we have a lot of material to cover today, so please pay close attention. We're a little behind in our science study. We have to reach Chapter Eleven by January, so let's have your fullest cooperation. Now turn in your books to the section we are studying on 'parts of the flower.' Today we will learn the function of the anther, the pollen, and the pistil."
>
> Being enslaved by the textbook sequence, the class could not investigate the early snowfall--something that affected their lives immediately. The students had firsthand information about the weather change, and they had questions they wished answered, but their needs and interests were denied.[6]

[6]R. Murray Thomas, Way of Teaching In Elementary Schools, New York: Longmans, Green and Company, 1955, p. 319.

Good elementary teachers with a background in science organize their own science program and build it around the children's science problems or bodies of knowledge directly related to their lives. They use the textbook as a resource book and usually have many other science books available for the children in developing their teaching unit.

Science units organized by science teachers will, of course, vary with the background and experience of the teacher. This is as it should be for each teacher will be assigned different children and education is concerned with developing critical thinking and should not be concerned with conformity to subject matter content.

Teachers who like to develop their own instructional unit whether in science or any other subject area would do well to give much thought to the fourteen characteristics of a good unit of study which has been developed by Lee and Lee:[7]

1. Problem-centered.
2. Involved with many areas of knowledge.
3. Develops understanding of the interrelatedness of knowledge.
4. Deals with significant knowledge and understandings.
5. Deals with materials and understandings of concern to the child.
6. Directed towards the development of concepts and understandings as well as the acquiring of knowledge and skills.
7. Set up to obtain changes in the behavior of children which will result in more effective living for them.
8. Planned with the understanding of how learning takes place.
9. Planned and developed cooperatively by pupils and teacher.
10. Uses a wide selection and range of resources.
11. Provides for a wide range of experiences, learnings, and activities.
12. Provides for continuous as well as culminating evaluation.

[7] J. Murray Lee and Dorris May Lee, The Child and His Curriculum, (Third Edition), New York: Appleton-Century-Crofts, Inc., 1960, p. 174.

In considering all of the units taught during the year
there are two additional characteristics with which
the teacher must be concerned.
They are:
13. Contributes to the total development of the child.
14. Provides for continuity in the development of the
    child.

The increasing knowledge and understanding of children and how they learn and the recognition of the importance of science in the education of children has given a new
impetus to science instruction in the public schools. Science today with its demand for critical thinking and better
understanding of the world and its demand for exact observation and intelligent planning has been recognized for its
important contribution to the education of children. Administrators and teachers through united and committee action
are planning for continuous growth in science experience
throughout each year of study but also from one year to the
next.

Younger children do not think of science in terms of
special fields of living and they react to it as a subject
without bounds. Only as they grow older and begin to classify knowledge or have it separated and classified for them
do they begin to enroll in courses such as earth science,
biology, chemistry or physics.

Physical and biological science has generally been
divided into five broad areas of study: the universe, the
earth, conditions necessary to life, living things, physical
and chemical phenomena and man's attempt to control his
environment.

The Illinois Curriculum Program Committee[8] has
suggested a desirable program of elementary science experiences which may be developed by the teacher around five
questions concerning our environment.

1. Here is our environment--what is in it and how can
   we understand it? An inventory of the community

[8]Illinois Curriculum Program, Strengthening Science Teaching in Elementary Schools,
Springfield: Superintendent of Public Instruction, 1960, pp. 30-31.

is necessary to open the eyes of the pupil to make him aware of things he contacts daily. Interrelationships between organisms and environment factors should be stressed.

2. Here is our environment--how do we use what is in it? The use of things as we find them in nature-- physical, chemical, biological are brought out.

3. Here is our environment--how have we changed it to better meet our needs? Utilization of the devices created by man to make a comfortable life for himself brings out many of the scientific principles stressed in all the major sciences.

4. Here is our environment--how have we damaged it? Careless, wasteful use of our natural resources such as soil, water, minerals, wildlife, and forests have impoverished many areas and reduced their occupants to submarginal existences.

5. Here is our environment--how may we restore it? Development of the conservation aspects of science are brought out which will curtail the damages to our environment that have been wrought by man's occupancy. Restoration or repair methods which will return the environment to productivity should be brought out.

With the recent emphasis on science instruction, many school systems are employing science consultants to assist classroom teachers in developing instructional material and developing techniques for instruction.

New York City has a department of science and gardens with consultants working with teachers on a sign-up basis. Other systems employ science teachers for teaching science in the upper grades and serving as consultants in science to teachers in the elementary grades.

Science in the primary grades is to be introduced and not exhausted. The child must be motivated by curiosity and enthusiasm. Teachers eager to give children an excellent background can sometimes kill interest in science by trying to give the children too much. Science instruction should be closely related to real things in the children's environment. It should deal with things children can see, feel, smell, hear, handle and study at firsthand.

Emphasis should be placed on learnings which come through the senses, seeing, hearing, feeling, tasting, and smelling. Feelings are of primary importance; the multi-sensory rather than the intellectual approach is emphasized; and abstractions are secondary to concrete and real experience.

In the primary grades children should be given first-hand experiences over the whole range of their physical and natural environment. Science should be simple. It should be specific and limited rather than broad and general. It must be interesting.

As children enter the intermediate grades emphasis will still be on firsthand learning, stressing the sensory approach, a wide variety of activity and somewhat greater detail in observation and study. As children grow older the teacher will call for more thinking and more accurate generalizations. The intellectual approach to science will supplement the multi-sensory so that skills and science concepts will begin to take form. Teachers will begin to place emphasis on problem solving and the development of a scientific approach to problems.

Simple and interesting experiences dealing with the broad generalities, rather than specialization, should guide the teacher in science instruction and activity in the intermediate grades.

A science program beginning with the child's own experience and covering the full range of activities from firsthand contact with real things, then through vicarious experiences to ultimate abstractions in the high school grades should give a basic foundation in science which will be suitable for use in modern day living. A plea to all teachers, especially to the teachers of high school science is to not let scientific abstractions become useless material for memorization by divorcing it from the process of science or from the process of living.

The primary purpose of the public schools is not to make scientists but citizens who are intelligent about science. There is plenty of time for universities to develop scientists for those who have unusual interest and ability in investigation, experimentation and in critical thinking.

SCIENCE AND OUTDOOR EDUCATION

Science teachers have probably used, or need to use, the outdoors more than any other teacher. It is hard to visualize a teacher presenting science materials entirely from a textbook inside a classroom completely isolated from the world of living things.

Since it is desirable to make learning experiences as direct and concrete as possible, outdoor education can provide a natural setting for developing science concepts. Just outside the classroom door, across the street in a vacant lot, two blocks away at the city park or within a short distance of the school, children may have an opportunity to learn about their environment in context, thereby gaining greater interests and understandings. Some schools own a garden, a farm or a forest which is available to all classes throughout the school year for investigation and exploration.

More and more school systems are developing camps where children may have an extended experience in living and learning close to nature.

Living close to nature in a camp setting, children get a true picture of man and his relationship to his environment. They learn that man is just another link in the wonderful balance of nature; that man uses the same environment and utilizes the same basic biological, chemical and physical process as other living things. The air he breathes is used and reused by other organisms. The oxygen he needs for life has just been released by surrounding plant life. The food and clothing he uses are obtained from plants and animals. Heat and light from the sun benefit all living things, not just man. Without such experience direct with nature, children too often get an exaggerated picture of man's importance to the process of life.

Science instruction, including health and conservation concepts, approached in this manner will bring new insights into man's relation to nature and will develop a reverence for those things beyond man's power to control.

Traditionally, the public schools have turned to textbooks, microscopes, and other instruments as the most important method of instruction. Perhaps this fact explains one of the reasons why schools have been so slow in accepting their responsibility for teaching the conservation of natural resources.

Although there is marked improvement in the use of these techniques in recent years, too few books emphasize realistic problem-solving techniques. Many students are provided with laboratory manuals which add experimental work to the text. The answers to important scientific problems are in the back of the book. Yet, little experience is provided outside the classroom in the local community or in nearby fields and woods where students may relate and interpret facts and principles to their daily living.

Because of the informality of the out-of-doors, the vastness of the educational setting, and the magnitude of materials which challenge the class, many teachers find it safer and easier to remain in the confines of the four walls of the classroom.

Teachers who gradually introduce children to outdoor education find that their instruction becomes much more stimulating and effective as they master the techniques of the outdoor education method.

Opportunities for teaching science in a meaningful and interesting way abound in the out-of-doors. It would be impossible to list all the projects or areas for science instruction for science is as broad as the universe. Some of the more obvious activities involving science in the out-of-doors may include such activities or projects as the following:

General Nature Walks
Bird Observation Walks
Wilderness Exploration
Star Observation and Study
Prospecting for Minerals
Nocturnal Hikes
Tree Identification Projects
Collecting Rock and Mineral Specimen
Collecting Driftwood
Recording Bird Songs
Collecting Natures Seed
Tracking Animals
Soil Testing

Planting Trees
Stream Improvement
Weather Observation
Fish Management
Erosion Control
Feeding Birds
Earthworm Culture
Care of Pets
Cocoon Culture
Growing Plants from Seed
Making a Wildlife Sanctuary
Collecting Materials for Crafts
Gardening
Gathering Edible Plants
Making Weather Stations
Use of Compass
Map Making
Observe Ant Hill and Ant Life
Observe Shadows Cast at Various Hours During Day
Observe Sunrise and Sunset
Visit Abandoned Farm Site
Collect Interesting Shells in Gravel Pit
Visit a Fish Hatchery
Prepare a well-balanced Meal in the Out-of-doors
Examine the Parts of a Flower
Hike in the Rain or Snow
Determine distance of Storm by Thunder and Lightening
Observe various Cloud Formations
Study Echoes
Repair Hillside or Gully Erosion
Make a Relief Map of the Area
Practice Conservation of Natural Resources
Study the Effect of Weather on Man and Nature
Study the Interrelation of Man and His Environment
Study how Plants and Animals Reproduce
Study the Economic and Recreational Value of Wildlife
Identify Snakes and Reptiles
Observe Man's Dependence on Sun and Rain
Descriptions of Natural Phenomena
Observation of How Animals Take Care of Themselves

Selected References

Blough, Glenn O. and Huggett, Albert J., *Elementary School Science and How To Teach It,* New York: Dryden Press, 1951.

Burnett, R. Will, *Teaching Science In The Elementary School,* New York: Rinehart and Company, 1953.

Chicago Public Schools, *Teaching Guide For Science, Pre-School Through Junior College,* Chicago: Board of Education, 1955.

Department of Instruction and Guidance, *Comprehensive Curriculum Guide for Elementary Teachers,* Kalamazoo, Michigan: Kalamazoo Public Schools, 1959.

Jeans, James, *Physics and Philosophy,* London: Cambridge University Press, 1943.

Lee, J. Murray and Lee, Dorris May, *The Child and His Curriculum,* (Third Edition), New York: Appleton-Century-Crofts, Inc., 1960.

National Society for the Study of Education, *Science Education in the American Schools,* (Forty-sixth Yearbook), Chicago: N. S. S. E., 1947.

State Superintendent of Public Instruction, *Science for the Elementary School,* Raleigh, North Carolina: North Carolina Public Schools, 1952.

Superintendent of Public Instruction, *Strengthening Science Teaching in Elementary Schools,* Springfield, Illinois: Superintendent of Public Instruction, 1960.

Thomas, R. Murray, *Ways of Teaching in Elementary Schools,* New York: Longmans, Green and Company, 1955.

Chapter 14

HEALTH
———

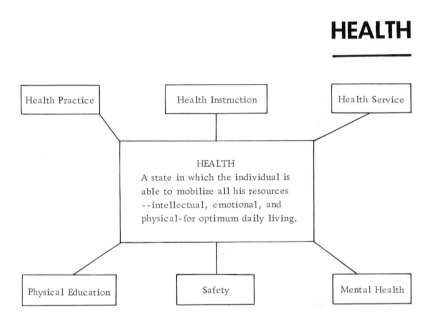

| Health Practice | Health Instruction | Health Service |

HEALTH
A state in which the individual is able to mobilize all his resources --intellectual, emotional, and physical-for optimum daily living.

| Physical Education | Safety | Mental Health |

    Health, physical education, and safety are closely related. In the study of any one of the three subjects children find a need for the other two and can easily see the relationship of one to the others. Children must be in good health to participate in physical activities and must have basic knowledge and attitudes in safety in order to enjoy such activities. Health involves the whole organism, both mentally and physically. One cannot be physically sick and mentally strong, or vice versa.

    In keeping with the concept of the unity of the individual, it becomes apparent that health education, physical education and safety have a definite place in the school curriculum. Today, more than ever before educators and parents alike realize that a well-planned curriculum for boys and girls must consider the health of the child, and health, physical education, and safety must be considered as an integral part of the educational process. The aim of this phase of education is to guide the child in those experiences which will help him attain total fitness in order to live democratically in an interdependent world.

The purpose of health, physical education, and safety is the realization of a condition in which body, mind, and spirit work in harmony throughout a person's life for maximum efficiency in living. Experience in health, physical activity, and safety are a part of every phase of living. They are more than subjects in a curriculum or perhaps better stated they are not curriculum areas in the sense that tool subjects are.

Physical education is a laboratory of health education, safety, and rules of conduct for play and safe living at school, in the home, and in the community. Through the activities of the physical education program, health and safety are promoted.

In the past teachers have approached these important aspects of living with an academic viewpoint as separate and isolated bodies of factual knowledge. Health education required memorization of the bones in the body, physical education was concerned with the rules of the athletic games, and safety required memorizing the rules of conduct on a special trip or school activity.

Today more and more educators are beginning to realize that health, physical education, and safety cannot be isolated from the process of education. Health is an integral part of all phases of living and all phases of the school program. It includes not only instruction in physical skills and safety concepts but even more important, it involves attitudes which will make the child health conscious and safety conscious in every aspect of his living.

President John F. Kennedy spells out the importance of health and physical fitness for modern living in a recent article in Sports Illustrated. Kennedy states that:

> For physical fitness is not only one of the most im-
> portant keys to a healthy body; it is the basis of
> dynamic and creative intellectual activity. The rela-
> tionship between the soundness of the body and the ac-
> tivities of the mind is subtle and complex. Much is
> not yet understood. But we do know what the Greeks
> knew: that intelligence and skill can only function
> at the peak of their capacity when the body is healthy
> and strong; that hardy spirits and tough minds usually
> inhabit sound bodies.[1]

The entire school staff is responsible for the health of the children entrusted to their care. The school nurse, the administrative staff, custodians and consultants, and the teachers play interrelated roles in the promotion of objectives set for safe and healthful living.

Health is considered as a vital part of the total fitness of man; it is his capacity for living in all its aspects; his capacity for enjoying the activities required for a happy and successful life.

The relationship of outdoor education and fitness-- mental, physical and spiritual--is increasingly clear. The out-of-doors offers new outlets for healthful living which can become an important part of life. People naturally love the out-of-doors and turn to it for opportunities to play in the open spaces, to camp, to hike, and to explore the woods, the fields, and the mountains.

The increasing availability of time that people have to themselves can be one of the greatest achievements of our times, or it can become one of the most severe social problems, depending on the degree of success in teaching people how to live. Current strides have been made in the improvement of school and college programs to equip children, youth, and adults with the skills, attitudes, and opportunities that will help them to live a more meaningful life. One of the most recent developments in the changing curriculum is outdoor education.

Outdoor education is good education. Its implications

---

[1] John F. Kennedy, "The Soft American," Sports Illustrated Magazine, December 28, 1960.

for fitness are extremely significant, from Ex-President Eisenhower with his golf and fishing to the proverbial "bare foot boy with cheek of tan."

Outdoor education has as one of its goals or by-products the immediate development of better physical fitness and the long range goal of attitudes and skills for maintenance of fitness all through life.

It is not hard to understand why normal human beings need outdoor activities for physical restoration. Automation, mechanism, and daily, sedentary classroom sessions have made it difficult, if not impossible, for many youth and most adults to get exercise, to say nothing of engaging in activities that supply both fun and physical development. All too often they have been taught only organized games and sports which require a group to participate, and which are unsuitable for most of those past the teenage years.

There is a great lack of training in skills for outdoor activities, which are suitable for all age groups and are appropriate and exciting for lifetime participation. These include camping, hunting, fishing and boating, canoeing, swimming, archery, nature study, gardening, hiking, and many other simple pursuits that require little organization and equipment yet promote a great deal of physical development.

In pioneer days, it was taken for granted that boys and girls would learn these activities in the home and in the community. While many youth agencies and outdoor interest groups are providing some outdoor programs, the great majority of the children have been deprived of contact with nature and of real experiences in the out-of-doors.

In outdoor education the mind and body are not separate entities, but are a part of an intricate interdependent system that make up the whole person. In order to be physically fit, the attitude or state of mind need be considered and an over-all fitness strived for.

The case of mental fitness through outdoor activities is obvious. With all the abstractions, the verbalizations, the rush to and fro, the tensions and stifling frustrations to the inner self brought on by competition in life and in the classroom; with so little opportunity to be creative and expressive and to actually participate in satisfying activities, the out-of-doors, the open spaces, offers true recreation.

How often has the time spent at the lake, or a hike through the woods, or a camping trip, relieved a tired mind? Outdoor education is superior to the classroom in this area.

The outdoor activities in which so many people engage can provide excellent opportunities for physical rejuvenation and muscular development through exercise that comes voluntarily. While outdoor activities are not substitutes for other planned types of exercise, it is only realistic to believe that people will do the things in which they have interest, experience, training, and which provide release from modern tensions. Outdoor activities are among the things that people do for themselves for their enjoyment of living. Thus, outdoor education becomes one of the effective means for physical fitness today.

HEALTH EDUCATION

Modern civilization has been both a blessing and a burden to the health of man. On the one hand, modern science has helped man conquer many dreaded diseases, but on the other it has made him a small cog in a world of machinery. It has increased his anxiety and placed him under greater stress and strain. As pointed out in Philosophy of Outdoor Education: [2]

> The incessant change in man's habit patterns, the rigid and scheduled urban life, the relentless pressures of the modern competititve society, the worry over war and world conditions and many other characteristics of modern life, together with a relatively sedentary existence, tend to adversely affect the health of man.
>
> Man has not always led a sedentary life. For century upon century his existence required hard work involving the use of his body in the open. He ate heavy foods and fed a hungry body that needed lots of energy.

[2]William H. Freeberg and Loren E. Taylor, Philosophy of Outdoor Education, Minneapolis: Burgess Publishing Company, 1960, p. 353.

> Modern life has taken away the necessary toil but man
> has not yet learned to make physical and mental health-
> ful adjustment to this life. He gets too little recre-
> ation, too little exercise, and too many calories.

In order to meet the needs and anxieties of the present day competitive society, the school curriculum is being revised. Unfortunately, health education is still being given a relatively minor role in this total revision. It is somewhat unique that society advocates a school curriculum which will produce more scientists, engineers, and technical personnel, but remains in a state of apathy regarding the improvement of the total health status of these individuals. Considering the physical condition of modern day youth as evidenced by the results of military examinations and the White House Conference on Youth Fitness, how can the future "rocket makers of America" be expected to produce to their fullest capacity in an efficient and effective manner if they do not possess good physical health. Vitamins, drugs, tranquilizers, and scientific medical advances are not the answers. Improvement of the total health status of today's youth can only be achieved through education. Considering the present day health education programs which are being conducted at the elementary level throughout the country, the primary question is how can a more adequate and beneficial program be developed.

The educational process at the elementary school level introduces the child to a variety of facts, information, and concepts regarding his total health status. Through periods of instruction in such areas as dental health, nutrition, posture and grooming, safety, communicable disease, and personal hygiene, the elementary school age child becomes aware of what constitutes good health practices. The individual is provided with classroom experiences and motivated to develop positive habits and attitudes concerning personal health with the underlying idea of total growth.

The principle theory of health instruction is ideal, but how effective is the actual practice and method of procedure? Are the children making practical application of this knowledge which is being imparted, or is health instruction merely the transferral of factual information from teacher to pupil?

The fact that over 90 per cent of all elementary school children have some form of dental caries, and that the United States does not hold a particularly high rank in the world in terms of the physical fitness of youth seems to cast a shadow of doubt regarding the effectiveness of the entire procedure of health instruction in the public schools. What are the problems, where does the fault lie, and how might these program deficiencies be improved?

One of the major problems seems to revolve around the fact that there is a great variance in the amount of time that is allocated to health education within the total curriculum.

The authors' survey of elementary school curriculum guides throughout the country reveals that past programs in health education were offered in the following ways:

1. Health education is integrated with all subject matter.
2. Health education is integrated with physical education.
3. One class period per week is devoted to health instruction.
4. Health education is taught twice a week for half hour periods.
5. The total curriculum includes two or three regular class periods per week for health instruction.
6. There are some educational systems which do not allocate any time within their curriculum for health instruction.

Taking the above information into consideration, and there may be additional methods and procedures which have not been cited, it is understandable that the development of good health habits and attitudes among school youth is a difficult procedure. In many of the elementary schools throughout the country there simply is not an adequate amount of time devoted for the teacher to organize a worthwhile and concentrated program of health instruction.

In many instances health education is taught because school districts are required to do so by state law. Under these circumstances any teacher within the school system who might have a little background in health is often allowed to instruct health courses. In addition to the lack of class time which is offered for health instruction, the lack of training and background on the part of the teacher is another problem which must be considered.

Actually every teacher should have a background in health education, for the health and safety of the elementary school child is the concern not only of all teachers, but of the administrators and staff. Such factors as lighting, adequate space to work and play, heat, ventilation, sanitation, safety, and other aspects of the physical environment is the responsibility of all members of the school faculty and staff.

Schools that try to teach from the book without providing a healthful place in which to live and learn defeat their own purpose. Health education in the public schools resolves itself into creating and maintaining living conditions, learning experiences, and instructional opportunities which will enable the pupils to do their work with maximum efficiency, satisfaction, and enjoyment. Not only must the schools assume responsibility for the life of the children entrusted to their care but they must instill health habits, skills, attitudes, and appreciations which will carry over into their community living and enable them to live to their fullest capacity throughout life. History, arithmetic, or English has very little appeal to a sick or unhealthy person. The cliche phrase "sound mind in a sound body" is loaded with implications for the classroom teacher.

The public schools are beginning to assume their rightful responsibility in teaching health to all children. The better schools are combining health experience with instruction and are providing health service and a healthful and safe environment in which to work.

BASIC CONCEPTS IN HEALTH EDUCATION

1. Good health is a state of complete physical, mental, social, and spiritual well-being, as well as the absence of disease or infirmity.

2. The welfare of the individual, his family, his community and nation depend upon the support and cooperation of all individuals in maintaining an adequate health, welfare and recreation program.

3. Research programs for prevention and treatment of illnesses, both mental and physical, should be supported.

4. An understanding of the nature of the human being--physical, mental, emotional, and social--is basic to application of the principles of healthful living.

5. Good programs in health, physical education and recreation will help people achieve total fitness for tasks to be performed, courage and morale, skills for survival and protection, leisure time skills and interests, democratic beliefs and skills in human relationships, moral and spiritual values.

6. The state of an individual's health, physical and emotional, should be considered in the choice of a vocation, for it is a factor in success.

7. There is a place in society for the physically, emotionally or mentally handicapped individual.

   Voluntary and official health and welfare agencies are essential to the maintenance of good community health.

8. Participation in vigorous play and exercise, out-of-doors when possible, helps develop fitness and is important to the development of muscular strength and coordination.

9. Physical and mental health are closely related.

   Experiences in infancy and early childhood establish the foundation for mental and physical development of the individual.

10. A knowledge of the mechanical correlation of the various systems of the body and of the function of muscles and organs will lead to maintenance and improvement of functional posture and body mechanics.

11. Growth and development--physical, mental, emotional, spiritual, and social--are a continuing process throughout the life of the individual. Both are influenced by diet, exercise, rest, relaxation, recreation, and by freedom from sickness and accident.

12. Keeping oneself in good physical and mental health helps one meet more successfully the mental and emotional problems in everyday living.

13. Practices of wholesome and unwholesome living have certain physical and psychological effects upon the human being.

14. Physical or emotional disturbance, or a combination of both, may interfere with growth.

15. Proper application of body mechanics to activities associated with everyday living helps the individual to use his body efficiently and gracefully.

16. Maximum educational and social values may be obtained by promoting wholesome boy-girl relationships through co-educational activities.

17. Active participation in sports satisfies basic human needs: the need for robust physical activity, for companionship, for stimulation and excitement.

18. Avocational interests offer rich opportunities for companionship, and help build strong friendships.

19. Individuals differ in their rate of growth and ability; therefore, each reacts uniquely to a situation.

20. It is natural to feel, at times, both positively and negatively toward people and situations. There are acceptable ways of expressing unpleasant feelings.

21. Adjustment to life consists of changing a situation when possible or accepting unalterable realities.

22. Recreation is an essential part of normal life, and a wide range of interests contributes to the development of a well-rounded personality.

23. Competence in skills leads to increased social pose among one's own and the opposite sex and acceptance by the peer group.

24. Every individual has the right to make his own decisions, provided he takes into consideration the responsibilities and rights of others.

25. Both constitutional factors and environment, physical and emotional, are important in explaining individual differences.

26. Sound family relationships form the foundation for emotional stability.

27. People who share the same interest have a common bond.
28. Development of ability to make acceptable adjustments to social situations dependent on desirable attitudes and cooperative participation.

BASIC SKILLS IN HEALTH EDUCATION

1. To evaluate one's health habits, and make needed changes.
2. To know and use correct terms when discussing physical and mental health.
3. To care for oneself after exposure to the elements.
4. To control one's emotions.
5. To organize time to provide for balanced living.
6. To dress properly for all occasions and seasons, and to exercise good taste in personal appearance and and wearing apparel.
7. To avoid use of drugs, tobacco and alcoholic beverages during the growing period and excessive use thereafter.
8. To follow rules of safety and accident prevention at work and play.
9. To learn the principles of first aid applicable to each activity.
10. To take care of oneself and others in unfamiliar surroundings--water, fire, forest, crowds, heavy traffic --or in the event of a disaster, and to be responsible for the prevention of accidents.
11. To recognize early signs of illness and to seek and follow professional advice.
12. To select and prepare foods for maximum nutritional value.
13. To exercise judgment in self-medication, to distinguish between sound medical practice and quackery, and to seek proper medical and dental advice.
14. To use the body in an efficient, graceful manner in sports and daily life activities.
15. To develop neuromuscular skills, organic power, coordination, maneuverability, creativeness, aggressiveness and initiative; to establish feelings of success, ease, and poise.

16. To practice first aid in simple emergencies, and to know accident prevention and civil defense procedures.
17. To acquire sufficient skill in motor activities to participate with competence in a variety of physical activities and derive satisfaction and enjoyment from participation and achievement.
18. To carry out essential practices of cleanliness and sanitation.
19. To work easily and comfortably with people of all ages and both sexes.
20. To evaluate advertising claims for patent medicines and all health adjuncts.
21. To practice initiative, courage, self-control and cooperation in individual and group activities.
22. To develop consumer judgment in regard to selection and care of equipment.
23. To explain or interpret to an observer or listener the merits of a skilled performance.
24. To distinguish between expert and inexpert performance.
25. To recognize that health, physical education and safety practices are based upon scientific knowledge gained in physical, biological and social sciences and enriched through cultural arts. Through research, attempts are made continually to define needs, improve methods and evaluate results.
26. To engage in competitive or tournament play under desirable conditions in individual, dual and team events, and to experience worthy team membership in a wholesome activity.
27. To learn that avoiding injury and developing a sense of security is dependent on a knowledge of health and safety factors applied in the correct performance of activities.
28. To learn that accidents are sometimes caused by hidden emotional factors.
29. To appraise the abilities, limitations, and potentialities of self and others and try new activities within this framework of understanding.
30. To learn to cooperate as a contributing member in affairs of the group.

DESIRABLE HEALTH ATTITUDES

1. Readiness to accept responsibility for maintenance and improvement of the best health possible for oneself.
2. Willingness to make decisions and to respect rights of others to make their own decisions.
3. Respect for both work and play as contributory to happiness.
4. Respect for health laws and safety regulations which protect health and life.
5. Willingness to explore and to choose alternative goals for those one cannot reach.
6. Readiness to accept and to give constructive criticism.
7. Understanding that relief from stresses and strains can come through participation in a wide variety of wholesome leisure time activities.
8. Desire for gaining and maintaining good health and physical fitness through physical activities.
9. Readiness to evaluate the physical education program objectively in terms of growth, skills, and social relationships in order that one may become increasingly self-directive and self-confident.
10. Realization that improvement comes through maturations as well as through conditioning and improvement of technique.
11. Willingness to look for causes when behavior in others becomes unacceptable to society.
12. Appreciation of the family and the role of its various members.
13. Appreciation of the history and development of various activities and sports.
14. Acceptance of change.
15. Realization of the importance of developing desirable character traits--good sportsmanship, leadership, followership, loyalty, self-confidence, poise and co-operation.
16. Readiness to accept consultation and care for physical, emotional or social problems.
17. Acceptance with tolerance, understanding, and consideration of those who are not like us in ability, who are

physically or mentally handicapped, or who are finally recovering from an illness.
18. Readiness to select activities according to needs, interests, abilities, and limitations.
19. Wholesome interest in the opposite sex.
20. Desire for and appreciation of the importance of mastering physical recreation skills.
21. Cooperation in carrying out good health and safety practices.
22. Friendliness toward others with whom one comes in contact.
23. Respect for creative self-expression through activity.
24. Appreciation of the responsibility of each individual to make the community a safer place in which to live.
25. Appreciation of the contribution made by science to the conquest of disease.
26. Readiness to seek new interests and develop new skills.
27. Willingness to submit to necessary discipline involved in mastery of an art, craft, or sport.
28. Receptivity to the stimulation offered by many forms of leisure time activity.
29. Appreciation and enjoyment of sports and skilled performance from the standpoint of a spectator.
30. Understanding that continuance and modification of activities in accordance with individual differences should give satisfaction and enjoyment that will sustain interest and participation in wholesome recreational activities in adult life.

HEALTH EDUCATION AND OUTDOOR EDUCATION

The purpose of any health program as a part of learning experiences in the out-of-doors is educational in nature. Children should have a safe and healthy environment, and the related experiences should be in accord with acceptable standards and practices.

Outdoor education is not the complete answer to the development of positive habits and attitudes concerning the personal health and well being of the individual child. In order to implement health instruction in the most efficient and beneficial way, there must be a correlation between the factual information which is learned in the classroom and the practical application of acquired knowledge through outdoor educational activities. One method of education complements the other. By combining in-class procedures with an educational program in the out-of-doors, the theory of providing experiences for the purpose of influencing habits and attitudes can be accomplished to a greater degree.

One variable must be seriously considered if the integrated program of outdoor education and classroom instruction is to be successful. No matter how meaningful and realistic health instruction might be for the child, a positive attitude regarding health practices must also prevail within the home and community. If parents and local citizens fail to realize the importance of developing good health habits, school youth will not be overly concerned about their health status; they will not take particular pride in their well being; and health education, no matter whether it is conducted inside or outside of the classroom, will have little or no value to the elementary school child.

PHYSICAL EXAMINATION

The physical examination should be a standard examination which is given the week prior to going to camp and should include a record of the doctor's inspection and the general condition of the individual, his general physical appearance, and any history of disease or allergies. Because the children are taking a physical examination for a definite purpose and due to the fact that they cooperate with the school nurse and/or doctor in the actual construction of health examination forms, these youngsters develop a better understanding of the meaning and purpose of a physical examination. An attitude of confidence toward the school nurse is achieved, and the individual is less fearful about consulting her and seeking general and specific information about any type of illness or abnormality. The carryover values resulting from this practical experience are:

1. The children become more observant and critical

of the condition of their bodies, their general appearance, and their health status both at school and in the outdoor educational environment.

2. There is less hesitance on the part of the child in seeking information and guidance from parents, teachers, and the family physician regarding normal development or unusual physical characteristics, and

3. Greater understanding and insight is acquired pertaining to the limitations which are invoked upon children with handicaps.

PERSONAL EQUIPMENT

Proper personal equipment for outdoor education experiences is an important item to take into consideration. Knowledge of what clothing and equipment is needed and the realization of why these personal items are necessary is the basis for group discussion which includes such considerations as the weather, time of the year, length of the program, general individual health, camp facilities, and program activities.

Through these informal discussions and the fact that the students usually help in preparing a clothing and equipment list, the whole area of personal welfare, care and cleanliness of clothes, and knowing the proper type of clothing to wear during periods of mild or inclement weather is better realized through practical experience.

FOOD PLANNING AND PREPARATION

By the time children have reached the sixth grade, they have received some factual information concerning the nutritional value of foods, but few children have had the actual opportunity to plan menus. Studying the measure, quantity and quality of foods, and methods of cooking in preparation for menu planning and food ordering provides a meaningful experience. It is thrilling to have a menu served exactly as the group has planned it, and quite often the fact that the meal has been planned by the children encourages them to eat something they have never really wanted to eat previously.

Through this practical experience and the factual information that has been learned, the importance of eating proper foods becomes more realistic. In many instances the children prepare their own meals at "cookouts" and from these opportunities they are able to understand the importance of food preparation, sanitation and menu planning.

Good table manners are also learned through direct experiences in the out-of-doors. A meal where the children are relaxed, where the meal is attractively served, where good manners are practiced, and where the table is properly set and appropriately arranged will be conducive to good eating and good digestion.

Many opportunities for learning experiences exist in the dining hall procedures or when meals are eaten in an outdoor setting. Students learn to serve the food, act as hosts or hostesses, and take turns carrying food from the kitchen to the table, scraping the dishes, and clearing the table after a meal and washing dishes. Through practical experiences they realize the importance of cleanliness in the handling of food and dishes. Actual participation in mealtime activities provides the child with worthwhile and enjoyable experiences because there is a sense of accomplishment.

PERSONAL HYGIENE AND SANITATION

One of the most important areas of health which is influenced by an outdoor education program is that personal cleanliness becomes a normal part of the daily living routine and is taken care of in a natural way. Because of the close association with classmates on a 24 hour basis, keeping clean and neat is an expected procedure. The facilities are available and time is allotted for washing and showering. It is quite amazing to watch the reaction and enjoyment of a youngster as he cleans himself through the use of a homemade shower or washes the soap off with a bucket of creek or spring water.

Group pressure also plays an important part in the development of habits and attitudes pertaining to personal hygiene. An individual child does not want to be excluded from the small group or from participation in activities because he is not clean. Quite often the positive habits of selected leaders within the peer group are influential upon daily habits of the group members from the standpoint of personal care. Counselor guidance is also helpful in the development of good habits and attitudes among these pre-adolescents. There is a tremendous carry-over value from these direct experiences.

The same educational learnings hold true for sanitation. The need for cabin cleanliness, making beds and keeping personal items neat, keeping an area free of litter, garbage disposal, and water purification becomes a learning by doing procedure. The children realize the significance of sanitation because they are directly effected by the condition of the camp in general and the cleanliness of their individual living areas.

PHYSICAL EDUCATION

Physical education is education by means of physical activities. The word "physical" in physical education denotes a means or an avenue of approach, and not the end of education. The general objectives of physical education are the same as for all educational activities and the program should be planned with the general objectives of education in mind.

Actually physical education is the oldest form of education. Man's very existence depended upon his success in physically battling his environment. His first education involved climbing trees, wading streams, throwing spears, shooting bows and arrows, and other activities that were necessary for survival in the simple tribal life of uncivilized man.

The Greeks, and then the Romans, were the first to give physical education an important place in their educational program. The Greeks were the first to see the importance of a healthy body to a good citizen and a strong nation. They saw beauty in the human body and exalted it in art. Education in ancient Greece stressed the moral and the physical. Citizens of Greece were taught to "give their all" for the glory of Greece and this required good militaristic training. Their education from an early age consisted of gymnastics, calisthenics, military drill, corrective work, strict discipline, feats of endurance, and other similar activities.

There was little need for physical education in colonial America. The business of settling a new continent, building a new home and carving a livelihood from the wilderness took every waking hour of every member of the family old enough to work. About the only time the family took from the many demanding chores was on the Sabbath and even the day of worship would not allow them time for the "pleasures of life." Play was regarded as a sin against God and a crime against society punishable by imprisonment.

Although there was little need for physical education, the colonist had great need for recreational activities to break the monotony of their hard struggle for subsistence Even this was not acceptable in many circles. The early Puritans had little use for leisure or leisure activities. Time off from work was to be spent either sleeping and resting for another day of work or was to be spent in prayer. The colonist passed laws in the early 1600's aimed at prohibiting all forms of amusement and mis-use of time.

This strong influence and indoctrination of thinking regarding the righteousness of work and the contempt for play in any form was passed from generation to generation and still exists in some parts of the country today. The old religious philosophy of "what is good for the body is bad for the soul" has retarded the acceptance of physical education and play for centuries.

Following World War I and increasing with every decade, there has been a changing attitude in favor of physical education. There are quite a few reasons for the increased emphasis on physical education and one was the world war itself. Draft statistics showed that one out of every three men selected for military duty failed to pass the physical examination. Public apathy soon became public pressure. In the 1920's many states passed laws making physical education a compulsory subject in the public schools.

Some states appointed directors of physical education, pre-scribed courses, and set standards for training. Normal schools organized departments in order to meet the in-creased demand for physical education teachers.

A second basic influence which resulted in a demand for physical education in the schools was the influence of the Industrial Revolution. With the trend from hand to ma-chine production, from home to factory production, and the movement of workers from the farm to the city, the social and economic scene brought a new way of life. As machines took over the work, man became an operator of an automat-ic machine. He is required to perform little or no physical exertion. Life in the city and work in the factory has cut down on the usual forms of exercise which were a part of man's life only a few generations ago.

Recent scientific progress, often referred to as "Cybernation," has caused a greater re-awakening on the part of educators for a greater need for physical needs of man--now they are designed to replace much of the thinking and creative work of man.

Closely related to the need for physical activity and the public demand for such is the emergence of our modern philosophy of education. For many years education con-cerned itself with training the mind. Modern day educators are concerned with the education of the whole child. They have abandoned the older notion that the schools should only be concerned with the mental and not with the physical edu-cation of children.

In the daring attempts to include physical education in the school curriculum, it is interesting to note the early statements of psychologists, physicians, and famous states-men who came to the aid of the educators. Among a few of the pertinent statements made in the 1920's and early 1930's were:

> Since the manner in which a child will react to a giv-en situation may be either good or bad, adult leader-ship and instruction are necessary. The results of self instruction in reading, writing or arithmetic may likewise be good or bad, probably bad in the case of a pupil; therefore, instructors or guides are provided.

The problem presented in physical education, including play, is no different, except that the activities in the physical education program are more closely related to the pupil's pre-school and extra-school experiences. These experiences are developed, built upon and interpreted to the pupil. It is not intended that native spontaneity should be curbed, but rather that it should be guided into more beneficial channels.

_____Allen G. Ireland, M.D.[3]

Of all the activities of the school curricula, none is as rich with educational outcomes as the play, games, sports and athletics of physical education.

_____Jesse Feiring Williams[4]

Let our young folks play manly games which train the eye and the hand and the spirit, which subordinate the individual to the team, the vanity and the egotism of the one to the honor of the whole company. The playing field is truly the trial practicing ground for the grand game of life.

_____Sir J. Ramsay MacDonald[5]

Modern life demands artificial living for our children. If God gave the child the instinct to play, man must provide the playground.

_____James E. Rogers[6]

In our thinking of play we have been prone to think of the earliest manifestations of it in the field of physical activity principally, and thereby have neglected the most important features. . . .Play does not mean being amused, and it is not synonymous with aimlessness and lack of results.

_____N. Norsworthy and M. T. Whitley[7]

[3]Connecticut Board of Education, A Program of Physical and Health Education For Connecticut, Hartford: State Board of Education, 1931, p. 7.

[4]J. F. Williams and W. L. Hughes, Athletics in Education, Philadelphia: W. B. Saunders, 1930, p. 36.

[5]Journal of Health and Physical Education, November, 1932, p. 18.

[6]James E. Rogers, "Teachers Training For Our Health and Physical Education Programs," School Life, November, 1930, p. 16.

[7]N. Norsworthy and M. T. Whitley, The Psychology of Childhood, New York: The MacMillan Company, 1926, pp. 215-216.

> With the young child, his work is his play and his play
> is his work.   Habits of mind and muscle are formed in
> this impressionable age which endure for life.
> White House Conference[8]

THE OBJECTIVES OF PHYSICAL EDUCATION

The general objectives of physical education are to contribute in every way possible to the development of the whole personality of the child. In educating through the physical the good teacher does not neglect the mental, social, and emotional phases of education.

Because the teacher is concerned with the whole child, it is practically impossible to list objectives of physical education that do not relate to objectives of other areas of learning. While educating through physical activities, many good habits and attitudes are being developed in health and safety, much is being learned about early history in folk dancing or Indian dances, and music or dramatics may be enriched in the rhythm and movement of the body.

The major objectives of physical education should be:

1.   To develop wholesome attitudes toward physical activity, exercise, and toward play.

2.   To aid the child in physical development, motor skills, coordination, and body efficiency by providing big-muscle activity. This includes the development of organic efficiency such as muscular strength, physical vigor, correct posture, and proper functioning of the vital organs.

3.   To provide physical activities, especially carry-over activities, which will be used not only in school but outside school and after graduation for the enrichment of leisure time.

4.   To provide situations through physical activities which will aid in the development of skills, attitudes and ideals which are essential for democratic living. Physical education through games, rhythms and athletics under competent leadership may increase the qualities of citizenship such as courage, fair play, loyalty, self-sacrifice, team play, leadership and "followship."

---

[8] White House Conference Report, 1930.

5. To assist in the wholesome development of each
child to his maximum capacity in the physical, mental, social and emotional qualities which will help him live a responsible and a happy life.

Teachers of physical education in the modern school
are not only stressing the concept of educating the whole
child but are interested in the child in the total educational
program. There is something wrong with a teacher that
demands good citizenship and good behavior of a child in a
particular class but is not concerned with his behavior in
other classes, in the home, and in the community.

SUGGESTIONS FOR TEACHERS OF PHYSICAL EDUCATION

There are many excellent textbooks and curriculum
guides in physical education which offer suggestions for
developing a physical education program. The authors will
mention here only the most obvious to most educators; they
are ignored in too many public schools:

1. Activities should be selected that are appropriate
to the ages, maturities, and abilities of the pupils. Every
elementary teacher knows that elementary school children
vary widely in interests, needs, abilities and maturation.
Special teachers of physical education sometimes try to
teach materials that are too advanced for a particular grade
level resulting in feelings of insecurity and failure on the
part of the pupils.

2. Physical education in the elementary school should
be taught by the classroom teacher and not by special physical education teachers. This implies that every teacher
must become familiar with content and methods of physical
education. Teachers must be prepared in physical education activities and in methods of teaching them to children.
It is most important that young children be taught by teachers who know them. It is impossible for a special teacher
to get acquainted with children meeting them for only one
period a day. It would be more ideal to have a physical
education consultant to work with the teachers who need
help and guidance in physical education. While the special-

ist in physical education is in a position to know his subject better, he cannot know the needs and interest of the child as the classroom teacher does. The obvious solution is for them to get together. This may be accomplished through workshops and in-service education.

3. Physical activities which have a carry-over value should be stressed in physical education. High schools and colleges tend to stress such activities as football, basketball, baseball and track and other team sports which are dropped from life after graduation. While it is true that athletic games have educational value for the students who participate it is reasonable to conclude that activities that can be carried over into adult life would be of more value. Activities such as golf, tennis, handball, softball, horseshoes, swimming, bowling, volleyball, skating, and dancing may be of value throughout life.

4. Winning interschool athletic contests is not an objective of physical education. Too many people judge the success of a physical education program on how many games the school has won in football or basketball. Too many coaches are not educators or have let public pressure and glowing headlines warp their sense of values.

Schools are supported by taxpayers which means that every boy and girl has equal rights to the use of gymnasia or athletic fields. A sound program of interschool athletics is most desirable and can be of extreme educational value under sane supervision but the athletic program should be the apex and not the base of the physical education program. In brief, interscholastic athletics should not be emphasized; winning should not be the main objective of athletics; the school and community should be instructed in the real value of athletics and the position of the coach; and athletic programs should be increased and broadened to provide more opportunities for participation.

5. Physical education should stress more co-educational activities. Too many schools begin segregation of boys and girls in elementary school and wonder why they act as wall flowers during junior high school. The physical education program should choose games boys and girls can play together through the first six grades. An occasional

segregation for such games as softball or volleyball should be the exception and not the rule. They should have a wide variety of experience in rhythms and dance, self-testing activities, individual and dual games, the team games in which all can play.

On the junior high level, boys and girls will have to be separated because of a difference in physical development, interests and abilities. But they should be brought together often for co-recreational activities such as social and square dancing, volleyball, tennis and other sports which they can play together both in and outside the physical education class. Classes in which girls dance with girls, which are all too prevalent on the college level should be eliminated immediately as unnatural and unenjoyable.

6. More fun and recreation should be injected in the physical education classes. One of the purposes of physical education is to provide and stimulate an interest in play. This cannot be done through the memorization of rules of games which change every year or meeting rigid standards set by physical education committees who are more interested in memorization of content than in the thrill and joy of education through physical activities.

PHYSICAL EDUCATION AND OUTDOOR EDUCATION

Physical education began in the out-of-doors for it was there that early men wrested his livelihood from his environment. One of the objectives of outdoor education is healthful exercise and the outdoor contributes more to healthful living than the indoors. In fact, it is hard to understand why physical educators do not take advantage of the out-of-doors in providing more functional exercise to achieve their objectives. Gymnasiums and rooms full of equipment are not only expensive but do not have fresh air and sunshine that is so necessary to healthful living.

Historically physical educators turn to sports activities for maintaining physical health and vigor. Practically all the research in the field has been on the benefits derived from certain sports and physical games but very little has been concerned with the benefits of exercising in the out-of-doors. Doctors prescribe walking as the best exercise. Walking along the lake shore or in the woods not only benefits the physical but is conducive to good mental health.

The outdoors is rich in interesting and recreational activities which contribute to the objectives of physical education. Among the many activities which may be listed as physical exercise are:

> Cutting and gathering firewood
> Hiking in the fresh air and sunshine
> Playing informal games
> Swimming, boating and canoeing
> Bait casting
> Fly casting
> Work activities around the camp
> Building bridges and other projects
> Laying out hiking trails
> Participating in informal camp games
> Gathering specimen for nature study
> Searching for native arts and crafts material
> All activities associated with learning and living in the out-of-doors

SAFETY EDUCATION

The number of deaths and injuries from accidents increases with each passing year. Never before has safety education been so important in the lives of young people. In this dangerous age of mechanical devices and speeding machines home and highway accidents are responsible for about one out of three deaths of school age children. The increasing complexity of society and the growing variety of situations in the daily life of man demands greater attention to the extension of safety education.

Safety education is concerned with helping children make wise choices when they are confronted with hazardous conditions. It deals with experiences through which children may make these choices when the possibility of injury to themselves and others is one of the factors involved.

OBJECTIVES OF SAFETY EDUCATION

The objectives of safety education are well stated in practically every safety education curriculum guide in the United States. The Iowa Department of Public Instruction[9] has listed ten worthy objectives of safety education which seem to be most frequently quoted by teachers and administrators setting up a program in safety education:

1. To help children recognize situations involving hazards.
2. To develop habits of conduct which will enable children to meet situations of daily life with as little danger as possible to themselves and others.
3. To develop habits of carefulness and obedience to safety rules at home, on the streets, in school, or at play.
4. To teach children to read, understand, and obey safety rules and regulations.
5. To teach children safe conduct in the use of streetcars, private automobiles, and buses.
6. To develop habits of orderliness and carefulness in the use of playthings, tools, common articles of the home and school, and in the use of fire.
7. To develop alertness, agility, and muscular control through rhythmic exercises, play, games, and other physical activities.
8. To teach children to cooperate in preventing accidents and to avoid unnecessary risks involving physical dangers.
9. To develop wholesome attitudes concerning:
    (a) law and law enforcement officers;
    (b) the safety of themselves and others;
    (c) organized efforts to assure safety for all.
10. To give children actual experiences in desirable safety practices.

GUIDING PRINCIPLES IN SAFETY EDUCATION

Basic considerations or guiding principles in teaching safety to boys and girls should develop out of the experience

[9] Iowa Department of Public Instruction, Instructional Units in Safety for Elementary Grades and Junior High Schools, p. 12, Des Moines, Iowa: Department of Public Instruction, 1940.

of all teachers.   The following list is by no means complete
but are common areas of agreement by authorities in safety
education:

1.   Since hazards to life and health are real and numerous in the everyday lives of children, safety education
must be planned in terms of the needs of children.

2.   Since safety is something to be lived and not memorized, pupils must be given an opportunity to live safely
through actual experience.   Pupils are not safe when they
memorize the rules on what to do.   They are safe only when
they know what to do and why it is done.

3.   The program of safety should incorporate accident
and fire prevention.

4.   Safety education should stress all the safety activities that lead to a safer way of life not only in the school
environment but in the home and in the community.

5.   Since all subjects of the curriculum contain instructional material involving safety understanding, habits
and attitudes, each teacher should share the responsibility
for safety education.

6.   Teachers should guide children in safe living in
all activities.   With children in on the planning and emphasis always on safety they soon learn to make safety a part
of all their activities by:

    a.   Realizing and understanding hazards,
    b.   Removing all unnecessary hazards,
    c.   Compensating for hazards that cannot be eliminated
    d.   Creating no new hazards.

SAFETY EDUCATION AND OUTDOOR EDUCATION

Rules of safety can be learned and practiced in the
classroom, but actual participation is necessary in order
to make safety procedures more meaningful to the child.
School children having had an opportunity to ride on a bus
can visualize from their experience the value of the application of safety rules which have been previously learned
in the classroom.   Running, pushing, horseplay, hanging
out the windows and similar forms of activity are simply

not accepted or tolerated. The individual develops an attitude of concern not only for his personal welfare, but also for the safety and protection of others.

John Locke once said that we know only what we experience. It is an important duty of every teacher to see that safe and sane attitudes, appreciations and skills become a part of the student's daily experience. As his experience is broadened into new activities and his world is enlarged through travel and broader education, his concepts of safety should likewise be broadened. The same attitudes and appreciations of safety in the classroom are necessary at home, in the community, on a field trip or at a school camp.

Once the children have arrived at camp, safety becomes an important aspect of living and learning in the out-of-doors. They quickly realize that the right way is the safe way and that courtesy and consideration are the main essentials of safe living. Prevention rather than cure is always emphasized. Some of the more specific aspects of safety in outdoor education have been outlined by Patty:[10]

1. Have a thorough medical examination before starting the camping trip. Camping is enjoyable and usually safe for the healthy camper.
2. Sleeping accommodations should be safe, even though primitive. If permanent cabins are not available, the following precautions should be taken:
   a. Locate the tent or other sleeping arrangement on high ground.
      (1) This provides drainage in case of rain.
      (2) Protects from hazards of cloudbursts.
      (3) Gives comparative freedom from mosquitoes, and
      (4) Gives benefit of breeze, if any.
   b. Dig a trench around the tent to drain water in case of rain.
   c. Take mosquito bar along to cover windows and door of tent or to cover one sleeping on ground in open air.

[10]Willard Walter Patty, Teaching Health and Safety in Elementary Grades, New York: Prentice-Hall, Inc. , 1940, pp. 322-324.

        (1)   Protects from mosquitoes and flies and permits sound, restful sleep.

        (2)   Protection from mosquitoes and flies is important to prevent disease and infection.

3. Clothing and shoes should be suitable for the time of year and the activity.

    a. Clothing should be loose-fitting.

    b. High shoes with broad toes and low heels are safest and most comfortable.

    c. Wool hose are best for hiking and climbing.

    d. High boots are safest for walking through tall grass, weeds, and brush.

    e. Adequate bedclothing should be taken.

4. Drinking water should be carried or secured from officially tested and approved sources. Almost all streams, springs, and lakes are polluted and unsafe for drinking purposes. Typhoid fever is the most usual disease resulting from drinking unsafe water. If a safe tested water supply is not available, boil all drinking water. It will have a satisfactory taste after cooling. Water in which you wash your hands before eating or handling food should be boiled.

5. Sanitary latrines or temporary outdoor toilets should be constructed where permanent facilities are lacking.

    a. They should be made flyproof.

    b. They should be located a hundred yards or more from the cooking place.

    c. Trenches should be dug for one-night stops. Fill in with clean dirt before leaving.

6. Poisoning from various sources constitutes one of the principle hazards on camping trips.

    a. Snake bites are not very common, but they do occur frequently enough to warrant elaborate precautions. One should wear high boots when going through undergrowth. Special care should be observed not to thrust hands into dark pockets and crevices in cliffs. Learn from first-aid text what to carry as medicine for snake bites and how to treat them

    b. Know how to identify and treat poison ivy.

    c. Know how to identify and treat poison oak.

    d. Blood poison may result from a neglect of cuts and bruises. This danger is greatest in hot weather.

    e.   Ptomaine and other food poisoning result from the use of spoiled food. Since most camping expeditions are taken in hot weather when food spoils quickly, care should be taken that only canned goods of first quality and condition are used. Other foods should be prepared only as they are needed. "Leftovers" are dangerous where refrigeration is lacking, and should be buried.

    f.   Teach the child to refrain from collecting and eating mushroomlike growths found on camping trips.

7.   Sunburn is a hazard. It is not necessary to burn in order to develop a sun tan. Expose the bare skin to the sun for only a few minutes at a time until a substantial tan is acquired. Severe burns also may become infected and may result in blood poisoning, if they are neglected. Carry a supply of sunburn lotions.

New experiences and in a new environment for most children offers an opportunity to apply rules of safe and healthful living to a new situation. Concepts of safety are broadened and become a part of the learner's being as he puts to practice his knowledge and skills for living comfortably with nature and the elements. As children experience discomforts in outdoor living they learn to make adjustments for a more comfortable life. Under the guidance of skilled teachers, children learn to put rules of safety to immediate use. They are learning safety in the best way possible; in the way advocated by John Dewey--they "learn by doing."

Selected References

Freeberg, William H. and Taylor, Loren E., *Philosophy of Outdoor Education,* Minneapolis: Burgess Publishing Company, 1961.

Hindman, Darwin A., *Handbook of Active Games,* New York: Prentice-Hall, Inc., 1951.

Iowa Department of Public Instruction, *Instructional Units in Safety for Elementary Grades and Junior High*

School, Des Moines: Department of Public Instruction, 1940.

Nash, J. B., *Teachable Moments,* New York: A. S. Barnes and Company, 1938.

Neilson, N. P. and Van Hagen, Winifred, *Physical Education for Elementary Schools,* New York: A. S. Barnes, 1932.

Patty, Willard Walter, *Teaching Health and Safety in Elementary Grades,* New York: Prentice-Hall, Inc., 1940.

Seaton, Don Cash and others, *Physical Education Handbook,* New York: Prentice-Hall, Inc., 1954.

Smith, Charles F., *Games and Game Leadership,* New York: Dodd, Mead and Company, 1932.

Chapter 15

CREATIVE EXPRESSION

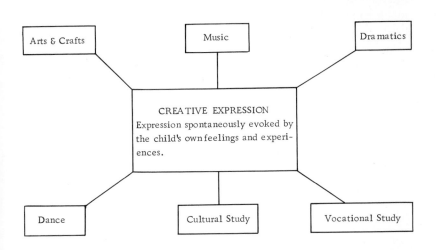

Since the turn of the century when John Dewey fought the "listening school" and advocated the activity school, educators have been concerned with the nature of creativity. Yet in spite of all the research and probing of educators, scientists, psychologists, and artists themselves, many teachers know very little about the creative process. As Lowes says, "Creation, like creative, is one of those hypnotic words which are prone to cast a spell upon the understanding and dissolve our thinking into haze . . . The ways of creation are wrapt in mystery; we may only marvel, and bow the head."[1]

[1]John Livingston Lowes, The Road to Xanadu, Boston: Houghton Mifflin Company, 1927, p. 428.

Research reveals that educators are making inroads into the complex and mystic quality of creativity and agree on many of the basic concepts. Practically all authorities recognize that creativity is not an academic subject or an area of study for children. It is an approach, an educational process in which something new and original is produced from past learnings and past experience. Creativity is a way of teaching for adults and a way of learning for children. Lease and Siks say creativity is the "sharing, feeling, thinking, and being that comes from active participation in creative group experiences."[2]

Creativity is conceived not primarily in terms of the product and its extrinsic qualities but in relation to the process through which the individual goes and the intrinsic quality of that process. If the experience is unique for the individual, involving markedly new combinations of factors, and if these combinations serve to express for him with unusual effectiveness the nature of the situation, then there is a significant creative expression.

In a broad sense, creativity includes the making of new interpretations and the seeing of new relationships in thinking and learning. In a more restricted sense, it is the interpretation of one's own ideas, thoughts, and feelings into a tangible form which is original with the person concerned.

Creativeness lies in the child doing the activity himself, prompted by his own imagination and his own inventiveness.

In the past a widely accepted view both within and without the school has been that only the select few, the elite group of artists, musicians, writers, and actors are blessed with the gift of creative expression. The truth is that everyone has creative potentialities although some are more creative than others.

In order to give more understanding to the meaning of creativity, Hockett[3] contrasts two groups of words. On the

[2]Ruth Lease and Geraldine Brain Siks, Creative Dramatics In Home, School, and Community, New York: Harper and Brothers, 1952, p. 1.

[3]John A. Hockett, "The Significance of Creative Expression," California Journal of Education, February, 1941, p. 159-65.

one hand is originality, ingenuity, inventiveness, experimentation, uniqueness, initiative, freshness, newness and change; on the other, habit, custom, routine, conformity, imitation, standardization, conventionality, uniformity, rigidity, repetition, memorization, training and indoctrination. All these words may be used to describe an activity. An activity involved originality or conformity, or some of both. The extent to which the activity possesses qualities indicated by the first list of words is a fair indication of the level of creativeness experienced in the activity.

The traditional association of creative expression with music, arts, crafts, literature, drama and similar activities must be viewed in a broader context. Creativity may be a quality in the everyday living of all people and not a privilege for the gifted few. It is not private property and it cannot be bought with money. It belongs to humanity. Thomas Edison was just as creative in his labor as the artist or the musician; for creativity is in the laborer, the artist and the musician and not in the results of their efforts.

Creativity is learning, but all learning is not creative. The learnings necessary to make automatic the skills or techniques are not creative. Creative learning must enable the child to see new relationships and increase his understanding. Systems of teaching where learnings are in the nature of rote drill and practice offer little opportunity for creative activity.

With this background and with the understanding that creativity is possible in all aspects of life and in all school subjects the authors will examine the place of arts and crafts, music, literature, dramatics, rhythms and dance and recreation in the educational framework. The above areas of expression to be sure offer wide opportunities for creativity and are certainly more than tool subjects but they do not have a monopoly on creative expression.

ARTS AND CRAFTS

This discussion on arts and crafts will concern itself with the activities of the graphic art media (painting, drawing, printing, photography), the spatial art media (sculpture, architecture, landscaping, interior decorating), and the crafts media (wood, metal, leather, weaving, ceramics).

Contemporaries in the fine arts are apt to be scornful of including crafts in with what they like to feel is the aesthetic. There is a tradition that the fine arts are for the art galleries and crafts or appreciative arts are really not art at all because they are useful.

Fortunately, this misconception of art is rapidly being discarded by educators. The ancient idea that art is divorced from life would make it, of course, irrelevant and unnecessary.

Educators today are in agreement that art grows out of everyday experience and a philosophy of art is really a philosophy of life. Art is generally a direct expression of what a person thinks and feels about a given experience.

Since art is inseparable from the everyday experiences of children it should be an important phase of every child's education. Through a wide range of art experiences, children develop the ability to express ideas and feelings and develop an appreciation for beauty and the ability to recognize beauty in everyday life.

The art committee of the National Education Association states that:

> Society has suffered merciless penalties for the neglect of art in our educational programs; the results are all too obvious, cities unbelievable ugly; homes devoid of comfort and the benevolence of beauty; dwarfed and distorted personalities; marred and disfigured landscapes; crude manners; and a world of things uglier than need be.[4]

Arts in schools today do not aim so much at making artists as at giving young people a chance to express themselves with various materials.

Almost every art department in our public schools has innumerable opportunities to contribute to community activities in such ways as making posters for special drives,

---

[4]Art Committee, National Education Association, 1951 Convention.

painting scenery for community plays, and contributing ideas for home decorating campaigns.

Students might organize their own art gallery, select work created by their own members, invite local artists to exhibit, and invite parents to the exhibition.

BASIC CONCEPTS IN ART EDUCATION

Some of the changing concepts in art education in our modern schools include:

1. Creative activities and self-expression are essential for the growth of children. Adult standards and imposed techniques must be introduced only when the child sees a need for help--not when the adult sees the need.

2. All children are artists and need opportunities for success and emotional satisfaction in creative expression.

3. The art education program should be designed, not only for the gifted pupils in art expression, but for all children as potential artists.

4. The teaching of art is too big a job for the art teacher; all teachers are art teachers in varying degrees and methods.

5. Art is broader than painting or drawing. Any product which is produced through the manipulation of materials or arrangements of materials to produce a more pleasing or harmonious effect is art.

6. Individual differences in abilities, ideas, and background experience must be recognized by the teacher and used as a basis for enriching the art program.

7. In addition to providing periods for specific study of art, the art program should be integrated into every period of the day and in any activity or area of study possible.

8. A variety of experiences with different art media is necessary to a well-balanced art program. A well-balanced art program should include opportunities for working in four areas: (a) painting and drawing (easel, water paints, finger paints, crayons, chalk, charcoal), (b) pottery and sculpture (clay, plasticene, soap, wood, papier-mache, wax, plaster of Paris, stone, wire, paper cardboard), (c) textiles (weaving, block painting, stamp printing) and (d) con-

struction activities (wood, leather, metal, plastics, cardboard, papier-mache).

9. While the school does not purposely try to develop
skilled artists, it is incumbent upon every school to provide
materials and opportunities for creative self-expression for
all children.

10. In order to evaluate an art education program criteria must be applied to the learner as well as the product.
It is not always possible to discover the inner values of
creative expression by a study of its product. It is more
important for the teacher to recognize what art is doing to
the pupil than what the pupil is doing to art.

OBJECTIVES OF ART EDUCATION

1. To promote growth in children through experiences
with a variety of materials and media.

2. Strengthen the powers of observation, awareness
and sensitivity in the child.

3. Develop imagination and creativeness through art
activities of special interest to children.

4. To develop appreciation of beauty in nature and
everyday life.

5. Develop good judgment and taste in personal appearance.

6. To increase proficiency in the use of tools and
the various media of artistic expression.

7. To develop some understanding of good line, space,
color and design.

8. To foster profitable use of leisure time for vocational and avocational uses.

9. To develop satisfaction and confidence in the
child's ability to express himself.

10. To develop understanding of three-dimensional
media made from clay and other materials.

11. To develop a feeling for systematic arrangement
and good spacing.

12. To stimulate creative art through crafts and to
dexterity in manual skill.

13. To provide an outlet for imagination and self-expression.

14. To extend understanding and appreciation of the lives and cultures of other people as reflected in their art.

15. To improve the child's ability to enjoy works of art as an accepted criterion of culture.

16. To develop an understanding of appropriate materials for use in art expression.

ART EDUCATION AND OUTDOOR EDUCATION

Without the fields, the streams, mountains, valleys, and outdoor life there would be no art. The greatest art of the past was based on rural life or on religion. America has depended upon rural scenes for inspiration and achievement in art. Even today artists and art teachers leave the artificiality of the city to seek the outdoors, the meadows, the mountains, the streams, the woods, the valleys--for subjects.

The beauty of form and the materials which enrich the culture of America comes from her natural sources. America has succeeded in art to the degree that her art has been integrated with life and developed through the everyday contact with nature.

Today, educators are striving to make all classroom learnings as closely related to the children's experience as possible. Learning concepts that can be put into practice not only assure longer retention but also strengthen understanding and appreciation. If the learner can see a need for learning the job of teaching is greatly simplified.

Arts and crafts in outdoor education is closely related to life and to practical application. Both art and handicrafts offer a splendid media for original design and creative expression. Handicrafts with proper guidance can approach a high art form and can blend in with the everyday experiences of the children.

The out-of-doors not only gives children an opportunity for self-expression, but provides a setting for appreciation of beauty in the commonplace and a recognition of beauty in all nature. In the out-of-doors art is truly the heritage of all.

Some of the possible arts and crafts activities which can be carried on in the outdoor studio are:

Observing cloud formations
Observing the rising sun or the setting sun
Observing the many beautiful phenomena of nature
Sketching scenes in nature
Modeling with native clay
Building bird feeding stations
Making primitive camp furniture
Wood carving and whittling
Making primitive musical instruments
Arrangement of table center pieces from native materials
Weaving baskets and mats from barks and grasses
Painting or drawing scenes from nature
Spatter painting leaves
Photography in nature
Map making
Making bouquets and corsages
Drawing murals for the classroom wall
Making attractive scrapbooks on birds, plants, farm life and outdoor life
Making models of farm scenes
Making signs for the nature trail

MUSIC

Music has taken years to be recognized as a worthy subject of the school curriculum. Until recently, it has been regarded as a frill subject, a little extra offering if the school can afford it.

Today, educators realize that no school can afford to omit music education from the school program. Music, like art, provides an important medium for growth and creativity and is an important aspect of every child's life. Practically every school in the country makes a conscious effort to improve the knowledges, skills, and appreciations

of children in music. A thorough knowledge of the fundamentals of music is as necessary for enjoyment and participation of music as the multiplication tables is to mathematics.

The basic philosophy of music education is well expressed in the Child's Bill of Rights in Music:

I. Every child has the right to full and free opportunity to explore and develop his capacities in
the field of music in such ways as may bring him
happiness and a sense of well-being; stimulate
his imagination and stir his creative activities;
and make him so responsive that he will cherish
and seek to renew the fine feelings induced by
music.

II. As his right, every child shall have the opportunity to experience music with other people so
that his own enjoyment shall be heightened and
he shall be led into greater appreciation of the
feelings and aspirations of others.

III. As his right, every child shall have the opportunity to make music through being guided and
instructed in singing, in playing at least one
instrument both alone and with others, and, so
far as his powers and interest permit, in composing music.

IV. As his right, every child shall have opportunity
to grow in musical appreciation, knowledge, and
skill, through instruction equal to that given
in any other subject in all the free public educational programs that may be offered to children and youths.

V. As his right, every child shall be given the
opportunity to have his interest and power in
music explored and developed to the end that
unusual talent may be utilized for the enrichment of the individual and society.

VI. Every child has the right to such teaching as
will sensitize, refine, elevate, and enlarge not
only his appreciation of music, but also his
whole affective nature, to the end that the high
part such developed feeling may play in raising
the stature of mankind may be revealed to him.[5]

[5]Music Educators National Conference, "The Child's Bill of Rights in Music", Music
Educators Journal, April-May, 1951, p. 25.

In the past it was often held that music, like art, could only be enjoyed by the gifted few who were talented in music. Today educators are in agreement with Flagg who states that:

> Music is not a marginal phenomenon, intelligible to the gifted few, setting apart those capable of its special functioning from the "unmusical" mass of individuals. It is, rather, an approach to human everyday life for practically everyone. It is as natural as breathing and taken almost for granted. There is no separation between the living, experiencing individual and the music that speaks to him, so directly does music operate within the human organism.[6]

For purposes of clarification most music educators consider music education as having five major aspects which are overlapping and integrating in nature and not separate and distinct:

1. Singing
   The present day stress is on singing for enjoyment. Singing is probably the most basic of all music experiences for children. It involves active participation for children of all ages in songs of all types (patriotic, fun, folk, comedy, devotional, popular, operetta) and in a variety of environments children should be taught in interpretation musical notation and development of part singing. Attention should be given to diction, phrasing, and a pleasing tone.

2. Appreciation and Listening Activities
   Children should be helped in developing an awareness of things to listen for, to recognize instruments by sight and sound, to develop an acquaintance with many kinds of music, to recognize characteristic styles of music of other countries, and to learn more about the various purposes of music.

3. Rhythmic Activities
   By studying music of other countries, past civilizations and cultures, and folk music of various sections of their own country music may be integrated with social studies, physical education, and other areas of instruction.

[6] Marion Flagg, Musical Learning, Boston: C. C. Birchard and Co., 1949, pp. 31-32.

Interpretation of song materials, musical games, dramatizations and expressive body movement activities add to the wholesome growth of children.

4. Instrumental Music

Children who become interested in playing an instrument require a more specialized educative process. Rehearsals are held for school bands and orchestras during school time and children usually are required to augment their study by private lessons and individual practice on their individual instruments.

5. Creative Activities

Creative activities include the development of original melodies, putting new words to familiar tunes, dramatization of songs and recordings, making simple rhythm band instruments and writing rhythms for them.

BASIC CONCEPTS OF MUSIC EDUCATION[7]

1. Music in the schools must be based on a general core for all. It should provide a meaningful contact with all phases of music as a form of aesthetic expression--singing, listening, responding to rhythm, playing, and creating.

2. The general core should be required of all during a period when common cultural values of music are stressed. Those who wish further experiences with music should have the option of electing a class with materials and methods adapted to the increasing maturity of the learners.

3. In order to emphasize common cultural values of music without de-emphasizing music as both an art and a science, it is necessarily at the elementary level that the general core be taught by: (a) a music specialist who is capable of synthesizing music with the total school program; or (b) a general classroom teacher capable of teaching the technicalities of music; or (c) some combination of specialist, supervisor, or consultant with the classroom teacher, in which the right relationship is maintained between music as general cultural

[7] Adapted from C. A. Burmeister, The Role of Music in General Education, Chicago National Society for the Study of Education, 57th Yearbook, Part I, pp. 221-224.

experience and growth in musical skills.

4. The curriculum should reflect co-operative planning by teacher and pupils, or by supervisor, teacher, and pupils.

5. The curriculum should consist of real musical experiences.

6. Skills should receive proper emphasis, but they must be related to needs which are apparent to the learner.

7. Without sacrificing opportunities for participation, the program should emphasize qualitative, rather than quantitative.

8. Throughout the music program it should be recognized that the child is primarily a potential consumer of music. The school music program should be designed to foster musical independence.

9. There should be no dichotomy between instrumental and vocal music either in the general core or in the pursuit of elective specialties.

10. The music educator should seek ways to develop general educative aspects of elective activities, and even of those based on a high degree of selection.

11. The choice of musical materials should reflect an awareness of functional values. The quality of music should not be defined solely by authoritarian standards. Music which might not be acceptabe in the concert hall can be used in a program of music education if it is eminently suitable for the purpose for which it is intended.

12. Goals and standards should be high enough to challenge each learner but should not be out of the realm of attainability of any of them.

13. There must be adequate provision for music specialties growing out of the general core. In this way music education contributes to the need for recognition of unusual interests and abilities. It should be possible for a school pupil to have satisfying and worthwhile experiences with music throughout his school career without once taking part in a musical specialty if he so desires.

14. The music program should reflect an underlying psychology which is organismic rather than additive, with its primary emphasis on musical growth.

OUTCOMES OF MUSIC EDUCATION

The San Diego County Schools[8] has listed excellent goals of music education in terms of attitudes, knowledges and understandings:

Attitudes and Interests

Be interested in and enjoy participating in the various musical activities.

Find relaxation and social and emotional satisfaction in the various musical activities.

Have developed greater appreciation and understanding of other peoples through their music.

Have grown in ability to evaluate their own and group musical experiences.

Carry their interest in music over into their out-of-school experiences.

Have developed greater poise and self-confidence while performing musically in groups.

Have discovered their own particular musical talent.

Show an increased desire for worthwhile music.

Continue to develop appreciation and love of music.

Have developed more effective relationships with others through their musical experiences.

Knowledges and Skills

Have grown in musical discrimination, in listening with a sense of pleasure, and in selecting appropriate instruments to enrich other activities.

Have expanded their general musical ability and understanding through their various music activities.

Have refined their pitch discrimination.

Have improved considerably the tone quality of their singing.

Have grown in their understanding and knowledges of rhythm and of various rhythm patterns and elements.

Have increased their understanding of note values and tempo and their ability to apply it in the various musical activities.

Have become more able to interpret music in a variety of ways.

[8] Music, (San Diego, Calif., San Diego County Schools, 1956), pp. 5-7.

Have increased their understanding and use of harmony.

Have developed a large song, dance, and listening repertorie.

Be able to play various rhythm and melody instruments and, possibly, some Orchestral instrument.

Have increased their knowledge of and sensitivity to the various instruments and their musical possibilities.

Have grown in their ability to respond rhythmically to music.

Be able to use their imagination to discover new ideas in music.

Be able to create original melodies, songs, verses, rhythms, accompaniments, dances, descants, etc.

Be able to read music notation phrase-wise and think tone in connection with it.

Have developed understanding and knowledge of tonal concepts, like and unlike phrases, tonal patterns, rhythm patterns, and musical terms and symbols.

Understandings

Realize that music is a way of communicating ideas and feelings through a combination of sounds that are pleasing and intelligible to the ear.

Understand that music consists of melody, harmony, rhythm, and form.

Realize that music expresses different moods.

Be aware that there is music in many things; there is a variety of sounds and rhythm in the environment.

Realize that the music of an age expresses that age.

Realize that we can develop an understanding of others, of other nationalities, and of other cultures through studying their music.

Realize that music is a universal language common to all mankind.

MUSIC AND OUTDOOR EDUCATION

Many of the great musical compositions were inspired in the out-of-doors. Children can gain an appreciation of nature through listening to such selections as Afternoon of a Fawn, Blue Danube, The Brook, Vienna Woods and other such selections.

There is something about the outdoors that inspires interest in music. The informal atmosphere found in the woods and fields greatly contributes to the inspiration and appreciation of music. The song of the robin, the thrush, the bob-o-link, the babbling brook, wind playing melodies as it rustles the leaves, the chirps and songs of the cricket and the insect family, the spring refrain of the frogs, and all of nature's music, especially its nocturnal symphony orchestra await the trained ears of music lovers.

Music supplements experiences in science and conservation and brings immediate satisfaction to the interests of the children. Many activities in the out-of-doors provide a natural approach to rhythmic response. Movement of growing plants or the grace of movement of the various animals and birds can be interpreted in body movement to depict natural form, motion and beauty. Music contributes to the development of good citizenship and aids children in the appreciation of the unbroken continuity in nature.

There is a place for every kind of music at a school camp. Various musical activities in which children themselves may participate include:

Singing camp songs and rounds
Marching, skipping, clapping and keeping rhythm to music
Listening to musical recordings
Composing camp songs
Distinguishing animals by their sounds
Imitating bird calls
Matching tones
Playing singing games
Making and playing on primitive instruments
Songs of the trail
Creative singing
Inspirational singing
Listening to nature's music

DRAMATICS

Today interest in children's dramatics as a tool in education is ever-increasing. Educators and leaders in recreation are beginning to realize that activities in dramatics provide opportunities for rich educational growth and development for all children. Furthermore, there is an increasing emphasis, both in education and recreation, upon the value of creative activities in modern day living. Dramatics of various kinds offer many avenues for children's creative expression.

Dramatics can make a unique contribution to the major objectives of education. The young child lives in a world of imagination and play acts many roles. Many teachers use the natural dramatic flair of children for enhancing their education. For instance, history teachers may use dramatic play as an outgrowth of learning experiences when children play act scenes of history and identify themselves with the people about whom they are learning.

Children enjoy planning plays in connection with their school work; they may put on shows, programs, assemblies, and pantomimes in connection with units of study in practically every area of instruction.

Educational Values of Dramatics[9]

In an evaluation of the importance of dramatics in an educational program, a comprehensive understanding of the value of experiencing activities in dramatics, the objectives of education, and the implication for education should be established. Research reveals that dramatics has many worthwhile values which can contribute to a creative program in education.

There is joy in dramatics

In contrast to earlier times when play, recreation, and leisure were frowned upon as idleness, the play of people today--both adults and children--is widely approved.

---

[9] Loren E. Taylor, Dramatic Activities in Recreation for Children (unpublished Doctoral Thesis, Teachers College, Columbia University, 1957) pp. 7-29.

Modern educators recognize that one of the purposes of both education and recreation is to help the individual achieve a richer and more abundant life. Educators have joined recreation authorities in the realization that an activity may be worthwhile for the sheer joy of playing, for the fun and enjoyment afforded the participant. Children need to participate in pleasurable activities. Opportunities for creative and enjoyable activities in dramatics can bring surprising and delightful results.

Dramatics provides opportunities for creative effort

The expression of creative ideas may be spoken or written, sung or played on a musical instrument, drawn or constructed through one of the art media, expressed through bodily activity in dance or rhythmic movement, or through combinations of these activities as in dramatization.

John Dewey points out that the sole purpose of appreciation is enjoyment. Good music should be listened to, good pictures seen, and good literature read and heard. Because so many teachers have forgotten, or never understood, that appreciation is enjoyment, much of the appreciation for creative expression has failed. Teachers have tried to teach the knowledge and skills for creative expression in the same manner as they have taught the academic skills; facts are presented for memorization and tests are given to determine whether the pupils pass or fail. The enjoyment of that which is truly creative, of that which has for its main purpose the increase of the child's appreciation and pleasure is one of the most valuable and integrative experiences one can have. Moreover, creativity is completely beyond the understanding of anyone who has never experienced it.

Every child has creative potentialities and should have opportunities for self-expression. Studies in child development indicate that there is need for children to express their individual thoughts and feelings in various ways.

Dramatics stimulates sociability

Through friendly, stimulating environment; through teamwork and cooperation in producing a play; and through the sharing of friendly criticism, children learn to develop socially.

Teamwork is at the very heart of a creative dramatics activity, for in every experience children learn to work together for the purpose of creating a fine and satisfying play. As a child takes part in many creative dramatic activities and plays many different parts, he begins to understand how other people think and feel, and he gains a better understanding not only of others but also of himself. Ward says, "Along with interest in and sympathy for the characters in the story comes an ability to adjust socially to the group of boys and girls who are cooperating with him in creating a play."[10]

Although the activity is participant-centered rather than audience-centered, children have opportunities to practice leadership as well as "followship." Children share ideas and together they plan the action. The audience is not left out. They may be made to feel just as important as the players by being asked to observe the group in action so that they can find the good and bad points and make suggestions for improvements.

Dramatics has therapeutic value

The use of drama for group therapy as in sociodrama, and the use of drama for individual psychiatric treatment as psychodrama, are well established therapeutic tools of competent psychologists. A teacher with a good background in child psychology as well as dramatics may contribute much to the emotional growth and stability of normal children. Virginia Axline in her book, Play Therapy, shows how a child brought out his personal problems while playing with puppets, and through the process he understood himself better and found his place in the group. [11] While a great deal is being done with dramatics for the physically handicapped children, much can be done for normal children of therapeutic value in releasing pent-up feelings and emotions. The shy child, the anti-social child, and the extreme extrovert with the help of a patient and understanding leader may

---

[10] Winifred Ward, Playmaking With Children, (New York: Appleton-Century-Crofts, 1947), p. 22.

[11] Virginia Mae Axline, Play Therapy, (Boston: Houghton Mifflin Company, 1947), pp. 46-50.

find his way into enthusiastic participation in a group activity in dramatics. Since dramatics has therapeutic value and is used by psychiatrists for the handicapped, it seems that it may be used as a preventive rather than a cure with normal children. Children from disturbed families as well as from happy homes seem to find in dramatics the help they need in meeting their problems and releasing feelings, particularly when they have a sympathetic and understanding leader. Dramatics, dealing as it does with situations in daily life, enlarges concepts of character and action and so deepens perception and increases sensitivity. The individual seeking to identify himself with another person is released from self-centered pre-occupations. Drama may in this way relieve repressions and inhibitions.

Drama makes use of children's interests and experience

Activities in dramatics serve as a basis for the child as he organizes his experience. As he plays a character in a certain situation, he relies upon experience to interpret the situation and the reaction of the character. Therefore, the need of carefully chosen experiences by an understanding adult who recognizes the interests and needs of children is most essential. An alert teacher discovers interests in the first few meetings of the group. Children are eager to share where there are willing listeners. A teacher may discover interests through such leading questions as: "If you could open this package and find something you have always wanted, what would it be?" "Think about someone else about whom we have read. If you had an opportunity to be one of these people, who would you choose to be?"

While the child is busily engaged in dramatic activities, he is working with others, gaining insights and ideas, adjusting to situations, and acquiring social and emotional experience important to his living in a democracy.

Dramatics develops inner security

When given security in creative dramatic activities where no one tells him what to do, no one nags or goads him on, or pries into his private life the child feels acceptance and can express himself more fully. As children play strong and vigorous characters in dramatization, strong inner feelings so often curbed in everyday living are brought into the open and channelled into healthy activities.

Through creative dramatics a child may express his personality through independent thought and action. He is releasing his feelings and attitudes and frees himself for independent thinking. He gains a security within himself and draws upon his inner resources to express himself.

Dramatics motivates the learning of communication skills

Because of an intense desire to be in a play, a child may be willing to spend more time toward learning to read, write, or improve his speech. Children tend to add to their vocabularies and to be selective in their choice of words when they see recognition given for good speech habits. Activities in dramatics point up this need and develop a growing interest in words. When a child identifies himself with the characters in good literature, he expresses himself in like manner in order to be selected for the play.

Furthermore, the released atmosphere of dramatics enables a child to speak with ease. Each child is made to feel that he has something to offer and is given time to express himself. The child who raises his hand to offer an idea and forgets what he has to say is encouraged to think about it and share his idea when it comes back to him.

Dramatics develops fine attitudes and appreciations

As a child accomplishes things that seem to him worth while, he is building appreciations of similar things offered by others. The wider such experiences a child has, the wider and deeper will be these appreciations. Dramatics makes stories, legends, history, and poetry come alive and have real meaning to children as they think out, feel, and be what they are learning. The greatest possibilities for artistic and imaginative growth come through the creative development of a story into a play. Thus, as children learn to appreciate good literature, they ask and search for more.

Dramatic activities develop an appreciation for beauty as children live the wonders of nature. Under the direction of a skilled leader, dramatics provides children with the opportunity to learn about beauty by living beauty. Children develop a sensitivity and an appreciation which is evidenced through joy, reverence, and a desire to share.

Dramatics provides a cooperative environment

Experience in dramatics tends to give every member of the group a share in planning and a shared basis for action.

"How did everyone help to make this a good play?"

"What did you see that you liked?"

"How can we make the play better?"

With the approach, children are encouraged to share ideas in evaluation. Each one is made to feel that his contribution is important to the improvement of the activity. Each child strives to do the best he knows how. When children work together there seems to be a more positive behavior than when they compete for an individual prize. They tend to forget themselves and act for the good of the group.

When the spirit of working together exists, skills and techniques of working together are practiced and tend to become a habit. Children may grow into adults who know how to work together if they have opportunities for the development of good habits in childhood.

Dramatics provides a barrier to provincialism

The value of dramatics to promote international good will and understanding is attested to by the fact that the United Nations' Educational, Scientific and Cultural Organization (UNESCO) promotes an International Theatre.

Children develop their understanding of people of all times and races as they interpret the characters in a story. UNESCO encourages Children's Theatres of all lands to produce plays of other countries so that the children may learn of the customs and habits of their neighbors in our "one world."

Dramatics offers constructive use of leisure time

It has been demonstrated beyond doubt that recreation, adequately and properly organized, contributes to the social, cultural, and moral well-being of the individual, family, and community.

Churches through Bible stories, public libraries

through storytelling, playgrounds and other agencies through dramatizations and children's theatre, all help in building sound physical and mental health, molding character, reducing crime and delinquency, and enriching life and fostering creative living for all children.

Too many children, today, have become spectators instead of participants. They listen to music instead of making music, see plays instead of creating plays, and watch professional ball games instead of playing ball. No one can deny that creative experience may be had by being a spectator, but there must be a balance between activity and passive enjoyment. It is the duty of the teacher to stimulate interest in activity and encourage a good balance between active and passive recreation. A good program in recreational dramatics gives boys and girls an opportunity to express their feelings in pleasurable activities as well as an opportunity to become members of an audience.

DRAMATICS AND OUTDOOR EDUCATION

Creativity is defined as a point of view, one's feeling about their home, an animal, or the things in a surrounding environment. It calls for willingness to experiment, to be independent and to express one's self. What better place than the out-of-doors can this creativity take place? Outside, nature with her green grasses, birds, towering trees, beautiful sunsets and laughing, sparkling brooks provides the setting for children to express themselves freely, the setting where they will learn to feel appreciation.

Since dramatics is a form of expression and the out-of-doors is more conducive and stimulating to children's expression, the wide open spaces offer a good stage for play acting. In an outdoor setting children can have drama experiences, in various forms, which can be a positive and vital element toward the creation of an atmosphere which is most beneficial for the entire group. Group participation, group cooperation and group rewards are only a few of the values gained in such an experience. However, dramatics should be more than these; it should first of all, be fun for the children. No competition for the better parts, no rigid rehearsals for a perfect production, no "star" parts make for a more enjoyable play, or whatever the performance may be. The performance should be done in terms of the fun and the learning through doing.

Informality is the keynote for all creative activities. Formality and conformity are not conducive to healthy expression and creative work. The freshness and originality of nature and the excitement of living in the out-of-doors frees the spirit of children and brushes away inhibitions as they partake in democratic group living. A few of the many activities in which children may gain experience in dramatics include:

> Composing stunts and skits
> Taking part in campfire ceremonies
> Construction of puppets
> Writing puppet plays
> Putting on puppet plays
> Participating in choral dramatics
> Dramatizations of animals and birds
> Imitation of animals
> Dramatization of poems and stories
> Participation in storytelling

RECREATIONAL ACTIVITIES AND CREATIVITY

In relation to the environment of today recreation seems as important as the basic human needs. It has become a vital part of daily living in all communities. Today, with increasing leisure time, the word "recreation" is heard on every hand. It is fast moving into its proper perspective and has taken its place along with education and social work in the struggle for the betterment of society. At every turn, the growing importance of recreation clearly appears as a fundamental element in the life of the individual.

Recreation, in order to attain full professional status, has developed, and is developing, an intellectually sound and socially acceptable philosophy or system of values.

420

Although authorities in recreation do not completely agree on the scope and meaning of recreation, they are in unanimous agreement on the importance of wise use of leisure time as a safeguard to the integrity of our society. In recent years, authorities are getting closer and closer together on common goals and the fundamental issues of recreation. The ideas, statements, and opinions of these authorities have, over the years, crystalized into a sound philosophy of recreation upon which can be structured a rich and creative activities program.

Early leaders in recreation, with a narrow physical education background, usually saw but one channel through which people could be recreated, the physical. Even today, many specialists working in recreation view the problem from their own personal training and experience. The dancing teacher recommends dancing; the librarian recommends reading; the dramatics teachers like dramatics; and the art teacher sees arts and crafts as the ideal medium for recreation.

Recreation is not limited; it embraces all phases of a person's being--the mental, physical, social, emotional, and spiritual. As Harbin explains:

> Recreation is more than the playing of games. It takes in all of the cultural and creative activities that modern recreation leaders are now including in their programs for leisure time guidance. It includes music, art, drama, the chance to converse with friends, the thrill of a hobby, the song of a cardinal, the enjoyment of nature, a lovely sunset, a quiet moment of worship, working in a garden, a trip through the woods, the fellowship of a friendly game, the fun of a sports program, and a thousand other joys.[12]

Howard Braucher, writing the editorial for the first issue of the new Recreation magazine, stated that:

> The word "recreation" has come without our willing it, to be the rallying word of those who work for a cre-

[12] E. O. Harbin, The Recreation Leader, (New York: The Cooperative Publication Association, 1952), p. 21.

ative, cooperative, expression of personality through sports, athletics, play, and also through certain art forms.[13]

Definitions of recreation vary from amusement, entertainment, and play to leisure time activity and off-the-job living. Authorities have been much concerned and much confused in their approach to recreation. Many have regarded it as an activity, others have viewed it as being more inclusive. Many have spent their lives trying to draw fine lines between recreation and education, work and leisure, and play and recreation. Today recreation is considered by most authorities as an attitude toward life. Jacks expresses this idea very clearly:

> The art of living is one and indivisible. It is not a composite art made up by adding the art of play to the art of work, or the art of leisure to the art of labour, or the art of the body to the art of the mind, or the art of recreation to the art of education. When life is divided into these or any other compartments it can never become an art, but at best a medley or at worst a mess. It becomes an art when work and play, labour and leisure, mind and body, education and recreation are governed by a single vision of excellence and a continuous passion for achieving it. A master in the art of living draws no sharp distinction between his work and his play, his labour and his leisure, his mind and his body, his education and his recreation. He hardly knows which is which. He simply pursues his vision of excellence through watever he is doing and leaves others to determine whether he is working or playing. To himself he always seems to be doing both. Enough for him that he does it well.[14]

In the out-of-doors children enjoy a freedom that is not possible in the more formal classroom. Informality and freedom are essential to creativity and self-expression. Formal classroom procedures and the very formality of the

[13] Howard Braucher, "Editorial," Recreation, (January, 1931), p. 4.
[14] Lawrence Pearsall Jacks, Education Through Recreation, (New York: Harper and Brothers, 1932), pp. 1-2.

physical environment are deterrents to creative expression
even with the best of teachers. The physical arrangements
even at best hinder freedom of movement and are an obstacle to the natural movement of children.

Teaching and learning in the out-of-doors is a more
natural and permissive setting for freedom of movement
and thought; it is an ideal laboratory for a creative and enjoyable learning situation both for the teacher and the students.

Selected References

Axline, Virginia Mae, *Play Therapy*, Boston: Houghton
Mifflin Company, 1947.

Burmeister, C. A., *The Role of Music In General Education*, Chicago: National Society for the Study of
Education (57th Yearbook).

Flagg, Marion, *Musical Learning*, Boston: C. C. Birchard
and Company, 1949.

Harbin, E. O., *The Recreation Leader*, New York: The
Cooperative Publication Association, 1952.

Hockett, John A., "The Significance of Creative Expression," *California Journal of Education*, February,
1941.

Jacks, Lawrence Pearsall, *Education Through Recreation*,
New York: Harper and Brothers, 1932.

Lease, Ruth and Siks, Geraldine Brain, *Creative Dramatics
In Home, School and Community*, New York: Harper
and Brothers, 1952.

Lowes, John Livingston, *The Road to Canada*, Boston:
Houghton Mifflin Company, 1927.

Music Educators National Conference, "The Child's Bill of
Rights in Music," *Music Educators Journal*, April-
May, 1951.

Taylor, Loren E., *Dramatic Activities In Recreation For
Children*, Unpublished Doctoral Thesis, Columbia
University, 1957.

Ward, Winifred, *Playmaking with Children*, New York:
Appleton-Century-Crofts, 1947.

Part 4 Evaluation and Research

Far must thy researches go
Wouldst thou learn the world to know;
Thou must tempt the dark abyss
Wouldst though prove what Being is;
Naught but firmness gains the prize,
Naught but fullness makes us wise,
Buried deep truth ever lies.

—Confucius

It took man century upon countless century to lift him-self from a state of barbarism. His slow march toward civilization was due chiefly to his inadequate tools of learning. Trial and error and chance were his chief means of discoveries; guesses and hunches his chief means of interpreting his experience. The accumulation of knowledge was thus slow and inaccurate. Man was further hindered in his climb from intellectual darkness because of his slavery to habit, dogma, authority and divine rights.

Research was born of science and science is the father of man's fantastic achievements. Science was born when man devised new ways of thinking and new ways of gathering and recording data. Science freed man from tradition and authority; science accelerated man's accomplishments; science increased man's achievements; and, science brought about the most cataclysmic period in all history.

Research is a method of study or scientific inquiry by which all ascertainable facts are carefully and exhaustively investigated in the solution of a particular problem. Research is a relatively new tool of learning.

To most Americans research brings visions of a microbiologist setting long hours at the microscope searching for a cure for cancer; a physicist pondering on the intricacies of a new atomic reactor; a horticulturist developing a beautiful new flower or a seedless watermelon; or, a chemist mixing strange concoctions to blow up the world.

America's unbelievable technological advances, her unparalleled industrial productivity and her unsurpassed standard of living is the result of industry's investment in research. The pace of progress in America is set by research and over four billion dollars is spent each year on research.

Ezra Taft Benson, former Secretary of Agriculture said recently, "Take away the results of the past 75 years of agricultural research and education in this country and you would reduce this country to a fifth-rate nation."

Through research in medical science man has conquered many dreaded diseases and pushed the frontier of health to undreamed of heights. Past accomplishments will surely be dwarfed by the future promises of research.

Why cannot research be equally outstanding in teaching and education? Why has research failed in education? How is it that every field of endeavor has spent billions of dollars in research and has made tremendous progress while education is still debating the same age old questions? Why is there yet so much disagreement surrounding education?

Many centuries have elapsed since man first undertook to pass on some of his knowledge to another, since the beginning of what we now hopefully call the teaching profession. Teaching techniques have been tried, revised, discarded, revived and debated. Libraries throughout the nation are filled with millions of volumes on the history, philosophy, theory and practice of education. A tremendous number of studies and surveys are made in university after university on educational problems.

It would seem that after all the centuries of passing knowledge from one generation to another and with all the data available from research in education that modern educators would be in fair agreement as to what direction they want public education to take, what should be taught and how it should be taught.

However, this is not the case. There is as much or more confusion today in education as ever before. Educators are debating the same age old problems that baffled Aristotle and Socrates in ancient Greece over 2500 years ago.

Why?

There are at least two reasons why research in education has not kept pace with research in other professions.

In the first place, research is not regarded with the same excitement and enthusiasm by educators and students of education as in medicine, industry and other areas of human endeavor. In most colleges of education students regard the term "research" as a fearsome graduate course that must be passed, the last obstacle to an advanced degree. Library shelves are filled with rows of dust gathering theses on all sorts of descriptive titles which are conjured up by students in order to fulfill the requirements of an advanced degree. Research, instead of leading to exciting and worthwhile findings which may improve or change educational methods is used as a criteria for granting advanced degrees.

Research papers in graduate schools of education are presented to professors who seem more interested in finding points for criticism than in finding new ideas. Very seldom are the strong points of a paper mentioned but always deviations from accepted pre-set research patterns are cause of great concern. A student's career is at stake each time he presents a research paper.

Secondly, modern colleges of education give the student a choice of either becoming a teacher with comparatively little pay and prestige or a researcher with prestige and high pay. This practice has spread to other colleges and is especially telling on the liberal arts colleges where gifted teachers are beginning to move into research and to regard teaching as a nuisance and a waste of talent. The title "research man" has become a badge of honor in higher education. University professors often complain because they are asked to teach a course.

The fact is that the really great teachers, those who have made major contributions to human knowledge, are both gifted in research and in teaching. They enjoy being with students and draw them into debate and stimulate student thinking as well as their own in the search for truth. In their humble way they earn prestige and everlasting gratitude from students by their deeds and their accomplishments. They have combined research with teaching. They have a respect for and an obligation to their students. Teaching to such creative and research minded scholars is truly a profession.

Chapter 16

EVALUATING
THE OUTDOOR
EDUCATION PROGRAM

Measurement and evaluation of pupil progress in outdoor education is a productive field for research. Little has been done to appraise the program and techniques of outdoor education in terms of the measurement of progress toward established objectives both of general education and outdoor education. Although empirical evidence builds a strong case for firsthand direct learning, there is a need for scientific evaluation of the school camping program and outdoor education experiences.

Both teachers and school administrators often fail to differentiate between measurement and evaluation. Teachers use measuring devices as ends in themselves. The pupil's score on a test too often becomes the most important goal of the educative process. Many teachers spend too much time debating whether Johnny should have a C+ or a B- on the report card and spend more time testing than they do teaching. The acquisition of knowledge and the understanding of how to use it is far more important to the pupil than the exact points scored on a test or where he ranks in his class.

Evaluation is more inclusive than measurement. Measurement is only a part of the evaluative process. It provides the information and data necessary for good evaluation. Measurement without evaluation and guidance is of little value.

PURPOSE OF EVALUATION

The purposes of evaluation in outdoor education as in the classroom are twofold:

1. Evaluation helps the teacher to determine the degree to which the objectives of general education through outdoor education have been achieved, and

2. Evaluation helps the teacher identify changes in the behavior, attitudes and personality of children.

The above mentioned purposes of evaluation imply certain basic principles in the evaluative process. The teacher, counselor or persons involved in evaluation must:

1. Know the philosophy, purposes and objectives of outdoor education.

2. Use evaluation as a continuous process every day, every hour and every minute the child is under their guidance.

3. Evaluate children and program in cooperation with other teachers, counselors, the children themselves, their parents, and administrators.

4. Use a variety of techniques and devices in evaluating progress and be sure that such devices are suited to the maturity of the children or group being evaluated.

5. Never consider any one measuring device as being infallible for even at best a test cannot measure all the aspects of maturation and growth. If a reliable test shows that a child is not progressing according to expectations then further diagnositic tests should be used.

In evaluating to determine the degree to which the objectives of school camping or other outdoor experiences has been achieved implies implicitly that the teacher must know the purposes and objectives of outdoor education in general and must have specific objectives in mind for each unit of instruction involving work outside the classroom. Nature hikes and school journeys, of course, must be purposeful and objectives should be formulated by the pupils and the teacher before making the trip.

Extended experiences in outdoor education such as school camping should grow from the short-term experiences just outside the classroom, in the school garden or

on the school farm. The general objectives of school camping will be greatly expanded because of the increased opportunities for learning on a 24 hour basis. The objectives of
outdoor education, conservation education, healthful outdoor
living, democratic group living, and leisure-time education
are more easily carried out in an extended experience in a
wilderness setting such as one should expect to find in a
school camp.

In any outdoor education experience, in fact, in any
educational activity, evaluation should be made in terms of
the general objectives of education. Specific objectives of
outdoor education should contribute to the over-all objectives
of education.

The American Camping Association Committee on
Camp Standards have formulated excellent standards which
are applicable to camps of various purposes and objectives.
It is well for outdoor education staff to keep these standards
in mind in evaluating camp programs. The standards set
by the American Camping Association[1] which apply to program are:

A. The Camp should develop objectives in the following areas:
   1. Outdoor living.
   2. Fun and adventure.
   3. Social adjustment--for example, the develop-
      ment of independence and reliability, ability
      to get along with others, and values in group
      living.
   4. An understanding of individuals and groups of
      varied backgrounds.
   5. Improvement of health.
   6. Skills and appreciation, particularly as re-
      lated to the out-of-doors.
B. The program should be so planned, administered and
   supervised as to lead to the achievement of the
   general objectives of camping and the special objectives of the particular camp.
        It is recommended that these objectives be
   stated in writing.
        Essentially, the program should be related to

[1]American Camping Association Resident Camp Standards.

the central theme of living together in a natural environment and learning to enjoy the out-of-doors.

C. Within the general framework of the program, there should be opportunity for co-operative planning of activities by campers and camp staff and an opportunity for some choice of activities by individual campers.

D. Program activities should be geared to the ages, abilities and interests of camps.

E. The program should provide opportunity for individual activity, for rest and quiet, for small group activity and for occasions involving the whole camp.

F. The pace, pressure and intensity of the program should be regulated so that campers will have time for leisure and can participate in activities of their own will and at their own tempo.

G. The program should include occasional parent-participation activities and/or other techniques to strengthen family relationships and parent understanding of program objectives.

H. Camps designed to offer a general program in camping should include a variety of situations in which the campers will have an opportunity:

1. To acquire a feeling of competence and to enjoy himself in the natural outdoor setting through camp skills and other activities common in camp life.

2. To participate in group projects, special events and ceremonies, and social activities.

3. To share in the care and improvement of the camp.

4. To increase his knowledge and appreciation of the world in which he lives.

5. To learn his relationship to his camp environment through activities designed to promote such understanding.

6. To participate in the planning and preparation of meals.

7. To create spiritual responses to camping experiences.

I. The tent or cabin camper group should be small (not more than eight in number for children eight years old and over, not more than six for younger children) and should have a counselor.

J. Supervisory and living units or sections should be
    organized on a homogeneous basis (age or otherwise)
    and should consist of not more than 40 campers.

Unless the outdoor education program brings about
changes in the children's behavior, attitudes and personality, it is not functioning as an educational technique. This
is the basic purpose of all education. Teachers and counselors should not only be concerned with the level of achievement of their pupils but also must watch their pattern of
progress.

Evaluating a child's progress and growth in education
is much broader than testing for subject matter. Education
is concerned with every aspect of the child's total growth.
The child must be evaluated not only in terms of his academic progress but also in terms of his ability to work with
a group, accept responsibility, share experiences, live
healthfully and safely, and adapt to varying situations in
a camp setting.

Some purposes which evaluation can serve in outdoor
education include:[2]

General Planning:
-- Improve pre-camp planning.
-- Show importance of pupil involvement in school
   camp program.
-- Determine whether experiences are worthwhile in
   terms of additional administrative work involved.
-- Determine whether experiences are sufficiently
   valuable to warrant expenditure of funds by
   family and school.
-- Secure parent interest, sanction and aid.
-- Improve teaching climate.
-- Support school-camp curriculum planning.
-- Build enthusiasm for the out-of-doors among
   pupils, staff and community.
-- Help determine the goals.
-- Help determine experiences to be offered.
-- Aid in the appropriate selection of resource
   persons.

[2]Michigan State Department of Public Instruction, School Experience In Camp,
(Bulletin No. 420) Lansing: Department of Public Instruction, 1958, pp. 22-23.

-- Measure effectiveness of the program.
-- Determine whether individual needs and interests are being met.
-- Determine individual behavior transfer from camp to school setting.
-- Supply pertinent information for C-39 record.
-- Help see values and growth of children.
-- Produce understanding of objectives.
-- Improve teaching techniques.
-- Give guidance for present and future planning.
-- Provide a basis for making necessary program changes.
-- Give better understanding of individual problems.
-- Recognize changes in pupil behavior including skills, attitudes, and appreciations.
-- Recognize changes in pupil-teacher relations.
-- Understand the unique values of outdoor education.
-- Gives impressions of pupils, teachers, and parents about the camp experiences.
-- Helps promote community-school relationships.
-- Provides an excellent opportunity for parent-school cooperation.
-- Builds support for future programs.
Suggestions for Daily and Weekly Evaluation:
Daily evaluation provides opportunity to:
-- Discuss the daily program.
-- Review work responsibilities.
-- Evaluate each project in terms of materials covered.
-- Discuss various activities in terms of objectives.
-- Appraise the nature of individual accomplishment.
-- Discuss with campers their general responsibilities.
-- Express oneself and give leadership in the group.
-- Keep program at a good tempo.
-- Involve all pupils in projects.
-- Improve continuity of planning.
-- Assimilate information and learning of the day.
-- Provide opportunity to seek pupil comments on progress.
-- Develop leadership, make suggestions for improvement.
-- Keep a daily account of the day's activities.

Weekly evaluation provides opportunity to:
  -- Summarize the week in camp and to interpret the
     value of the learning activities.
  -- Plan for improvements for next year's experi-
     ences.
  -- Provide basis for parent reports.
  -- Become better acquainted with conservation prac-
     tices and problems.
  -- Review accomplishments of the week.
  -- Focus attention on individual progress of
     campers.
  -- Seek comments on the total camp environment.

INSTRUMENTS OF EVALUATION

Outdoor education programs must constantly be appraised in terms of the degree to which they are meeting
the objectives of education. The evaluation process, if well
planned, helps to appraise the strength and weaknesses,
the significance and the scope of the school camp, the school
forest, the school farm, the school garden or other types of
outdoor education.

Since all schools are different each school must establish outdoor education objectives in terms of its own needs.
Specific objectives for children of urban schools may differ
from those of rural schools because of the difference in experience and background of the children. Objectives formulated for primary grades will differ in scope and degree
from those formulated by children and teachers of upper
grades.

Factors affecting the evaluation process include the
school's administrative policy, time and facilities available,
skill of the staff and the maturation level of the children.

Generally speaking, too little time is spent on evaluation in outdoor education programs. Usually teachers feel
that there is so much to do in such a short time that evaluation can wait. Such a situation should not exist and can be
eliminated either by better planning for outdoor experiences
or for the allotment of more time in the out-of-doors. Actually, evaluation should be a part of every learning expe-

434

rience and should work in constant and continuous relationship with the objectives and program of outdoor education.
The evaluation process itself can be a vital learning experience if made an integral part of the program.

Teachers and counselors will want to use all available
techniques necessary for obtaining more information about
children and the effectivenss of the instructional program in
bringing about desirable changes in their behavior. Education becomes stagnant and somewhat stifled by too much
dependence on existing standardized tests. Teachers should
not be afraid to experiment with a new battery of tests. New
tests and new techniques of evaluation in the spirit of seeking truth will add zest and interest to the teaching process
as well as assure the teacher of more nearly meeting the
stated objectives of the activity or lesson.

The most common instruments of evaluation used in
schools are listed below. Many of these may be employed
in outdoor education, however, some lend themselves to the
informal outdoor classroom more than others.

STANDARDIZED TESTS

Schools should be interested in strengthening and supplementing academic learnings in outdoor education and may
use any one of many standardized tests on the market for
this purpose. Because the experience is for a relatively
short duration, however, it will be impossible to determine
the extent to which the experience in the outdoors contributed to the academic achievement.

Standardized tests are available for the measurement
of intelligence, achievement, personality, interests, attitudes and readiness.

LOGS OR ANECDOTAL RECORDS

Logs or anecdotal records are an attempt to obtain a
full picture of the child through brief, clear accounts of
significant and unusual happenings involving the child.
These logs or recordings are "on the spot" observations
of the child in a variety of experiences.

Recordings should include brief, clear accounts of

significant comments of the child, description of typical or unusual behavior, examples of leadership, cooperation, or other characteristic abilities and quotations from the children's peers.

Through logs or entries concerning behavior or conversation of children, teachers and counselors may gain valuable insight in a child's personality by watching for recurrence of behavior, signs of gaining security, contributions to group activity or any gains or losses in ability to live and cooperate in informal outdoor education.

Examples of such logs might be:
"Johnny joined group singing today.
Johnny volunteered to help with the dishes.
Johnny helped plan the Indian dance at campfire ceremony.
Johnny went on his first overnight camp-out and told Tommy, "Gee, it was fun!"

AUTOBIOGRAPHIES

Autobiographies are another means which contribute to a better understanding of the child. It is helpful for children if the teacher will provide a general outline to serve as a guide in the preparation of the autobiography. The outline for their stay at camp may include my home in the woods, my fishing trip, social activities, my most enjoyable experience, my most boring experience, my best friend at camp, and why I would like to (or would not like to) return to camp next year.

Through the use of autobiographies, a teacher can appraise the child's growth and development in many areas. They may give the teacher insight into early childhood jealousies, adjustments, maturity, needs and hopes.

SELF DESCRIPTION

It is always helpful for the teacher to know how a child feels about himself. Information concerning family attitude, cover-up behavior, role in family life often give teachers important insights for guidance and help in their personality development. Such revelations as "my mother

always picks on me, " "my older sister can do no wrong, "
"the counselor won't let me help with cooking, " or "I like
camp but I wish mother were with me, " help the teacher
gain information that would not come to light for several
weeks or not at all.

SOCIOGRAMS

Another way for a teacher to learn about a child is
through the sociogram. By indicating choices of friends
and classmates with whom they would like to work and play,
children reveal to the teacher the interrelationships within
the group.

The basic material collected from the boys and girls
is used to construct a sociogram. Through the construction
and study of the sociogram, the teacher gains added insight
into the existing situation of a group of children. The sociogram helps the teacher to determine certain aspects of
group structure and raises questions concerning group
relations.

Examples of some statements and questions which
could be used in the construction of a sociogram for a cabin
unit follow:

Write the name of your best boy friend.

Write the name of your best girl friend.

Write the name of the boy you think gets along best
with our group.

Write the name of the girl you think gets along best
with our group.

Who would you choose for your pup-tent on an overnight camp-out?

Who would you choose to represent your cabin at
camp council?

GROUP EVALUATION

One way of providing an evaluation of a group project
is through group discussion. Through group discussion the
strong points and weaknesses may be recognized and the
group is able to build on their strengths and overcome their
weaknesses. The group evaluation might concern the goals,

the achievements, and the methods of the group.

An example of a group evaluation following a nature hike in the school ground might be guided by the following questions:

In what ways has our trip been good?

Each student tell or write about one important thing you learned.

How could our trip have been better?

SELF-EVALUATION OF PUPILS

The pupils own interpretation of the meaning and value of what he does in a camp setting, in a school garden, a school forest or other outdoor activity is a necessary part of his learning and development. No teacher or counselor can successfully impose his own evaluation upon his pupils. Basically, the values a person holds and the judgments he makes are products of his own experiences and his own interpretations.

Efforts to promote self-evaluation on the part of children may seem time consuming and difficult at first but the results are more beneficial to both the teacher and the children than external teacher evaluation.

When pupils are allowed to set up purposes and formulate objectives to be sought in their work, they learn to make judgments. As children learn to set their own goals and to appraise their own efforts toward reaching these goals their learning becomes more meaningful and the teacher is more able to observe growth and to provide more adequate guidance.

The teacher and counselors should exercise caution in making sure that the evaluative process is used to promote self-confidence rather than discourage it. Self-evaluation teaches children to be true to themselves and is a personal experience.

The method of self-evaluation employed should determine the techniques of self-evaluation to be used. Suggested methods of self-evaluation used by pupils and teachers include: weekly evaluation reports both academic and social, letters to parents, and self-rating sheets.

The teacher may guide the pupils in their weekly report by suggesting such questions as: "What did I enjoy about camping most?" "What are my weaknesses at camp?" "What can I do best?" and "What did I learn?"

The self-rating sheet may be mimeographed by the teacher and should include questions to fit the situation. Evaluation after a week at camp might include such items to be rated as:

Respect for others.
Accepted responsibility.
Responded to counselors' directions.
Completed tasks required.
Accepted criticism graciously.
Followed camp rules and guides.
Practiced good health habits.
Was a good member of my group.
Cooperated with others.

The Wausau (Wisconsin) Public Schools use the following evaluation of school camping experience for the child's evaluation of his activities.

CAMPER'S EVALUATION OF SCHOOL CAMPING EXPERIENCE

1. Would you like to go back to school camp again?

   Yes_____   No_____

2. Did you take part in any unusual experience, such as an exciting adventure of something you will always remember?

   Yes_____   No_____

3. Did you learn anything at camp which can help you take care of yourself or others more safely?

   Yes_____   No_____

4. Did your camp experiences help you understand some of your school work better?

   Yes_____   No_____

5. While at camp did you learn to like anyone you had not liked before?

   Yes_____   No_____   Do not know_____

6. How did you feel about such jobs as dishwashing, bed-making, etc.?

   Enjoyed_____ Did not mind_____ Disliked_____

7. How did you get along with the other boys and girls at camp?

   Better than at school_____

   The same as at school_____.

   Not so well as at school_____

8. List the three activities you enjoyed most:

   a.

   b.

   c.

9. List the three activities you liked the least:

   a.

   b.

   c.

10. On the back of this paper, write a short paragraph telling about the school camp.

Because self-evaluation is more closely related to the everyday lives of children and is a part of their learning experience it seems to be most appropriate for outdoor education activities.

TEACHER OR COUNSELOR EVALUATION

The teacher or counselor will be in a position to give a more objective evaluation of the children. Comparison of the teacher's evaluation with that of the child's self-evaluation should in itself be worthwhile in revealing certain hidden problems or attitudes.

Following are two teachers evaluation forms used by the Newton Public Schools:

440

KEY: A=Always   S=Sometimes   N=Never

A. Personal and Social Adjustment

  1. Shows respect for others . . . . _____

  2. Shows respect for property . . . . _____

  3. Offers to do more than required tasks . . . _____

  4. Shows a willingness to carry full share of
      responsibility . . . . _____

  5. Shows leadership ability . . . . _____

  6. Is a good fellow . . . . _____

  7. Appeared friendly . . . . _____

  8. Responds to counselor and/or teachers'
      directions . . . . _____

  9. Cooperates with others in work and free
      activities . . . . _____

  10. Shows willingness to change to meet new
      situations . . . . _____

  11. Shows initiative and resourcefulness in
      work and free activity . . . . _____

  12. Completes tasks required . . . . _____

B. Health and Safety

  1. Meet requirements for sleep and rest . . . . _____

  2. Has good eating habits . . . . _____

  3. Keep self and clothes clean . . . . _____

  4. Has good health habits . . . . _____

  5. Dresses properly for weather . . . . _____

C. Camp adaptability

  1. Shows interest in camp activity . . . . . . _____

  2. Was on time . . . . _____

  3. Follows camp rules and guides . . . . _____

  4. Adjusts well to outdoor life . . . . _____

D. Growth in knowledge and understanding

   1. Contributes each day to:

      a. Science . . . .   _____

      b. Arithmetic . . . .   _____

      c. Language arts . . . .   _____

      d. Social studies . . . .   _____

      e. Health, physical recreation and safety.   _____

      f. Creative expression . . . .   _____

OUTDOOR EDUCATION   NEWTON PUBLIC SCHOOLS
                                         NEWTONVILLE, MASSACHUSETTS

TEACHER EVALUATION OF FIELD SCIENCE AND CONSERVATION TRIP

1. Did you note any specific changes in social growth:

   _____

   _____

   _____

2. What activities do you think contribute to better health
   habits?

   _____

   _____

   _____

3. What specific needs of your group were met by the camping experience?

   _____

   _____

   _____

4. What situations do you think contribute to better appreciation and knowledges of the outdoors?

   _____

   _____

   _____

5. Looking at camp as a children's community, did you note growth in the following?

                              Yes   No

    Responsibility_____

    Co-operation_____

    Friendship_____

    Work habits_____

    Personality growth_____

    Group work_____

OUTDOOR EDUCATION   NEWTON PUBLIC SCHOOLS
                                      NEWTONVILLE, MASSACHUSETTS

EVALUATION FORMS (PARENTS)

The Newton (Massachusetts) Public Schools wisely include the parents in their evaluation. Not only are parents in a position to offer valuable information concerning their own children, but they are also brought closer to the program through participation in the evaluative process.

Dear_____

Your child has recently completed an educational experience at _____ Camp. Since this is a pioneering venture in New England, we are evaluating it very carefully and would greatly appreciate your answers to the following questions:

1. Had your child ever been to camp before? Yes___ No___

2. What part of the cost of the trip did your child earn?

3. How do you feel about the experience as a whole?

    _____

    Extremely   Valuable   Of doubtful value   Practically
    Valuable   worthless

4. Would you endorse such an experience for all children at some time in their school careers? Yes_____ No_____

5. What particular values (if any) do you see in the experience?

_____

6. What disadvantages (if any) do you see in the experience?

_____

7. Will you list any comments that your child made about the trip?

_____

Your frank answers to the above questions will be extremely helpful to us in indicating whether or not to continue this kind of experience and extend it to a greater number of children. We would appreciate your returning this form to your child's teacher as soon as possible.

The Wausau (Wisconsin) Public Schools sends a follow-up questionnaire to parents of children who participate in the school outdoor education experience.

FOLLOW-UP QUESTIONNAIRE FOR PARENTS

Your child participated in the Wausau Public School Outdoor Education Program this spring. We want a program that best serves the students and the community. Will you please let us know how you feel about this experience by answering the following questions:

1. Has your child ever attended camp before this experience?

   Yes_____   No_____

2. Would you be willing to send your child to school camp again?

   Yes_____   No_____

3. Do you feel you were adequately informed as to the camp program and procedures?

   Yes_____   No_____

4. Would you recommend that each sixth grade student have an opportunity to attend a school camp?

   Yes_____   No_____

5. Should the camp period be longer than three days?

   Yes_____   No_____

6. Was the cost reasonable?

   Yes_____   No_____

Comments about this year's school camp:

Suggestions for future school camps:

The DuQuoin (Illinois) Public Schools have had a camping program for their sixth grade children for several years. At the end of their camping session last year they sent the following questionnaire to all parents of those children who went camping. The questions asked, and typical responses to the questions follow.

1. Do you feel that your child's school camping experience was worthwhile?

   Many children never have an opportunity to live in the woods and enjoy a more natural environment. This is an experience they will always remember because it is adventurous, exciting, and different. I think they also develop a closer relationship with their classmates after being together this way.

   In this age of technology and man-made environment, I am happy that my child has an opportunity to get better acquainted with the things I knew as a child--the world in its more natural state. At camp children are acquainted with things more real and this becomes important to them. The camp program was apparently good as my child was enthusiastic and inspired. She has written several letters to her relatives and friends telling about her experience.

2. Do you have any suggestions for improving the program?

   I believe children should have at least two weeks of experience offered in the school camp. The first two days of camp, they are very excited with a new adventure and the last day is spent in preparation to break camp. It is very worthwhile, but should be extended.

   I know school camping is supposed to be educational, but there needs to be more fun too. Recreation such as fishing, swimming, and other things children like to do are important. How can we continually stress education when man has more and more leisure hours? Isn't recreation important too?

Selected References

Baxter, Bernice, *Teacher-Pupil Relationships,* New York: American Book Company, 1950.

Caswell, Hollis Leland, *Education In The Elementary School,* New York: American Book Company, 1950.

Cutts, Norma Estelle, *Providing For Individual Differences In The Elementary School,* Englewood Cliffs, New Jersey: Prentice-Hall, Inc., 1960.

Lindberg, Lucile, *The Democratic Classroom,* New York: Bureau of Publications, Teachers College, Columbia University, 1954.

Strang, Ruth, *Reporting To Parents,* New York: Bureau of Publication, Teachers College, Columbia University, 1947.

Thomas, R. Murray, *Judging Student Progress,* New York: Longmans, Green and Company, 1954.

Winkle, William L., *Improving Marks and Reporting Practices,* New York: Rinehart and Company, 1947.

Chapter 17

RESEARCH IN
OUTDOOR EDUCATION

Research in any field of endeavor or any area of study is essential to its orderly growth and development. The rate of progress is usually governed by the amount and quality of research conducted in any given field.

Education has failed to keep pace with industry, medicine, and other fields of human endeavor both in the amount of money spent and the amount and quality of research conducted. If business spent proportionately as little money on research as the public schools do in educating children, business would fail. Dr. Robert J. Schaefer, director of the Graduate Institute of Education at Washington University, said in a recent speech:

> We do not know what the teacher needs and we are not doing much to learn more. Our universities have not put much money into educational research.
> We are in a state of ignorance. It's about time we faced up to this, and stop acting as if we knew the answers.

Education cannot expect to fulfill its aims in a democratic society without adequate research funds. Education should not become a charity case depending upon tax-exempt grants from foundations to advance its goals through study and research. It is hard to understand how any nation can spend such little money, relatively speaking, on the education of children of today who will be leaders of our country tomorrow. More money, research and better education is needed for the future success of our nation.

Unfortunately, in too many cases, educational research begins and ends with the requirements for advanced degrees. It has become an essential hurdle in the struggle to acquire a Masters Degree or a Doctor Degree in education. When teachers complete these requirements and graduate, they usually return to the classroom where they become over-loaded with formal teaching and seldom have additional de-sires or the necessary time to conduct research.

Research in education should be an on-going process and should not end once the professional educator has gained his advanced degree. The most productive, educational re-search should come from experimentation and study con-ducted by teachers "on the job" who have classroom instruc-tion responsibilities. Qualified teachers with years of ex-perience can contribute most toward improving educational methods. The outdoor education program could stimulate research of this kind and in many instances would penetrate the entire school system from kindergarten through grade twelve. Research in education should be conducted by teach-ers and administrators who have the skill and ability to en-gage in research at the same time they are on the job in administration and in the classroom.

Research must become the immediate tool of every classroom teacher and every student from kindergarten through college. It cannot be regarded as a tool for those too intelligent or too gifted to teach. Education can never become a profession until theory and practice is combined by the scholar-teacher working in the field.

Perhaps one reason for the shortage of skilled and creative classroom teachers is the fact that the public and too many college professors of education themselves do not hold enough respect for the teaching position. There is an attitude that anybody can teach and as long as this at-titude prevails, education can be called a profession only by courtesy. When teaching is made an exciting and chal-lenging profession, when teachers have the same zeal and respect for research as the medical profession, education will then attract more scholars and more dedicated teachers.

Sir Edward Appleton, Vice Chancellor of the Univer-sity of Edenburgh, said, "Learning in a situation without

448

research can be likened to drinking from a stagnant pool, while learning in a situation with research can be likened to drinking from a running stream. "

When education reaches the point where classroom teachers are allowed to drink from a running stream, it will then truly become a profession.

Although outdoor education is the oldest technique in education, it has not been universally recognized by educators until the last decade. Each year brings scores of new camps into existence. Over 100,000 boys and girls in California go to a school camp each year. Michigan and Wisconsin have over three hundred school camps. Illinois is moving forward very rapidly in outdoor education programs. Many public school systems in other states are establishing outdoor education centers and turning to nature as a technique for bringing meaning and life to the lessons of the classroom.

A number of individual and isolated cases of research have been conducted within these various programs. The research has been very good and to a certain degree has substantiated the values of outdoor education. However, we have not made an overall study or a comprehensive approach as to methods and techniques of research that should be applied to the outdoor education field.

Many educators today who are acquainted with outdoor education programs and who have introduced such programs into their school system, maintain that outdoor education provides a meaningful and vital setting for meeting the objectives of education.

Learning by doing, learning by firsthand direct experience, and learning in a democratic group situation are the chief claims of proponents of camping education.

Outdoor educators have yet to prove conclusively their claims for furthering the objectives of education. As in many other areas of education, there are so many intangible factors and there is too little money and too little leadership for the quality and caliber of experimental research necessary to prove the claims of outdoor education.

The need for research in outdoor education is pointed up by two educators. Mason states that:

> The business of youth in taking on experience, and
> camping is still in its youthful stage. To settle
> down within our accepted view, to establish policy,
> whatever they may be, is stagnation. It is only as
> we maintain the experimental spirit of youth that we
> grow. There is much need that the research, experi-
> mentation and thought of the leaders and students of
> camping be constantly passed on and integrated with
> the experience of others.[1]

The need for more research work in the field of camping is also expressed by Dr. Howard Y. McClusky of the
University of Michigan as follows:

> Camping ought to be an object of systematic research
> much more so than has been done in the past. When I
> think of the rich experiences you have throughout your
> years in this work, I think of the need for systemati-
> cally gathering that experience and working it back
> into great sources of teacher training and for training
> institutions of higher learning.[2]

Educational values of outdoor education although supported by many outstanding educators seem at this writing
to be largely theoretical. Empirical evidence and experiences and statements by educators and leaders in the field
of education seem to indicate that outdoor education and
camping can be utilized for a number of purposes in strengthening the educational program and in reaching the stated
objectives of education.

However, the difficulty is in evaluating the outcomes
of outdoor education. Much experimental research and objective measurement has been done in areas related to outdoor education. Research dealing with material things,
with things that lend themselves to scientific experimentation seem to give great prestige to those areas of science
where objective measurement is possible.

Educators through research know their subject matter
but they don't know people. Farmers know their land but

---

[1] Bernard S. Mason, Camping and Education, New York: McCall Company, 1930, p. IX.
[2] Howard Y. McClusky, "Camping Comes of Age," Camping Magazine, 19:14, November, 1947.

they don't know people. In the modern age of mass leisure with greater emphasis on mass education and recreation it is time to do more research on the needs, attitudes and appreciations of people and their behaviorial changes brought about by education, recreation, and outdoor education. Until this is done the educational values of outdoor education will lie chiefly in the form of suppositions and claims.

Although in recent years much more research has been done in outdoor education, it has not been done in the field of educational and personal-social growth. There are good reasons for this. The chief reason is the time required and the money necessary for such experiments. Secondly, the study of social and personal changes or growth is still in its infancy or pioneer stage. This type of research is most difficult.

The most noteworthy attempt in measuring the value of outdoor education as it contributes to the objectives of education was conducted by Dr. L. B. Sharp, Executive Director of the Outdoor Education Association. The study was conducted in 1947 in cooperation with the New York City Board of Education. Two control groups were involved in the study--one group spending a three-week session in camp and the other group remaining in the classroom. Evidence seems to indicate that those children in the camp setting not only kept pace academically with the children in the classroom, but gained valuable insights, attitudes and appreciations that were more long lasting.

Tests were designed with the help of Dr. Wayne Wrightstone, the city school psychologist, to measure gains in the various subject matter areas. The most highly significant gain was in the area of arithmetic.

Little has been done in research of this type which is necessary to substantiate the claims of outdoor education and bring about its universal acceptance into the educational curriculum of the public schools of America. Great care must be exercised in applying the tools of research that we now use for formal classroom work to the outdoor education program. Tools of research must be worked out and devised that will more nearly measure the real values of outdoor education. Standardized tests which are used to meassure knowledge gained from texts and other references which are based primarily on memorization of accumulated facts will not adequately measure the success of outdoor education instruction.

Below is a list of questions and concepts regarding outdoor education that need a great deal of scientific research.

1. Does the textbook in various subject matter areas at certain grade levels serve as a governor on educational learnings?

2. Is grade placement the best approach to our educational systems? Can fifth or sixth graders comprehend the same learning at the same time?

3. Can outdoor education experiences be interesting enough and learned well enough to cause children to learn and comprehend subject matter now found in textbooks they will have two or three years hence?

4. Can the natural science curriculum be integrated and taught more successfully in the out-of-doors?

5. Can the socio-economic learnings be more meaningful and learned better through outdoor education?

6. Can creativity in education be more successful and possibly be measured more easily through outdoor education?

7. Are teacher-pupil relationships actually improved through outdoor education experiences? If so, what are the distinguishing educational features which cause this?

8. Does the outdoor education program cause parents to be more interested in the educational program? How, why, and to what extent? Is this good or are there some weaknesses?

9. What subject matter or subject matter areas seem to benefit most from outdoor education?

10. Can English, foreign language, mathematics, physics, chemistry, poetry, art and other subjects benefit from outdoor education? How, through what kind of activities? How much, in relation to what things in nature?

11. What personality qualifications of teachers are essential in conducting outdoor education programs?

12. What is a proper administrative organization for

developing and perpetuating an outdoor education program in the grade schools, the junior high schools, the high schools, and the universities?

13. Can health habits and safety habits be taught better and more meaningful in outdoor education?

14. Can we actually develop proper attitudes towards conservation of natural resources through outdoor education?

15. What are the time elements recommended for outdoor education programs? What proportion of time for various subject matter areas are used in grades one through twelve? These times are now designed for formal classroom teaching. Some times are designated as a matter of law. Is there or is there not a need to specify amounts of time for subject matter instruction?

16. Does outdoor education stimulate students to do additional readings and further investigation in things they learn through outdoor education experiences?

17. Do outdoor education experiences allow students to develop new interests and skills in leisure time pursuits that have carry over value for later life?

18. What administrative changes are need to implement an outdoor education program? Teachers, transportation, scheduling, insurance, food service, other services, relationship of outdoor education program (particularly camps) to the total school curriculum.

19. Is in-service training necessary? Who should be included? How should it be conducted? How long? Where? etc.?

20. How can we evaluate the program? What tests? Other methods? When are evaluations scientifically sound? Who should evaluate? How often? etc.?

Selected References

Ackoff, Russell L., *The Design of Social Research,* Chicago: The University of Chicago Press, 1953.

Board of Education of the City of New York, *Extending Education Through Camping,* Carbondale, Illinois: Outdoor Education Association, 1948.

Good, Carter V. Barr, A. S. and Scates, Douglas E., The *Methodology of Educational Research,* New York: Appleton-Century, Crafts, 1941.

Harrison, Raymond H. and Gowin, Laurence E., *The Elementary Teacher In Action,* San Francisco: Wadsworth Publishing Company, 1958.

Hillway, Tyrus, *Introduction To Research,* Boston: Houghton Mifflin Company, 1956.

Mason, Bernard S., *Camping and Education,* New York: McCall Company, 1930.

McClusky, Howard Y., "Camping Comes of Age," *Camping Magazine,* November, 1947.

Rugg, Harold and Shumaker, Ann, *The Child-Centered, School An Appraisal of the New Education,* Yonkers-on-Hudson, New York: World Book Company, 1928.

INDEX